For Marx

'Richard Peet leads the reader on a broad sweep through the post-positivist debates that have dominated human geography during its progressive engagement with social theory. Unlike most previous books on this topic, it is a pleasure to see the work of feminist geographers placed squarely within these debates. Detailed introductions to the philosophical underpinnings of different positions, and in-depth readings of key contributions by geographers within the different paradigms, provide vital information for those new to the field. The verve and passion of the writing, and the explicit positioning of Peet within these debates as he engages critically with each paradigm, will stimulate students to continue the debate themselves. A thought-provoking text for advanced courses on geographic thought.' **Professor Eric Sheppard, Department of Geography, University of Minnesota**

'Impressive in its grasp of a wide variety of literatures, both inside and outside of human geography, it is a clear advance over other books . . . The judgements and interpretations have been carefully thought through and show a nice sense of balance. In this book Richard Peet makes an important contribution to the growing literature on the history of thought in human geography. At the same time it will be a significant resource for all those geographers anxious to find out what else has been going on in a field that has become noted for its diversity of viewpoint.' **Professor Kevin Cox, Department of Geography, Ohio State University**

Modern Geographical Thought

Richard Peet

Blackwell
Publishing

BLACKWELL PUBLISHING
350 Main Street, Malden, MA 02148-5020, USA
9600 Garsington Road, Oxford OX4 2DQ, UK
550 Swanston Street, Carlton, Victoria 3053, Australia

First published 1998

6   2006

Library of Congress Cataloging-in-Publication Data

Peet, Richard.
  Modern geographical thought / Richard Peet.
     p.   cm.
  Includes bibliographical references (p. -) and index.
  ISBN 1-55786-206-0 — ISBN 1-55786-378-4 (pbk.)
     1. Geography – Philosophy. I. Title.
  G70.P375 1998
  910'.01—dc21   97–27639
                                              CIP

ISBN-13: 978-1-55786-206-8 — ISBN-13: 978-1-55786-378-2 (pbk.)

A catalogue record for this title is available from the British Library.

Set in 10 on 12 pt Sabon
by Grahame & Grahame Editorial, Brighton, East Sussex

The publisher's policy is to use permanent paper from mills that operate a sustainable forestry policy, and which has been manufactured from pulp processed using acid-free and elementary chlorine-free practices. Furthermore, the publisher ensures that the text paper and cover board used have met acceptable environmental accreditation standards.

For further information on
Blackwell Publishing, visit our website:
www.blackwellpublishing.com

Contents

Figures

Preface

I have frequently asked myself, especially in the closing months of this book's completion, why I ever started the damn thing. It was a fairly casual commitment originally, to write a short work on contemporary thought in geography, but it grew larger as the years rolled by (seven to be exact) until the book reached its present gargantuan size (even this has been cut by a third). I was familiar with recent debates in and around the discipline, having taken part in some, while watching others from the sidelines, sometimes with amusement, often troubled. Yet I did not realize until this project was well under way how many there had been, nor how intense they often became. Nor did I see, at the beginning of this "writing experience," how intricate the connections are between contemporary geographical thought, social theory, and philosophy. Finally, in my naiveté, I did not understand that even the simple, straightforward summary of main positions to which this book pretends would cost so much in terms of time increasingly precious in my years of decline. Yet as these realizations dawned, rose, and I settled into accepting them, I resolved literally to make the most of my original commitment by doing as good a job as I could to produce a thorough survey of recent ideas. Here it is!

A few words of caution and guidance are necessary before the main contents are perused. A first point is that this is not a catalogue of quick summaries in the style "Smith (1990) says this, but Jones (1991) says that." I do not see much point in such a style, except perhaps to show how extensive the author's reading has been. So I have limited the usual "quick mentions of a few obscure writers and many references to the famous," although bad habits may crop up occasionally. Instead, I try to engage fewer authors in more detail, giving long accounts of their work – often too long I know – even though this sometimes detracts from the flow of the main argument. The idea is to respect the ideas of the authors of the works I deal with, to place their ideas in their own contexts, as well as appropriating them for my own, sometimes devious, purposes. This also, I hope, allows the thoughtful, careful reader a more sustained relation with ongoing projects. After all, you do not have to read everything just because you paid good money for this book. So where the reading drags on (and on), or the pages become simply too intense to bear, with dense summary after dense summary, well, put the book down, or skip a bit – the ideas will still be there should you wish to return. The reader may notice that the book gets sparser in its comments as it goes along. This is not because there is not much to say, but rather that the author reached a state of mental exhaustion from too many ideas, even in the several years it took to write them. Let me say too that I do not refer to other surveys of recent geographical thought, such as Derek Gregory's *Geographical Imaginations*, not because they are of little worth, but because they are, and I did not want merely to reinterpret the existing interpretations. Intertextuality definitely has its limits, and these were reached some time ago!

A second point concerns my own involvement with the debates "recorded herein," and my own often fierce, but increasingly mild, reactions to them as I wrote the book. A quick glance at the bibliography shows a whole bunch of entries under "R. Peet." Yet I tried to minimize my own involvement in several key debates, even to the point of cutting out some (but not all) of the really clever replies I thought of long after the fact. Most of the main contents of the chapters are written from some distance with a degree, at least, of "objectivity," whatever that means ("accurate, neutral representation," I suppose). Yet each chapter has critical assessments at the ends of sections and in the innocuously termed "Conclusion," which definitely express my own point of view. Let me therefore explain what that view is, just in case you missed the book's dedication or, like the late Abby Hoffman (of Worcester, Mass.), think that Marx means Groucho rather than Karl. Originally I was a positivist in geography and a socialist in real life. I was then an anarcho-Marxist and basically remain so, even after all those years of criticism, including a few of self-criticism. More recently, I have been largely persuaded by socialist feminism and partly persuaded by poststructuralism, yet remain unconvinced by most of postmodernism, except Baudrillard, with whose notions of sign-domination I basically agree. The book is therefore written from the perspective of a kind of materialist poststructuralism which remains committed to a radically humanist socialism defined as reproductive democracy – that is, direct, popular control of the basic institutions of society. So, reader, be forewarned: committed critical intention prowls beneath each summary, even the choice of who to mention and who to ignore or dismiss with merely a "Jones (1991)."

I have taught this book several times while writing it. I had a memorable experience teaching an early version while visiting the University of Iowa, where Rebecca Roberts and David Reynolds often sat in and commented, Mark Lawrence gave me the benefit of his profound yet informed skepticism, and many other graduate students proved to be excellent discussants. From my Geography and Social Theory seminar at Clark University Gavin Bridge, Elaine Hartwick, Stuart Lorkin, Sunita Reddy, Rachel Slocum, Genese Sodikoff, Phil Steinberg, Susie Steinemann, Elliot Tretter, and the "German contingent" (especially "Walter Martin") stand out; Stuart Lorkin and Rachel Slocum worked on chapter 7 and I thank them for permission to use portions of papers they plan one day to write. The book was originally commissioned by John Davey, long geography's best friend in publishing, and it has been ably brought to completion by Jill Landeryou. Thanks to Hazel Coleman for thorough copy-editing. Kathy Olsen helped me considerably with the early drafts of several chapters. My son, Jim Peet, the best computer draftsperson in England, drew the figures, except for figure 1.2, for which I thank Jeremy Tesch. John Pickles read chapter 2, Andrew Sayer chapter 5, and each was generous with his critical comments, unbelievably so considering that I end up disagreeing with positions they hold dear! Neil Smith almost gave me some written comments on chapters 4 and 5, but at least made encouraging sounds. I worked with Michael Watts editing another book (*Liberation Ecologies*) while writing this one, and I have to say that Michael is great to work with, one of the few people I know who actually does well that to which he commits himself. Piers Blaikie was supportive and gave good advice when I really needed it, even though I didn't follow it. Most of all I appreciate the helpful discussions and constant encouragement of Elaine, without whom the book could not have been finished.

Richard Peet
Belchertown, Massachusetts

Chapter 1

Introduction: Geography, Philosophy, and Social Theory

What is this thing called geography? Outside the discipline, geography is usually the memorization of "facts," when geography can be distinguished from geology. Within the discipline, there is confusion too. The problem in part derives from the corpus of organized geography containing separate spheres of interest in what often appear to be discrete topics. Region, place, landscape, space, natural environment – all these give rise to traditions apparently with little relation, one to the other. Indeed, adherents to these traditions are often mutually antagonistic, as the space and regional traditions were in the 1950s and 1960s, or place and space in the 1970s, or again (to a lesser degree) space and natural environment in the 1970s and 1980s. Geography has a permanent identity crisis because what geographers do is complex. This complexity is inherent in the disciplinary viewpoint but it intensifies as the different aspects of geography shift in pragmatic importance, for example as environmental relations come into heightened crisis, or global space increases in significance. Such a shifting complexity should be regarded as dynamic, interesting, and intellectually fertile. Yet some degree of definition might help in organizing the controversies which are bound to happen. So let us begin this journey through modern geographical thought by briefly defining the subject, talking about its component parts, and discussing some ways of approaching geographical knowledge.

Defining the Field

Geography is the study of relations between society and the natural environment. Geography looks at how society shapes, alters, and increasingly transforms the natural environment, creating humanized forms from stretches of pristine nature, and then sedimenting layers of socialization one within the other, one on top of the other, until a complex natural–social landscape results. Geography also looks at how nature conditions society, in some original sense of creating the people and raw materials which social forces "work up" into culture, and in an ongoing sense of placing limits and offering material potentials for social processes like economic development. The "relation" between society and nature is thus an entire system, a complex of *inter*relations. What was once a causal relationship mainly in one direction (the formation of humanity during natural evolution) becomes an equally causal interrelationship in the reverse direction (social evolution alters the "natural" environment). In this way, human activity continually remakes its natural context – nature comes to be socially constructed, in the sense both of social and economic forces remaking landscapes, and of the intervention of ideas and discourses. Understanding this system of relations requires that geographers be sophisticated natural *and* social scientists, find ways of combining the two, know the methods and be excited by the insights of both aspects of knowledge. Thus, the synthetic core of geography is a study of nature–society interrelations.

While this is increasingly realized in theory, it becomes increasingly difficult to realize in practice as the two parts separate, becoming specialized and intensely complex in their own rights. But also the idea inherent in all this, that human mentalities and social activities alter their natural origins, has proven particularly difficult to theorize adequately. Social theory swings wildly from natural determinism to social constructionism in a number of fields – cultural geography and feminist geography to give but two disciplinary cases. Perhaps such a socio-natural synthesis is effectively impossible, and perhaps too that is one reason for interminable debates over "what is geography?" Yet it is vitally necessary not only for narrow reasons of disciplinary coherence, coverage, and competence, but because compatible society–nature relations determine the very possibility of a future for human beings.

The notion of geography as the study of society–nature interrelations appears to stress one aspect of the field (resources, physical environments) at the expense of another (space, spatial relations). But this is only an apparent misplacement of emphasis. For what is space but surface stretches of natural environment? And what are society–nature relations but (in part) the influence of spatio-natural forces, like gravity and the friction of distance, on human activities, and the return effects of social processes on the (natural) qualities of space? Space was artificially separated from natural environment during the "quantitative revolution" of the 1950s and 1960s, when the need for simplification in the service of spatial science overcame a previous concern with disciplinary coherence. Now that the urgency for a spatial *science* is passed, we are at liberty to recombine space with its natural base, space as that part of nature most involved in human activity, yet an aspect of nature retaining much of its original naturalness. Unless space is considered to be the surface of a still-natural world it is a dry desert of a topic, as with central place studies in the early 1960s. But also the separation of space into a distinct, non-natural arena reduces the potential interest in the compartments of space, its regions and places, which (with such a separation) become disruptive nuisances preventing spatial generalization rather than what they are, natural foci *for* general geographic statements drawn from spatial particularities. The most interesting spatial compartments are areas of natural difference where raw materials, energy, and geomorphic landscapes are sources of cultural differences. For in an era when travel too frequently brings only more of the same, regional differences, originally derived from physical and environmental sources, are a precious resource – regional geography is the historical record of socio-natural differences. So too with locality and place, defined often in the arid spatial terms of labor markets (in locality studies) or shopping centers (in geographies of consumption), but best understood as environmental niches differentially transformed through local histories of social activity. Places are particular and different also because space, a natural force, applies frictional resistance to the diffusion of power and influence; otherwise our worst fears would be realized – all places would indeed be the same and we would die from geographical boredom! Yet let us not romanticize local difference in whose name millions are killed – think of the incessant culture wars in the Balkans, or the exhuming of fields of skulls and skeletons in Bosnia. Difference is dangerous as well as interesting and vital. In other words, there are simultaneously generalities of space and particularities of place which are aspects one of the other, or of a whole that is the humanized earth surface. The physicality of space and the natural origins of local specificity are integral moments of this space–place interaction. The political task of geography is to enable people to understand their similarities and differences in appreciative rather than destructive ways. Joined with geography's direct environmental quest, preventing the destruction of nature, this places a heavy burden of responsibility on our disciplinary shoulders. What a difference the definition of geography makes!

Levels of Abstraction

Understanding this complex set of interrelationships entails investigating empirical particulars and constructing general abstractions. In this book, empirical investigation is largely bypassed so that attention can be focused on theorization. Here we discuss several types, or levels, of generalization – metaphilosophy, philosophy, social theory, theory, and practice. All are divorced from real geographical phenomena and material practices by mental processes of simplification, generalization, and essentializing – that is, all involve trying to give, through short, dense statements, the essence of a myriad empirical cases. These generalizing processes should not be thought of as pure reasoning, or some kind of inherent ability of the universal mind to see through details into structures, but instead are influenced (in what they find to be essential or whether essentializing is indeed possible or desirable) by metaphilosophies as cultural and political viewpoints. Thus, two people can regard the same set of "facts" and see different general structures – hence the importance of getting straight the different levels of abstraction.

Metaphilosophy

By metaphilosophy we mean the most general perspectives which guide thinking. Metaphilosophy is the link between world views and cultures and thinking organized around theoretical concerns; metaphilosophy is a conduit carrying cultural values into theory, yet it is active too in carrying theoretical and philosophical persuasion and informed thinking into culture. It expresses the general aim of thinking at the level of its purpose – what people seek in thought, what they appeal to for justification, the standards of truth or efficacy applied to thinking. Philosophies can be grouped metaphilosophically around a few main themes and arranged historically from premodern through modern to postmodern as the preoccupations of thinkers change over time. Thus, metaphilosophy refers to attempts at thinking the fundamentals of existence: the presence of God, the meaning of life, the truth of thought, the emancipation of humanity or, conversely, the absence of firm grounds for thinking and believing, perhaps even the meaninglessness of existence. In premodern times, philosophical contemplation tried to discern God's intention behind patterns of events. In the modern era, the best philosophies sought truth, meaning, and emancipation. Postmodern philosophy supposedly abandons such essentialist foundations and tries to think without established grounds, bases, or appeals to metadiscourses. Metaphilosophical purpose has shifted over time from the most fundamental, mystical discovery to postmodern skepticism, a process referred to here as the "disenchantment" which accompanies human conquest of the natural world and its forces. But metaphilosophies do not disappear even when replaced as intellectual dominants, so that in any period several coexist usually under the hegemony of one, although dominance can vary with place, class or political persuasion. Philosophies may express several metaphilosophies so, for example, Marxism is a search for truth and meaning under the dominance of the quest for human emancipation (figure 1.1).

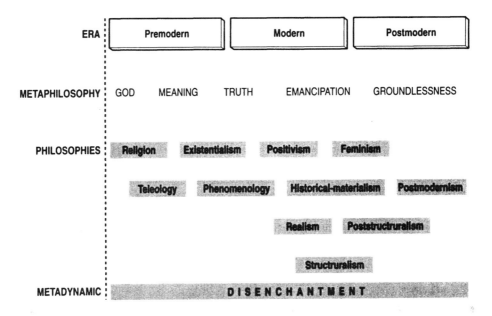

Figure 1.1   Metaphilosophy, metadynamics, and schools of philosophy.

Philosophy

Philosophy is an abstract way of thinking which employs logic to organize imaginaries, beliefs, and notions of purpose into formal systems of understanding. To achieve pragmatic efficacy, philosophy has to claim that human practices are informed by ideas. It must claim also that ideas are not just random sparks of imagination, but form sequences which, while derived originally from experience, are partly autonomous from material reality. Philosophy organizes these ideas into coherent patterns, and employs the results in the endeavor of understanding existence. Here, the key terms are "logic" and "rationality" derived, in the western tradition, from the Enlightenment revival of Greek classicism. In the western tradition, minds are supposed to have innate rational structures derived from similarity of experience in a world already characterized by order – natural evolution, for example, or transhistorical similarities in the life course (birth, life, death) or in basic structures in the production of existence. Inner logic replicates this outer order in mental forms which can be expressed symbolically. One can think, speak, and write in symbols and thus give the essence of myriad events. No wonder Plato advocated philosopher kings!

The idea of innate logical structures is challenged by notions of social, political, and cultural construction – ways of thinking are culturally and socially imposed on the mind rather than merely brought to realization by socialization (education in ideas, for example). From this second perspective there can be no single, universal philosophy, but only historical systems and regional forms. Whatever their origin, the point remains that there are logics of an age common to many people which can be studied and at least partly replicated by philosophy. Philosophy involves basic positions on the structures people employ in making their livelihoods – what might be called social ontologies. Philosophy also contains evaluations of the truth and validity of the statements which can be made about reality – what might be called epistemologies. In other words, philosophies are thought to be self-evaluating modes of understanding which are extremely useful to know. All of this – replication, ontology, epistemology – is the province of philosophy.

Theory

Theory has a more direct contact with the occurrences, events, and practices of lived reality. Theory is inherently inductive – that is, constructed originally from empirical sources. Theory tries to replicate in the imagination a certain, particular sequence of events or category of real occurrences using the device of generalization, usually (or conventionally) looking for commonalities or similarities, but also (perhaps) systems of difference or, maybe, just difference. While theory is clearly a component part of philosophy, it is limited in scope, with more direct contact with a certain sphere of life, yet still containing important elements of speculation. Hence, theory is also deductive in that from a knowledge of one part, aspect, sequence, or difference, the mind can deduce through logic the probable characteristics of other aspects or even, daringly, entire sequences or structures. This kind of deductive leap between parts known with varying accuracy, or leaping ahead from the partly known into the unknown, is almost automatically a part of theorizing. Every thinker does this with varying degrees of care, even when formal methods of hypothesis formulation and testing are being consciously carried out, and it is increasingly the central activity of theorizing with the abandonment (more in boredom than disgust) of empirical forms of positivism. In this book, we investigate a particular kind of theory called geography.

Social Theory

Social theory occupies the middle ground between philosophy and theory. As the term suggests, social theory is more restricted in scope than philosophy, more directly dealing with social, political, and cultural tendencies and characteristics in real societies. As a consequence it is phrased in less abstract and more socially engaged terms. Social theory is particularly important as a combination of storage and bridging device, storing the summarized results of work in one area in the form of ideas which can be transferred across theoretical bridges to other fields. Increasingly this allows the formation of general social theory developed for its own sake. What used to be separate disciplines, like geography, become dedicated to furthering social theory's interests and causes rather than their own disciplinary ends – this is somewhat different from the previous "interdisciplinary studies" which used the coinage of comparison to facilitate interchange rather than the syntax of synthesis to enable unification. Increasingly, scholars are social theorists with disciplinary specializations, rather than disciplinary specialists with social theoretic inclinations. Increasingly too, specializations overlap and transcend disciplinary boundaries, as, for example, with the postmodern upsurge in social-theoretic interest in space. This growth of a generalized social theory rather than a set of separate disciplines is an exciting development particularly of the last few decades. Hence, this book uses most of its space to explore the connections between social theory and geography.

Like many new things, social theory results from a number of previous and ongoing frustrations. In terms of the other "levels" of thinking outlined earlier (metaphilosophy, philosophy, theory), social theory derives from criticisms of the idea that the mind has an innate logical structure. Instead, social theorists see logics as social and cultural in origin and political in intent; logics are influenced by non-logical beliefs and cultural meanings, and by body and emotion as well as mind. From this derives the suspicion that philosophy is phrased too abstractly, certainly in the tradition of analytical philosophy, with its mathematical equations which supposedly replicate the logical components of thought processes. Hence, philosophy is better phrased as social theory, ideas in cultural context rather than universal generality. But social theory also comes from a frustration with just plain old theory, especially empirical–positivist notions of theory, the slow aggregation of inductively derived fragments through the observation and measurement of discrete "facts." Frustration with the confining rituals of positivist theory stems not only from the realization that all supposedly neutral facts are "in fact" partly opinions, but also from the snail's pace of hypothesis formulation and exact testing in a world of crisis – for example the suspicion that by the time global warming is finally "scientifically proven" we will be frying on land and boiling in ocean water! As these frustrations suggest, social theory is also intensely political – in a critical sense, that is – dedicated to changing the world in some way for the better. Social theory is almost always leftist in style, character, and intent – that is, dedicated to changing the world to make it a better place for poor and oppressed people, dedicated to human emancipation even in many of its most skeptical (postmodern) forms. Hence, the social theories we deal with in this book are almost exclusively critical, leftist, even social revolutionary in adherence and intent. Finally, social theory is different from other types of theory not only in terms of level of generality and politics but also in that it specifically theorizes human beings in social groupings. Theories about people are different from theories about atoms in several ways, but in this way particularly – people respond to circumstances through intent, emotion, consciousness, and choice. People interpret the forces that affect them, and theorists interpret these interpretations in a double hermeneutic. While this only begins to reveal the complications of human life, it is enough to cause physicists or chemists to throw up their hands in disgust. For the social theorist, however, human complexity is exactly what intrigues – that is the reason we are social theorists!

Practice

Social theorists engage in praxis (or practice) in a number of ways inside and outside academia. Intellectuals are basically involved in the production, eternal discussion, and dissemination of ideas, with ideas being representations of real events and practices. Research discovers the factual, empirical basis of these representations. Theoretical contemplation elaborates ideas from facts and puts them into systems. Writing displays these ideas in discursive formats. Critique challenges structures of ideas and tries to replace them. Teaching and publication disseminates ideas but also reformulates them into simpler structures. In the sense of the social nature of theory, these again are not neutral processes, but instead, research, thinking, writing, and teaching are political processes immersed in power relations. Ideas are not neutral "facts" but are instruments of persuasion. Relations between teachers and students, between academics, and between researchers and outside institutions such as grant-giving agencies, constitute intellectual power fields with relations of domination and control just as severe, and in many ways nastier and more vicious, than those of the corporate world or even the family. In academia, status reigns and power informs every sentence and gesture.

Geographical Thought

This book investigates metaphilosophy, philosophy, and social theory and their equivalents in the theoretical study and practice of geography. By "study of geography" we mean, primarily, the discipline that has been allocated geographical topics in the existing academic division of labor, although often the course of investigation takes us into cognate areas like regional science (caught between economics and geography), sociology (especially urban sociology), and other fields. But the notion of allocation by a division of labor while adequate as a first impression, creating a guiding picture so to speak, is too anonymous and structural for our purposes.

Geographical Praxis

"Geography is what geographers do" is more than a cliché. It expresses the making of geography through daily praxis – for example, teaching actively shapes the ideas being transmitted, research constantly reveals inadequacies and potentialities, even the act of writing constantly throws up new notions as the sequential logic of sentences unfolds sometimes seemingly "by itself." (How do I know what I think until I see what I write?) Teaching and research practices react to the broader context of societal crises, urgencies, and pragmatic requirements while disciplines contend for position in meeting or responding to practical, social exigencies. This is an intensely political reaction, for it involves utility or critique, accommodation or opposition, to the existing social order. Then too there is the notion of a scholarly quest for understanding, which has some truth beneath its obvious, selfish trappings. All this suggests that groups of scholarly practitioners constantly make and remake their discipline in a complex political process of reactions to external social pressures, competitive internal contentions for status, power, and money, fights over boundaries and contents with surrounding groups, the almost selfless quest for truth, and so on. These groups produce specialized discourses composed of formal statements, with rules establishing who is listened to, with what degree of intensity, and what is accepted as truthful or valid. In this process, there is no such thing as neutral assessment either of the structure of social existence in the sense of ontologies or of the truth or even adequacy of theories in the sense of epistemologies – there are only political ontologies and political epistemologies,

Philosophy of Geography

In such processes of the making of geography through practice, a leading role is played by histories and philosophies of the discipline. At its best, the "philosophy of geography" is that system of general ideas concerned with the direction and content of geographical work which practitioners elaborate during praxis. That is, teaching, writing, and practicing geography at the level of exact theory leads to the formation of abstract notions which both summarize multiple realizations or practical insights and project these in speculative ways into scarcely theorized new directions. The philosophy of geography basically concerns the main themes of a group of practitioners, the fascinations of a time and place among people thinking about similar topics. It is an arena where geographers meet to discuss their practice in general ways, to put it simply. At its worst, the "philosophy of geography" is where those who have read philosophy in general and disciples of "more advanced ideas in other disciplines," exercise ideological power over those who remain with practical concerns. Even so, the philosophy *of* a discipline constantly interacts with philosophy *as* a discipline and thus with the current of ideas in general. Yet this "interaction" is most productive when geographers interpret philosophy to apply its summarized knowledge in furthering the system of ideas formed through contemplating discrete forms of theoretical practice. Then too the "philosophy of geography" has a dynamic structure of its own represented by "the history of geographical thought" – that is, the temporal sequence of general notions about the content and themes of a study. All these contribute to a disciplinary philosophy. But, to repeat, philosophy is best when formed though empirical and theoretical practice rather than abstract speculation, reading philosophy in general, or reading theoreticians through the lens of other theoreticians.

Philosophy as Social Theory

Increasingly, abstract thinking in the tradition of the philosophy of geography resembles social theorizing rather than disciplinary navel contemplation. Social theory is preferred to philosophy in part because philosophy often seems remote from anything resembling practical concern. In part, this is because disciplinary boundaries at last melt away leaving social theory as the meeting ground for generalized yet still practical ideas. A change occurs too in the quality of philosophizing about geography. Earlier geographical thought was naturalistic in form and content, societies being approached from the perspective of their natural qualities, with humans seen as natural creatures in the literal sense of "creations" whether of purely natural forces or, almost inevitably, God acting through the Nature "He" designed. The philosophy of geography still resembled religious contemplation whose aim was to find God's intention in the pattern of earthly events. Even in its "positive" forms, environmental determinism for example, early geographic thought had mystical qualities as the thinker sought original cause and teleological direction in the depths of God's will or Nature's destiny. Mysticism has hardly disappeared, indeed it stages a come-back among lost souls seeking evangelical distraction in a world of crisis. In the twentieth century, the philosophy of geography became more a materialist history of real processes. In other words, there is a change in the purpose of thinking in general from spiritual contemplation to practical intellectual activity.

In this chapter, we look briefly at several schools of modern geographical thought which precede contemporary geographic thinking (see figure 1.2). By "modern" geographical thought we mean post-Enlightenment and European – that is, since the rationalized structures of thinking of seventeenth- and eighteenth-century western Europe. Modern western geography arose under the impetus of two developments of this period: the need to catalogue and interpret the mass of geographical information collected by European "discovery and exploration" (the quotation marks signifying that non-western people already knew they were there!); and the use of rational, scientific forms of thinking and expression to organize this data, rather than religiously and mystically interpreting it to divine God's will. In other words, modern geography serves the societal function of theorizing facts about the "world as the

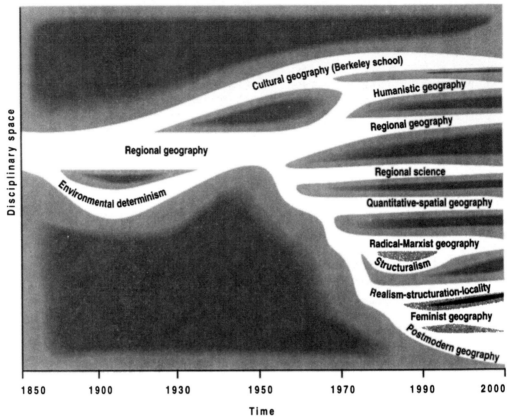

Figure 1.2   Schools of modern and postmodern human geographical thought.
An increasing variety of schools of thought have emerged over time in the discipline of geography.

home of humankind" or, more accurately, the "world as controlled by European people."

Geographical thought elucidates theoretical frameworks for the organization of data about this world. To give a simple, familiar example, a map is a model, a symbolic device for organizing spatial data in summary form. Or a more complex example, the theoretical notion of societies as organisms is a conceptual device for organizing natural and cultural facts in synthetic forms. Thought abstracts from the immediacy of fact to form systems which rebound to structure the recognition and collection of facts. Indeed, abstract thought systems often precede fact, ideologically construct it, discursively guide what is construed as "fact." Theoretical organizational devices are political tools of power formation. So the map may give a "bird's-eye" view but the bird is an eagle, symbol of the state, and soaring on high, rather than a working sparrow, pecking up the crumbs of its localized existence. Hence, the geographic device of mapping might be termed a form of "militaristic and bureaucratic abstraction." Likewise, the organismic analogy is a naturalistic device for relating social dynamics to evolutionary causes in the service of political contestation and state expansion. Returning to the discussion of philosophy and social theory outlined earlier, ontologies are therefore political ways of understanding the world, while epistemologies only pretend the neutral arbitration of fact over fiction in an effort at disguising not their direct political motives but their social functionality (hence the notion that facts are social constructions). The modern history of geographical thought can only be read politically.

Early Modern Geography

Geographical thought occurs when geographers and others interested in society–nature relations abstract from the immediacy of facts to think generally about systems like landscapes, regions, or spaces. The first modern thinkers who specifically and institutionally were practicing geographers, with recognizable, organized theoretical views, are conventionally taken to be Humboldt and Ritter (histories of premodern geographical thought are given in Glacken 1963 and Livingstone 1992; for a simple introduction to geographical thought see Unwin 1992). While geographical information piled up in western Europe, center of the mercantile world, these German geographers set about constructing systems by which this data could be understood at more than a directly factual level.

Modern Beginnings

Alexander von Humboldt (1769–1859) was a scientific traveller, conveniently of independent means (i.e. wealthy), who searched for the universal patterns underlying particular, observed phenomena. His idea was "to depict in a single work the entire material universe ... in a vivid style that will stimulate and elicit feeling" (Botting 1973: 257). This resulted in *Cosmos: Sketch of a Physical Description of the Universe* (1847: xviii), which tried to "discern physical phenomena in their widest mutual connection, and to comprehend Nature as a whole, animated and moved by inward forces." That is, Humboldt wished to find unity in a diversity of earth phenomena discovered using accurate measuring devices with the graphic display of information on iso-maps (isobars etc.). Cannon (1978: 105) describes early nineteenth-century Humboldtian science as "the accurate, measured study of widespread but interconnected real phenomena in order to find a definite law and a dynamic cause." In brief, this was an aesthetic form of positivism, tinged perhaps by the remnants of scholastic mysticism (the "inward forces" of Nature), a point of transition between a metaphysics of God's existence and a metaphilosophy of truth. Carl Ritter (1779–1859) also saw unity in geographical diversity but rested his regional synthesis more directly on a teleological foundation:

> Geography, taken most comprehensively, regards the Earth as the dwelling place of Man
> ... The Earth is the grand floor, so to speak, of Nature; the home, or rather the cradle,
> of men and of nations, the dwelling place of our race ... the theater where all the forces of
> Nature are displayed in their variety and independencies. Besides this, it is the field of all

human effort, and the scene of a Divine revelation ... grander than its relation to the system of *things*, is its relation to an unseen world, to an unseen hand, even that of the Creator ... a revelation of Divine wisdom, in the form of a visible world. (Ritter 1874: xiv–xvi)

Ritter's 19-volume *Erdkunde* tried to infuse the multitude of geographical data with a sense of cosmic unity and purpose in the philosophical tradition of German idealism. Ritter followed the philosopher Immanuel Kant's division of the senses into outer, geographical forms (sight, hearing, etc.) and inner, historical forms (soul, self), with science as the search for the laws of nature, and teleology as integrating device (May 1970: 109–10, 150–1). Humboldt and Ritter were transitional thinkers caught to differing degrees between premodern religious mysticism and modern scientific theory.

Environmental Determinism

In the second half of the nineteenth century, geographical thought shifted in its conceptual basis from natural theology to evolutionary biology. Dereck Stoddart (1966) thinks that Darwin's biological theory, establishing the human's place in nature, made possible the development of geography as science; specifically, the organismic analogy (between society and nature) overcame the dualism inherent in the study of human–environment relations. Actually, the missing link between nature and society was forged with particular effect by the sociologist Herbert Spencer's (1864; 1882) notion that societies are social organisms which diversify and specialize under the influence of external environment and their own intrinsic structures. The tendency was to draw more on Jean Baptiste Lamarck's (1914) theory of the inheritance of acquired characteristics rather than on Darwin's (1964) theory of random mutation and natural selection for, as David Livingstone (1984: 17) puts it, Lamarckism allowed the religious concepts of holistic design and teleological purpose to be retained, easing the "transition from Providential design to natural law as the source of social legitimation."

This notion of legitimation theory is crucial for understanding geography's entry into modern science in the form of environmental determinism (Peet 1985). Friedrich Ratzel (1844–1904), a student of the ultra-Darwinist Ernst Haeckel, took the notion of the unity of organic life, and the Spencerian organismic analogy, in the direction of a geopolitics of the state. Every living organism, he said, requires a territory – its *lebensraum* or living space – from which to draw sustenance. The growth of population leads to increased demands for sustenance and thus for space, with a "flowing over" of excess population and the acquisition of larger territories in an interstate struggle for societal existence – hence the necessity for European expansion overseas (Bassin 1987). Thus, the rise of modern geography can be interpreted as "serving the interests of imperialism in its various aspects including territorial acquisition, economic exploitation, militarism, and the practice of class and race domination" (Hudson 1977: 12). Geography legitimates, excuses, rationalizes, in its very act of origination.

Thus, we consistently find environmental determinists prominent in the institutionalization and theorization of early modern geography. (Sir) Halford Mackinder (1861–1947) synthesized natural and cultural geography to provide the naturalistic basis for British foreign policy (Mackinder 1911). Mackinder (1931: 326) thought that natural regions have flows of sap and blood coursing through their plants, animals, and humans, "on loan for the moment in the 40 million bodies of the present generation [of English people]," giving them the fluid essence of their supposed superior national characteristics. (For such intellectual gallantry he was knighted, rather than benighted!) Social Darwinist ideas found a ready audience in the United States (Hofstadter 1955) with its strong needs for evolutionary legitimation as the Euro-Americans wrested the continent from its aboriginal inhabitants in a spatial process resembling genocide in methods and effects. Hence, the importance of Ellen Churchill Semple's *American History and Its Geographic Conditions* (1903), with its tale of the sturdy energy of the Anglo-Saxon race reinvigorated under the frontier conditions of North America and its updating, or scientific specification, of the nineteenth-century ideology of "manifest destiny." Semple imported Ratzel's ideas into United States geography under the aegis of "science" using a strong admixture of poetry as disguise and excuse for what otherwise would obviously be deemed severe lapses in logic:

> Man is a product of the earth's surface. This means not merely that he is child of the earth, dust of her dust; but that the earth has mothered him, fed him, set him tasks, directed his thoughts, confronted him with difficulties that have strengthened his body and sharpened his wits, given him his problems of navigation or irrigation, and at the same time whispered hints for their solution. She has entered into his bone and tissue, into his mind and soul. (Semple 1911: 1)

Interpreting Ratzel through the scientific racism current at the turn of the century Semple thought that earth regions produced people with different "temperaments" – northern Europeans as energetic and thoughtful people, southern Europeans as improvident, emotional yet imaginative, qualities which "among the negroes of the equatorial belt degenerate into grave racial faults" (Semple 1911: 620). Likewise with Ellsworth Huntington's (1915: 9) hypothesis that where a certain type of (mid-latitude) climate prevails human energy is at its height and great civilizations arise – "therefore, such a climate seems to be a necessary condition of great progress." So too with William Morris Davis (1900), prominent American geographer of the early twentieth century, finding Ritter's teleology no longer adequate, turning to geographical evolution, a combination of geology and biology. David Livingstone (1992: 210), a historian of geographical thought at Queen's University, Belfast (Northern Ireland), argues that Ratzel, Mackinder, Davis, and others were engaged in a "geographical experiment ... a manoeuvre designed to hold together the natural and social worlds under one explanatory umbrella ... [using the vocabulary] ... provided by the Neo-Lamarckian construal of evolutionary theory." Putting this differently, the organismic analogy, and the conception of a natural humanity, allowed geography entry into modern science not only because they enable logical synthesis of the natural and the human (as with Livingstone), but more importantly because this synthesis could be employed in the service of power, specifically to legitimate as natural the expansion of Europe into world dominance. Behind the collection of geographical facts into organized systems of thoughts lay a sense of social and political purpose! Unless histories of geographical thought emphasize legitimation theory they too join that conspiracy of silence which disguises the relations between power and knowledge.

This is a clearly a contentious issue. Speaking of the relations between colonial power and modern geography during the "age of empire" Felix Driver (1992) criticizes the notion that geography was "simply a tool of capitalism" and wants to develop a more complex explanation drawing on the many aspects of the culture of imperialism. Thus, Edward Said's *Orientalism* (1979) maps the "imaginative geography" of the Orient represented by a range of scholarly, administrative, and popular texts: the recurring theme, Said finds, is binary opposition between west and Orient, the one rational, mature, normal, the other irrational, backward, and depraved. Here, geographical knowledge is a critical axis in the colonial process – geographical ideas were necessary for acquiring and subordinating space. For Driver, this initiates a series of studies examining the images and fantasies ("Darkest Africa") about the colonial world created within geographical texts. But Driver's critics might reply that this only makes geography a somewhat complex tool of capitalism, yet a tool nevertheless! Complexity should not be used to hide complicity.

Cultural Geography

The trouble was that soon after geography became environmental determinism the direction of legitimation theory was already shifting from (external) imperial conquest to (internal) control over consciousness in what was becoming a consumer-capitalist (Fordist) society. It was this shift in societal demands for legitimation, rather than pure intellectual criticism, that revealed the logical inadequacies of environmental determinism. Specifically, the organismic analogy has the quite obvious deficiency that while human beings are indeed animals, and societies resemble herds, flocks, or even swarms, the two kinds of entity are also profoundly different, at least usually. Humans have consciousness to the point of reflexivity (we know we exist, can think about our existence, can think about thinking). Social change among humans occurs primarily through cultural transmission (i.e. learning processes) rather than genes or biological inheritance. Thus, we find the Berkeley (California) cultural geographer Carl Ortwin Sauer (1889–1975) argued in the 1920s that a transposition of divine law into omnipotent natural law had produced in geography a "rigorous dogma of naturalistic cosmology" (cosmology meaning science of the universe). But, as he added later, "natural law does not apply to social groups" (Sauer 1963: 320, 343). Here, Sauer followed a line of anthropological thinking moving from Franz Boas to Alfred Kroeber which draws from the philosopher Wilhelm Dilthey the existential notion that natural science deals with explanation but social science seeks human understanding – the two, in other words, are quite different. Sauer learned from Kroeber an antipathy to environmental determinism but also an enthusiasm for comparative cultural history, which he combined with the notion, learned from German landscape studies, of the transformation of natural landscapes into cultural artifacts.

This complex of influences and reactions resulted in what came to be known as the Berkeley school of cultural geography. In this school, regionalism takes the form of the study of culture areas and cultural landscapes (Sauer 1963; Livingstone 1992: 292–300) from the deep perspective of long-term history. William Thomas, editor of *Man's Role in Changing the Face of the Earth* (1956), a huge work (1,193 pages) representing the culminating triumph of the Berkeley school, describes its views as follows:

> geography is the study of what has been happening to the earth's surface during the last million years or so – the period of human occupancy. It has a proper concern for the results of physical–biological processes in creating regional differences on the earth, but it builds upon this knowledge by asking questions (relating to human cultural history) about the varying interpretations and uses that different cultural groups have made of earth resources, about the diverse ways in which they have organized their respective portions of earth space, and about the cumulative effects of man's actions in changing the face of the earth. (Thomas 1959: 4)

Strong elements of naturalism and organicism remain in this school of cultural thought. Its politics are vaguely critical but anti-modern: in *Agricultural Origins and Dispersals* Sauer (1952: 4) reaches the critical conclusion that civilized man has the arrogance to believe in "an ever-expanding system that places no limits upon himself other than his individual mortality ... his knowledge giving him powers which he has lacked the wisdom to control." Similarly, the final pages of Sauer's (1956) "The Agency of Man on Earth" contain vivid, sweeping condemnations of such "human failures" as commercialism, speculation, technocentrism, rampant consumption, immediate profit-orientation, lack of consideration, Eurocentrism and industrialism related to the destruction of the environment in a statement reminiscent of Heidegger's later period. Sauer thinks that living beyond one's means may encounter the limits of physical matter, or be stopped by people growing tired of getting and spending as measure and mode of living, or be checked by fear of the growing power of government. "The high moments of history have come not when man was most concerned with the comforts and displays of the flesh but when his spirit was moved to grow in grace. What we need more perhaps is an ethic and aesthetic under which man, practicing the qualities of prudence and moderation, may indeed pass on to posterity a good earth."

There are similarities between the Berkeley school of cultural geography and the French tradition of human geography. In this version of human geography, most prominently represented by Vidal de la Blache (1845–1918), modern geography is the scientific study of places – scientific in terms of a series of carefully designed regional studies employing field study which result in meaningful generalizations. The idea is to look at the influence of natural milieux (the "organically integrated physical and biotic infrastructure of human life on earth" – Buttimer 1971: 45) on human associations, groups, and societies, emphasizing the life styles, or *genres de vie*, which evolve through history. Here, the difference from environmental determinism lies in the active role of the social system mainly, in the rural areas where French human geographers did most of their work, the cultivation system, but emphasizing also the creative force of human intelligence in overcoming natural obstacles – the relative autonomy of this intellectual force is the kernel notion of environmental "possibilism" as opposed to environmental determinism (Buttimer 1971: 44–54). Critical of this formulation, Lucien Febvre (1925: 236–7, 367) rephrased possibilism in Marxist terms as the fashioning of natural conditions by human labor, a process which ended natural determination as it produced new effects on nature as well as society. Yet with the notion of small area studies the Vidalian school begins also to resemble the hegemonic idea of the time – regional geography.

Regional Geography

The leading form of regional geography in the Anglo-American tradition was theorized by the University of Minnesota geographer Richard Hartshorne (1899–1992). According to Nicholas Entrikin (1989: 1), Hartshorne's *The Nature of Geography* (1939) was symbolic of a particular style of descriptive regional geography with roots in German geography, especially the ideas of Alfred Hettner (1895–1941). For Hettner (1927), geography is not the study of the distribution of phenomena spread over the entire earth's surface (as with Humboldt), but is instead a *choro*logical (i.e. regional-descriptive) discipline focused on causal relations between the assemblages of phenomena which lend individuality to particular places (Elkins 1989: 22–3). Hartshorne (1959: 13) reads Hettner's definition of geography as "the chorological science of ... earth areas and places in terms of their difference and their spatial relations" with the goal of the discipline being "to know the character of regions and places through comprehension of the existence together and interrelations among the different realms of reality." For Hartshorne (1939: 460–9), as with Kant, geography and history are integrating sciences, geography in terms of earth spaces, history in terms of periods of time. The main features of Hartshorne's conception of the geographical part of knowledge can be summarized as follows:

Geography seeks to acquire a complex knowledge of the areal differentiation of the world ... Phenomena significant to areal differentiation have areal expression ... Consequently, in studying the interrelation of these phenomena, geography depends first and fundamentally on the comparison of maps ... In systematic geography each particular element, or element-complex, that is geographically significant, is studied in terms of its relation to the total differentiation of areas ... In regional geography all the knowledge of the interrelations of all features at given places – obtained in part from the different systems of systematic geography – is integrated, in terms of the interrelations which these features have to each other, to provide the total geography of those places. (Hartshorne 1939: 463–5)

Putting this a little less turgidly, geography is basically a regional study dealing with unique combinations (interrelations) of characteristics in specific areas of the earth's surface; it is also largely descriptive: "no universals need to be evolved, other than the general law of geography that all areas are unique" (Hartshorne 1939: 468). If we turn to statements by other regional geographers, notions of uniqueness and the impossibility of generalization emerge even more clearly. So for Preston James (1952), of Syracuse University, the regional concept, core of geography, marks off areas of distinctive character or focuses attention on particular places for the purpose of a more complete understanding of the face of the earth. James (1952: 197–8) says:

> The things geographers deal with on the face of the earth are not uniformly distributed over it. As Hartshorne points out geographers have long selected for study things which are not uniformly distributed and have rejected as lacking geographical interest those things that are uniformly distributed ... The phenomena associated in a particular place are unsystematically related because they are produced by different processes ... [the geographer's] particular mission is to study each process as it operates in particular places, and as it is actually modified in its action by the presence of other unsystematically related phenomena grouped naturally together on the face of the earth.

Exactly these ideas of naturalness, particularity, unsystematic, and non-generalizable spatial association proved anathema to the new scientific geography which erupted out in the Middle West and on the West Coast of the United States only a few years later!

For Neil Smith (1989: 91), a geography professor at Rutgers University in New Jersey, and no stranger to the techniques of penchant criticism, Hartshorne's *The Nature of Geography* sought a logical rationale for geography as an academic study. But in doing so the work isolated geography within a museum-like existence. Smith traces Hartshorne's isolation of the discipline through Hettner to Kant and the neo-Kantian resurgence in German philosophy in the late nineteenth century. Kant (1965) believed that real world "things-in-themselves" engender sensations in knowing individuals who try to create order from them, the two (sensations and ordering) combining in a "phenomenon." The thing-in-itself is left inaccessible to conceptual manipulation while Kant emphasizes the intuition of the knowing subject in his "transcendental idealism." Hartshorne (1939: 362) says similarly that the regional concept exists "only in our thoughts" with regions being "not inherent in the world." The severance of regions from the material world, Smith (1989: 103–4) claims, "nurtured an anti-intellectual relativism in mid-century regional geography ... the central concept of geography was effectively denied any material referent ... Hartshorne's neo-Kantian idealism justified and indeed promoted the sterility of a regional concept and approach at precisely the time when real-world landscapes were being dramatically restructured."

Philosophical Origins

This needs explaining further by placing Kant's theory of time and space in philosophical context. Seventeenth- and eighteenth-century thought concentrated on the epistemological problem of the self as an experiencing subject. In the tradition of British philosophical empiricism, founded on the scientific revolution of the sixteenth and seventeenth centuries, human beings have no knowledge of the world other than that derived from experience. For John Locke (1632–1704), knowledge begins with sensations and is developed by reflection; David Hume (1711–76) reduced the person to a series of sensations and ideas; George Berkeley (1685–1753) thought that the mind could have no knowledge without the senses (Dunn, Urmson, and Ayer 1992). The British empirical approach to knowledge was counterpoised to a continental European tradition of rationalist philosophy which stressed inherent reason rather than experience. Hence, René Descartes was thoroughly skeptical about the senses and experience – the only thing that could not be doubted, he said, was the thinking thing, the I (*cogito*) having often false encounters with the world (hence experience cannot be trusted). With Leibniz (1953) a priori sensation, or reflection, is a question of the immediate experience of the self; while, for Spinoza (1959), the mind reflects on the body's experiences. Into this intellectual milieu Kant introduces the philosophy of "transcendental idealism." In this, knowledge is inevitably empirical yet the subject contributes so much that without the subjective component experience would not be possible. In *Critique of Pure Reason*, Kant (1965) argues that we do not experience things in themselves but only the representations they occasion in our sensibility (Smith 1933). Through "transcendental deduction" Kant reaches the conclusion that the self connects these impressions, and imposes an objective order on them, so that experience is subject to the a priori laws of understanding (Forster 1989). Specifically, Kant argues that space and time are not properties of things in themselves, nor do they represent things in relation to one another. Rather, Kant deduces, space can only be a subjective form of representation – space reflects the nature of the knowing subject rather the object known – space is a form of intuition (Guyer 1989; Melnick 1989).

We should add that Kant's transcendental idealism has gone through several phases of rejection and rejuvenation. After being widely rejected, along with all forms of idealism, in the period 1830–48, Kantianism began to be revived (1849–65) and disseminated in the neo-Kantianism of Friedrich Albert Lange and then the Marburg school of philosophy (1865–81), coming into a second full glory in the period 1881–1914, after which it rapidly lost prominence, only to be revived again recently (e.g. Deleuze 1984). In Willey's (1978; cf. Kohnke 1991) interpretation, the neo-Kantianism of the late nineteenth century was an attempt at redeeming German liberalism. Kant's moral philosophy of the primacy and autonomy of conscience, his argument that ethical obligation derives solely from pure reason, and not from circumstances, or the empirical nature of humans, was used to posit the existence of a free, rational, moral being, incompatible with any form of tyranny. In the Marburg school, this became a form of ethical (rather than Marxist) socialism, part of the rise of German social democracy in the 1890s. More generally, Kantianism in philosophy, and geography too, is used to oppose empirically based science and materialist understanding, even though this probably misinterprets Kant's intention. Thus, Hartshorne's Kantian regionalism was opposed by spatial science drawing on positivism, the logical successor to the British empiricism of the seventeenth and eighteenth centuries.

Geography as Spatial Science

Hartshorne's discourse on geography as an exceptional, synthesizing study of regional uniqueness prevailed, without serious or at least open criticism, as the hegemonic, defining disciplinary philosophy between 1939 and 1953. During the Second World War geographers engaged in government service began to pragmatically stress what Hartshorne called "systematic geography" – practical notions about transportation and industrial location, rather than academic ideas about unique regions – as their functional contribution to the war effort (Ackerman 1945; 1958; 1963). During the immediate postwar period frustration grew with geography as it had been, in several senses: the emphasis on regions; the lack of modern, scientific methodologies; the remoteness of the discipline from practical and social utility; thus the lack of prestige on campus and in government and industry. Systematic geographical topics were being successfully studied outside the discipline. In the 1940s, a group of "social physicists" (amalgamating physics with social studies) advocated a modern science of human activity with a strong emphasis on space. G. K. Zipf (1949) argued that "the principle of least effort" governed the entire range of individual and collective behavior, even language and preconceptions, as a natural law, an orderliness that could be studied by means of the "exact sciences"; Zipf specifically applied this general law of human behavior to "the economy of geography" by which he meant the effect of distance on movements and distributions in space (Zipf 1949: chapter 9). In an article in *Geographical Review* on the distribution of population in earth space, the astronomical physicist John Q. Stewart (1947a: 485) told (what must have been) a startled audience that there was no longer any excuse for ignoring the fact that human beings obey mathematical rules resembling the "primitive 'laws' of physics." A new science of social physics was within sight, he said, a scholarship unprejudiced and truly modern, one benefiting humankind through planning – "When we have found it, people will wonder at the blind opposition its first proponents encountered." In a companion piece in *Science*, Stewart suggested how this new science might develop:

> principles resembling some of those in physics apply not only in demography but in related aspects of economics ... When celestial mechanics was being developed, in the sixteenth and seventeenth centuries, the order of advance was: (1) the collection of quantitative observations (Tycho Brahe); (2) their condensation into empirical mathematical regularities (Kepler); and (3) theoretical interpretation of the latter (Newton). If there is to be a social physics, its beginnings must follow the same standard pattern. (Stewart 1947b: 179)

While this crudely outlined the development of a new, realist, scientific geography, it took for granted certain preconditions necessary for the very possibility of a social physics of space. Geography as the study of regional uniqueness could never use the methods of physics which depend fundamentally on the recognition of regularities. For geography to be modern science it had to be redefined away from the irregular and towards the study of space as regularity; that is, space had to be reconceptualized not as the irregular characteristics of natural environments describable in metaphorical, poetical terms, but as distance pure, simple, and quantifiable. A geography truly modern in the sense of a modern mathematical science dedicated to the pursuit of truth required a "spatial revolution" against what was judged to be a prescientific notion of geography as "areal differentiation." Space understood in this quantifiable way thus became synonymous with scientific modernity.

The mouthpiece for this growing frustration was Fred K. Schaeffer (1953: 226), emigré professor of geography at the University of Iowa. Schaeffer complained in the *Annals of the Association of American Geographers* (posthumously as it unfortunately turned out) that "the methodology of geography is too complacent." Schaeffer criticized Hartshorne's notion of geography as a unique integrating science and proposed instead that spatial relations are the discipline's real subject matter. While it may be true, he said, that regions contain unique combinations of phenomena which can be described, this is only a first stage before systematic geography examines these phenomena as instances of causal factors describable in terms of general laws. The purpose of scientific geography is to formulate generalizations and laws about spatial relations. Edward Ullman (1953: 60), a professor of geography at the University of Washington, thought that geography as areal differentiation implies that "we are not seeking principles or generalizations or similarities, the goal of all science." He too found geography's main contribution to be a concern with space and spatial interrelations, which were the common denominators of all geography's different types. Ullman (1953: 56) related this idea of spatial interaction to the existing notion of regional geography: "By spatial interaction I mean actual, meaningful, human relations between areas of the earth's surface, such as the reciprocal relations and flows of all kinds among industries, raw materials, markets, culture, and transportation." Space in this view is the medium through which areas are related through flows (Ullman 1957).

Similar ideas of a theory of space had been developing outside geography and on its fringes for some time. The basic notion of simplifying space into "isotropic plains" was used by the nineteenth-century German landowner and amateur scientist J. H. von Thunen (1966) to look at the distribution of agricultural land uses around cities, while Alfred Weber (1929) uses a similar notion for the distribution of industry in space. Walter Christaller (1893–1969), playing with maps of southern Germany, noticed regularities in the distribution of cities of like size which he idealized as a hexagonal, hierarchical structure (Christaller 1933). He too expresses notions of spatial regularity, in this case the distribution of cities in space, or central place theory, in terms of universal physical principles:

The crystallization of mass about a nucleus is part of the elementary order of things. Centralistic principles are similarly basic to human community life. In this sense the town is a center of a regional community and the mediator of that community's commerce; it functions, then, as the central place of the community. Central places vary in importance. Those of higher order dominate larger regions than those of lesser order, exercise more central functions, and therefore have greater centrality. For all however, "the sum of the distances which rural residents travel to the central place is the smallest conceivable sum". (Berry and Pred 1961: 15)

Likewise the writings of the economist August Losch (1906–45) on space are expressed optimistically and positively in terms of opening new scientific vistas (in this case space as a new formulation of the entire theory of economics), but with an emphasis on spatial economic science for the benefit of humanity:

The real duty of the economist is not to explain our sorry reality, but to improve it. The question of the best location is far more dignified than determination of the actual one ... I see in my mind's eye an economic science that ... creates rather than describes. (Losch 1954: 4, 508)

These ideas were carried to Sweden by Edgar Kant, an Estonian geographer; Kant's research assistant, Torsten Hagerstrand (1952), used similar notions of space to investigate the diffusion of innovation in central Sweden (Holt-Jensen 1988) and for a decade or more Lund became Mecca for a new kind of geographer, mathematically, scientifically, spatially oriented. We should add to this list of qualities the notion of a spatial geography positivistic in the finer sense of the word, that is dedicated to using geographical science to rationally improve society.

Then too Walter Isard, an economist at Harvard University in the late 1940s and early 1950s, developed the notion of "space economy" investigated using mathematical models and graph synthesis (Isard and Cumberland 1950). Thus, the years 1954–7 saw the appearance of a series of works mainly by economists, such as Edgar S. Dunn (1954), Walter Isard (1956) and Melvin L. Greenhut (1956), together with translations of works originally in German by August Losch (1954) and Walter Christaller (1933; trans. 1957), dealing with the location of economic activities in space. The Regional Science Association, at first mainly populated by economists, expanded rapidly in the middle 1950s and, for the next fifteen years or so, regional science, rather than economic or urban geography, was the frontier of a new spatial science.

In economic geography, signs were already appearing of a new kind of geographical discourse in industrial studies beginning in the 1940s. But the basic approach of "spatial science" emerged most fully in the area indicated by the social physicists and by Christaller and Losch, the distribution of cities in space and the principle of least effort expressed as distance minimization in journeys to service centers. A series of articles by William Garrison, Duane Marble, and teaching associate Brian Berry, all of the University of Washington, began to use an entirely different terminology of "rigorous proof of theorems" (Garrison and Marble 1957) and "patterns of city sizes . . . observed to be quite regular from one area to another" (Berry and Garrison 1958: 83). In Germany, Dietrich Bartels (1973) elaborated a critical rational geography as a science of space combined with systems theory. These developments were summarized in a crucial series of review articles in the *Annals of the Association of American Geographers* by William Garrison (1959a: 238; 1959b; 1960) in terms of the "mutual relations between geographic and economic forces." Altogether the decade 1953–63 witnessed a shift from geography as regional description to geography as spatial science, in the belated entry of a reluctant discipline to scientific modernity.

In 1963, Ian Burton, a geographer at the University of Toronto, proclaimed the discipline radically transformed:

> In the past decade geography has undergone a radical transformation of spirit and purpose, best described as the "quantitative revolution." The consequences of the revolution have yet to be worked out and are likely to involve the "mathematization" of much of our discipline, with an attendant emphasis on the construction and testing of theoretical models. Although the future changes will far outrun the initial expectations of the revolutionaries, the revolution itself is now over. It has come largely as the result of the impact of work by non-geographers upon geography, a process shared by many other disciplines where an established order has been overthrown by a rapid conversion to a mathematical approach. (Burton 1963: 151)

Burton saw this "revolution" coming from the spread of scientific methods into a world dominated by concern with the exceptional and the unique. To be accorded respect in society, social science "needs to acquire demonstrable value as a predictive science" (Burton 1963: 154). The quantitative revolution was thus inspired by a genuine need to make geography more scientific, nomothetic (law-stating) instead of idiographic (descriptive). The nomothetic approach to geography basically meant observing and describing regularities, as with spatial arrangements of human activities, with theory providing a sieve to sort meaningful from meaningless facts, or forming the measure against which exceptional events could be compared and recognized. Referring to the logical positivist R. B. Braithwaite (1953), Burton found the function of science to be the establishment of general laws governing the behavior of empirical events. The core of scientific method, he said, is organizing facts into theories which are tested or validated through prediction of the unknown. Given the rigorous dictates of this method, the best tool is mathematics, which could help theorists avoid "self-deception." It follows, he concluded, that any branch of geography claiming the status of science needs to develop theory, and theory necessitates quantitative techniques. Theoretical geography was a direction worth following.

The revolution was completed a year later in a "synthesis of regional analysis" by Brian Berry, by this time a professor at the University of Chicago, who put forward a series of basic theses on the new geography:

1 Like other scientists geographers are identified not so much by the phenomena they study as by their integrating concepts.

2 The geographic point of view is spatial.
3 Geography's integrating concepts relate to spatial distributions, spatial integration, spatial interaction, and spatial processes.
4 These concern the worldwide ecosystems of which humans are the dominant part. (Berry 1964: 2–3)

In formulating these theses, Berry proclaimed basic adherence to systems theory (von Bertalanffy 1951) and the scientific method outlined by Braithwaite (1953) and Nagel (1962). A science, Braithwaite says, observes facts and makes simple inductive generalizations from them; it also makes abstract logical statements, and constructs theories, stated initially as hypotheses; but hypotheses are assumed to be valid only when the simple inductive generalizations coincide with the final deductions of the abstract logical constructs. In brief, geography for Berry is spatial science, and science is logical positivism. Similarly for William Bunge (1966: 36), then a graduate student at the University of Washington, geography is theoretical and mathematical. With these statements geography joins in a metaphilosophical search for truth organized in theoretical terms. The high priests of this metaphilosophy are the "logical positivists."

Logical Positivism

Most of this geographical work accepted, virtually without discussion, let alone question, the main precepts of logical positivism as philosophy and positivism as method of analysis. We might therefore divert to render this more specific. Positivism derives originally from the "positive philosophy" spelled out in Auguste Comte's *Introduction to Positive Philosophy* (1988), itself based on the attacks on metaphysics launched by British empiricism (Hume, Locke, and others) and the French Enlightenment philosophers. For Comte, the sciences form a hierarchy of generality and complexity, with sociology (in the sense of social physics) at its apex. Scientific understanding progresses through theological and metaphysical stages to reach positive knowledge. In positivism, the science of society shares the same logical form as the other sciences, but has to develop its own methodological procedures because its subject matter is more complex. Sociology relies on observation, experiment, and comparison but finds isolated empirical observation idle and theory basic to science and progress – theories direct attention to certain facts rather than others. Human social development, Comte says, may be governed by laws similar to those in nature, but variations in the operation of social laws make deliberative action possible in the rational facilitation of progress. These Comtean notions influenced Anglo-American social thought through John Stuart Mill, Herbert Spencer, and the sociology of Emile Durkheim. Thus, for Mill, deductive arguments depend on inductively derived cases while, as Giddens (1978) points out, Durkheim regards social facts as things whose observed regularities can be made into inductive generalizations as parts of a functional and positivistic sociology.

More profoundly, Comte influenced twentieth-century positivist social science, including geography, through the "logical positivism" of the Vienna Circle, a group of natural and social scientists formed originally in 1907, but most active in the 1920s and 1930s (Ayer 1959); the most prominent members were Schlicke, Neurath, Hahn, Waissmann, and Carnap, with a Berlin school composed of Reichenbach, von Mises, Grelling, and later Hempel, and also Scandinavian, Dutch, and Polish philosophers, together with North American sympathizers like Nagel, Morris, and Quine, and British analysts like Russell, Wittgenstein, von Wright, Braithwaite, and Ayer. In its early days, this school put forward an uncompromising positivism which respected scientific method, believing that problems can be solved by logical analysis, thus completely rejecting metaphysics, religion, and mythology. In the Vienna Circle's later years, this position was modified to show greater respect for empiricism – examples, illustrations, common sense – while in Ayer's (1959: 8) still uncompromising words "the metaphysician is treated no longer as criminal but as a patient: there may be good reasons why he says . . . strange things." The key events were the publication of Ludwig Wittgenstein's *Tractatus Logico-Philosophicus* (1922), a 1929 manifesto "The Vienna Circle: Its Scientific Outlook," together with numerous international congresses and a journal, *Erkenntnis*.

This school recognizes the significance of logic and mathematics as systems of symbolic representation in scientific thinking. Here, the mediating ideas between positivism and logic were formulated by the physicist Ernst Mach (1959). Like Comte, Mach saw the scientific outlook as historically triumphant (over metaphysics and religion) and morally progressive in that it facilitated the welfare of the human species. Again, as with Comte, philosophy could no longer be metaphysical speculation, but was the logical clarification of the bases of science (i.e. separating the factual from the imaginary). Logical positivism drew also on British philosophy, especially Bertrand Russell's insistence that philosophy should elucidate the language in which theories are expressed if it is to reveal logical structures underlying the play of appearances. For the logical positivists, differentiating the scientific from the non-scientific turns on the method of verification or testability – that is, the verification principle of the meaningfulness of a statement. In Mach's original thinking, experience is derived from the relations between elements, the sensations of which form the basis of statements. However, this fails to distinguish statements concerning experiences from statements about other statements ("syntactical sentences"). Mach's positivism is transformed into logical positivism by treating the elements which derive from sensations syntactically – that is, as components of a formal language through which experience is described.

In the work of Rudolf Carnap (1935; 1958), Mach's elements become "protocol sentences," statements of experience immediately recorded. The original view of the Vienna Circle was that scientific knowledge rests on a bedrock of indubitable fact accurately represented by these protocol statements. This view was eventually revised and elaborated to place greater emphasis on the elaboration of theoretical concepts. The idea became that the observation language and the theoretical language are connected through "correspondence rules" in which observations are interpreted in the light of theories, and theories are interrogated through observations. In R. B. Braithwaite's analogy, correspondence rules are like zippers pulling theory and observation together into a system of knowledge.

Eventually the dominant logical positivist account of scientific explanation in modern empiricism was developed by Hempel and Oppenheim (1948) as the "deductive–nomological" model of explanation. In this, explanation of an event involves information supplied by two types of statement: general laws and statements specifying the circumstances in which laws apply. A statement referring to the event or phenomenon to be explained is deduced as a necessity from the conjunction of the two. Objective testing involves empirical confirmation of the statements describing laws and conditions, and logical confirmation of the deduction of necessity. For Carl Hempel (1952; 1965), predictions are deduced statements about future events and are therefore symmetrical with explanations. While deductive–nomological explanation is integral to all empirical science, Hempel (1965) says, social scientific theory and history differ from natural science in that their laws are often derived from common sense while their empirical basis cannot be stated with precision – historians mostly offer explanation sketches, although these can be made more scientifically acceptable by empirical testing of their laws and conditions. In Ernst Nagel's (1962) version of this position, most generalizations in a still-youthful social science are statistical uniformities (i.e. regularities) rather than universal laws; these are complemented, however, by functional generalizations explaining the maintenance of system states through feedback. Likewise, Hempel (1965) sees functional analysis in the social sciences explaining patterned, repetitive forms of social behavior in relation to larger social systems; in functional explanation systems meet the exigencies necessary for survival and propositions about self-regulation yield predictions which can be objectively tested. For both Hempel and Nagel, interpretative understanding, *verstehen*, or "the method of empathetic understanding," can only suggest hypotheses which have to be established in deductive form and tested empirically to become science (Giddens 1978; Ayer 1952; 1959).

This orthodox model of science has long been criticized from positions ranging from post-positivism to scientific anarchism. To give some examples: Karl Popper (1972) completely rejects induction and sensory certainty and substitutes falsification for verification – that is, the criterion of the scientific status of a theory is whether it can be falsified, refuted, or tested rather than verified; if a hypothesis survives falsification it is confirmed to some degree. All observations are theory impregnated, interpretations of facts, and there is no foundation of certain knowledge. Popper comes to this position, falsification as marking science off from non-science, as a result of critically reflecting on certain types of social theory, such as Marxism, which he says gain their support from quasi-religious conversion rather than the capacity for providing explanations that can be shown to be mistaken on empirical grounds. Imre Lakatos (1968) distinguishes various kinds of falsification to arrive eventually at a sophisticated type in which discarded theories are replaced by superior ones with surplus empirical content (predicting facts excluded by the theories they replace). Similarly, Thomas S. Kuhn's *The Structure of Scientific Revolutions* (1962) argues that the pattern of natural scientific development reveals a picture of scientific inquiry different from the version of strict methodological rules propounded by the descendants of positivism – science, he said, only appears to develop in a linear cumulative fashion (Maier 1986). Instead, accepted paradigms of "normal science" are disrupted by revolutionary periods when contradictions emerge in their puzzle-solving activities. In the work of W. V. O. Quine (1953) and Mary Hesse (1974), scientific knowledge takes the form of networks of statements, with the observable and theoretical distinguished in pragmatic, relative ways and (with Hesse) scientific language growing by metaphorical extension from natural language. The most extreme form of this growing, post-positivist skepticism about scientific method is expressed by Paul Feyerabend (1978). Science, for Feyerabend, is an anarchistic enterprise in which theoretical proliferation is beneficial while uniformity endangers the free development of the individual. How far this deviates from logical positivism may be seen from Feyerabend's (1978: 15) statement that:

> science is much closer to myth than a scientific philosophy is prepared to admit. It is one of the many forms of thought that have been developed by man, and not neces-sarily the best. It is conspicuous, noisy, and impudent, but it is inherently superior only for those who have already decided in favour of a certain ideology, or who have accepted it without having ever examined its advantages and its limits. And as the accepting and rejecting of ideologies should be left to the individual it follows that the separation of state and *church* must be supplemented by the separation of state and *science*, that most recent, most aggressive, and most dogmatic religious institution. Such a separation may be our only chance to achieve a humanity we are capable of, but have never fully realized.

For Feyerabend, the idea of a fixed method or theory of rationality rests on a naive view of humans and their social surroundings; it is a craving for intellectual security in the form of clarity, precision, objectivity, and truth. In contrast, for Feyerabend, the only scientific principle that can consistently be defended is "anything goes."

The change in thinking can perhaps best be represented by the work of Ludwig Wittgenstein (1895–1941). The early Wittgenstein asked what kind of simple, essential nature the world must have if a purely logical language could represent it? In the *Tractatus* (1922), the subject attains meaning by making pictures for itself of facts about a separate world. But in the later Wittgenstein of *Philosophical Investigations* (1968), ordinary language (grammar or the possibilities of use of language) was the essence of the world and philosophy its custodian. Here, grammar consists in conventions and thus has a cultural context, but is also autonomous, not accountable to any reality – hence, language misleads and holds people captive, bewitching them to misunderstand – hence "language games" as activities or forms of life. For Finch (1995: 168), Wittgenstein's philosophy introduces an epochal change from "vertical hierarchical abstraction" (the dominant "progressive" force of modern mathematics, logic, and science) to "horizontal metaphoric connections" which permit the sanity and intelligence of everyday humanity to shine through. We encounter these ideas again under the aegis of poststructuralism and postmodernism (chapter 6).

Explanation in Geography

Most of geography's early work in spatial science followed a pragmatic bent in which quantitative methods were borrowed and applied under what was assumed to be a positivist philosophy rather than a rigorously derived logical positivism or a deductive–nomological mode of explanation. Between the late 1950s and the late 1960s regional–descriptive and spatial–theoretical geographies coexisted uneasily, with sharply demarcated groups of followers, the young (spatial–scientific) turks and the old (regional–descriptive) guard. There was no way of deciding between the two positions except personal preference, the ability to learn new statistical skills, or the desire for status in an up-and-coming new approach to the field. For many, the matter of which path to follow was finally resolved through the writings of David Harvey, then a professor of geography at Bristol University in England. *Explanation in Geography* (Harvey 1969; see also Paterson 1984) was written with these disciplinary quandaries in mind.

Harvey begins with the statement that "geography is concerned with the description and explanation of the areal differentiation of the earth's surface," clearly derived from Hartshorne. This is a statement, Harvey says, composed of two parts, one of disciplinary objective (areal differentiation), one of method (description and explanation). Objectivity is arguable on grounds of belief and values, what Harvey calls the philosophy of geography – that is, distinctive views of the nature of the study. Yet the philosophy of geography is crucial to the prosecution of substantive work and thus implies method: "most methods cannot be evaluated independently of objectives and purpose" (Harvey 1969: 8). "Description," Harvey argues, usually means cognitive description – that is, coherent, patterned, rational, and realistic explanation. And, as opposed to philosophy, such a method can be disputed directly on logical grounds. Thus, the concern of logicians and philosophers of science is to deepen understanding of the logic of explanation by setting up criteria for judging its soundness. The task of a methodologist of geography is to consider the application of evaluative criteria to ensure sound and consistent explanations of geographical phenomena.

Explanations, Harvey says, come from conflicts between expectations and experience; explanations make unexpected outcomes into expected ones, making a curious event seem natural or normal. Of various ways of doing this, Harvey favors the deductive–predictive approach (Braithwaite 1953; Nagel 1962; Hempel 1965) based in classical physics. In this approach, the objective is to establish general laws which are assumed to be universally true statements governing the behavior of events. The basic issue is judging whether a particular explanation is reasonable. Science sets up conventions or rules of behavior for scientists to follow if they are to explain in a reasonable manner: this is the scientific method. Somewhat problematically, Harvey adds Kuhn's (1962: x) notion of paradigms as "universally recognized scientific achievements that for a time provide model problems and solutions to a community of practitioners" – that is, paradigms establish criteria for choosing problems assumed to have solutions within accepted rules and conventions. Thus, scientific activity ("normal science") is "puzzle solving" and scientific revolution occurs through accumulation, to the level of crisis, of problems that cannot be solved by reference to a prevailing paradigm. Basically Harvey takes the position that formal analysis provides deep insights into complex methodological problems. The "standard model" of scientific explanation derived from the natural sciences, especially physics, provides the most consistent, coherent, and empirically justified body of information on which to base understanding of the real world. Scientific inquiry aims at providing "systematic and responsibly supported explanations" (Nagel 1962: 15) or "general laws governing the behavior of empirical events" (Braithwaite 1953: 1), while scientific method prescribes rules dealing with the generation of hypotheses, the provision of responsible support for conclusions, and the linking of these into coherent bodies of organized knowledge.

In this argument, statements made by science about the real world are hierarchically organized into factual statements (sense perception), generalizations or empirical laws and, at the highest level, general or theoretical laws. Of the two routes for establishing a scientific law, induction from particular instances to universal statements, and deduction from a priori premises to particular sets of events, Harvey says that the latter has won wide acceptance and is systematized in the hypothetico-deductive system. Hempel (1965) suggests that explanation aspiring to scientific status should be rendered in the deductive–nomological form as follows:

$C, C, \ldots C$ (a set of initial conditions)
$L, L, \ldots L$ (a set of appropriate laws)
therefore E (the event to be explained)

This involves stating a set of initial conditions (C) and a set of laws (L) which, taken together, show that an event (E) must necessarily occur. Prediction and explanation are symmetrical and deduction ensures the logical certainty of the conclusion. Harvey (1969: 49) follows Hempel (1965) and Popper (1965) in arguing that this "covering law" model of explanation should be used in history: "Historians *must* use this kind of rigorous form in offering explanations." Historians resist this, claiming that they study unique historical events and that subjects like theirs use idiographic methods (exploring particular connections) rather than nomothetic methods (establishing generalizations). This notion of uniqueness and the idiographic method is also claimed by some social sciences, and by geography through Hettner and Hartshorne's notions of regional description. But the uniqueness thesis in history is challenged (Joynt and Reschler 1961) by the argument that all (natural and social) events are unique, and that categorization, classification, and generalization occur only in thought. The historian may face particular difficulty formulating generalizations or laws in precise ways and be forced to offer "explanatory sketches" (Hempel 1965: 236). Weak forms of explanation like this are indeed common to the early stages of development of a discipline. But Harvey interprets these arguments as resistances against deductive theory, resistances he finds to be self-defeating. This brings him to the difficult question of explanation specifically in geography.

For Harvey, extending the scientific form of explanation to the social sciences and geography is an ultimate goal worth pursuing – indeed Harvey's book can be read as a primer in scientific-geographic methodology from a logical positivist perspective. Harvey argues that geography is remote from discussions of scientific method – Hartshorne, for example, scarcely mentions modern analytical philosophy. This provokes the worried reaction that geography is isolated from the advancing front of science (Ackerman 1963) or the vividly stated criticism that geographers "preserve the *status quo* by bathing in a euphoria of inertia" (Chapman 1966: 133). Modern science enters geography anyway as subfields develop their own methodological frameworks. Most geographers assume their discipline to be science but often deny the rigorous employment of scientific method (Hartshorne 1959: 167). For Harvey, the issue of the scientific nature of geography rests on whether law statements can be made, especially in human geography. Resolving this issue depends, in turn, on whether clear criteria can be established for the lawfulness of such statements. Harvey concludes that with less rigid criteria (than physics for example) it can be assumed that laws may indeed be developed in geography, as in biology or economics. Yet most geographers abandoned such a scientific endeavor in the 1920s and 1930s as a critical reaction to the "laws" of environmental determinism. A powerful new orthodoxy came into force associating a particular set of objectives (description and interpretation of small, unique areas) with a particular explanatory form (the idiographic method). Here, the argument centers on the "exceptionalism" of geography.

This exceptionalist position, Harvey says, is based on Kant's statement, expanded by Hettner and Hartshorne, that geography studies an unlimited class of objects and must therefore be defined by its distinctive method of approach, its point of view rather than the range of its subject matter. This implies that geography is the spatial study of unique collections of objects and unique locations, hence description and the idiographic method are used rather than the nomothetic formulation of general laws. Hartshorne also derives from Kant the view that geography analyses the interaction and integration of phenomena in terms of space. Harvey thus turns to Kant's theory of space. This theory shifted from a relative view (space as a system of relations between substances) to a Newtonian absolute view (space has an existence of its own independent of matter), to a transcendental idealist view (space as a conceptual fiction). For Harvey, Kant's eventual position is that space is neither thing nor event but a system of pigeon-holes or a filing system for observations. Space and time are abstract frames of reference which can be examined independently of matter. This Kantian view, amounting to an absolute philosophy of space, or a container view of space, is the source of much of the philosophy of geography: thus the Hettner–Hartshorne notion of regionalism and uniqueness. But Harvey (1969: 208) claims that "the absolute view of space has not been general in the philosophy of science for the last hundred years" and that Kantian views on space and geometry were discredited during the first half of the nineteenth century. Absolute and relative views of space are in conflict in geography; much of the discipline's philosophy relies on a Kantian conception of absolute space, while practitioners operate with relative views of space.

Thus, for Harvey, geographers had accepted an absolute view of space at variance with the philosophers of science and this assumption had relevance for the issue of uniqueness in geography. For Harvey, a major modification, or an outright rejection, of the notion of uniqueness was called for. This centers on the notion of the uniqueness of locations – that is, regional entities as "geographic individuals." Given a relative view of space the idea of uniqueness of locations has to be profoundly modified – locations are not unique, or at best are relatively unique. In turn, this leads Harvey to conclusions about theory in geography. With a Kantian view of absolute space and unique locations, geographers are content with an implicit definition of their point of view, avoid specific theory, or theorize in speculative and non-scientific ways. Yet theory is the "hall-mark of a discipline" (Harvey 1969: 74). For Harvey, the Popper–Hempel thesis about covering laws forms the basis of rigorous explanation in geography. This requires appropriate mathematical methods for handling the complicated multivariate systems which geography tries to analyze. Harvey continues:

> More generally we may conclude that there is no logical reason for supposing that theory cannot be developed in geography or that the whole battery of methods employed in scientific explanation cannot be brought to bear on geographic problems. (Harvey 1969: 77)

This may entail many practical difficulties. But for Harvey (1969: 78) the implication is that: "The Kantian thesis . . . needs profound modification if it is to be satisfactory for the current needs of geography as an independent discipline embedded in an over-all structure of knowledge." Specifically, Harvey advocates the deductive theoretical route to scientific geography – that is, the formulation of theories yielding testable hypotheses. By comparison, Hartshorne's inductive logic (classifying observations and forming principles) is a weak route to the formation of covering laws: it avoids unification of general principles into theoretical structures. Basically Harvey proposes that geography become a hypothetico-deductive discipline, and implies serious consequences should it not do so. He outlines a number of explanatory forms (ecological, functional, systems analysis, etc.) which can satisfy this requirement of hypothetico-deductive science, depending on the kind of question asked. Much of Harvey's book consists in methodologically elucidating these explanatory forms.

In the conclusion to *Explanation in Geography*, Harvey argues that geographical problems cannot be solved merely by selecting some logically consistent methodology. Something more is needed, an adequate philosophy of geography. "Philosophy provides the steering mechanism, methodology provides the power to move us closer to our destination" (Harvey 1969: 482). The geographer, he says, "*needs to identify the particular domain (or set of domains) with which he is specifically concerned*" – Harvey's (1969: 483) speculation about the basic tenet of geographic thought (i.e. its point of view) being that "general theory in geography examin[es] the interactions between temporal process and spatial form." The domain of geographic thought seems to revolve around questions of scale, in practice the "regional scale of resolution" (Harvey 1969: 484), although "regional" may vary over time from the local to the international. A closer definition of domain, he concludes, must await a well-articulated, well-validated geographic theory, by which he means mathematical models, geometry, and probability theory, answering the challenging questions raised by "the complex relationship between geographical conceptualizations on the one hand and syntactical mathematical systems on the other" (Harvey 1969: 485). For Harvey, therefore, theory formation using logical positivist methods was geography's most important priority.

From a position of hindsight, given the subsequent trajectory of his career, and those of others sharing similar views, it is interesting where this takes Harvey as logical positivist. The Vienna Circle had a left wing (Hahn, Neurath, and Carnap); Neurath was a Marxist (Giddens 1978: 251, 255); however, we might note that Mach was called a reactionary philosopher by Lenin (1972b). In a brief mention of Hegel and Marx, Harvey (1969: 425–7) terms the Marxian dialectic a mechanistic form of historical explanation akin to environmental determinism! Instead his fascination is with geography as a positivist science of space, a "discipline in distance" (Watson 1955), fraught with "operational problems" like measuring distance. This implies that geometry is the language of geography – hence Harvey's discussion revolves around geometric concepts, the study of interactions, migrations, theoretical patterns in space, map transformations, hexagonal markets, and so on: "formal geometric theorems may be used to yield meaningful geographic results" (Harvey 1969: 212). Logical positivism thus served to reinforce the notion of geography as spatial science against geography as the description of unique regions. Yet spatial science is conceptualized only in the restrictive sense of spatial causation of spatial events, with geometry rather than dialectics as language of scientific discussion. It was exactly this conceptualization that humanistic and Marxist geographers were soon to rebel against. Supreme irony dictated that David Harvey led the anti-positivist rebellion from within the Marxist camp!

Conclusion

With Harvey's book the description of unique regions was finished as the leading theme of modern geography. A modern discipline consists of two related dimensions of knowledge: a set of objects regarded from a distinct perspective and a methodology sufficient for providing an adequate knowledge of these objects – "adequacy" being decided not only by practitioners but also by the social users of geographic theories. Geography took a century and more to emerge in modern form. It was made possible, indeed necessary, by the collection of a universe of facts needing classifying and arranging in theoretical formats. Two main means of classification were developed between the middle nineteenth and twentieth centuries: regional synthesis and environmental causation. Regional synthesis proved difficult to formulate in exact scientific terms; also it is not clear what pragmatic use regional descriptions have other than teaching facts about the world. By comparison, environmental determinism had direct social functionality in legitimating imperialism as a necessary stage in the evolution of humanity; its logical deficiency stems from a crude analogy between human societies and natural organisms. A disciplinary reaction against environmental determinism resuscitated regional studies in descriptive, idiographic terms rather than as a nomothetic, scientific syntheses – this has to be explained not only in terms of the difficulties inherent in such a synthesis, but also by the revulsion against geography as science with environmental determinism as model case. By the 1940s geography was again secure internally as regional description but vulnerable externally in terms of criticisms of its scientific nature and its practical utility. The postwar period saw geography redefined as the science of space – space not in the Berkeley school's sense of earth surface transformed through human action into cultural landscape, but space made to resemble physics, space reduced to distances between points, with spatial behavior as distance minimization, and geometry as disciplinary language. With such a space, modern scientific methods could be employed, initially as statistics inductively measuring regularities, eventually as mathematical logics in a deductive science. About this period of change Peter Gould (1979: 140) was to say:

> It was not the numbers that were important, but a whole new way of looking at things geographic ... It was a generation that, without exception, was completely conventionally trained, but one that knew in its bones that there was something better, more challenging, more demanding of the human intellect than riffling through the factual middens and learning the proper genuflections from *The Nature of Geography*.

The changes of the 1950s and early 1960s were misinterpreted, by Burton among many others, as a quantitative rather than a scientific and spatial revolution in the interests of humanity. This latter aspect is captured in retrospect by Gunnar Olsson in a paper titled "Toward a Sermon of Modernity":

> What I and some others were searching for was the truth of human spatial interaction. Our ambition was to catch that truth in the most precise net we knew, that is to translate statistical observations into the clear and non-ambiguous language of causal relations in which the error term had been minimized. Out of the rich manifold of specific experience we wished to wring the certainty of general knowledge. The goal was to specify, and verify, a set of parameter values by which reality could be tied down and eventually tamed. We were after the kind of "truth" that is necessary for the construction of an optimal world. (Olsson 1983b: 82)

Olsson continues that "reality was more evasive than our naive minds had been taught to believe" and dismisses the "quantitative–spatial–theoretical revolution in human geography" as "simply a matter of passing time, of innocent war babies playing in a field of intellectual blind shells" (Olsson 1983b: 83). Yet this is said with the easy irony of hindsight. At the time, substituting a positive spatial science for regional description was deadly serious in a disciplinary field full of primed shells. Thus, David Harvey's book *Explanation in Geography* turned the heavy artillery of logical positivism and scientific method against the "mere description" of unique regions, blasting it to smithereens. While this entry into modern science saved the discipline, especially in the United States, where geography has only a precarious existence, it limited the kind of work that could claim scientific status to spatial distributions, spatial flows, and interactions conceived geometrically and purely spatially rather than *socio*-spatially. Despite its greater functionality human geography as science of space was still isolated from social science in general, which had difficulty recognizing the significance of "all this theory about space." The spatial revolution also produced a dualism between space and environment, ironically at a time when environmental problems proved to be of rising concern (geography as the study of social effects *on* nature). Geography as spatial science linked the discipline with a philosophy, logical positivism, already suffering (in social science) even from the limited attacks from its post-positivist critics, let alone the critiques from phenomenology and its successors in postmodernist epistemologies; the metaphilosophy of truth, with truth defined as accurate representation, was already under attack as geography belatedly joined it! Positivist geography thus contained the seeds of its own critique. These seeds germinated quickly under the hothouse political conditions of the long radical decade of the 1960s (that is, extending well into the 1970s); from such criticism sprang humanistic and radical geographies quite unlike anything seen or known in the past. This brings to a close the first phase of what we (somewhat arbitrarily) define as modern geographical thought. This chapter serves merely to summarize some tendencies which form the prelude to the main work, human geography as social theory.

Chapter 2

Existentialism, Phenomenology, and Humanistic Geography

"Humanistic geography" emerged in the late 1960s as the most sophisticated of a series of critical reactions against the logical positivist forms of knowledge dominant in the established, academic discipline. Humanistic geography's critique of society took an ethical and moral turn, with a politics more implicitly understood than stated, than the radical geography developing at the same time. Yet humanistic geography's critique of positivist theory was, if anything, more deeply radical, more strongly stated and extensively developed than for the (politically) radical geographers. For humanistic geography immediately drew on the powerful critiques of positivist science long theorized by existential and phenomenological philosophy. These had quite direct applicability to a criticism of the quantitative, theoretical geography of the 1950s and 1960s. There was a tendency also to find continuities between humanistic geography's ideas and certain pre-positivistic themes in geography, especially notions of place and landscape. Thus, in *Humanistic Geography*, the first major collection of essays in this area, David Ley and Marvyn Samuels (1978a: 8–10) traced the lineage of the movement to Vidal de la Blache and French human geography, the Berkeley school of cultural geography, the writings of John K. Wright (1965; 1966) on the history of geographical lore and those of David Lowenthal (1961) on the personal experience of landscape, among other predecessors.

Ley and Samuels (1978b: 9) found little enthusiasm for epistemology and theory in "traditional humanism" which took the position of the humanities rather than the social sciences. In contrast, they thought, "modern humanists" place geography in the social sciences: "A principal aim of modern humanism in geography is the reconciliation of social science and man, to accommodate understanding and wisdom, objectivity and subjectivity, and materialism and idealism." For Ley and Samuels, the main tasks of humanistic geography were clarifying the philosophical base of humanism in geography, developing methodologies, and making substantive contributions to an understanding of the human's place in the world. In other words, it differs from positivism in the *type* of theory it employs, rather than the degree of interest in theory. As Nicholas Entrikin (1985), a prominent humanistic geographer teaching at the University of California at Los Angeles, later argued, humanistic geographers contrast their theoretical approach with positivism's naturalism – that is, its methodological unity between natural and human science, and its advocacy of causal explanation. Humanistic geography, Entrikin said, is anti-naturalistic and seeks "understanding" rather than causal explanation.

In an early review of the emerging field, Entrikin (1976: 616) argued that contemporary humanism gives existential meaning to concepts of traditional significance in geography. Place is redefined as "center of meaning or a focus of human emotional attachment" rather than mere physical point in space. The humanistic approach, he said, is a reaction against an overly objective, mechanistic view of human beings. Instead, the idea is to study the distinctively "human" aspects of humankind – meanings, values, goals, and purposes. Humanistic geography's approach to such issues lies in phenomenology, a position advocated in geography in works by Edward Relph (1970) and Yi-Fu Tuan (1971), and subsequently adopted by others (Mercer and Powell 1972; Buttimer 1976). The early to middle 1970s witnessed an absorbed interest by humanistic geographers in phenomenology and existentialism which, up to that time, were only briefly mentioned, and then rarely, in the geographical literature (e.g. Sauer 1963: 315–16). We therefore outline the main positions in existential and phenomenological philosophy before turning to an exposition of what soon became an existential–phenomenological humanistic geography. The chapter then returns to humanistic geography before concluding with some criticisms of this school of thought.

Existentialism

Existential thought has been plagued by a bad case of mistaken identity. This results as much from its own elusiveness as from vulgarization by others. As opposed to idealism, existentialism is a philosophy of the human subject in the whole range of its existence. Existence for existentialists is characterized by concrete particularity and sheer "givenness," as compared with the abstract and universal concepts of humanity and life common to positivist thought. This notion of "existence" is used in a special sense. For Søren Kierkegaard (1813–55), the first modern existentialist, "existence" means the unique, concrete being of the individual human, the particular which refuses to fit into any system constructed by rational thought (Kierkegaard 1941). Martin Heidegger (1889–1976) restricts the German word *Dasein*, meaning the condition of *existence*, to the human in respect of his or her being, with the "essence" of existence (*Existenz*) constituted by possible ways of being (Heidegger 1962). Jean-Paul Sartre (1905–80) asserts that "existence precedes essence," defining existence to mean concrete individual being, here and now (Sartre 1958); in elaborating this notion of "being," Sartre distinguishes between the being-in-itself of the object and an emergent being-for-itself of the conscious subject, free to choose its essence, yet paradoxically finding in freedom a lack of being. Finally, with Karl Jaspers (1883–1969) *Dasein* simply refers to humans finding themselves in the world, in the sense of an unreflecting experience of life, whereas *Existenz* implies potential, transcendence, and individuality (Jaspers 1967; Macquarrie 1972). Kierkegaard wished to free people from the domination of objectivity. For Kirkegaard, objectivity makes people into observers, while abstract thinking is thought without a thinker. Kirkegaard wanted to destroy the scientific myth that everything is causally determined and, therefore, can be objectively explained in terms of general laws. Subjective knowledge, by comparison, always has the nature of paradox, is concrete rather than abstract, and is known by means of faith rather than rationality. *What* is believed is less important than *how* it is believed. Freedom means being free to choose whether to move from one stage of enlightenment to another, being free to inwardly grasp truth, being free to think for oneself without recourse to rules or laws (Kierkegaard 1936). Likewise, Friedrich Nietzsche (1844–1900) found objectivity, in the sense that there are hard facts in the world to which correspond definite truth statements, to be the main enemy of understanding. Instead, concepts used to describe the world and predict its behavior are chosen to suit our purposes. There are no sharp lines between describing and evaluating. Our very sense perceptions are permeated by inescapable valuations (Nietzsche 1968).

In existentialism, there is no "world" apart from human beings. This does not mean (as with idealism) that the material universe depends for its existence on the minds that perceive it, but rather that humans organize phenomena into some kind of unity or "world." Existentialists differ on whether people bring order to a meaningless chaos, or whether meaning can be projected on earthly things only because the possibility of mental order is given by the order of things. Conversely, there is no human existent apart from the world in which she or he exists – to exist is to be in the world. To exist is to confront that which is other than oneself. The existent constitutes her or himself by an act of separation from the rest (Sartre 1957). The many human interests and perspectives give rise to multiple worlds, with the everyday world being fundamental for existentialists. Thus, for Heidegger (1962), living or dwelling means being related to the world in multiple ways, and practical "concern" constantly puts new natural and human-made objects to use, with the world deriving unity and meaning from the human's organizing concern. Yet people can become slaves to the things they have (Marcel 1949).

Gabriel Marcel, Jean-Paul Sartre, and Maurice Merleau-Ponty give particular attention to the body as a mode of human participation in the everyday world. They occupy space as bodies. They are located at particular points in a space which, from the beginning, is organized in terms of bodily participation – hence, left and right, above and below, front and behind are fundamental (bodily) ways of organizing space. Humans organize space in systems of places related to concerns (places *for* something) with geometrical space subsequently being measured by considering existential space in an objective and detached (scientific) way. The self is seen as an active bodily agent rather than (as with western philosophy since Descartes) the self as a thinking subject, as pure consciousness. Existentialism recurrently deals with the emotional life, the feelings, moods, and affects through which people are involved in the world. Existentialism, then, differs from positivist science in its emphasis on inner experience, knowledge by participation rather than observation, and its celebration of subjectivity over objectivity. Like idealism, existentialism is a philosophy of the subject, but whereas the idealist begins with ideas, the existentialist begins with "mere" existence confronting things themselves. Existentialism is critical in that it rebels against establishment, accepted authority, and traditional canons. Radical questioning and readiness to doubt are its trademarks (Macquarrie 1972).

Phenomenology

Literally the study or description of phenomena (a phenomenon being anything that appears or presents itself to someone), phenomenology involves the description of things as one experiences them. Experiences include seeing, hearing, and other sensory relations, but also believing, remembering, imagining, being excited, getting angry, judging or evaluating, and having physical relations, like lifting or pushing things. In conventional philosophy, phenomena are usually conceptualized dualistically as: (1) appearances; (2) essences (something beyond or behind appearance), essence being misrepresented by appearance. A distinction is often made between an inner world of private experience and an outer world of public objects, as with Descartes' dualism of mind and body or consciousness and matter. These conventional dualisms are rejected by phenomenologists. In phenomenology, experience is always *of* something, always refers to something beyond itself, and therefore cannot be characterized independently while, similarly (and distinct from scientific realism), objects cannot be characterized as a separate external world. Phenomenology calls this feature of an immersed conscious experience *intentionality* while the phenomena experienced are termed *intentional objects*.

Husserl's Critique

Phenomenology originated in criticism by Franz Brentano (1839–1914) and Edmund Husserl (1859–1938) of the realist, empiricist, and scientific positivism developed in the nineteenth century (Husserl 1970: 5–6). Normative, evaluative questions, Husserl said, demand answers. The empirical sciences cannot provide them; given the identification of rational human knowledge with the empirical sciences recourse is made to irrational solutions. There is a cultural crisis.

For Husserl, the crucial episode in forming this crisis was the emergence of a modern, Galilean science aimed at discovering laws of nature expressed as mathematically specified functional relationships between measurable variables. The main mistake, according to Husserl, was Galileo's claim that the only real properties of objects were those which could be mathematized – shapes, sizes, etc. (or, we might add, distance in the study of space); all other properties (color, smell, qualities of places) were subjective effects of these real properties. Husserl rejected this identification of science with the objectively real, with its relegation of the "lifeworld" (the world as experienced in everyday, prescientific life) to the status of subjective appearance. Furthermore, he said, this realist position was soon extended to a general dichotomy between "inner experience" (including all perceptual experience) and the "outer world" of material objects (as depicted by the physical sciences), a duality of subjective experience and objective nature. Such a split was clearly expressed in Descartes' philosophy where it served to separate humans as conscious beings from the rest of the world, and to give a dualistic picture of each human being as consisting of a mind and a body (Husserl 1970; Hammond, Howarth, and Keat 1991).

Husserl's Transcendental Phenomenology

Thus, for Husserl, positivism's "scientific rigor" required the scholar to exclude all valuative positions, and to define objective truth exclusively in terms of establishing facts. "But," asks Husserl (1970: 6–7), "can the world, and human existence in it, truthfully have a meaning if the sciences recognize as true only what is objectively established in this fashion?" Such positions led earlier critics, like Kierkegaard and Nietzsche, to repudiate system-building in philosophy. Husserl wished instead to make a new, yet still rigorous, *science*. For Husserl, the "crisis of science" refers to the unclarified status of scientific knowledge, a lack of awareness of its ontological and epistemic foundations. Science is impaired by its unfounded and unclarified assumptions, particularly its empty-minded ("container") theory of consciousness, and its conception of the human subject as passive receptor of discrete, simple, atomistic impressions from a distinct "outside" world. Instead, Husserl wants phenomenology to unearth the experiential roots of all thoughts in their original "noetic" (intentional) contact with real phenomena. Husserl wishes nothing less than to discover the radical, primary foundations of all knowledge!

In *Cartesian Meditations* (1977), Husserl opposes phenomenology to philosophical realism. For Husserl, realism involves a philosophically naive misinterpretation of "the natural attitude" – the assumption of the independent existence of what is perceived and thought about. Instead, one must suspend, or put into abeyance, this assumption and investigate experiences without it – this suspension is termed the phenomenological *epoche* or *bracketing* (putting in parenthesis), closely related to Descartes' "doubt." The eventual objective of the exercise is a propositionless philosophy beginning with the experiences of conscious human beings, living and acting in worlds which make sense to them, and dealing with this world through a spontaneous intentionality. For the original moment of intuition to be recovered (and for science to be reconstituted) Husserl suggests the method of phenomenological reduction (epoche), suspending all empirical, rational, and scientific judgment to bring to light the essential intentional contact between consciousness and the world. The epoche yields apodictic evidence of: the I (the *cogito*, consciousness of self); the world phenomenon intended by transcendental consciousness (the *cogitatio*); and the fundamental conjunction between the two. This *cogito* is not, as with Descartes, the indubitable knowledge of thinking being. Rather, with Husserl, understanding the *cogito* is "the grasping of self outside of the natural world ... as transcendental subjectivity, that is to say as origin of all meanings, as the sense of the world"; making the world appear as a phenomenon involves understanding its meaning, as something intended by the *cogito* (Husserl 1977; Thevanaz 1962; Hammond, Howarth, and Keat 1991).

The Lifeworld

Husserl's phenomenology thus brings together Cartesian themes of evidence, intuition, and seeing, with Kantian themes of the constituting or creative activity of consciousness. The world reveals itself to the view of consciousness which confers on it its meaning. Husserl called the moving historical field of lived existence the "lifeworld" (*Lebenswelt*) and proposes the disciplined exploration of its essential structures and manifestations. Some areas of investigation include the oriented space of the lifeworld, lived time and human historicity, the human body as it is lived, and a human freedom deeper and broader than that traditionally called freedom of will. In philosophy, this led to a new approach to understanding humans (a kind of philosophical anthropology) expressed in the existential phenomenologies of Heidegger, Merleau-Ponty, and Sartre among others (Wild 1962: 7–9; Edie 1962: 13–36). In geography, it leads to a disciplined but subjective investigation of the places constituting the lifeworld.

Existential Phenomenology

Existential phenomenologists adhere to Husserl's method of description (i.e. his phenomenology) but not to his transcendental idealism. For existential phenomenologists, the existence of the world is definitely not something to be bracketed out in producing pure descriptions. Nor is it the task of philosophy to find foundations for knowledge. Instead, the world is intelligible in the world by virtue of human *action* on it. Rejecting the notion of a transcendental ego, the philosophizing subject standing outside the world, the existential aim is to characterize the ordinary experience of human beings living *in* the world. Thus, as opposed to Husserl, existential phenomenology takes activities, or what Sartre calls "conducts," as a starting point. The world of objects acted upon, and the conscious active subjects, are interdependent – any conduct presupposes the existence of both. The task of philosophy is to find the characters of existent objects and active subjects, given their interaction. While the idealist subject is outside, the existential subject lives inescapably in the world. And while the realist subject is an integral part of the world, a natural object among others, the existential subject is distinctively different – all that is determinate and intelligible in the world is so solely by virtue of human action.

Heidegger's Method

Martin Heidegger's lifetime preoccupation was with the ultimate existential question: "What is the meaning of being?" His "hermeneutic method" consists of phenomenologically uncovering, or making explicit, the forgotten fundamental structures of being. Opposing the ontic (the existent, what is) to the ontological (the meaning of what is), Heidegger searches for a radical foundation, not only for knowledge (as with Husserl), but also for the quality of being. Heidegger's existential phenomenology attempts to go beneath the level of consciousness into the *Dasein*, the original condition of "being there," or "being-in-the-world," the area of "opening up" where something manifests itself. For Heidegger, the original encounter with the world does not consist of knowing it, or being separate from it (as with Husserl), but dealing with it in a more practical way ("concern"). The world does not consist of entities recognized as "things" but as entities used before they are recognized ("equipment"). The human being, then, is originally practical, yet ultimately concerned about itself, concerned with the search for self-identity. By virtue of this concern *Dasein* relates to other persons, to objects, and even to itself. "Heidegger's philosophy is a working out of this essential quest, finding out what (who) we are" (Solomon 1972: 208).

Being and Time

Heidegger's ambition was to regenerate philosophy by removing the conceptual rubbish to recover a clearer understanding. His best-known work *Being and Time* (1962; original 1927) argues that a philosophy of humans must arise from, and return to, the whole existence, and not merely the disengaged attitude of knowing (i.e. humans as disembodied consciousnesses). The problems in philosophical thinking, he argues, are due to a peculiarly western way of understanding the nature of reality: "substance ontology" – the view that reality "stands under" properties and remains continuously present throughout all change – this is also called a "metaphysics of presence" (cf. Derrida in chapter 6). Since Descartes, substance ontology has bred a series of either/ors that generate the problems of philosophy; e.g. either there is mind, or everything is just matter. Heidegger tries to undercut this position by challenging the idea that reality must be thought of in terms of substance. His claim is not that mind and matter do not exist, but that they are derivative, regional ways of being for things. He sees the history of philosophy from Plato to Husserlian phenomenology as one extended misinterpretation of the nature of reality, inevitable once one adopts the detached standpoint of theoretical reflection (i.e. stepping back to get an impartial, objective view of things), for then the world goes dead, i.e. things lose their meaningfulness. Following the lead of "life philosophy" (Nietzsche, Bergson, Dilthey), influential at the turn of the nineteenth century, Heidegger hopes to recover an original sense of things by setting aside the view of reality derived from abstract theorizing and focusing instead on the way things show up in the flux of everyday, prereflective activities.

To do this, *Being and Time* asks the traditional question of ontology: what is the being of entities? But this fails to inquire first into the meaning of being – i.e. since what things are (their being) is accessible only insofar as they become intelligible (show up as relevant) we need a fundamental ontology that clarifies the meaning (conditions of intelligibility) of things in general. Since "being-there" (*Dasein*) is the horizon in which existence becomes intelligible, fundamental ontology must begin by clarifying the possibility of having any understanding of being at all – this makes up the content of *Being and Time*; that is, an investigation of our own being as the basis for inquiring into the being of entities in general. In doing this, Heidegger brackets the assumption that there is mind or consciousness as a self-evident starting point, and starts with people in the midst of day-to-day practical affairs (engaged agency), prior to any split between mind and matter, caught up in the lifeworld: for Heidegger there is no pure external vantage point which gives a disinterested view. Fundamental ontology thus begins with a description of phenomena that become manifest (show themselves) in relation to purposes as these are shaped by forms of life. The goal of inquiring into mundane activities is to identify the essential structures that make up the formal scaffolding of any *Dasein* (i.e. being human). The phenomenology of everydayness is coupled with a hermeneutic, or interpretation, designed to bring to light the hidden basis for the unity and intelligibility of the practical lifeworld.

When human being is thought of as the temporal unfolding of a life course, three structural elements can be identified as making up human existence for Heidegger. First, *Dasein* always finds itself thrown into a concrete situation and attuned to a cultural, historical context – "facticity." Second, agency is "discursive," in the sense that we articulate with the world along guidelines of interpretations embodied in public language. Third, *Dasein* is "understanding," in the sense of a general tacit knowhow, taking a stand on life and projecting possibilities of meaningfulness for things and ourselves ("future" in the sense of realizing some outcome – being toward the future). Hence, for Heidegger, the meaning of being (i.e. basis of intelligibility) is an "absence of ground" or "abyss" in that there is no *ultimate* foundation for the holistic web of meaning that makes up being-in-the-world (Kockelmans 1965; 1984).

In his "Letter on Humanism," Heidegger (1977) takes these arguments a step further to criticize the modern project as the subjection of nature to the mastery of a rational will – that is, the modern subject represents and manipulates an objective world, dominating nature according to its own priorities (Bernstein 1992: 104). This fundamental critique of modern humanism is picked up by contemporary French Heideggerian philosophers and passes into poststructural and postmodern thought through the anti-humanism of Michel Foucault (Johnson 1994: 5–6, 12–13).

Being and Space

Being and Time (Heidegger 1962) can also be read as offering "an existential interpretation of space as localized and qualitative, grounded in an analysis of our practical dealings with the world … space, thought existentially, is equi-primordial with temporality" (Frodeman 1992: 34). In this view, Heidegger finds inadequate the western philosophy of space as container; a more adequate view is spatiality as involvement, the ready-to-hand quality of tools, the regions of everyday concerns (home, workplace …) that generate a fundamental sense of space. The spatial characteristics of *Dasein*'s relation to the world are deseverence and directionality – these define a space prior to objectively measured geometric space. Deseverence is the "de-distancing" resulting from *Dasein*'s relations with things (i.e. familiarity or understandability). Directionality denotes *Dasein*'s directedness towards a region as well as an object's orientation in space. Deseverence and directionality demonstrate that a primary sense of space is not abstract and geometric but embodied and erotic, directed and oriented towards desired regions; these are fundamental determinants of *Dasein*'s being in the world.

Additionally, understanding and attunement, conditions of the possibility of consciousness and world, may best be understood in terms of existential spatiality. The "thrown" character of existence (*Dasein* finding itself already being in a predefined space) is human attunement to the world, the lived experience of thrownness. Understanding can be thought of as the space-creating aspect of *Dasein* – through understanding room is created for manoeuvering within a social space, breathing space is made in the sense of letting the place provide its own categories. Heidegger's notion of care for mortal entities also has an irreducibly spatial element. An analysis of conscience shows that *Dasein* is always involved with, and indebted to, others. Hearing the call of conscience, care is a category of authentic spatiality, authenticity being a matter of responding to one's place in the world. Thus, Heidegger's thought can be completed through a topology of being that reconciles time and space in terms of the places inhabited by being – but place is the marker of an absence as well as a presence (Frodeman 1992).

Phenomenology of the Social World

Heidegger's ideas are fundamental to understanding many subsequent philosophical, social theoretical, and geographical conceptual tendencies: these ideas recur in structuration theory, underlie deconstructionist versions of poststructuralism, are part of feminist critiques of scientific objectivity, all movements with vital implications for geographical understanding. But for existential phenomenology to affect social geography it needed translating sociologically, and here the crucial interpreter was Alfred Schutz.

Alfred Schutz (1899–1959) moved existential phenomenology in the direction of a phenomenological sociology. For Schutz, experience is always experience of something; direct experiences occur in the everyday lifeworld; and individuals pursue interests by manipulating objects, dealing with other people, conceiving and carrying out plans. In the natural attitude, individuals are pragmatic and utilitarian. They deal with specific situations which limit and condition interests and present opportunities. The individual brings to the situation a chain of prior lived experiences which are unique – the person in a "biographically determined situation" brings to bear a (partly contradictory) store of experience and a stock of knowledge stratified according to its relevance and preciseness. The lifeworld is prestructured for the individual who takes it as given along with the interpretations of the person's cultural in-group, especially its central myths or world view – Schutz, however, thinks that individuals have their own versions of this world view. Exposure to culture and its selective interpretation presuppose a common language as means of communication and instrument of cognition: the terms and phrases of the vernacular contain pre-interpretations of the world and are endowed with particular meanings. Any specific individual interest brings a sorting of knowledge into zones of relevance. Also any social group establishes its own domains of relevance each with a particular hierarchical order.

In the lifeworld, individuals take the existence of others for granted. Spontaneously the individual endows the sensory configuration of the other with a consciousness and feeling similar to his or her own. The shared interactive and communicative environment allows for mutual understanding and consent. The individual not only experiences self in a situation, but also the experience of the situation by another. Genuine subjective understanding can be achieved by putting oneself in the place of another and grasping their motivations – subjective understanding is motivational understanding. The dynamic of mutual understanding involves a reciprocity of motives (one's intentions becoming the other's) and a reciprocity of perspectives (reasoning in the other's place). For Schutz (1967; 1970), a "thou-orientation" springs from face-to-face interaction with another person – if it is reciprocated, if both turn intentionally towards one another, a "we-relationship" results. Face-to-face involvement with others is the dominant form of social encounter. But situations also arise where the individual is not a direct participant, but only an observer and indirect interpreter of motives, actions, etc. For Schutz, the objective point of view is the perspective of the uninvolved observer. The implications are profound for cultural and intersubjective spaces.

Phenomenology of Perception

Maurice Merleau-Ponty's (1908–61) introduction to *Phenomenology of Perception* (1962) presents a sustained critique of empiricism and intellectualism (rationalism) from the point of view of existential phenomenology. The task of phenomenology, for Merleau-Ponty, is describing rather than causally explaining in a "scientific" way. Merleau-Ponty opposes the realist notion of the existence of the world as independent of one's knowledge of it, and to the idea that such knowledge can be gained through empirical science. Yet he also opposes transcendental idealism, in which the world is constituted by a conscious subject not a part of that world. Realism depends on scientific explanation, and transcendental idealism on analytical reconstruction, neither of which, Merleau-Ponty argues, can be successful. Additionally, realism and idealism have in common a view of the world which he calls "objective thought." According to this, the "universe" consists of identifiable objects with definite locations which interact with each other in a single spatial framework. Objective thought characterizes the world in a way which makes it suitable for scientific treatment. But Merleau-Ponty finds this fundamentally in error in attempting to understand perception. For the world people actually perceive is not "objective," but consists of objects in a lived world with non-determinate, ambiguous properties, with relations of meaning and reciprocal expression rather than causal determination, objects variously situated in relation to the human agent's specific field of action. Empiricism and intellectualism, then, misdescribe the lived world, systematically distorting their descriptions through the prejudices of objective thought. Merleau-Ponty says, what one actually perceives can never be precisely specified, objects cannot be fully described, properties may or may not adhere, and the properties of objects may be mutually incompatible. This makes ambiguity an inherent feature of the lived world; the determinacy of the objectivist's universe is at odds with it.

Also, objective thought recognizes causal or functional relationships between things, but Merleau-Ponty denies that relationships in the lived world are external – rather they are internal between things which cannot be independently specified; this is true of all relationships in the lived world, even those between organic and inorganic entities, despite their important differences. Merleau-Ponty claims too that objective thought sees every object as having a determinate location in a unified spatial framework yet as not being affected by its position in space – whether it is upright or upside-down for instance. But this is not true of one's actual experience of things in the lived world, where things are always situated in relation to specific human actions. Finally, objectivism makes a radical distinction between the properties objects genuinely possess and those which they only apparently possess (to the perceiver) but, Merleau-Ponty argues, there is no more reason for denying such perceived properties as there is for denying any others. Thus, Merleau-Ponty insists that what objective thought regards as purely metaphorical should instead be taken as literally true (Hammond, Howarth, and Keat 1991).

Bodily Knowledge

Merleau-Ponty criticizes in particular the objectivist conception of the human body. Objectivist thought fails to recognize the active, purposive nature of the body, its practical attitude toward the world. Empiricism fails in assuming that the body is a mere object, while intellectualism errs in separating the human subject from the body or more broadly in dichotomizing the subject (for-itself) and the object (in-itself). Merleau-Ponty develops an account of the kinds of knowledge, understanding, and intentionality possessed by the body as the subject of action. Acquiring new skills or habits involves conscious analysis and mental imagery, but also there is an irreducibly bodily element of "understanding" involved. The body grasps relationships, senses how things should be done, feels incipiently what new movements would be like. Without this practical bodily knowledge a purely intellectual grasp of things would be to no avail. Hence, one must accept that "it is the body which 'understands' in the acquisition of habit" (Merleau-Ponty 1962: 144). Indeed, he claims, the body's practical knowledge is irreducible, or original, and is primary in the sense that it provides the foundation for other forms of knowledge. Hence, abstract spatiality is rooted in, and derived from, the practical spatial knowledge displayed in movements. Additionally, the fundamental form of intentionality is one's ability to act in the world; in such intentional action the body is directed towards the world. Thus, for Merleau-Ponty, intentionality belongs to the body, and provides the basic connection between humans and world.

Being and Nothingness

Sartre agrees with Heidegger that the initial distinction between acts of consciousness and objects (of consciousness), between *cogito* and *cogitato*, is philosophically disastrous – by polarizing the two, and emphasizing the dependence of the world on the subject, Husserl adopts an idealist stance. Sartre (1957; 1958) criticizes Husserl's phenomenological method, especially the distinction between the transcendental ego as subject and the intended object as object. For Sartre, the transcendental ego is neither necessary for explaining experience, nor detectable in experience. Likewise, Sartre criticizes Husserl's conception of the objects of consciousness as too dependent on the subject. Sartre puts forward an alternative conception of "translucent" consciousness: "the object with its characteristic opacity is before consciousness, but consciousness is purely and simply consciousness of being conscious of that object" (Sartre 1957: 40); or later "Every conscious existence exists as consciousness of existing" (Sartre 1958: xxx). In other words, consciousness is an act rather than a subject, an awareness of being rather than a transcendental intentionality.

By contrast Sartre, in *Being and Nothingness* (1958), denies the distinction between objects and objects for consciousness: objects simply *are*. The true distinction lies between perception and imagination as ways of grasping objects in consciousness. While the act of perception is not free (the objective is obtrusive), consciousness (by imagining) can ignore, destroy, or go beyond objects in a creative act Sartre calls "nihilation." The bracketing of existence is impossible for perception, whereas it is just this possibility of bracketing (or nihilating) that characterizes consciousness. Every act of consciousness includes the possibility of nothingness, or that things might be different from what they are: hence the human is a being of possibilities. In reflecting on one's past and future selves, one is no longer one's past, not yet one's future self: "Consciousness confronts its past and its future as facing a self which it is in the mode of non-being" (Sartre 1958: 34). Transcendence is the human capacity to go beyond a present state towards a future one, while "anguish" is the awareness that one is both free and responsible. "Bad faith" involves fleeing from both these realizations, acting as a being-in-itself. An object obeys the principles of self-identity (it is just a set of properties), but a human being, conscious of its properties, can dissociate itself from them. Human freedom, then, is the ability of consciousness to wrench itself away from the actual world. Sartre's "nothingness" is the equivalent of the existentialist notion of freedom. Even so, Sartre's freedom of intention remains restricted by situations. That is, human beings are free to choose their own "projects" and impose their own interpretations, but only on situations in which they find themselves. How far Sartre lies from the vulgar concept of freedom to do anything one chooses may be seen from his statement that: "man being condemned to be free carries the weight of the whole world on his shoulders: he is responsible for the world and for himself as a way of being" (Sartre 1958: 707). We note again that Merleau-Ponty's critique of science and Sartre's notions of project, freedom, and agency are fundamental to later developments in social theory and geography.

Hermeneutics

Originally, hermeneutics was a tool used by disciplines concerned with understanding texts, for example in biblical interpretation. Friedrich Schleiermacher expanded this interpretative process to a broader understanding of the linguistic expression of thought, both the words of texts and the author's intention, the task of hermeneutics being "to reconstruct the inner course of the compositional activity of the writer" (Schleiermacher 1977: 188). For Schleiermacher, interpretation could in some sense be scientific, while for Wilhelm Dilthey (1833–1911) and the German theorists of the nineteenth century, hermeneutics was definitely scientific, of a kind different from the natural sciences in the sense that texts have a unique meaning determinable by the reader.

Heidegger's project in *Being and Time* was a "hermeneutic of *Dasein*." As we have seen, he means by this that phenomenology must be turned from letting *things* become manifest as what they are without forcing categories on them, to interpreting *being*, rendering visible the hidden structure of being-in-the-world in a hermeneutic of existence. Here, hermeneutics is still the theory of understanding, but understanding is defined as the power to grasp one's situation and the possibilities for being within the horizon of the lifeworld. Heidegger's later work turns increasingly to the interpretation of texts, in the broad sense of revealing the questions that the "text" of western thought was trying to answer. He argues that the western tradition conceptualizes truth as "correspondence," while correct-seeing and thinking comes to mean the proper manipulation of ideas, placing an idea before the mind's eye, the presence, appearance, or perception of what each being is. The world becomes subject-centered and philosophy becomes consciousness-centered, i.e. modern "subjectivism" in which the world has meaning only with respect to humans whose task is domination – the great metaphysical systems become expressions of will, whether phrased in terms of reason (Kant), absolute spirit (Hegel), or will-to-power (Nietzsche). For example, the will-to-power grounded in subjectivism knows only the thirst for more power, expressed in the contemporary frenzy for technological mastery, concepts that give control over both objects and experience. Western thinking represents the "text" of this thematization. Hermeneutics, for Heidegger, thus involves asking what the text does not say, doing violence to the text, retrieving the original event of disclosure, understanding the author better than her or himself (Heidegger 1963; Palmer 1969: 140–61).

The crucial hermeneutical question, for Heidegger, thus becomes not merely the nature of being but how to *think* being. In this, true thinking is not the manipulation of that already disclosed but disclosing that which was hidden. In terms of texts, Heidegger (1959) outlined a hermeneutics of questioning which reaches into unmanifest being and draws it into concrete, historical occurrence. Heidegger was also increasingly interested also in the linguisticality of being or, later, language as an appearance of being. And finally, Heidegger saw art as a way of revealing the being of beings. Art is a way of capturing the tension between earth, as primordial source, and world, as lived by humans.

This reconception of understanding was bought to full systematic expression in Hans-Georg Gadamer's "philosophical hermeneutics." According to Heidegger, we understand not with empty consciousness but with an already established way of seeing, with certain preconceptions, with a prestructure of understanding. For Gadamer in *Truth and Method* (1975), this means that the past is a stream in which we move and participate in every act of understanding. Tradition is the fabric in which we do our thinking. Thus, there can be no presuppositionless interpretation, inside or outside the sciences; what we call "reason" is a philosophical construction – tradition furnishing our stream of concepts; and the notion of one "right" interpretation is impossible. So, in terms of the interpretation of historical texts, understanding is a matter of participation in the tradition of the author, within the event that transmits tradition, in a movement that applies historical meaning to the present situation (Gadamer 1975; 1977; Palmer 1969: 162–217).

By comparison, Paul Ricoeur (1965) defines hermeneutics as a theory of rules governing textual exegesis – "text" being interpreted broadly as a collection of signs – which goes from manifest content and meaning to latent and hidden meaning. Hermeneutics, for Ricoeur, is particularly concerned with symbolic texts of equivocal symbols with multiple meanings. With Freud, he distrusts conscious understanding as a web of myths and illusions. This leads Ricoeur to propose two different syndromes: a hermeneutics dealing sympathetically with the symbol – recovering meaning from it; and one seeking to demystify the symbol (e.g. religion) as representation of a false reality (cf. Marx, Freud, Nietzsche). Because of the opposition between the two, there are no universal canons of interpretation (Palmer 1969: 43–5).

To summarize: this was the substantial body of ideas which humanistic geographers found "ready-to-hand," so to speak, as they began criticizing positivistic geography in the late 1960s. Humanistic geography drew three main aspects of a transcendental critique from existential phenomenology and hermeneutics: a critical analysis of the objectivity of realist, positivist science; alternate phenomenological and hermeneutic methods; and a spatial ontology derived from existentialism. Existential phenomenology is critical of the notion that science consists in the recognition of facts and the formulation of causal laws through a practice of scholarly separation from the world using abstract, objective methodologies; such objectivity it finds the enemy of understanding. But the problem is that phenomenology cannot settle on an alternate methodology because basic ontological problems remain unsolved: so, for Husserl, transcendental subjectivity is the origin of meaning, whereas for Heidegger and the existentialists, it is the forgotten, fundamental structures of being; the common theme, however, is the intentional creation of order rather than its discovery already formed. Yet the problem remains, what is the nature of this "intentionality"? In a more immediate sense, humanistic geography derives from existential phenomenology an interest in the lifeworld, the field of lived experience, which it interprets as the ontological basis for an interest in the spaces occupied by experiencing, interpreting subjects – that is, humanistic geography derives an abiding interest in places. We return to an examination of this interest.

Phenomenology and Humanistic Geography

The substantive (disciplinary) difference that emerges between positivistic and humanistic geographies involves competing conceptions of the human's place in the world. Positivist geography looks at environment and sees space. That is, positivist geography sees stretches of homogenized earth surface, characterized by extension measurable in standard units (miles); with the human relation to space theorized as the expenditure of effort needed to overcome the friction of distance (transport costs, travel times); this having predictable effects on human activity in space (less interaction as intervening distance increases); and with a notion of location as mere position in an abstract spatial extent (industrial plants, central places, etc.). Hence, there can be objective laws of human behavior in space, "objective" in two senses: space and people are treated as objects; and the observing scientist can maintain objectivity as the main standard of scholarly behavior. *Humanistic geography* looks at environment and sees place – that is, a series of locales in which people find themselves, live, have experiences, interpret, understand, and find meaning. Yet the mere mention of place as center of life experience evokes in the positivist mind the suspicion that humanistic geography is unscientific, new age sentiment, incapable of producing generalizations beyond personal opinion. For example, R. J. Johnston (1983: 84), long at Sheffield University, and now a professor at Bristol University, who has written extensively on the recent history of geographical thought, sees humanistic geography as involving simple, personal understanding. Neil Smith (1979: 367–8) compares phenomenology's naive delight in the individual with the brute realities of everyday experience. There may be more than prejudice behind such views. But such reactions, which usually prevent further serious investigation into existentialism, phenomenology, and humanistic geography, merely reinforce the existential phenomenological claim that a narrow-minded, highly particularistic view of "scientific knowledge" monopolizes knowledge, and that to be schooled in this pale, insipid understanding is to be blind to many, if not most, forms of human experience, including the scientific. More importantly, the notion that the study of place is entirely personal mistakes the arguments particularly of humanistic geographers in the strict phenomenological tradition that: practical experience (of place) is the original source of scientific notions; that positivist geography describes (badly) one quantitative aspect (distance, transportation) of spatial relations; that other aspects are equally significant (dwelling, locality); and that geographical science needs to start again by building theories which encompass the wide range and experiential depth of life in places. To further this *scientific* endeavor, humanistic geographers turn to existential phenomenology and hermeneutics, bringing these to bear on traditional geographic concerns with place, space, environment, landscape, and region. An in-between position, between positivism and existentialism, occupied by "behavioral geography" (Gould 1963; Wolpert 1964; Cox and Golledge 1969), involves a more limited search for models of humanity different from the spatially rational beings of normative location theory, a redefinition of environments as other than objective and physical, and an interest in psychological, social, and other theories of human decision making and behavior (Golledge and Timmermans 1990). Here, however, we cover the ideas of some of the founders of the humanistic geography school of thought – Edward Relph, Yi-Fu Tuan, Anne Buttimer, and David Ley – rather than behavioral geography (which many humanists criticized as complicit with positivistic approaches). Of these, probably the most important early statements came from Relph, a professor of geography at the University of Toronto.

Relph's Phenomenology

For Edward Relph (1970), phenomenology is a branch of modern philosophy concerned with the reorientation of science and knowledge along lines which have meaning and significance for human beings. Relph finds the idea of the human as ultimate point of reference for all objects and facts of nature well recognized by geography. The idea that natural objects exist only through their utility for humans, and are discovered only through practical pursuits, is similar to widely held views of resources, such as those of Zimmerman (1933). Similarly, the idea that formal geographical knowledge is based on a more fundamental everyday contact with the world is well recognized (Lowenthal 1961). Such anthropocentric views give the possibility of understanding humans and nature as a single system unified by reference to human needs, intentions, and existence – this enables the unification of the field of geographical enquiry (i.e. physical and human geography). But this, he says, is not a field which can be comprehended using positivist methods, such as those outlined by Harvey's *Explanation in Geography* (1969). The positivist assumption that humans are predictable, rational, and behave in a measurable manner, conflicts with the phenomenological belief that humans are describable in terms of consciousness rather than behavior and live in a set of subjective, meaningful worlds that change with their intentions. "From the basis of these phenomenological assumptions attempts to develop mathematical models and theories of man's behavior in space are seen not as a contribution to an understanding of some 'real' geography of man's activities, but as the reflection of the limited intentions of those geographers presenting the explanations" (Relph 1970: 198). If geography is concerned with developing objective laws and theories, Relph said, the criticisms of phenomenology might be ignored. But if geography is concerned with understanding people on the human level, the concepts of phenomenology have much to offer. What this might be is shown by Relph's empirical work.

Place and Placelessness

In his highly original work *Place and Placelessness*, Relph (1976) argued that a practical knowing of places is essential to human existence. Place is a profound, complex aspect of the human's experience in the world: as Heidegger (1958: 19) declared, "'place' places man in such a way that it reveals the external bonds of his existence and at the same time the depths of his freedom and reality." Yet architects, planners, even geographers fail to adequately explore the concept of place. Even conceptions which understand place, and everything occupying it, as an integrated and meaningful phenomenon (Lukerman 1964) are unsatisfactory because they preserve an earlier confusion between the concepts of place, region, area, and location. Clarification must be sought by examining the links between place and the phenomenological foundations of geography, in the direct experiences of the world which all formal geographical knowledge presupposes (Dardel 1952). Relph therefore explores place as a phenomenon of the geography of the lived-world of everyday experiences.

For Relph, location or position (as in positivist geography) is an insufficient condition of place. Nor is it possible to understand all place experiences as landscape experiences (as with the Berkeley school). Instead, there is a powerful relationship between community and place, in which each reinforces the identity of the other, so that "people are their place and a place is its people" (Relph 1976: 34). In both the communal and personal experience of particular places, there is often a close attachment that constitutes "our roots in places" (Relph 1976: 37), a familiarity involving not just detailed knowledge, but a sense of caring and concern for places. Relph finds such attachment to places to be an important human need: "To have roots in a place is to have a secure point from which to look out on the world, a firm grasp of one's own position in the order of things, and a significant spiritual and psychological attachment to somewhere in particular" (Relph 1976: 38).

Relph discusses various levels of the intensity of the experience of outsideness and insideness in places: existential outsideness, in which all places assume the same meaningless identity; objective outsideness which, Relph critically claims, has a long tradition in the academic geographer's objective cataloguing of information and neutralization of thought in order to explain "scientifically" the spatial organization of places; incidental outsideness, in which places are experienced as little more than backgrounds for activities; vicarious insideness, in which places are experienced in a secondhand way via paintings, poetry, etc.; behavioral insideness, involving deliberately attending to the appearance of a place; empathetic insideness, which involves more emotional and empathetic involvement in a place; and finally existential insideness, when a place is experienced without deliberate and unselfconscious reflection, yet is full of significance. "Existential insideness characterizes belonging to a place and the deep and complete identity with a place that is the very foundation of the place concept" (Relph 1976: 55).

Authentic and Inauthentic Places

This preamble brings Relph to his central question of "authentic" place-making, placelessness, and manifestations of the two in the landscape: a sense of place may be authentic and genuine, or inauthentic and artificial. The notion of authenticity, taken from phenomenology, connotes "that which is genuine, unadulterated, without hypocrisy, and honest to itself, not just in terms of superficial characteristics, but at depth" (Relph 1976: 64). In existentialism, authenticity refers to a mode of being, *Dasein*, which recognizes a human's freedom and responsibility for its own existence, whereas the inauthentic person transfers responsibility to large, nebulous, unchangeable forces about which nothing can be done. Thus, an authentic attitude to place is:

> a direct and genuine experience of the entire complex of the identity of places – not mediated and distorted through a series of quite arbitrary social and intellectual fashions about how that experience should be, nor following stereotypical conventions. It comes from a full awareness of places for what they are as products of man's intentions and

the meaningful settings for human activities, or from profound and unselfconscious identity with place. (Relph 1976: 64)

An authentic sense of place involves being inside and belonging to a place (home, hometown, region) as an individual and member of a community, and knowing this without having to reflect on it. Such an authentic and unselfconscious sense of place remains important for it provides an important source of identity for individuals and communities. But the very possibility of the development of a sense of place has been undermined in technologically advanced cultures by the possibility of increased spatial mobility and a weakening of the symbolic qualities of places. For the modern city dweller, a sense of belonging to place is rarely in the foreground and can usually be traded for "a nicer home in a better neighborhood" (Relph 1976: 66).

There is a widespread sentiment that the localism and variety of places and landscapes characteristics of preindustrial societies are being eradicated. In their stead, we are creating "flatscapes" (Norberg-Schulz 1969), lacking intentional depth, providing only commonplace and mediocre experiences. The possibility thus exists of a "placeless geography" lacking diverse landscapes and significant places. We subject ourselves to the forces of placelessness and lose our sense of place. Such an "inauthentic attitude of placelessness" is now widespread, in that we neither experience nor create places with more than a superficial and casual involvement. So, while authenticity consists of an openness to the world and an awareness of the human condition, inauthenticity is an attitude closed to the world and to the human's possibilities. Inauthenticity is expressed through the "dictatorship of the 'They'" (Heidegger 1962: 168), in which the individual is unwittingly governed by an "anonymous they." A second and more self-conscious form of placelessness is linked with the objective and artificial public world where decisions are taken in a world of assumed homogeneous space and time. "Uncommitted 'cold, prying thought' [Nietzsche] which characterizes the philosophical approaches of positivism, and the technical approaches of much physical and social planning, is clearly inauthentic because of its very detachment and narrowness" (Relph 1976: 81). It is manifest in technique, an overriding concern with functional efficiency. For Relph, inauthenticity is the prevalent mode of existence in industrialized, mass societies. An inauthentic sense of place is essentially no sense of place, for it involves no awareness of the deep and symbolic significances of places and no appreciation of their identities. Inauthentic attitudes to place may be: unselfconscious, stemming from an uncritical acceptance of mass values ("kitsch"); or self-conscious and based on a formal espousal of objectivist techniques aimed at achieving efficiency ("technique"). Inauthentic attitudes, directly or indirectly transmitted through diverse media (mass communications, mass culture, big business, central authority, and the economic system that embraces all of these) encourage "placelessness" – that is, "a weakening of the identity of places to the point where they not only look alike, but feel alike and offer the same bland possibilities for experience" (Relph 1976: 90). The trend is toward an environment of few significant places, a placeless geography, a flatscape, a meaningless pattern. Placelessness, then, describes an environment without significant places and the underlying attitude which does not acknowledge significance in places. At its most profound it consists of a pervasive and perhaps irreversible alienation from places as the homes of people. Yet there is a deep human need for associations with significant places. If we choose to ignore that need, allowing the forces of placelessness to continue unchallenged, the future can hold only an environment in which places simply do not matter. If, on the other hand, we choose to respond to that need and transcend placelessness, the potential exists for the development of an environment in which places are for people, reflecting and enhancing the variety of human experience. Which is more probable Relph finds far from certain, but one thing is clear to him, responsibility for the world, placeless or placefull, is ours.

Topophilia

Yi-Fu Tuan, a professor of geography at the University of Wisconsin, uses similar humanistic ideas and also is concerned with environment and place but comes to somewhat different conclusions from Relph, placing greater emphasis on the environmental imagination. For Tuan (1976: 266), humanistic geography looks at "people's relations with nature, their geographical behavior as well as their feelings and ideas in regard to space and place." Humanism is an expansive view of what the human person is and can do, while humanistic geography tries to understand how geographical phenomena reveal the quality of human awareness. The basic approach is by way of human experience, awareness, and knowledge. Humanistic geography serves society essentially by raising its level of consciousness.

In *Topophilia*, a widely read and much appreciated book, Tuan (1974) explores the affective bond between people and place with emphasis on ways of perceiving environment. "Topophilia" is a neologism meaning human love of place, or more broadly all the human being's affective ties with the material environment. Humans respond to environment in various ways, from visual and aesthetic appreciation to bodily contact. The most intense aesthetic experiences, he says, tend to come from surprise, but a personal and lasting appreciation of landscape endures when mixed with the memory of human incidents, or when aesthetic pleasure is combined with scientific curiosity. An awareness of the past is important in the love of place. Patriotic rhetoric stresses the roots of a people, patriotism meaning the love of one's natal land. Local patriotism feeds on an intimate experience of place, whereas imperial patriotism feeds on collective egoism and pride – topophilia rings false when claimed for large territories. Tuan trusts instead more compact sizes scaled to the human's biologic need- and sense-bound capacities. People also more readily identify with a natural area, the home region (*pays*), a physiographic unit small enough to be known personally.

This said, Tuan turns to the role of place in providing images. Such a making of images does not mean that environment "determines" them, nor that certain environments have an irresistible power to excite topophilic feelings, but rather that environment provides the sensory stimuli which lend shape to human joys and ideals. Three material settings appeal strongly to the human imagination: the sheltered sea or lake shore may have been one of humankind's earliest homes (cf. Sauer 1963);

valleys or basins of modest size appeal as highly diversified ecological niches promising easy livelihoods; islands captivate the imagination. People pay attention to aspects of the environment commanding awe, or promising support and fulfillment in the context of life's purposes. As interests change so do the images taken from the environment: contrast the Greeks' environmental imaginary of sea, fertile land, and islands, with early European landscape painting of mountains, river valleys, and forests, with Chinese landscape gardening stressing the verticality of the mountain against the horizontality of alluvial plain and water.

For Tuan, a person is a biological organism, a social being, and an individual. Perception, attitudes, and values reflect all three levels of being. Humans are biologically able to register a vast array of environmental stimuli, but most people make only limited demands on their perceptual powers, with culture and environment very much determining which senses are favored. People respond to the environment in multiple ways, some of which, based on biology, transcend particular cultures. While all humans share common perspectives and attitudes, each person's world view is also unique. However, the group strongly affects the perceptions, attitudes, and environmental values of its members. Tuan claims that the group influences perception to such a degree that people see things that do not exist. The physical environment also has an effect on perception, with culture mediating: thus, the development of visual acuity is related also to ecological qualities of environments.

Environments also provide the major building blocks of autochthonous cosmologies and world views. For Tuan, the world views of traditional societies differ from those of the modern, which have been influenced by science and technology. It has often been said that in a prescientific age people adapted to nature whereas now they dominate it. But a truer distinction is that traditional peoples lived in a "vertical, rotary, and richly symbolic world" whereas modern people live in a world "broad of surface, low of ceiling, non-rotary, aesthetic, and profane" (Tuan 1976: 267), with the change taking place in Europe after AD 1500. And whereas the ancient city was a symbol of the cosmos, with public symbols concentrating and enforcing ideas of power and glory, modern cities are often tagged by a single image or piece of dramatic architecture.

For Tuan, attitudes towards wilderness and countryside had their origins in the city. Wilderness signified chaos, the garden and farm an idyllic life; the city signified order, freedom, and glory, but also worldliness and the corruption of natural virtues and oppression. In the west, however, after the nature-Romanticism of the eighteenth century and the industrial revolution of the nineteenth, public opinion stressed the merits of the countryside and nature at the expense of the city; with wilderness now standing for (ecological) order and freedom, the central city being a chaotic jungle ruled by social outcasts, and the suburb gaining prestige. The meanings of core and periphery are thereby reversed. From this Tuan (1974: 248) deduces:

Human beings have persistently searched for the ideal environment. How it looks varies from one culture to another but in essence it seems to draw on two antipodal images:

the garden of innocence and the cosmos. The fruits of the earth provide security as also does the harmony of the stars which offers, in addition, grandeur. So we move from one to the other; from the shade under the baobab to the magic circle under heaven; from house to public square, from suburb to city; from a seaside holiday to the enjoyment of the sophisticated arts, seeking for a point of equilibrium that is not of this world.

The thrust of the humanistic enterprise, for Tuan, is to increase the burden of awareness.

Grasping the Dynamism of Lifeworld

By contrast, the humanization of the earth, in the view of Anne Buttimer, long a professor of geography at Clark University, and subsequently at the University of Dublin, can be seen as a process in which people have sought styles of dwelling in space and time. Social science lacks ideas and languages to explain the human experience of nature, space, and time, but phenomenologists, she says, are articulate spokespersons for this endeavor. Phenomenology can be defined as "a philosophical mode of reflection on conscious experience, and an attempt to explain this in terms of meaning and significance" (Buttimer 1976: 280). Existentialists, by comparison, have been more concerned with issues of life – anxiety, despair, hope – than with problems of knowledge and mind; most disclaim generalization and, it seems to Buttimer, enjoy the quagmire of ambiguity which surrounds human existence. Combining the two approaches, existential phenomenologists use the phenomenological method to penetrate the lived world context in which experience is construed, exploring the preconscious, organic, and sensory foundations which precede intellectual knowledge.

For Buttimer, relating the notion of lived world to geographic language raises problems. In existential phenomenology, human subjects are seen as the primary initiators of experience, world and milieu being construed as passive. Geographers are more aware of the active role of milieu. But it is the spirit of phenomenological purpose Buttimer suggests we should follow rather than the practice of its exact procedures. For the phenomenologist, "world" is the context within which consciousness is revealed. Broadly speaking, *Lebenswelt* (lifeworld) can be defined as the all-encompassing horizon of individual and collective lives. The notion of lifeworld connotes the prereflective, taken-for-granted dimensions of experience, the unquestioned meanings and routinized determinants of behavior. Bringing these precognitive givens into consciousness, she advocates, can elicit heightened self-awareness and empathy with the worlds of others, whereas in positivism lived experience is objectified. We must therefore shrink from positivist models inspired by physics and consistently return to direct experience:

One must reject any scientific cause–effect models of subject and object, and conceptualize the relationship between body-subject and world as reciprocally determining one another ... Scientific procedures fail to provide adequate descriptions of experience because of their implicit separation of body and mind within the human person. Similarly, if one separates person and world the wholeness of experience escapes. Person (body, mind, emotion, will) and world are jointly engaged in the processes and patterns observable in overt behavior. (Buttimer 1976: 283)

This stance is translatable into language and procedures amenable to geographical description. Three avenues of enquiry are identifiable. First, space is seen by phenomenologists as a mosaic of special places stamped by human intention, value, and memory. Each person is surrounded by concentric layers of lived space from room to home to city and region. Phenomenologists affirm that environments ("world") play a dynamic role in human experience, even though they tend to subsume this dynamism within a dialogue in which human agents ascribe meaning and significance to place. The sense emerges of lifeworld as preconsciously given facets of everyday place experience, one returns to Vidal de la Blache's notion of *genre de vie*, and from phenomenology and geography one derives the notion of rhythm as everyday behavior shows a quest for order, predictability, and routine, as well as adventure and change. Second, studies of social space look at the experience of the world as filtered through social reference systems and interaction networks. Phenomenologists view society as an assembly of subjects and examine behavior in terms of intersubjectivity. Ways of relating to the world are transmitted through our socio-cultural heritage. Intersubjectivity can also be understood as an ongoing process whereby individuals create their social worlds. Phenomenology suggests therefore that geography may justifiably claim a focus on humans and environments without adopting a deterministic stance on their mutual relations. Third, the "time-geography" model of Hagerstrand (1970) can be used to investigate the dynamism of everyday environments. But no attempt has been made to assess the experiential meaning of scheduling in time and space; and this notion also assumes an undifferentiated space. By removing such assumptions one could uncover facets of the world which play a critical role in everyday experience.

The direction of such endeavors is a more experientially grounded humanistic orientation in geography. Buttimer (1976: 290) also stresses the beneficial effects of phenomenology on the geographer as person and researcher:

> if we hear its fundamental message, phenomenology will move us toward a keener sense of self-knowledge and identity; it will create a thirst for wholeness in experience and a transcendence of a priori categories in research ... it could also sensitize us to the uniqueness of persons and places.

She thinks that phenomenology's message rings most clearly in the realm of experience rather knowledge – indeed, phenomenology "offers ambiguity rather than clarity on several fundamental issues" (Buttimer 1976: 29l). Existentialism and phenomenology challenge social scientists to radically question their normal ways of knowing and being and, daringly, to accept the responsibilities of freedom.

Place Identity

Drawing out the relations between people, places, and language, Buttimer says that people's sense of personal and cultural identity is intimately bound up with place identity. She points out that in *The Poetics of Space* Gaston Bachelard (1958) claimed that "topoanalysis" (the exploration of self-identity through place) might yield more fruitful insights into the person than psychoanalysis. Places may be thought of in the context of two reciprocal movements observable among most living forms: most life forms need a home; and horizons reach outward from that home. Hence, universal experience includes the lived reciprocity of rest and movement, security and adventure, housekeeping and husbandry, community building and social organization. For any individual there are distinctions between the home and reach of one's thoughts and imagination, those of one's social affiliations, and the actual physical location of home and reach. If all three are harmonized we can speak of centeredness: one's sense of place is a function of how well it provides a center for one's life interests. This process of *centering* may be contrasted with the notion of rationally planned nodal *centralization* of power and social energy. The difference between centering and centralization may, in fact, symbolize the differences between insiders' and outsiders' views on place: "dwelling" as compared with "housing" for example. A first step in straddling the divide between insider and outsider worlds involves stretching conventional "noun" or "picture" language to accommodate the "verbs" and "process" language of lived experience. The *outsiders'* trap lies in reading the texts of landscapes and overt behavior in the picture languages of maps and models, inevitably finding in places what he or she intends to find. The *insiders'* trap lies in such an immersion in the particulars of everyday life and action that one sees little point in questioning the taken for granted, or seeing home in its wider spatial or social contact. The greatest challenge is to call into conscious awareness taken-for-granted ideas and practices within one's personal world and then reach beyond for a more mutually respectful dialogue. Buttimer thinks that the geographer might find such a pedagogical challenge attractive. We might examine our own experiences in places and use this as a testing ground for our disciplinary models, most of which have adopted an observer's stance on places. She contrasts this with formal disciplinary knowledge which gives only an opaque picture, insufficient, say, for any adequate planning. Her experience is that solutions to regional problems discovered by trial and error over several generations may still be more rational than those of the civil servant. Solutions which people do not consider to be their own will be resented, avoided, or rendered ludicrous. She hopes that there can be a place for reason in the highly rational worlds of liberal planning, and aspires to playing a mediating role between insiders and outsiders (Buttimer 1980a).

Geographies of Lifeworld

Because of Anne Buttimer's presence, Clark University was a center of humanistic geography in the 1970s. Looking back, Buttimer describes this work as reaching for "a language which might permit a more sensitive relationship between 'insider' and 'outsider', between 'supply efficiency' and 'demand appropriateness' in the organization of public services" and "a concerted attempt to probe the experiential grounding of concepts like place, community, at-homeness, movement and commitment" (Buttimer 1980c: 16–17). Typical of such work, David Seamon, a student of Buttimer's, now professor of architecture at Kansas State University, explores the human's inescapable immersion in the geographical world. A *Geography of the Lifeworld* (1979) focuses on people's day-to-day experiences and behaviors associated with the places in which they live. Seamon searches for basic patterns epitomizing human behavior and experience. In the past, behavioral geography explored themes such as spatial behavior, territoriality, and place preferences, reflecting the need felt in the social sciences for understanding inner psychological structures and processes underlying environmental behavior. But Seamon's (1979: 16) work differs in its use of phenomenology "to uncover and describe things and experiences – i.e. phenomena – as they are in their own terms." Whereas behavioral geography draws attention to one aspect of environmental behavior, phenomenology seeks a holistic view of the interrelatedness among environmental experiences and behaviors. And whereas behavioral geography begins with a theoretical perspective, definitions, and assumptions, phenomenology strives to categorize and structure as little as possible, turning instead toward "phenomena ... blocked from sight by the theoretical patterns in front of them" (Spiegelberg 1978: 658).

Take, for example, movement in space. Behaviorist approaches insist on explaining spatial behavior through imposed a priori theories: cognitive theorists assume on faith the cognitive map, behaviorists a stimulus–response sequence. Seamon seeks to break away and return to everyday movement as a phenomenon in its own right before it has been defined, categorized, and explained – hence, he brackets assumptions such as movement depending on cognitive maps. He argues that cognition plays only a partial role in everyday spatial behavior, which is, instead, very much precognitive, involving prereflective knowledge by the body. He also brackets the idea that movement is a process of stimulus–response, arguing that the body holds an intentional capacity which intimately "knows" the everyday spaces in which the person lives.

Movements then are often made habitually without, or before, conscious intervention, a form of intentionality which Seamon terms "body-subject" – the inherent capacity of the body to direct behavior intelligently, the body as an intelligent subject. Thus, Merleau-Ponty (1962) criticizes cognitive theorists for treating the body merely as a physical entity on which consciousness acts as an "exterior" cause. Instead, movements are directed by the body's connections via intelligent threads which run between the body and the familiar world. Body-subject learns through action as repeated movements are incorporated into prereflective understanding. The body has the power within itself to initiate directed movements before and without a need for cognition. Because of body-subject we can manage routine movements automatically, gaining freedom from everyday environments. Hence, body-subject is caretaker of life's mundane aspects. For Seamon, body-subject houses complex behaviors, extending over considerable times and spaces, which he terms *body ballet* and *time–space routine* for individuals, or when fused by many people sharing the same space, *place ballet*. So, body ballet is a set of integrated gestures and movements which sustain a particular task; time–space routines are sets of habitual body behaviors which extend through considerable portions of time; body ballets and time–space routines interact in a supportive physical environment to create place ballets. Such notions are valuable for geography, planning, and policy because they join people with environmental time–space. Western societies tend to fragment places and time into isolated units and, at the same time, suffer from growing personal alienation and the breakdown of community. Place ballet brings people together physically, helps foster a visible collective entity, and promotes interpersonal familiarity. Place ballet is an essential part of place experience and a lack of it reduces the meaning of human life.

Urban Social Geography

As a final case study of these ideas, David Ley (1977) adapts ideas of existential phenomenology, especially those of Schutz, to the study of urban social geography. Place, Ley says, should be seen phenomenologically as an object for a subject. Place, however, is not solely an object but also an image and an intent. Place always has meaning, is always "for" its subject. This meaning carries back to the intent of the subject and forward as a "separate variable," prompting the behavior of a new generation of subjects. Just as place is meaningless without a subject, so the subject has an uncertain identity when removed from place. Places may have multiple realities, their meanings changing with the different intentions of their subjects. Usually, however, a dominant meaning obtains and landscapes can act as indicators of the subjective intentions that mold them. Even mundane features – wall graffiti, for example – point beyond to local social values. Landscape settings offer "cues" for appropriate behavior. The meaning of a place systematically attracts groups with similar interests and values. As a result, the city becomes a mosaic of social worlds each supporting a group bound together by similar intent.

Within the lifeworld, Ley argues, there is a spatial counterpart to social designation. At the simplest level of experience, space is partitioned into near and far portions and private and public. Ley draws on Bachelard's (1958) notion of "felicitous space," the kind of space that can be grasped, defended, and loved, space which is eulogized, space which "concentrates being within limits that protect." The home is the core but this space can extend into the community through an intersubjective consensus derived from solidarity and shared identity. To have such meaning communities must be an object common to a plurality of subjects. For Ley, the post-industrial metropolis is characterized by the separation of subject from object. Dehumanized urban settings are little more than spaces or geometry; they are not "for" a collectivity. Capitalist and socialist cities alike manifest a materialist philosophy which has forgotten the human being. In response, grassroot movements attempt to reinstate meaning to land, land being a surrogate for identity. Thus, the relationship between landscape and identity is profound ("man in his place," in French phenomenology) even though that relationship goes largely unexamined.

A Phenomenological Critique of Geographical Phenomenology

These accounts, little more than quick summaries, enable an impression to be formed of the kind of work conducted under the label "humanistic geography" in the middle to late 1970s and early 1980s (see also Entrikin 1976; Ley and Samuels 1978a), when this school reached its height in terms of quality of work and influence on geographical thought and practice. It continues to exist (e.g. Entrikin 1991), often in relation to poststructural geography, as with the "landscape as text" school (Agnew and Duncan 1989). The philosophical bases of humanistic geography have never been widely understood; as the previous sections demonstrate, existentialism and phenomenology are not the easiest sets of ideas to comprehend. But in part humanistic geography declined eventually under the weight of its own contradictions. These were abundantly demonstrated in a devastating phenomenological critique of humanistic geography by John Pickles (1985), a professor of geography at the University of Kentucky.

A Critique of Humanistic Geography

Pickles's critique of what he calls "geographical phenomenology" centers on its connection with humanism: phenomenology was to be the philosophical underpinning for humanistic approaches to geography with a focus on prescientific awareness of environments. Humanistic geographers, Pickles says, claim that people's everyday experiences of the world are already geographical and the geographer's task is merely to thematize them. Such a phenomenology, he says, is not derived from Husserl's project, but is a Kantian conception in which extant phenomena are described as they "really are." In this, no explanation of the constitution of scientific objects, nor of objects in general, need be given by the geographer, nor is it necessary to account for the a priori framework of meaning by which the geographical perspective is constituted.

For Pickles, therefore, the relationship between phenomenology and science is misconstrued by humanistic geographers. Pickles finds that Buttimer's (1976: 283) concern with the integrity of lived experience and her criticism of the objectivism of positivist science results in the rejection of the fundamental principle of positive science, the positing of objects for a subject – thus, she says, "one must reject any scientific cause–effect models of subject and object ... scientific procedures fail to provide adequate descriptions of experience." From such a view, Pickles claims, phenomenology as critique of positivism easily passes into phenomenology as anti-science. Similarly, he interprets Relph's (1970: 193) rejection of hypothesis testing and reliance on evidence from direct insight as anti-theoretical, whereas for Pickles (1985: 55), "phenomenology is concerned with how phenomena are originally given, the constitution of what is acceptable as evidence and the a priori framework of meaning from which a hypothesis and a causal relationship can be framed as meaningful and relevant. Phenomenology seeks to ground the sciences." Pickles points out that the geographical literature contains few details of the phenomenological method – indeed, Buttimer (1976: 278) claims that phenomenology does not offer "clear operational procedures to guide the empirical investigator" and should not be understood as a method but as a perspective. Entrikin (1976: 629) similarly argues that phenomenology lacks a clear, defined methodology for ascertaining the structures or forms of human experience and should be understood as criticism. For Pickles, such views "misunderstand phenomenology completely."

Furthermore, Pickles argues that the imposition of humanist and anthropocentric concepts has encouraged a voluntarist and subjectivist interpretation of the key phenomenological idea of intentionality. In saying that "intentionality is man's striking toward a structuring of his world through caring, hoping, conceiving, feeling and meaning," Buttimer (1974: 38) psychologizes intentionality. Then, step by step, geographical phenomenology moves towards radical subjectivism, towards subjectivist philosophies (Hay 1979) and so-called philosophies of meaning (Ley 1981). It has subsequently been claimed that phenomenology is individualistic (emphasizes personal geographies), and fails to account for the great range of social behaviors. "In psychologizing the method and in reducing the rigor of its principles, this 'variation' of phenomenology became merely an undisciplined exercise in description, without clarification of a priori assumptions" (Pickles 1985: 74). There is a need, then, to rescue the phenomenological project from such subjectivist, individualist, and undisciplined interpretations. Pickles proposes moving from what passes for phenomenology in the geographical literature towards what is actually the case in phenomenology.

Phenomenology Restated

The aim of phenomenology, Pickles says, is nothing less than a clarification and revision of the basic concepts of science. The basic structures of any subject area of science have already been worked out in people's everyday ways of experiencing and interpreting the world: the concepts of formal geography, for example, are pre-given in the world. Heidegger's version is that the human's fundamental relation to the world is not one of awareness and spontaneous consciousness, but involvement in, and towards, the world. Science must formalize, thematize, and "reduce" the lived world to its domain of study in obtaining stable objects of theoretical reflection. But humanists, in geography as elsewhere, argue that non-objectification must be the goal of a truly human science: i.e. geography should deal with the world as it is actually lived by real people. Those who favor a "scientific" approach reply that this misunderstands the need for rigor and definition, and find in humanistic geography a romantic rebellion against necessary abstraction which is little more than bad poetry. The choice appears to lie between accepting the (positivistic) "scientific" methodological attitude, thereby losing involvement in the reality being studied, or retaining immediacy but giving up objectivity (Ricoeur 1973: 129). Before accepting such a predicament, Pickles suggests that we ask again what constitutes science, and how science relates to everyday life.

The objective of phenomenology is to outline the ontological genesis of the theoretical attitude as a precondition for the possibility of conducting scientific research – that is, it seeks an existential conception of science, understanding science as a mode of the human's being-in-the-world. In the traditional scientific understanding, knowing the world is interpreted as a relation between a subject and an object, an inner world of perception and knowing set against an outer world of things and physical nature. Knowing subjects divorced from involved concern with the world are presumed to be "proto-scientists" or "problem solvers." But Heidegger (1962; 1969b) claims that the kind of being belonging to this knowing subject is left unqueried. For him, knowing is grounded beforehand in a being already in, and toward, the world. Through a dialogue with the world people let things be what they are, uncover them, and bring their meanings to light. The human's primordial relation to the world is not cognitive or theoretical but one of *Dasein*, of being there. Theoretical knowledge involves standing back and observing something encountered within this primordial relation with the world. In this way, entities are encountered as merely there.

Thus, if phenomenology is understood as a method seeking to clarify science's concepts, for Pickles it would want to ensure that the thematizations of the world as object of concern, and the constructs presupposed by empirical geography, are relevant and meaningful.

Place and Space

Pickles argues that geography traditionally deals with themes of world, environment, and nature, particularly as related to humans. Place and space both derive from a fundamental spatiality. Understanding this requires a certain interpretation of the world, presupposed by contemporary geography, but in need of revitalization. The idea is to search for an ontological, existential understanding of the universal structural characteristics of human spatiality as the precondition for understanding places and space: "we seek to clarify the original experiences on the basis of which geography can articulate and develop its regional ontology if geography as a human science, concerned with man's spatiality, is to be possible at all" (Pickles: 1985: 155). Pickles's exposition seeks to demonstrate how Heidegger's ontological analysis of the spatiality characteristic of humans might ground the human science of geography anew on foundations which transcend the present limits of space in the Cartesian or Kantian senses of the term.

In this argument, the space which Galileo, Descartes, and Newton characterized as homogenous expanse, equivalent in all directions, and not perceptible to the senses, is neither the sole, nor the genuine, objective space. Likewise, the Cartesian and Newtonian ontology of the world, which sees things as substances characterized by extension (length, breadth, thickness), does not effectively grasp the character of the world. Phenomenology seeks to return to the original experiences of space prior to their thematization by scientific activity. As with Heidegger, the spatial ordering of entities thus occurs through human activity. In this sense, place is not mere location in geometric space, but the proper place of equipment – place belongs to an equipmental context. Work and equipmental context also determine the relations of places within regions. Consequently, human spatiality, in being related to several equipmental contexts, is hierarchical and worldly, and is not understandable independently of the beings organizing it. Humans do not discover space. Rather, space is given in the form of places created by equipment in their contexts. The environment is not spatially arranged in advance. Rather, a totality of places is articulated by a world of involvements (Pickles 1985: 162).

The final question is how space encountered in practical ways (through work, dwelling, etc.) becomes a theme for science? Through thematization, objectification, and formalization, abstract spaces of various kinds and degrees of generality can be projected in which places are reduced to multiplicities of positions and environments become homogenous space. Indeed, ultimately the possibility exists for a purely mathematical space constructed with any number of dimensions, a space of world points undifferentiated and undifferentiable. Spatiality, characteristic of humans as worldly, must have the character of directionality, where the world is already oriented through people taking a direction towards it, out of which arises the fixed directions left and right. In "bringing close," people make remoteness vanish; closeness or remoteness refer to the de-severant character of the human's being; this makes possible the measurement of distances; and so on. Human beings spatialize and this creates the possibility of spatial theorization.

Pickles (1985: 168–70) concedes that these are the early, unsophisticated ideas of a new conception of space. For him, the question is not which conception of space is most useful, but what does spatial behavior refer to? If we are discussing the activities of people as atomic particles in abstract space, then the space of the physical world is appropriate. If we are discussing human spatial behavior, conceptions of space which incorporate the human character of such behavior are appropriate. The phenomenologist asks what is necessary if a science of geography concerned with human spatiality is sought and how such a science is possible. The tasks of phenomenology, he concludes, are to clarify the ontological structure of the "geographical," to critique taken-for-granted conceptions of space, and to explicate a place-centered ontology of human spatiality.

Conclusion

Humanistic geography informed by existential phenomenology is at its best when criticizing positivistic scientific approaches to geographic understanding – science as distanced objectivity can neither replicate nor understand the subjective processes through which humans create their worlds. Empirical works carried out by existential geographers using the phenomenological method demonstrate a profound, sympathetic engagement with fundamental geographic elements of the human experience, like place, lifeworld, and context; thus Relph's experience of place, Tuan's perception and imagining of place, Buttimer's lifeworld, Seamon's bodily experience, and Ley's meaning of place. In its own way, humanistic geography is more critical than Marxism, anarchism, or perhaps even radical feminism, of the society built by modern science and technology. It mourns the loss of a world where places had meaning and life was conducted or constructed at recognizable scales.

Humanistic geography has a popular, ethical appeal in its insistence that "we" restore the lived world of experience to a prominent place in our theorization. Notions of practical knowledge, familiarity, caring, and care-taking, places as depositories of experiences, even the more nebulous "authenticity," all these are notions which conscientiously express and promote understanding committed to humanitarian goals. Furthermore, humanistic geography is intellectually radical in its insistence on a return to "original" experience rather than reworking second- and third-order impressions already distorted by suspect theories. A critique of humanistic geography can only start with such appreciations of its fundamental ontological and ethical qualities. Such a critique must quarrel not with the notion that theorizing begins with experience (what else is there?), but with the way experience is experienced in the theories which form the systematic content of an organized understanding. Here we develop the idea that while setting off to explore experience, humanistic geography diverts into intentionality, revealing an enduring idealism in its belief in a pre-existing consciousness, and that this has consequences for its politics and intellectual practice.

Existential phenomenology ranges politically from Heidegger's affiliation with the Nazis to Sartre's later Marxism (Waterhouse 1981; Kockelmans 1984; Farias 1989; Heidegger 1990; Dallmayr 1993). It makes no mention of class or gender, often substitutes nostalgia about an unrealistic, romanticized past (workmen, tools, dwellings) for what should be historical analysis, and pins its hopes for the future on an almost mystical moment of realization when the scales of scientific thinking drop from people's eyes and they begin to see again as though for the first time. In Husserl's transcendental phenomenology, we find the notion of an intentionality already present in consciousness which organizes the world – where does such a consciousness come from? In existential phenomenology, the emphasis shifts to experience in place, but not a place structured by power relations, or a place of oppression, or even a real place, but a sanctified lost realm producing an innocent intent.

This criticism can be elaborated through the central humanistic geographic notion of place. Humanistic notions of place are structured by a series of oppositions contrasting inside with outside, belonging with escaping, significance with superficiality, understanding with knowledge. These oppositions are consistently hierarchically valued, the first term favored over the second. What method of evaluation is used? Two types of appeal recur. First, there are continual mentions of "originality" in some historical sense, as though there was once a place where experience was genuine, but now that place has been lost. This lost place and its missed time are left unspecified – except perhaps that Heidegger looks to classical Greece or, on occasion, preindustrial southern Germany, while phenomenological geographers usually look to premodern landscapes. Exact specification would open this lost place to criticism – classical Greece was founded on slavery, feudal villages on serfdom or rent paid to landlords. "Originality," therefore, is necessarily transposed into vaguer, yet still "historical," terms of nostalgia, which evoke the past without specifying actual places or events. Nostalgia has exactly the sentimental appeal that critics of humanistic geography find unscientific. But rather than dismissing sentimentality we need instead to investigate its qualities. Sentimental nostalgia is selective in the qualities it preserves, exaggerates, and uses in ethically valuing places. It is a delightful yet dangerous way of cleansing the past to make it more appealing and supportive of actions carried out in a more brutal present. As such, nostalgia is amenable to political and religious manipulation, particularly when applied to territory, region, and locality, where it informs notions of the "spirit of place," nostalgia being an expression of spiritual connection between people and home, or more dangerously people "belonging" to "historic" homelands – hence, a connection between Heidegger and German geopolitics. Nostalgia thus produces a prejudiced view of place which forms the basis of nationalism and conservative versions of localism, as well as more benign views which see place as supportive community. All these qualities are invested in the place characteristics valued through nostalgia for a lost home.

Second, humanistic geography favors the practical, direct, and immediate as sources of authenticity. How does humanistic geography characterize practical lived experience in places? Places are said to be centers of significant experiences derived from multiple sources, but the main stress lies on the experiences of "dwelling" and "working." Here, nostalgia enters to disguise some aspects of dwelling to evoke memories of certain other aspects. In phenomenology, "dwelling" connotes home as center of care and affection between people and in relation to place. But "dwelling" must also mean reproduction in place, and (practical) reproductive activities and structured by social relations deeply flawed by power inequalities, as between the patriarchal father commanding the home and dependent women and children fearfully following and resisting his orders. Indeed, the phenomenological construct "dwelling" can be seen as an ideological conception which evokes nostalgia to hide power. Furthermore, practical activities in dwellings must be related to practical activities of production, in the home, in the surrounding community, or more distant in space. What role does domestic reproduction play when the commodity production system is economically and spatially separate and how do relations of production interact with those of reproduction? These are questions which must be asked of "dwelling." Similar problems beset working class, exploitation, etc. Yet humanistic geography maintains silence – class, gender, power are conspicuous by their absence. Practical activities and experiences are thus selectively preserved as "dwelling" or "working" in humanistic geography in a process of idealization which has conservative political consequences. Nostalgia for a time and place that never was, for working practices cleansed of their exploitative aspects, are then used as idealized values against which the qualities of places and practices are judged. Valuation occurs in relation to (political) values which are assumed rather than explained or justified.

These preliminary critical remarks lead to the main questions that must be posed of humanistic geography. What is this "meaning" of existence, or rather how can "we" come to find meaning through experience? It may seem that humanistic geography proposes a hermeneutic of experience of place in which meaning is derived entirely from its rich interplay of events and relations. Yet the interpreter does not start from nothing and become an understanding being entirely through the activity of interpretation. Rather, humanistic geography proposes "intentionality" (in the

Husserlian tradition) as the source of acts *giving* meaning to practice rather than experience manifesting *to* the individual broader social or natural meanings. Such intentionality can be appreciated as countering structural excess in which human behavior is motivated entirely by functional necessity, whether externally derived (the impress of existing institutions, for example), or internally appropriated (fitting into existing patterns to satisfy needs). Yet what is the source of an inherent intentionality? Phenomenology assumes a knowing or curious consciousness free to choose – even Sartre in *Being and Nothingness* (1958: 30) says: "Human freedom precedes essence in man and makes it possible" (Poster 1975: 79). Humanistic geography simply declares that people are free to choose and responsible for their choices – "we" are prisoners of our freedom. But what about the structuring of choice by need? It may be that people can choose to satisfy or neglect need, but only after it has been learned that life is not all it is supposed to be. That is, not only the mechanisms of choice, its structure of alternatives, but also the very act of choosing, whether to eat or not for example, is learned behavior, socially constructed on the basis not of being as inquisitive consciousness but being as need. Humanistic geography prefers an "original" innate capacity to choose as central feature of the bestowing of meaning. Various authors turn desperately to biological innateness (Tuan), the knowing body (Seamon), or more usually cannot bring themselves to address the implication that the innate freedom of a knowing consciousness is the essence of a human "spirit." Humanistic geography contradicts its scientific pretension by posing an unknowable yet "understandable" world of the human spirit.

This raises the fascinating question of the nature of "authenticity." With Relph, an authentic attitude to place is a direct and genuine experience of its complete identity, direct in that experience is not mediated or confined by intellectual fashion or stereotypical convention. Authenticity also involves awareness that places are the products of human intentions. Yet authentic places are seen through the prism of nostalgia rather than referred to via historical argument. They are original places in the sense of expressing a direct intentionality unsullied by rational intervention. Again, the question which must be answered is, what is the origin of this intentionality?

In this analysis, modern, scientific rationality is the enemy, not capitalism or elite power. Rationality is not class- or gender-produced (as with ideology) but derives from the fundamental misunderstandings of superficial people who have forgotten what they "once" were and can no longer experience things as they "really are." We will encounter again (in chapter 6) this notion of perverse modern rationality for, as one author puts it, after Descartes the master thinker of contemporary (poststructural) French philosophy became Heidegger (Rockmore 1995: 18–19). For the moment, let us note the arrogance of a philosophical position which claims to show others "how things are in themselves." And we have to add that the very question "what is the meaning of existence?" is unanswerable except in religious terms, for it assumes something more meaningful than existence, something beyond being, certainly in the Husserlian tradition, but also we suspect for Heideggerians. It is also a question asked only after existence has been secured, a question structured by the means and social relations which produce existence, at least in the understanding that we turn to next – Marxism. Thus, fundamental differences between phenomenology and Marxism divide radical from humanistic geography into occasionally collaborative but mutually suspicious camps. Eventually, the two split as humanistic "concern" was used conservatively to counter structural Marxism's theoretical "excess" (Duncan and Ley 1982). Yet suspicion had been there for some time.

Chapter 3

Radical Geography, Marxism, and Marxist Geography

The first intimation that there could be such a thing as a politically radical geography came in the middle 1960s as part of an oppositional politics (the "movement," as it was called) which coalesced around domestic issues like inequality, racism, sexism, environment, and opposition to the Vietnam War. Events of the late 1960s, such as the burning of large sections of cities in the western world, student–worker uprisings in Paris in 1968, massive anti-war protest actions, and the reformation more generally of a radical culture, made the concerns of the traditional discipline of geography, for all its quantitative update, and even its humanistic concern, seem socially and politically irrelevant, especially to radicalized students and junior faculty members. From the middle 1960s onwards, articles dealing with more "socially relevant" geographic topics (e.g. Morrill 1969–70; Albaum 1973) began to appear in some of the discipline's mainstream journals, and in 1969 *Antipode: A Radical Journal of Geography* was founded at Clark University in Worcester, Massachusetts, specifically to publish the new kind of work. Early issues of the journal dealt with urban and regional poverty, discrimination against women and minority groups, unequal access to social services, advocacy planning, Third World underdevelopment and similarly political topics. Only gradually, and with reluctance, did socially relevant radical geography turn into Marxist geography. This chapter follows the historical sequence of the move from radical to Marxist geography during the 1970s, develops Marxist notions of materialism and dialectics in some detail, before returning to a lengthy discussion of the main themes of Marxist geographic on environment and space. The chapter concludes with some criticisms of the Marxist approach.

Radical Geography

Early work in radical geography accepted the view that geography was a science of space and environment but argued for a change in the spatial topics of concern in the direction of urgent social issues. The language tended to be confrontational, optimistic, anarchistic, and the message in *Antipode* was often phrased informally, as drawings, cartoons, posters as well as the usual articles and reviews.

Social Relevance

The idea prevalent in the 1960s was that radicals were new kinds of intellectuals, not only in terms of class origin and political commitment, but as agents practicing their daily lives – that is (for academics), thinking, doing research, and teaching in new ways. Earlier scholars, it was thought, had entered academic life for different reasons than the new generation of radicals, who thought hard and taught well in an effort to transform society, and were uncomfortable with the usual trappings of intellectual power. For example, meetings of the Association of American Geographers were (and still are) held at prestigious hotels in major cities. These hotels always have a central hallway which is packed with socializing "academic conventioneers" (cf. Hurst 1973). Young radical geographers saw this as a status-driven activity, the discipline's power structure expressed spatially as a kind of central place hierarchy, with power/space patterns of who talks to whom on the convention floor; gods talk with gods, disciples hover, graduate students peck up occasional crumbs of condescending attention. Radicals vowed never to be like that. How could we know that within a decade we would become the new gods of the geographic intellect, invited all over the world to give polite talks on revolution? That structure would overcome intention in replicating only a slightly more relaxed power/space hierarchy?

The late 1960s–early 1970s were years of political involvement and intellectual excitement unique in the modern history of geography. Looking back from the future, when gains made then have become commonplace, even passé, it is difficult to realize how dramatic a shift took place between the kinds of interests and level of dialogue predominating in the geography of the middle 1960s, and those coming to the fore by the middle 1970s. "Social relevance," the key phrase of the time, was conceived not in a vague way, as "feeling sorry for one's fellow human beings," but as taking the side of the oppressed, advocating their causes, pressing for fundamental social change. Even those openly professing liberal values, like the quantitative geographer Richard Morrill, who criticized the revolutionary premises of the New Left, still maintained that the academic's role was "to help bring about a more just, equal and peaceful society" and "search for more 'radical' ways and means to achieve change" (Morrill 1969–70). The result of work like this was indeed a more socially relevant geography but, it was later concluded, one tied still to a philosophy of science, a set of theories, and a methodology compatible with the existing academic and disciplinary power structures (Peet 1977).

The development of adequate social theories proved difficult for geographers trained in the field-work traditions of regional description. Theoretically sophisticated ideas tended to form in areas of radical geography with clear connections with more heavily theorized streams of thought outside the discipline. Two examples were imperialism, long the focus of spatialized versions of Marxist social theories, and relations between women and environment, where feminist theory could readily be adapted to geographical topics. We quickly survey two examples of early radical geographic work in these areas.

Geography and Imperialism

Long-term geographic interest in the Third World (e.g. Bruhnes 1952) was revived by United States involvement in the Vietnam War, which many radicals interpreted as a contemporary symptom of an historic and endemic First World imperialism. A series of articles drew on the existing stock of sophisticated radical ideas dealing with questions of underdevelopment, center–periphery relations, and imperialism to provide theoretical insight. In the best of this work, James Blaut (1970), a professor of geography at Clark University, later at the University of Illinois (Chicago), argued that conventional western science is so closely interwoven with imperialism (defined as "white exploitation of the non-white world") that it can only describe and justify, but not explain or control. Imperialism, he says, is underpinned by western "ethnoscience" – that is, the cognitive system (beliefs about reality) characteristic of a given cultural–linguistic universe, in this case the white, European west, that provides the system of scientific ideas with which people think and work. European ethnoscience contains a set of historical beliefs and social-scientific generalizations about the world biased in favor of whites and congruent with the interests of western imperialism. For Blaut, the European model of the world has a unicentric form with a distinctive geometry, an inner European space originally closed from an outer non-European space. "The west" has some kind of unique historical advantage (race, environment, culture, mind, spirit) which gives it superiority over all other peoples. European civilization is supposedly generated mainly by inner processes – Europe makes history – while non-Europeans play little or no crucial role in epochal events – "the rest of the world" is traditional. Non-Europeans are characterized as primitive and unprogressive, barbarous and heathen, less intelligent and less virtuous than Europeans. The expansion of the Europeans is thought of as self-generated, a "striving outward," with progress diffusing and becoming less evident with distance from the center, so that whenever non-Europeans show evidence of progress this is proportional to the European impact on their society – this amounts to global diffusion model and the belief generalized is "diffusionism" (i.e. cultural processes flow from the European center to the non-European periphery).

Blaut (1976) compares this with a Third World ethnoscientific model of the world as multicentric, with centers of incipient or proto-capitalism springing up at strategic points throughout the Old World. In a Third Worldist understanding, the multi-centered pattern of relatively equal levels of development was disrupted by the European plunder of the New World (the European "discovery" being due solely to the fact that the Iberian centers of expansion were closest to America), the flood of bullion into Europe, and the resulting commercial, industrial, and scientific-technological development. "Thereafter the dialectic of development and underdevelopment intensified, and the world economy fixed itself in place" (Blaut 1976: 1). From this perspective, Blaut argues against the notion of the "European miracle" by undermining its more concrete theory of the autonomous rise of Europe.

Thus: (1) Europe was not superior to other regions prior to 1492; (2) colonialism and the wealth plundered from Third World societies were the basic processes leading to the rise of Europe; (3) Europe's advantage lay solely in the "mundane realities of location" – that is, nearness to the Americas (Blaut 1994).

Women and Environment

As part of the growing radicalization of social thought, questions of gender and gender relations were raised by some of the few women in academia at the time. In an "atmosphere of social and academic ferment" typical of the early 1970s, geographers began to inquire into relations between women and space (Mackenzie 1984: 3). This was exploration into nearly uncharted territory: but there were signposts in the growing body of feminist theory. At first work on gender and environment took the form of criticisms of the "invisibility" of women in the geographic literature or the "gender-blindness" of the neoclassical and behavioral models of spatial structure (Burnett 1973). In the 1970s, most work in liberal feminist geography tried to create a "geography of women" which documented the disadvantages systematically suffered by women, the constraints on women's activities, and women's inequalities in general. Hence, Tivers (1977) used Hagerstrand's time–space model to conceptualize constraints on women's spatial choices, arguing that problems of access result from constraints of gender role such as the social expectation that women should primarily be involved in family care. Other work influenced by humanistic approaches to geography explored women's more sensitive and perceptive ways of knowing the physical and social landscape (Bowlby et al. 1989: 161). Empirical work documented the legitimacy of treating women "as a geographic subgroup in their own right" as a way of "questioning the assumptions of many geographic models" but in Mackenzie's (1984: 6) later opinion this led to the definition of women as a deviant subgroup and implicitly elevated purely spatial restrictions to the level of causal efficacy.

In an article well in advance of its time, Alison Hayford (1974), subsequently a professor of sociology at the University of Regina, argued that women were as invisible in geography as they had been in history. Institutions expressing a dominant male role are taken as expressive of the entire social order, with women assumed either to have no role of their own, or to be continuously adjusting to the male-determined order. For Hayford, by comparison, women form a distinct geographical force, lending credence to the need for a geography of women. Her version of this was a "spatial dialectic" founded on the geographic contradiction between "here" and "there" and focused on the stress all people experience because of their inability to have direct contact with the totality of surrounding space. Women, she thought, embody the means by which people attempt to relieve the tensions which come from dealing with infinite space in finite time. Thus, women are almost universally the essence of locality. In traditional societies, women have main responsibility for types of production (gathering and agriculture) that reinforce locality: it seems likely that women discovered the gardening techniques which created the basis of a strong locality, a safe and definable "here." In such societies, there is little distinction between public and private spheres of activity. Women, she found, are central in space because of their role in the household, the main means people have devised to lessen the tensions of space:

> The household was the nodal point, in the spatial network of productive systems, and formed the point around which rights to the use of the earth were determined ... At the same time the household had tremendous symbolic importance; it contained the iconography of the locality – it was the ultimate and often the complete expression of "here." It was a concrete statement of group solidarity and of the ability to work in a cooperative manner ... It was the site of the most dependable personal relationships ... It was the one place where human obligations were most supportive and most fixed; the one place where people could spend their weakest and most private moments – sleeping, eating, childhood, old age – in relative security. (Hayford 1974: 6)

The household was also an important means of extending control over space, socializing labor, and allocating resources. As the center of the household, women had main roles in establishing the linkages through which the earth's surface was manipulated.

However, the growing separation of the public and private spheres of activity created a tension between the household and the larger society. With the development of class society, the separation of economy and politics subjects the household to external power, diminishing the symbolic linking significance of women. Under capitalism, direct and personal organizations with women at their cores are replaced by the impersonal, invisible power of capital. The private sphere of women is replaced in importance by the male-dominated public sphere. And the functions of women in the household are confined to reproduction, care of personal needs, and the security of the locality. Capitalism thus changes the position of women from centrality to peripherality. The safe space of the household still provides relief from the stresses of involvement in capitalist productive relations, but it is also under pressure from these relations. The separation of work from living space, and of the various other kinds of space from each other, subjects women to continual spatial tensions – for example, between an ideological commitment to the household and an economic need to function in a wider space. Women do not have the same freedom as men to move in space, or organize it, and have no power to change the structures on their lives. Such arguments, Hayford (1974: 17–18) concludes, make it important for geographers to investigate the spatial roles of women, in particular the meaning of the "continuing transition from centrality to the periphery, from being the pivot of society's relations to being nowhere."

Anarchic Leanings

In the early days of radical geography, typified by these positions on imperialism and women, the tendency was to draw freely on a variety of sources for political theory, including anarchism. The early radical geography was anarchistic in more than the riotously "irresponsible" behavior of its early adherents. Anarchism and geography have more than casual relations – there are structural similarities between the two in terms of anarchism's naturalistic interpretation of the human character (as essentially cooperative) and the spatial form of its decentralized vision of an alternative society. Peter Kropotkin, a leading anarchist theoretician of the late nineteenth and early twentieth centuries, was a geographer by inclination, training, and practice (Kropotkin 1978; Galois 1976). With such connections radical geography made numerous attempts at developing an anarchist base with a distinct political perspective on alternative forms of society, drawing on Kropotkin's writings (1898; 1902).

Kropotkin thought that we should learn from the great sweep of history in building an alternative to capitalism. For long time periods, humans lived in groups organized around principles of cooperation and mutual support, for it was found that cooperation and altruism were the only lasting bases of social life. Kropotkin believed that natural cooperativism forms the basis of people's ethical system. Yet competition also functions for individual survival in (relatively short) periods of struggle. Raising a short-term reactive emotion into a long-term social-organizing function makes capitalism contradictory. Kropotkin thought that we must return to societies based on cooperation and mutual aid, principles which have continued to be practiced (for example in the family) and which are propagated still via an underground people's history.

Myrna Breitbart (1975), then a graduate student at Clark University, and later a professor at Hampshire College in Amherst, Massachusetts, developed some of these ideas. Kropotkin thought that producers are so mutually interdependent that all labor is social in character, all people are equal inheritors of the past, and therefore scarce goods should be distributed according to need. Basing her ideas on such principles Breitbart advocates "integrated labor" rather than the division of labor as the basis of production. People should perform several different kinds of tasks in free associations with the means of production and products held in common by a decentralized society. Essentially self-sufficient regions would become "integrated cells" prepared to equally interchange ideas and products with other regions. From anarchist principles such as these Breitbart derives a "location theory" to guide the active construction of a new landscape. Anarchist economics, she says, sacrifices traditional forms of productive efficiency in favor of alternative social goals like equity, need, and creative work: these would form their own kinds of cooperative efficiency based on producing what is necessary in the most humanly satisfying way, with the time freed from work available for leisure, inventive, or artistic pursuits. Anarcho-communists believe in the gradual disappearance of the dichotomy between rural and urban land uses, the decline of large cities, and the formation of egalitarian spaces. Production decisions should be democratically made at the grassroots level by confronting needs with available resources, including alternative uses for labor. Centralized hierarchies should be replaced by directly connecting (horizontal) networks. Work places and living places should be nearer together, allowing greater integration of the various spaces in which life is lived. Such rudiments of people's location theory, Breitbart (1975: 48) suggests, might be considered a prelude to the making of landscapes which benefit everyone living in them (see also *Antipode* 1978–9; Breitbart 1978). Believing deeply in such ideals many radical geographers have long understood communism to be a radically democratic, decentralized society, where the people directly control the making of their own spaces, the very opposite of the state authoritarian "communism" practiced in the former Soviet Union. No wonder that when red-baited for being "authoritarian Marxist–Leninist communists" radical geographers react usually with horror, but sometimes with amusement!

Radical Geographical Practice

The early days of radical geography were characterized also by extensions of the political activism typical of the anti-war and civil rights movements into more obviously "geographical" arenas. In 1968, William Bunge, previously a leading quantitative-theoretical geographer, founded the Society for Human Exploration. This called for rediscovering geographic skills of exploration and using them for new purposes. For Bunge (1969: 3), "the tyranny of fact compels that geographers go into a state of rationally controlled frenzy about the exploration of the human condition" by forming "expeditions" to the poorest areas, contributing rather than taking, planning with (rather than for) people. Geographers, he said, should become people of the regions they explore, should discover the kinds of research people need doing, and address themselves energetically to these problems. Local people should be trained in geographic skills so they could become part of the solution rather than being objects of study. Thus, in response to a request from a black community organization, the Detroit Geographical Expedition prepared a report on school desegregation which maximized black control over black children's education. A report on Trumbull, a working-class inner-Detroit neighborhood, countered plans for expansion by Wayne State University (Detroit Geographical Expedition 1972). Furthermore, as part of the training program of the Expedition, courses were organized at Michigan State University which enrolled 670 students (Horvath 1971) before such expeditionary principles as community control and (more importantly!) free tuition led to the educational project being terminated by officials of the university. Also, by 1973 the Detroit Geographical Expedition ceased to function, beset by problems such as the "enforced mobility" (to Canada) of its founder and student members, and the refusal of nearby universities to grant tenure to supportive faculty members. Expeditionary movements were carried to Toronto (Canada), Sydney (Australia), and London (England) in the resulting diaspora (Stephenson 1974), where they survived into the late 1970s.

Within the discipline of geography, a Union of Socialist Geographers (USG), founded in 1974, organized 200 members in North America in its first year, and 100 more members in Britain soon after. Its most successful "union local" (at Simon Frazier University in Burnaby, British Columbia) enrolled 50 student members and participated in several expeditionary and advocacy activities in the city of Vancouver. Members of the USG organized special sessions at Association of America Geographers (AAG) conventions and Institute of British Geographers (IBG) annual meetings on topics like imperialism, women, and revolutionary theory, much to the dismay of the old guard in the discipline ("is this geography?"). As an active force the USG lasted until the early 1980s, when its place was taken by socialist specialty groups within the dominant disciplinary institutions – a sign that what was once oppositional had indeed been "disciplined."

The Radical Critique

In the early 1970s, self-consciously radical geographers began to seriously question mainstream ideas of quantitative-spatial geography, including modifications like behavioral geography. This critique went beyond the social relevancy issue, described previously, in its depth, political intensity, and transformational intent. The new criticism centered on geography's pervasive distinction between the spatial dimension of human activity and the full range of social activities concerned with the reproduction of existence, the key critical term being mainstream geography's "spatial fetishism." Thus, in the case of industrial location theory, quantitative geography's prize product, Doreen Massey (1973), now at the Open University in Britain, found incoherent any treatment of "the spatial" as a closed system analyzed via an autonomous (location) theory. Massey argues that industrial location theory is based on neoclassical economic analysis. This is ideological in that it asks questions allowing only limited answers, directs attention to certain aspects of location (the profits of industrialists rather than the interests of working-class people), and in general justifies the existing economic system. As a result, a gap widens between location theory and the formation of real world spatial problems (or, rather, socio-economic problems with spatial manifestations). Ideology, she says, makes conventional science ineffective. Likewise, in a similar critique of development theory, David Slater (1975), now at Loughborough University in Britain, claimed that spatial patterns could be described in the most minute mathematical detail without disclosing anything significant about causal social processes – for Slater, geography was caught in a methodological trap in which the collection and manipulation of spatial data are preferred over the elaboration of social theory. For both Massey and Slater, geographical location theory uncritically draws its basic frameworks of understanding from the bourgeois social sciences.

Perhaps the most sophisticated version of the notion of conventional science as ideology was elaborated by David Harvey (1974), by this time a professor of geography at the Johns Hopkins University in Baltimore. In what has to be termed a "significant reversal" (see chapter 1), Harvey now finds the argument that *the* "scientific method" guarantees objectivity and the ethical neutrality of "factual" statements to be an ideological claim. For the (normative) principles of scientific method can be justified and validated by appeal only to something external to science – metaphysics, religion, ethics, convention, human practice – realms which even scientists would agree are penetrated by ideological considerations. This does not reduce science to mere personal opinion but forces the further concession that "scientific" enquiry expresses social ideas and conveys social meanings.

By comparison, the only method capable of dealing with issues such as the population–resources relation in an integrated, dynamic way must be founded on Marx's dialectical materialism.

From Radical to Marxist Geography

This proposal for employing Marxist ideas brings us to the second transformation of the period. Radical geography was a quest for social relevance at a time of contradiction and crisis in capitalist society. But social relevance produced a contradiction inside radical geography, between political objectives which were virtually unlimited (i.e. aimed at the transformation of society) and analytical capacities which were claustrophobically constrained by the techniques, methodologies, and paradigmatic boundaries of conventional scientific concepts. Thus, radical geography was radical in topic and politics but not in theory or method of analysis. Truly radical explanations, it came to be believed, must trace social issues to their origins in societal structures. As the anti-war movement escalated into near political insurrection, and as many radical geographers became dedicated revolutionaries, the need for a politicized social ontology tying space to society became ever more compelling. The urgent need for an alternative mode of understanding became clear even to people reluctant to completely abandon positivism, with its quantitative methods which geographers had slaved over in a desperate attempt at becoming white-coated "scientists." Again, the transformation of radical into Marxist geography is typified by the trajectory of David Harvey, previously guru of positivistic geography. *Social Justice and the City* records Harvey's move from a liberal, critical position focused on ethics, to a Marxism based in the science of historical materialism. In this, *Social Justice* provided a guide to many others beset by similar dilemmas.

Social Justice and the City

After completing *Explanation in Geography* (1969), Harvey began to explore how ideas usually regarded as distinct from the philosophy of science, notions of social and moral philosophy, could be related to geographical inquiry. Harvey wanted to breach the gap between what appeared to be two irreconcilable modes of analysis, the ethical and the scientific. The essays in *Social Justice and the City* (Harvey 1973) represent stages in the history of understanding which subsequently evolved. For a while he remained within a normative conception of social justice (i.e. what "ought to be" from a moral viewpoint), a position familiar to location theorists whose dominant norm was societal efficiency in terms of spatial costs (i.e. optimal location). "In the long run," he thought at first, "social justice and efficiency are very much the same thing" (Harvey 1973: 97). But an interaction between ivory tower "ideas for ideas' sake" and his material experiences in the inner city of Baltimore challenged his conception of urbanism as well as his more general conceptions of space, theory, knowledge, and eventually, we might add, the politics of scientific inquiry. Frustrations of theory and practice led beyond moral liberalism into Marxism as ontology, epistemology, and ethic.

The Baltimore experience (e.g. Harvey and Chatterjee 1974) made Harvey critical of Kuhn's (1962) "idealist" formulation in which accepted paradigms of knowledge are transformed through internal anomalies – that is, through a purely intellectual process within the realm of ideas. Harvey moved instead towards Bernal's (1971) interest in the material basis for science, including the manipulation and control of scientific activity by industrial and financial interests, and work by Johnson (1971) on revolutions in economic theory brought about by failure to adequately conceptualize pressing social problems. Hence, the old regional geography, Harvey argues, focused on the qualitative and unique, had proven incapable of resisting a drive in the social sciences towards tools of social manipulation and control, requiring an understanding of the quantitative and in general leading to the "quantitative revolution" in geography. In turn, the quantitative movement of the late 1950s and 1960s, which quickly established itself as the hegemonic orthodoxy, showed disparities between its sophisticated theoretical and methodological framework and its ability to say "anything really meaningful about events as they unfold around us" (Harvey 1973: 128). In short, quantitative geography was not coping well and was ripe for overthrow. The emerging objective social conditions and geographers' inability to cope with them made necessary a further revolution in geographic thought. The question, for Harvey, was how to accomplish this.

For Harvey, there were several possible paths. One was to reject the positivist basis of the quantitative movement in favor of phenomenology – that is, "the concept of man as a being in constant sensuous interaction with the social and natural realities which surround us" (Harvey 1973: 129). But phenomenological approaches could lead to idealism or naive empiricism – the so-called "behavioral revolution" in geography showed this. A more fruitful strategy was to explore a Marxist understanding in which positivism, materialism, and phenomenology overlapped to provide interpretations adequate to social reality. Hence, like positivism, Marxism is a materialist analysis, but whereas positivism seeks merely to understand, Marxism understands in order to change the world. Put differently, positivism draws its categories and concepts from existing reality in a straightforward and uncritical way; but the Marxist dialectical method incorporates contradictions and paradoxes, and points to their resolutions. Hence, in the case of the geographic problem of urban ghetto formation, the Chicago school of urban geography (Berry and Horton 1970) produced a "true" theory of urban land use in the sense of empirical accuracy (e.g. Muth's [1969] application of von Thunen's theory to Chicago), but the culmination for that theory was merely an indicator of the problem for Harvey: "Our objective is to eliminate ghettos. Therefore, the only valid policy with respect to this objective is to eliminate the conditions which give rise to the truth of the theory" (Harvey 1973: 137).

Harvey examines the notion of rent as a central factor in urban land use allocation. For Marx, rent was a manifestation of surplus value produced by exploiting labor. This was exactly the discussion of origin missing in positivistic accounts, which covered everything except the most basic characteristics of capitalist market economies, and devised all manner of solutions except those challenging the continuation of the capitalist form of economy. Such limited discussions and superficial "solutions," Harvey said, make researchers look foolish. Hence the need for a revolutionary approach to theory that goes beyond mapping and measuring social problems to become "nothing more nor less than the self-conscious and aware construction of a new paradigm for social and geographic thought through a deep and profound critique of our existing theoretical constructs" and the production of "a superior system" which when judged against realities requiring explanation would make "all opposition to that system of thought look ludicrous" (Harvey 1973: 145–6). This leads Harvey to an alternative Marxian theory dealing with land use within cities and cities in space. As opposed to the neoclassical economic notion of rent as a positivistic rationing device sorting land uses into locations, Harvey counterposes a Marxian theory theorizing rent as payment to the monopolistic power of private property. He also proposes a general theory of urbanism which links cities to modes of production; that is, cities are formed through the geographic concentration of the social surplus product and function to stabilize socio-economic contradictions. Marxism, he finds, is the only method capable of grappling with issues such as urbanism in this general, system-connecting way.

In essence, Harvey reaches (slightly in advance) a position approached by many other radicalized geographers – that it was impossible to do radical geography without a truly radical social theory. This theory was increasingly found in Marxism, long the basis of critical thinking in Europe, but equally long suppressed (using ferocious means) by states, universities, and the popular cultural media in North America. In many geography departments, groups of committed radical geographers began subversive Marxist reading groups, particularly useful for getting over the infamously difficult chapter 1 in volume 1 of Marx's *Capital*, but more generally effective in building rapport as theoretical understanding interacted with the development of a revolutionary politics. From these reading groups emerged a new generation of geographers which moved towards intellectual maturity in the middle 1970s, a group which retained its committed radicalism well into the more conservative years of the 1980s – some members of these groups even remain radicals today. Indeed, while the saying in the anti-war movement was "Don't trust anyone over thirty" it later became "Don't trust anyone under thirty." We pass therefore to an extended consideration of Marxism as the political, philosophical, and theoretical basis of what became the new approach: Marxist geography.

Marxism

As many people began to read and understand Marx, in part stimulated by Harvey's work, geographical thought was transformed in content and philosophical depth. Simply put, the level of prevailing discourse changed from an obsession with the empirical and the quantitative to an equally committed obsession with the political–epistemological and the political–ontological, with philosophy, social theory, and geography's place within it.

Lenin (1972a: 180) said it is impossible to understand Marx's *Capital* without first having understood Hegel. Marx's thought derives from the philosophical tradition of German classical idealism (Kant, Fichte, Schelling, Hegel) even as its leading criticism. We must therefore retrace Marx's philosophical trajectory from critical idealism to historical materialism as philosophies of the world. This section discusses

Marx's epistemology, ontology, and economic theory in a long detour, before returning to Marxist geography.

Hegel and Marx

In a brief but brilliant geo-materialist analysis, Auguste Cornu (1957) sees G. W. F. Hegel (1770–1831) expressing conditions in economically backward Germany, dominated still by feudal regimes. In such a context, Hegel had to consider activity essentially from a spiritual point of view. As a result, Cornu argues, Hegel (1967) did not understand reality as the object of concrete, practical human activity, but thought that the development of spirit determines, and expresses, the evolution of the world.

In this, Hegel drew on earlier German romantic idealist philosophy. Fichte made reality into the creation of a thinking subject: the Ego sets up a non-Ego in order to define and raise itself by a dialectical process to greater autonomy and higher morality; relations between Ego and non-Ego, humans and the external world, generate dialectical development. Schelling considered spirit and matter as two expressions of the divine, different in form, alike in essence, with spirit penetrating nature and realizing itself until nature becomes spirit, and spirit becomes nature. Drawing on Fichte and Schelling, Hegel (1967) found a form of reason, the Absolute Idea, or World Spirit, a spirit higher than individual subjectivity, creating reality by alienating its substance in the world, then progressively reassuming substance back into itself, to arrive at full self-consciousness by eliminating irrational elements from the real. The union of spirit and being determined by this rationalization of the world is accomplished in the form of concrete ideas, or concepts, which are not mere representations which humans make of objects, but constitute the most essential aspects of reality itself. The laws of spirit form the necessities of the real world, and logic becomes the creator of the real. Hegel thus explains evolution by the unfolding of the virtual contents of the Idea, the march of history being subordinated to the march of logic, the sequence of events in time being determined by their rational order. In this scheme, the development of the world is subordinated to the end it is to embody (Hegel 1967; Cornu 1957: 17–25).

For Hegel, the evolution of the real is determined dialectically by the oppositions and contradictions inherent in every real thing, each contradiction expressing, however, a moment, or aspect, of the Absolute Idea. In this, the contradictory term, the negative element, is essential for change, becoming the living source of dynamic process. Thus, negation, in the Hegelian dialectic, takes an essentially positive value, becoming that active or fertile element without which there would be no development and no life. In Hegel, negation is the moving force asserting itself in the forms of opposition and criticism against everything that endeavors to persist. The antagonisms between contradictory elements (thesis and antithesis) are exacerbated to the point that they can no longer coexist, precipitating a crisis in which the contrary elements are reabsorbed into a higher and qualitatively different unity, the synthesis. In this way, spirit, in its effort to go beyond incessantly reborn contradictions, progresses from notion to notion, each uniting in itself a new stage of reality, spiritual and material. The dialectic is Hegel's method of showing how reality follows a rational path in its development and expresses the very movement of spirit (Cornu 1957).

Marx derives his dialectical method from Hegel but rejects its teleological, spiritual idealism. As Marx (1976: 102–3) puts it:

> My dialectical method is, in its foundation, not only different from the Hegelian, but exactly opposite to it. For Hegel, the process of thinking, which he even transforms into an independent subject, under the name of "the Idea," is the creator of the real world, and the real world is only the external appearance of the idea. With me the reverse is true: the ideal is nothing but the material world reflected in the mind of man, and translated into forms of thought ... [However], the mystification which the dialectic suffers in Hegel's hands by no means prevented him from being the first to present its general forms of motion in a comprehensive and conscious manner. With him it is standing on its head. It must be inverted in order to discover the rational kernel within the mystical shell.

The philosopher Sydney Hook (1962: 16) points out that the two positions, idealism and materialism, are in total opposition, yet "Hegelian elements in Marx are integral to his system." For both Marx and Hegel, the social system constitutes a whole, so that the various aspects of society are parts or aspects of the whole. Hegel's doctrine of essence also appears in Marx: however, in Marx, the essence of a system does not exist behind or beyond its appearances, but is expressed in them; the whole exists in its parts, the parts in the whole. Similarly, the key to the development of the whole is found in the specific character of its structural oppositions. But, for Marx, the extent, strength, and rate of interaction between the polar opposites in any situation depends on the specific factors involved and cannot be deduced from a general formula of dialectical movement. This lends the Marxian dialectic a significant empirical dimension and transforms it from an instrument of teleological necessity to a way of analyzing a determinable but open historical process (Hook 1962).

Marx and his collaborator Friedrich Engels concur with Hegel that the driving force in development is the conflict and opposition between elements. This entails looking at things in terms of their relations, their contradictions, and their place within wider systems of relations (wholes or systems). But whereas Hegel sees the principle of negativity as the way the Absolute Idea expresses itself, Marx begins with an examination of the actual economic relations within which humans find themselves. These relations take the form of oppositions between social groups (classes in class societies) which cannot be resolved without changing the whole society – in Marx the "dialectical principle" appears as social activity. The dialectical resolution of conflict is a productive synthesis of the conflicting elements in a definite situation. As Hook (1962: 68) points out, a true synthesis is not a simple destructive process, an addition, transformation, or repetition; it is all these and more: "Thesis and antithesis are resolved in such a way that the pretensions of each to constitute the whole of a relation are denied; yet aspects of each are retained or conserved in every new whole or situation; and are re-interpreted or elevated as subordinate moments in a more inclusive whole." Whereas Hegel was, in this, groping to express the logic of spiritual development, Marx reconceptualized synthesis, seeing development as socio-historical rather than logical, resulting in a succession of social systems in a determinate order – that is, the history of modes of production.

Marx's Theory of Society

Hegel's followers polarized after his death in 1831 between a right wing, which accepted Hegel's conservative notion that the Prussian state was the incarnation of the Absolute Idea, and a left wing (the young Hegelians), which critically demanded that this state conform, in fact, to the Absolute Idea. Left Hegelianism then took two main forms. On the one side, Otto Bauer and his followers abandoned Hegel's absolute idealism for a position similar to the subjective idealism of Fichte, in which the objective world is merely posited by the Ego in order for it to attain self-consciousness. On the other, Ludwig Feuerbach's more radical critique of Hegel reverted to the philosophical materialism of the French Enlightenment. For Feuerbach, the subject of the dialectic was nature, with humans as nature's highest development. Feuerbach accepted Hegel's account of the structure of the dialectic, but believed that Hegel had transformed nature into a manifestation of the Absolute Idea. This speculative feat was part of another inversion: the imagination of an alien being (a fictional deity) and the attribution of all the human's essential powers to it. The task of philosophy, for Feuerbach, was to demolish both this fictitious God and the Absolute, setting humans in their natural place. Since people are, for Feuerbach, essentially natural beings, the connections with nature (sense-perceptions and physical needs) provide the only certain sources of knowledge – this means that humanism becomes materialist and empiricist. For the young Hegelians generally, history with the Absolute removed was the development of self-consciousness, the progress of the human mind, the growth of enlightenment, and development of knowledge of self and the natural environment (Callinicos 1985).

Karl Marx (1819–83) and Friedrich Engels (1820–95) were originally radical fringe members of the (Feuerbachian) young Hegelians, advocating its materialist humanism, and believing that human alienation could only be abolished in a communist society. In his *Critique of Hegel's Philosophy of Right*, Marx (1964a) followed Feuerbach in arguing against Hegel's inversion of reality and thought. For Marx, human alienation has its origin in the structure of society rather than in the human consciousness. But in his early (Hegelian) phase, Marx still regarded the proletariat as a passive element, as an inert mass awaiting the enlightening, radical spark of philosophy. In the *Economic and Philosophical Manuscripts*, Marx (1964b) transformed his previous Feuerbachian and passive view of human nature to a conception based on the human's active relation to the environment. Now the human's "species-being" consists not in self-consciousness but in labor: through labor, people can redirect their activity to achieve new goals and, as productive powers are enhanced, new desires are created and people change. Likewise, production transforms nature so that while Feuerbach sees the world as a thing remaining forever the same, Marx sees even the most certain natural objects as mediated by an active labor process. At the core of the *Manuscripts* is a teleological philosophy of history in which the development of the social-productive forces of society culminate in communism, the complete return of the human to itself, the final resolution of the conflicts between people, and between people and the environment. The French philosopher Louis Althusser (1965; 1969; Althusser and Balibar 1968) argues that an "epistemological break" occurs in Marx's thought at this point. From the perspective of such a break, Marx's (1969) critical *Theses on Feuerbach* constitute the first systematic presentations of historical materialism. Hence, in the *Theses*, explanatory primacy shifts from the human being in a dialectic of alienation and reconciliation, to production, control over nature, and social organization: for Marx, it is not consciousness that determines life, but life that determines consciousness. Whereas the utopian socialists of Marx's time continued the Enlightenment view of social change as the product of intellectual development, from the time of their more fully developed *The German Ideology* Marx and Engels (1970) saw struggle within social relations as the driving force of history. However, this conception of social relations took a while to develop. At first, social relations are crudely understood as a "form of intercourse" between people, including all kinds of relations, such as trade and commerce. By comparison, Marx's conception of the forces of production (human labor power, means of production, controlled natural forces, and materials) was more advanced. These different levels of conceptual development gave the tenor of technological determinism to Marx's first summary of his overall social theoretic viewpoint. Summarizing his differences with Hegel over law and politics, Marx (1970) says:

> My investigation led to the result that legal relations as well as forms of state are to be grasped neither from themselves nor from the so-called general development of the human mind, but rather have their roots in the material conditions of life . . . In the social production of their life, men enter into definite relations that are indispensable and independent of their will, relations of production which correspond to a definite stage of development of their material productive forces. The sum total of these relations of production constitutes the economic structure of society, the real foundation, on which rises a legal and political superstructure and to which correspond definite forms of social consciousness. The mode of production in material life conditions the social, political and intellectual life process in general. It is not the consciousness of men that determines their being, but, on the contrary, their social being that determines their consciousness. At a certain stage of their development, the material forces of society come in conflict with the existing relations of production, or – what is but a legal expression for the same thing – with the property relations within which they have been at work hitherto. From forms of development of the productive forces, these relations turn into their fetters. Then begins an epoch of social revolution. With the change of the economic foundation the entire immense superstructure is more or less rapidly transformed . . . In broad outlines Asiatic, ancient, feudal, and modern bourgeois modes of production can be designated as progressive epochs in the economic formation of society. The bourgeois relations of production are the last antagonist form of the social process of production – antagonistic not in the sense of individual antagonism, but of one arising from the social conditions of life of the individuals; at the same time the productive forces developing in the womb of bourgeois society create the material conditions for the

solution of that antagonism. This social formation brings, therefore, the prehistory of human society to a close.

In this statement, the dynamic of forces of production drives change in the entire "mode of production of material life." By the time of Marx's (1976) mature work *Capital*, by comparison, the forces of production are subordinated to the relations of production, and social relations are conceived as relations between classes centered on the extraction of surplus labor time or "exploitation." Societies are exploitative when uncompensated surplus labor, or its products, are taken from the direct producers, the exploitation process being an arena of struggle, the dominant using a combination of economic, political, and ideological force, and the dominated resisting through overt means like social organization and rebellion, and hidden means, like reluctant compliance. In such a context, consciousness must take ideological forms which rationalize and legitimize exploitation, organized religion being one such form, conventional science being another.

In addition, a society characterized by exploitation and conflict must develop institutions for ensuring elite domination and for collectively reproducing the conditions and infrastructures of production (Hirsch 1978: 64–5). Many of these collective activities are accumulated in the state, governed by an appropriate kind of politics. However, for Marx, structural necessities do not functionally create institutional forms or empirical tendencies in direct, unmediated ways. Hence, the exact character of the state can only be found through examining its particular conditions of existence:

> It is in each case the direct relationship of the owners of the conditions of production to the immediate producers – a relationship whose particular form naturally corresponds always to a certain level of development of the type and manner of labour, and hence to its social productive power – in which we find the innermost secret, the hidden basis of the entire social edifice, and hence also the political form of the relationship of sovereignty and dependence, in short, the specific form of state in each case. This does not prevent the same economic basis – the same in its major conditions – from displaying endless variations and gradations in its appearance, as the result of innumerable different empirical circumstances, natural conditions, racial relations, historical influences acting from outside, etc., and these can only be understood by analyzing these empirically given conditions. (Marx 1981: 927–8)

Hence, for Marx, there are structural connections between the social relations of production (owners and workers in capitalism, peasants and landlords in feudalism, etc.) and the form of the state apparatus. Structural factors limit and direct the kind of state which comes into existence, but people living in specific times and places create its more exact social and historical forms (see figure 3.1).

For Marx, social transformations essentially involve a shift from one mode of the production of existence to another (figure 3.2). Marx envisions these as violent episodes undertaken by desperate people when all the productive possibilities of the old social order have been exhausted. Crises in material development sharpen and intensify ongoing social struggles, giving the potential for broad social change,

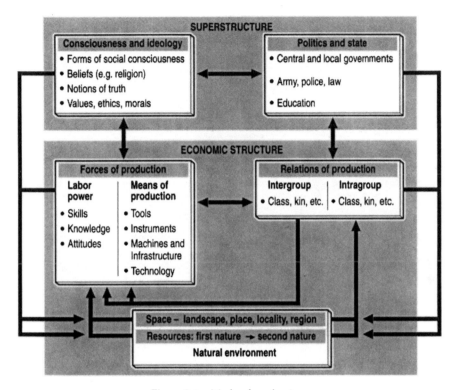

Figure 3.1   Mode of production.
Social relations direct the application of forces of production in the transformation of the natural environment. Politics and state activity guide this process of the production of existence, while forms of consciousness explain, legitimate, and justify its continuation.

including political and ideological transformations. The new social system gained through struggle does not materialize out of thin air, or from utopian desire alone, but is formed out of embryonic relations present already in the dying body of the old society. And communism may or may not result from the clash between worker and owner over control of capitalist production. For, by the time of *Capital*, history has no pre-determined, teleological end point for Marx: "With the introduction of the concept of the relations of production Marx finally abandons the teleological philosophy of history he inherited from Hegel and Feuerbach" (Callinicos 1985: 52). To summarize: Hegelian dialectical conceptions remain even in the mature Marx, although used in a different (materialist) way. For Hegel, contradictions in the real world are manifestations of contradictions in the Absolute Idea. For Marx, contradictions (such as between capital and labor) are the moving principles of social life giving rise to the struggles, conflicts, and crises endemic to class societies. In Marx's fully materialist dialectic, an open-ended conflictual theory replaces the still mystical teleology of Hegelian Idealism. For Marx, a scientific knowledge of societies can only be phrased in terms of the antagonistic relations constituting them.

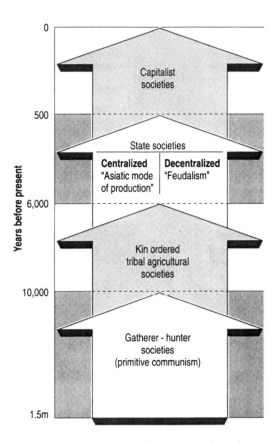

Figure 3.2   Modes of production through time.
Modes of production arranged in terms of their first appearance. Note that gatherer–hunter (primitive communist) societies predominate through 99 percent of human history.

Understanding this requires that we go further into Marx's epistemology and his ontology of internal relations. The next two sections are dedicated to these topics.

Marx's Political Epistemology

Dissatisfied both with pre-Hegelian Enlightenment thought, in particular with the dualism between "is" and "ought," and also with the idealism of Hegel's teleological dialectic, Marx involved himself in the creation of a post-Hegelian dialectical science in which the origins of the "ought" are found in the practical world, rather than in a moral code external to it (Murray 1988). Marx considered *Capital* to be a work of science, regarded science as a statement about truth, and thought that truth could guide political and economic practice (or praxis). However, Marx's conceptions of knowledge and truth were different from conceptions predominating in the positivism of the nineteenth century, bearing still a greater resemblance to Hegel's dialectical conception.

As Bhukhu Parekh (1982) argues, from a realist perspective (see chapter 5), Marx locates truth within the larger context of human existence. Humans are needful beings engaged in praxis which requires that they understand nature and society: humans initially pursue truth and knowledge because these are the basis of praxis and, ultimately, human wellbeing. Such a material grounding does not mean that knowledge lacks independent character, however. Practical problems become theoretical issues when they are redefined and transposed into an appropriate language, while theoretical inquiries have their own standards of truth and methods of investigation. For Marx, class conflicts of interest shape the practical pursuit of social knowledge and its dissemination: some interests "apologetically" favor the class domination embodied in the prevailing social order; others "critically" favor human emancipation. Society is conflict-ridden and the theorist is involved in, and affected by, such conflicts. The social theorist cannot avoid taking sides even when believing in the possibility of pure, neutral ("scientific") theory. Furthermore, apologetic social theory has a tendency to dehistoricize theory, employing ahistorical and abstract categories, and asking systematically biased questions. It cannot be used to criticize and change the social order. A critically oriented theoretical knowledge, by comparison, not only explains, but interrogates the existing social order. It explores dialectically society's internal contradictions, potentialities, and the ways society can be changed. For Marx, then, a body of knowledge contains political imperatives and recommendations: theory and practice cannot be disjoined and compartmentalized, but are interdependent moments of a single whole. In brief, the social theorist must decide what view to take of the fundamental structure of society (Parekh 1982).

Marx finds only the emancipatory interest to be justifiable. Humans seek truth to liberate themselves from natural and social restraints and only the emancipatory interest is capable of attaining truth. By comparison, the pursuit of knowledge in the interests of domination is locked into a system of assumptions which prevent it from probing the innermost nature of the social order and is therefore ideologically distorted. Marx thus finds a fundamental harmony between truth and freedom: only the truth can set people free. Yet truth has often been taken to be immutable and independent of human thought and action. Marx takes the view instead that truth consists of the conformity of ideas to reality (i.e. a correspondence theory of truth). Yet reality is also created and altered by praxis; in this sense truth creates reality. As humans alter social reality, they make true what once was false, and vice versa. Theory can make itself true by bringing the world into harmony with itself (this therefore is a quite different "correspondence" theory). Marx does not intend by this that humans create truth as they please or that human praxis is the sole criterion of truth (Parekh 1982).

With Aristotle, a rigid distinction was drawn between truth and falsehood – a statement is either true or false. For Hegel and Marx, by comparison, theories contain ideas which are neither wholly true nor false. For Marx, a theory is a complex body of thought containing true insights which its assumptions might not allow to be fully articulated or developed. Insights may be distorted, interpreted wrongly, put to questionable theoretical uses, or combined with false ideas. A theory has immanent dimensions, pointing beyond itself, saying more than it intends, sometimes containing criticism or even refutation of its own basic premises. For these and other reasons, and by comparison with positivism, a theory as a whole cannot be neatly categorized as true or false. A theory might offer a true account of the surface of society but not of its inner structure, be true at one level, false at another. As social reality is subject to historical change and geographical variation, a theory giving a true account at one time and in one context might give a false account in another. Even so, for Marx, scientific theory must still be judged by its ability to give a true account of its subject matter. For the realist Parekh, Marx subscribes to a modified version of the correspondence theory of truth, but in the following way: a theory is true if its conceptual structure reproduces the inner nature of its subject matter. This "inner nature" is not a matter of empirical observation. The theorist uses knowledge of an entity's inner structure to explain why it behaves in a particular way and displays specific forms – comprehension of inner structure should enable explanation of observable (outer) behavior. If an explanation of behavior is correct we are entitled to conclude that the theory corresponds to the inner structure of the entity. Thus, correspondence can (only) be indirectly verified. An explanation is correct if it shows that the behavior of an entity is not a chance occurrence but a necessary consequence of its inner constitution. Scientific explanation thus has the following logical form:

(1) an entity has a specific inner structure; (2) it has certain tendencies and must behave in a given manner; (3) the tendencies become manifest under certain conditions at certain times; (4) this leads an entity to behave in a given manner at a certain time. The primary task of a scientific theory is not so much general law making as articulating the inner nature, or constitution, of its subject matter. A scientist specifies how an entity must behave and the kinds of factors and circumstances frustrating the realization of its tendencies – in what ways and within what limits. For Marx, such tendencies are not transcendental but immanent in the behavior of the entity in question. Therefore, although every fact is not absolute in authority (as with positivism), it cannot be ignored either.

In Marx's view, theory should also give "theoretical satisfaction" through its originality, unity, simplicity, concentration, depth, novelty, and conciseness. In general, for Marx, a scientific theory should be judged by the explanatory powers of its truth, its critical coherence, its logical structure, and its elegant simplicity. For Marx, the discovery of truth requires a correct method of investigation leading to a well-structured and well-presented theory. A true theory is compelled by the force of its insight to develop an elegant conceptual structure (Parekh 1982: 186–210).

Marx's Social Ontology: The Philosophy of Internal Relations

If epistemology establishes the conditions of possibility of truth, ontology conceptualizes the structure of existence which true statements characterize. The version of Marx's ontology most affecting geographical thought (through the writings of Harvey, for example) was developed by the political scientist Bertell Ollman in *Alienation: Marx's Conception of Man in Capitalist Society*, originally published in 1971 (second edition 1976). In Ollman's reading, human nature and social relations together make up Marx's primary vantage point. Marx, he says, had a theory of human nature, different from other conceptions which he found unhistorical (i.e. human nature as given and unchanging). For Ollman, Marx's view of human nature was elaborated in the early works, *Economic and Political Manuscripts* (1844) and *The German Ideology* (1846) but, as opposed to Althusser, Ollman finds no significant breaks between these and Marx's later works (*Grundrisse, Capital*, etc.).

For Ollman, there are problems in interpreting these writings because, as Pareto (1965, vol. 2: 332) says, Marx's words appear like bats – one can see in them birds and mice. Hence, the notion that the mode of production of material life determines the life process in general is difficult to interpret because Marx uses the same expression (mode of production) to refer to different things (e.g. relations of production). Such inconsistency draws heavy critical fire and lends itself to misunderstanding. Thus, the position is taken that Marx's theory must have a separable "factor" (production) determining everything else (consciousness) and by a process of elimination this factor is said to be productive technology – hence, economic determinism becomes technological determinism. As technology can hardly be said to change independently (of science, law, etc.) Marx is found not only wrong but ignorant of the elementary facts of social life. Ollman calls this criticism "fundamentalism," thinks that economic determinism in this sense is a caricature, and sets out to show that Marx did not separate out such mutually exclusive social factors – hence the theory of internal relations.

In Ollman's reading, Marx uses theoretical categories as forms of expression or manifestations of social existence, and frequently one-sided aspects at that, rather than categories being simple means of description. In Marx, any social factor or activity (working, thinking) is composed of many tied facets or parts and is thought of as a definite social relation; hence, the concept representing this factor (labor, consciousness) must convey these facets and ties as part of its meaning. While in common-sense understanding a social factor is independent of others, for Marx, the relations between factors are internal to them, so that when a relation changes, the factor becomes something else: the term "relation" thus refers to the factor and its connections, or the factor in its relations. In this view, interaction is inneraction – Marx studies the inner connections between things. When something "determines" or "causes" something else, in a philosophy of internal relations this merely emphasizes one particular link or influence, for each factor develops under the direct and indirect influence of everything else. Also, each social factor is internally related to its own past and future forms, as well as those of surrounding factors. The relations bound into any factor make one kind of development more probable than others, and Marx uses "law" or "tendency" to refer to such relational tendencies in the real world and "logic" for these relations reflected in the meanings of the relevant categories. As Marx moves from one problem to another, new areas inside each relation become relevant and previously relevant areas cease being so – hence, the contents of the analytical categories varies.

How then does Marx decide which version of the meaning of a category to use? For Ollman, the problem lies in describing the precise ways that actual existence affects the way we conceive of it, and label it, and how that label reacts on what exists. Marx's practice in naming or labelling accounts for the real world as it is (the core notion of a factor) and his conception of what it can be (the function of the factor in the sub-system of society under examination). In the latter sense especially, each factor potentially may take the names of others when it functions as they do. So "theory" can become a "material force" when it is a driving factor in human life. Hence, the sense conveyed by Marx's concepts is unstable. Thus, instead of seeking a strict causal tie between mode of production and other social practices we must seek the many ways Marx believes effects proceed from economic factors. Justifying his belief that Marx has a philosophy of internal relations, Ollman points to the tradition of thought (Spinoza, Leibniz, Hegel) which intellectually nourished Marx; all sought the meanings of things and terms in relations inside wholes. Ollman also points to key statements in Marx (humans as assemblages of social relations) and views (humans and nature as internally tied) to support his position. Finally, this entire discussion can be presented in the dynamic language of dialectics – that is, Marx's dialectic sees things as moments in their own development in, with, and through other things (Ollman 1976: 3–69).

Using this approach, Ollman explores Marx's ontology of human nature in general and as modified during each historical period. Every human being, Marx believes, possesses certain powers and needs, some natural (shared with every living entity), some species (possessed by humans alone). "Power" means ability or faculty but also potential, while "need" refers to desire or want for something not immediately available. Power is coupled with need, powers fulfill needs, the two reflect one another. Similar to animal functions, natural powers exist as tendencies, abilities, and impulses (labor, eating, sex) seeking fulfillment outside the individual's body. The realization, or objectification, of human powers in nature is the transfer of suitably altered elements within an organic whole: the two spheres are bound together (inner related) practically and conceptually, and the human relation to nature includes bonds between individuals (e.g. sexual ties). As natural beings, humans are objective and sensuous, limited and conditioned, expending effort through labor to satisfy physical needs, as with all other animals. But as species beings, humans are self-conscious, aware of themselves as individuals active in pursuing their own ends, knowing that they exist as beings. Humans manifest themselves as species beings through activity of a distinct kind, quality, and pace. Natural powers establish a framework while species powers express the specific kind of life which humans carry on within it (Ollman 1976).

For Marx, relations between human powers and the rest of the world occur through perception (immediate contact through the senses), orientation (establishing patterns, assigning worth, setting a frame for action), and appropriation (powers using nature to realize ends), the last occupying a prominent place in Marx's thought. Appropriation means using constructively, or incorporating in such a significant way that perception and orientation are enhanced; one power reacts on others to make new achievements possible. The degree of movement towards human potential depends on productive development and social relations. For Marx, communism is the era of complete emancipation, when the richness of human sensibility is fully realized. In each historical era (and, we might add, each regional formation at any given time), the objects appropriated, and that which they are appropriated from, bear the tell-tale marks, or signs, of what humans have become, particularly in the case of material production, where the species powers are most evident, and where nature is the main object of production. How and what humans produce indicates who people are.

Objects are appropriated through activity, especially work, which creates use values, or the ability of a product to serve an intended purpose in satisfying a need. For Marx, productive activity creates material use values, combines the human powers, establishes new possibilities in extending the boundaries of nature, remolds nature, and enables, with each alteration, the powers to achieve new kinds and degrees of fulfillment – hence, Marx views the natural features of a locale as limitations and incentives. Yet work can also consume rather than enrich the human powers, as with the productive activity of the proletariat on the assembly lines of a capitalist factory. For Marx, activity must be done with and for others – humans are social as well as creative beings, "social" entailing cooperation, either active and conscious (production) or passive and unconscious (language). In this conception, "society" is the sum of all social relations between individuals. Need creates reciprocal links and production is the sphere where the social character of the human being emerges most clearly. For Marx, people appropriate each other in all their contacts, and suffer or gain according to the qualities of those they come in touch with – hence, an individual's stake in maximizing the accomplishments of another person could not be more personal. In communism, need or enjoyment lose their egotistical character – as Ollman (1976: 107–8) puts it:

> A person can no longer satisfy his own need by depriving others, since the effect of their disappointment would punish him along with everyone else ... extraordinary cooperation ... brings a revolution in the way each individual conceptualizes his relations with what we take to be the "outer" world ... The age-old conflict between man and society has been resolved ... in communism, "nature becomes man" ... communist society "is the consummate oneness in substance of man and nature – the naturalism of man and the humanism of nature both brought to fulfillment."

This brings Ollman to the culminating moment of Marx's ontology, the theory of alienation in capitalist society. For Marx, "free conscious activity is man's species character" and alienation is the result of the devastating effects of capitalism on the human character. For Marx, the connections which tie individuals to the external world have broken down and each element in these relations has become independent: people are separated from their life activity, their products, the material world and their species. In each case, the relation distinguishing humanity disappears and the constitutive elements are reorganized to appear as something else. The being left over after losing its human qualities is an "abstraction ... reduced to performing undifferentiated work on humanly indistinguishable objects among people deprived of their human variety and compassion" (Ollman 1976: 134). The split-off parts undergo their own transformations into alienated, independent life elements –

money, property, industry, religion – taking on "needs" which the individual is forced to satisfy. As a result of alienated work the product becomes an external existence, a power of its own confronting the individual either as a purchasable commodity, hence addiction to buying, or as privately owned means of production, as controlling capital. In the related theory of commodity fetishism, Marx (1976: chapter 1) argues that under conditions of market exchange of commodities, the social character of labor appears as an objective character of the product:

> the relations connecting the labour of one individual with that of the rest appear, not as direct social relations between individuals at work, but as what they really are, material relations between persons and social relations between things ... To [the producers] their own social action takes the form of the action of objects, which rule the producers instead of being ruled by them. (Marx 1976: 73, 75)

Thus, capital is said to "earn" a profit, money "creates" more money, consumption goods have the power to "generate" needs, and so on. From this comes also the overall structure of Marx's theory of religion. In *Capital*, Marx argues that the religious world is not an original presence, in the creationist sense, but a mental reflex of the real world – that is, God is a figment of the imagination. For societies based in the production and exchange of commodities, where the social production of existence is organized indirectly via markets, alienated social relations take the form of an abstract humanity, a humanized "God," which is substituted (in part) for earlier versions in which people worshipped Mother Nature as the force controlling existence. Hence, the development of the forces of production, the application of science and technology, leads only to a shift in the form of religious mystification rather than its eradication. In brief, alienation is Marx's theoretical explanation for that central feature of contemporary life: the greater the technical and economic power of humanity the less control exercised by individuals, classes, families, localities or nations. Controlled by structures, active but only partially effective, humans confront this central paradox of their existence. The theme of structure and agency recurs throughout the following chapters.

It scarcely needs adding that the philosophy of internal relations can be read in spatial and environmental terms. Objects exist in webs of spatial relations intrinsic to their constitutions and the formation of their powers. Spatial context, in this view, is not a passive surface, but actually creates the nature of the objects, investing them with causal powers. Societies are tied to natural environments through inner relations, displaying their most basic characters in the features of the landscape. Such notions had a powerful effect on geographic thinking.

Schools of Marxian Thought

Before these are discussed, we should digress briefly to explore further some other forms taken by Marxist thought in the twentieth century. Like other thought systems, Marxism passed through a scientific, positivist period in the late nineteenth century, symbolized by Friedrich Engels's proposal in *Anti-Duhrung* (1976) and *Dialectics of*

Nature (1940) that the "laws" of dialectics are the most general patterns of matter in motion, and thus apply to natural and social science as a unified whole. As we have seen (chapter 1), late nineteenth-century Germany in particular saw a reaction against materialism, science, and modernity and a revival of interest in the philosophy of Immanuel Kant. In Marxism, neo-Kantianism took the form of critiques of Darwinian evolutionism, materialist determination, and the notion (in Engels among others) that the human sphere of life is an extension of the natural world (subject therefore to the same dialectical laws) – nature, it was argued, knows nothing of human freedom, scientism can say little about moral issues, and so on. The leader of this "revisionist" movement was Eduard Bernstein, a prime figure in the German SPD (Social Democratic Party), and proponent of neo-Kantian ethical socialism. In this, he was vigorously opposed by V. I. Lenin, Rosa Luxembourg, Gergi Plekhanov, and the editor of the leading Marxist Journal *Neue Zeit*, Karl Kautsky (Sheehan 1985). Even so, the romantic, anti-scientific tradition of Marxism was carried into twentieth-century Marxian thought by Georg Lukács in *History and Class Consciousness* (1971), first published in 1923. In Lukács, there is no suggestion that science and industrialization have liberating effects. Science is merely one form of contemplation, while truth is relative to the standpoint of a given class. For Lukács, too, the essential features of capitalism are commodity fetishism and its product, reification – the process by which human relations take the appearance of relations between things, and the products of social activity (society, history, science) appear as alien forces, as external laws of nature. For Lukács, even the scientific method is a product of reification, active in that it destroys organicism and metaphysics to create a world of pure facts: in the words of Goran Therborn (1978: 94), "Immutable scientific laws of society were the expression of a world in which human relations had become things beyond human control, and the separation of different scientific disciplines revealed a specialization which destroyed the totality and historicity of human existence." With this, Lukács synthesizes neo-Kantian idealism and Marxism.

The Frankfurt School

However, the main route through which idealism, whether of the Hegelian or Kantian variety, was carried into contemporary Marxism lies through the Frankfurt school, originally Horkheimer, Adorno, Marcuse, the historian-geographer Wittfogel, more distantly, Eric Fromm and Walter Benjamin, and, more recently, Jürgen Habermas and Alfred Schmidt. "Critical theory," the theoretical program of the Frankfurt school, starts from the view of humans as the creators of history, whereas traditional theory's mode of cognition derives from the natural sciences – with this, in Goran Therborn's (1978: 88–9) interpretation, "critical theory explicitly announces its concordance with German idealism from Kant onwards ... Critical theory's epistemological basis is a metaphysical humanism." The Frankfurt school shares with Tonnies, Weber, Lukács, and Korsch a fascination with capitalist rationalization, but takes the critique of scientific rationality in the direction of science as domination. In *Dialectic of Enlightenment* (1991: 3), Max Horkheimer and Theodore Adorno ask why "the fully enlightened earth radiates disaster triumphant." For them, natural science, specifically Bacon's empiricist theory of knowledge, employs a logic contaminated by domination: "What men want to learn from nature is how to use it in order wholly to dominate it and other men" (Horkheimer and Adorno 1969: 4). They find Enlightenment reason institutionalized as domination in the capitalist economy, in international corporations, state bureaucracies, and the culture industry. Similar to Lukács, they see science and instrumental reason reproducing religion's blind obedience to superior powers in a new kind of rational totalitarianism.

This interest in the domination of instrumental reason is carried into the second generation of Frankfurt school theorists, and into contemporary human geography (Gregory 1989; Miller 1992), by its leading representative, Jürgen Habermas. Here, the approach is through a critique of positivism as a form of instrumental reason which refers only to efficiency of means and not ends. For Habermas (1971), science is embedded in anthropologically deep-seated technical interests, especially the domination of nature and the material reproduction of the species. Yet there is another practical interest, also necessary for socio-cultural reproduction, in maintaining intersubjectivity through ordinary communication. The domination of technical over practical interests in positivism fails to provide an adequate conceptual framework for understanding the rationalization of the world. In response to criticism that this constitutes a form of philosophical foundationalism, Habermas shifts attention to theories of language and action, while retaining a belief that there is a universalistic sense of rationality which applies even to the moral–political dimension of life. Hence, Habermas's later claim is that the speech acts of competent actors conform to a set of rules which establish the criteria of communicative rationality – language functions as a medium of intersubjective understanding and coordinated consensual action based on mutual recognition of validity claims. Here, Habermas performs a more complex critical analysis of modernity than Horkheimer and Adorno, arguing that the modern consciousness corroding religion (disenchanting the world, in Weber's terms) experiences itself as alienated: a search for self-assurance results, a project in which modernity creates normativity out of itself alone (and not out of religion or cultural traditions). In *The Theory of Communicative Action* (1984–7), Habermas argues that societies are simultaneously action systems integrated through communicatively achieved consensus and (with Schutz) lifeworlds linguistically organized by stocks of interpretative patterns. For Habermas, capitalist reification takes the form of systemic deformations as the lifeworld is colonized – this produces the cultural impoverishment and social pathologies of advanced capitalism. The task of critical theory then becomes providing a theory of rationality which allows reconciliation with the radical potential of modernity – this involves, in Stephen White's (1988: 136) view, a rejection of the domination instrumental modes of relating to nature, enhancing the moral–practical and aesthetic–expressive dimensions of everyday social life (McCarthy 1978; 1985; Outhwaite 1994).

Marxist Geography

Fired by encounters with ideas like these, of a different order than those exercising previous generations, radical geographers started to teach, carry out research, and write using consciously Marxist approaches and methodologies. As we have seen, in the middle 1970s radical geography gave way to Marxist geography as the main impetus of critical intellectual endeavor. The difference between radical and Marxist geography resides not so much in everyday political practice as in the depth and style of intellectual practice, the far greater contact made with other social theories via the corpus of Marxist works, and the reasons for doing research and publishing, which had even more sense of long-term mission. Revolutionary theorists are committed to developing the most insightful theories ever known and are determined to use the power that comes with persuasive ability to change society completely and for ever. If the radical geography of the late 1960s was exhilarating for its adherents, Marxist geography in the middle to late 1970s provided a deep sense of committed satisfaction, tempered by the occasional realization that acts of intellectually elitist arrogance occurred. For the interaction between Marxism and the knowledges of environment and space (hardly the least significant of human understandings) produced powerful theoretical insights into profound issues of human existence, and these in turn produce disciplinary power in its many guises. Here, we emphasize the difference Marxism makes to geographic knowledge of environment and space.

For much of the 1970s and well into the 1980s, Marxist geographers in the Anglo-American tradition were preoccupied with deriving analytical concepts and categories from the corpus of Marx's works and applying them to practical issues of immediate concern. As understanding matured into a fully Marxist geography, exegesis was gradually, although never completely, replaced by the creation of specifically Marxist geographic theories, mainly through interactions between the new insights and the old preoccupations with nature and space. Summarizing and extending many of these ideas, Neil Smith's *Uneven Development* (1984) can be taken as symptomatic of the best of Marxist geography. We shall explore this work in detail, first dealing with natural relations.

The Production of Nature

For Smith, real experiences in the social transformation of nature determine its "intellectual consumption" or, more specifically, industrial capitalism reshapes (pre-industrial) accumulated meanings of nature into more appropriate contemporary concepts. But, despite their variations, for Smith, the various conceptions of nature are organized into an essential *dualism*: on the one side, nature is external, a realm of extra-human objects and processes; on the other side, nature is universal, including human nature. The historical roots of this dualism, in the western philosophical tradition, can be traced to Kant, for whom external nature was the physical environment, internal nature was human passion, and the knowing mind (rational consciousness) experiencing nature as a unity was a means of overcoming the dualism. Smith thinks that this Kantian dualism now permeates western thought to the level of intuitive correctness. Dualism flows through the scientific and literary traditions: it is found in Francis Bacon's advocacy of the mastery of nature through science and technology, as well as in positive science's abstraction of natural phenomena from the social context; it is found likewise in the poetic tradition, as American wilderness to be tamed, yet (later) appreciated as repository of values, or in the romantic–idealist theme of the unity of a separate nature in the pastoral ideal and American transcendental literature (Emerson, Thoreau). For Smith, dualism is an ideologically necessary contradiction in contemporary thought. As externality, it legitimates natural subjugation. As universality, it invests certain forms of behavior, like competition, with natural (normal) status. Dualism, however, has disastrous consequences in fragmenting knowledge and reducing nature to mere "external factor" in capitalist economies and neoclassical economics.

By contrast, in his early work, Marx insisted on the unity of nature. For explication, Smith turns to the main theorist of the Frankfurt school dealing with natural relations: Alfred Schmidt's *The Concept of Nature in Marx* (1971) theorizes Marx's "dialectic of Subject and [Natural] object." For Marx, society was internal to nature, the mediating processes literally passing through "metabolism" (i.e. the process of building nutritive material into living matter), or "metabolic interaction," with labor as active force and unified science as mode of understanding – hence, Engels extended Marx's materialist (social) dialectic to include nature in one system. But Schmidt detects in Marx's notion of metabolism as eternal, nature-imposed necessity a "negative ontology" of the purposive human will's triumph over nature, with technology as its emancipatory, utopian force. In the Frankfurt school, by comparison, technology is seen as a dominating force. Smith finds this interpretation of Marx to be a figment of Schmidt's imagination. Indeed, Smith finds the Frankfurt school's theme of the domination of (external and internal) nature replacing a (preferred) Marxian emphasis on class conflict; Smith thinks this shift in emphasis (from class to a generalized domination) leads to a critical politics centered on the "human condition" rather than social relations, which inserts a flawed, dualistic conception of nature into the environmental movement.

In place of the Frankfurt school of Marxism's *domination* of nature, Smith wants to substitute what he finds to be a more complex notion of the *production* of nature. Theoretically, this entails reconstructing Marx's scattered ideas in a "logico-historical" understanding which moves from abstract towards concrete (exact) categories. Beginning at the abstract level of production in general, metabolism forms a use value relation between society and nature. People are originally natural beings with consciousness directly interwoven with material, natural activity. But this is a differentiated unity of people and nature: humans distinguish themselves from animals by *producing* their means of subsistence (the implication being purposive, deliberate production) which eventually yields permanent surpluses of products, which are material bases of class formation. With this, interactions with nature come to be mediated by unequal social relations. For Marx, this is a contradictory movement: social surplus begins a process of emancipation from natural constraint; emancipation is accompanied by internal social differentiation and institutions like the state, patriarchy, and the market; the precise resolution of the contradiction between emancipation from nature and social domination forms the specific kind of society.

A further transformation in human nature occurs: with development of the productive forces, and with division of labor and commodity exchange, the individual is alienated from work, product, and nature. When production comes to be primarily for exchange, "pristine" or "first" nature is separated from a "second," socially produced nature. Natural relations come to be primarily characterized by exchange, with nature as one more commodity. The production of second nature speeds up emancipation but sharpens social differentiation; this twin process (emancipation with differentiation) is key to the bourgeois revolution, the formative social process of capitalism, a class society of competition and accumulation (economic growth) for the sake of accumulation. While all societies have socially mediated relations with nature, capitalism differs in its complexity: "it is the abstract logic that attaches to the creation and accumulation of social value which determines the relation with nature under capitalism" (Smith 1984: 49) – by "abstract logic" is meant a law of value determined by blind forces of competition rather than deliberative human will. Under the abstract dictatorship of accumulation, capital must expand continuously, stalking the earth in search of raw materials, appending nature in its totality to the production process. This recast Marxist argument leads Smith (1984: xiv, 57) to the ultimate conclusion of his "production of nature" thesis: "Human beings have produced whatever nature became accessible to them" and "No God given stone is left unturned, no original relation with nature unaltered, no living thing unaffected." Yet, for Smith, the production of nature universalizes contradiction, as capitalism (rather than Schmidt's "human condition") creates new barriers – scarcity of resources, nuclear technology, and pollution of the entire earth environment. This suggests, for Smith, the "natural inevitability" of social transformation within the possibility of the "revenge of nature" (e.g. the greenhouse effect). Smith thinks that this analysis achieves what Schmidt's conception of nature could never accomplish, a politics of social and environmental action: "Truly human, social control over the *production* of nature ... is the realizable dream of socialism" (Smith 1984: 65).

Political Ecology

Responding to the environmental activism of the 1970s and early 1980s an important offshoot from such Marxist-inspired theories of society–nature relations emerged as a more pragmatic "political ecology." This involved, even more than with Smith's work, a sustained critique of previous geographic notions of human–nature relations. Thus, conventional geographic work carried out under an earlier "human ecology" perspective saw natural hazards as problems of mistaken perception or imperfect knowledge in the human adjustment to natural events, as flaws remediable by environmental policies, rather than as basic and necessary components of the reproduction of capitalist social formations (Wisner et al. 1976; O'Keefe et al. 1976; Susman et al. 1983; Watts 1983a). In place of this deficient approach, ecologically concerned geographers attempted to weld together issues of how communities are integrated into the global economy with issues of local resource management and environmental regulation and stability (Grossman 1984; Watts 1983b). During the 1980s, this attempt at synthesis met a second phase of environmental activism (the Green movements) driven by a recognition of the deepening *global* human-induced modifications of the environment. Forged in the crucible of neo-Marxian development theory, this new "political ecology" was inspired by peasant and agrarian societies in the throes of complex forms of capitalist transition. There was also an increase in the incidence of catastrophes which came to be seen as resulting as much from social, as from natural, vulnerability. And a media-driven upsurge in public awareness ("save the whales") had not yet reached that state of saturation, boredom, and incorporation which western environmentalism, in many of its guises, now displays (hence, we are all environmentalists, even Mobil Oil). In this context, a series of works wedding political economy to a critique of cultural ecology appeared in the early to middle 1980s (Peet and Watts 1996).

Michael Watts, a professor of geography at the University of California, examines the causes of famine in Northern Nigeria in *Silent Violence* (1983b), using a version of an articulation (combination) of modes of production approach which allows for specificity and contingency. Watts begins his analysis with an account of the pre-capitalist mode of production in the Hausaland region, incorporating French work on ecological history and Scott's (1976) concept of peasant moral economy. He finds that Hausa farmers traditionally possessed an adaptive flexibility to accommodate climatic risks at the levels of the household, community, and region; droughts were expected but there was an indigenous relief system integrated into the political-economic system. This system was eroded through articulation with an expanding colonial capitalism, which incorporated commodity production (groundnut, cotton) into the international economy but left subsistence production to reorganize itself. Yet export cropping substantially altered the food production system, the culture of reproduction, and the role of the state: the moral economy became a money economy. Hence, integration into capitalism dissolved many of the response systems which had buffered peasant households from the vagaries of a semi-arid environment, making them vulnerable to droughts which had long occurred. In other words, peasant households are not intrinsically pathological but are constrained in their ability to withstand threats, disturbances, and perturbations (Watts 1983b: 465).

The most renowned and best-argued political ecology to appear at the time was Blaikie's *The Political Economy of Soil Erosion in Developing Countries* (1985). Piers Blaikie, a geomorphologist by training, working in development studies at the University of East Anglia, argues that soil erosion in Third World countries was seen in the conventional (colonial) view as an environmental problem caused by irrational (peasant) land uses and overpopulation, with the solution found in involving peasants in market (capitalist) economies. Blaikie develops a critique of this position. He finds the physical context of erosion important but chooses to emphasize instead the political-economic context, especially the social relations of production determining the nature of land use. Following a bottom-up approach, Blaikie begins with the smallest decision-making unit, usually the (peasant) household operating under constraints of limited assets. The household is immersed in two kinds of social relations: local relations of production; and exchange relations with the world market. In both spheres, "surplus is extracted from cultivators who then in turn are forced to extract 'surpluses' . . . from the environment . . . and this in time and under certain physical circumstances leads to degradation and/or erosion" (Blaikie 1985: 124). Through incorporation into the global capitalist system, peasants are spatially marginalized, crowded onto lands of limited agricultural potential, where they adopt desperate survival strategies. Hence, political-economic processes are interrelated with natural processes; steeply sloped areas, with high natural propensities to soil erosion, are deteriorated by desperate farmers; soil erosion then exacerbates their predicament, intensifying the process. For Blaikie, underdevelopment rather than "false perception" or "peasant ignorance" lies at the heart of what is better phrased as a poverty–nature syndrome; small producers cause soil erosion under conditions of threat to livelihood, making cooperation difficult and state intervention ineffective, while the available ideas about soil erosion ignore these economic imperatives compelling peasant action. Hence, Blaikie finds the outlook for major success in soil conservation to be bleak indeed.

Blaikie's book was soon followed by a collection of essays elaborating many of these concepts. Blaikie and Brookfield's (1987) *Land Degradation and Society* raises a number of important issues including the social origins of degradation, multiple perceptions and definitions of ecological problems, the need to focus on the land manager (and his/her opportunities and constraints), and the pressure of production on resources. Three broad motifs explore the relation between poverty and degradation. First, political, economic, and ecological marginality can be self-reinforcing: "land degradation," as Blaikie and Brookfield (1987: 23) say, "is both a cause and a result of social marginalization." Second, the pressure of production on resources is transmitted to the environment through social relations which compel the land manager to make excessive demands ("the pressure of deprivation"). Third, the facts of degradation are contested and there will always be multiple perceptions and explanations – one person's degradation is another's soil fertility. All of this amounts to a radical critique of the pressure of population on resources view of environment and points to the need for a rethinking of both conservation and development.

Spatial Relations

Developments in the derivation of a Marxist theory of the production of nature were part of a more general process of exegesis, rethinking, and theoretical creation which focused even more intensively on the production of space. During the 1970s a series of articles, mainly appearing in *Antipode*, drew out the spatial implications of works by Marx and Marxist theorists in a kind of "capital logic" school of spatial thought. That is, the movement of theory was from contradictions in the historical dynamic of the accumulation of capital to manifestations of these contradictions in space, and then back again, as spatial effects became contributory aspects to contradictions in the form of uneven development. A main component of this position was the notion of the build-up of crises internal to regions expressed in outward movements in space; interregional social relations were theorized as spatial components of a more general internal–external dialectic. Two versions of this position appeared: from a decade or more of Marxist work, conducted mainly by Harvey and his students (Lata Chatterjee, Richard Walker, Neil Smith, and others at the Johns Hopkins University in Baltimore) emerged a theory of the expression of contradiction in uneven development; from Henri Lefebvre and those influenced by him (Soja 1980; 1996) came theories of the complex production of space and a socio-spatial dialectics. We discuss each in turn; further discussions re-examining similar questions more from consciously structuralist positions appear in chapter 4.

Internal–External Dialectics

For Harvey (1975), the Marxist theory of growth under capitalism puts capital accumulation at the center of a dynamic and inevitably expansionary mode of production. This dynamism encounters barriers (in labor, means of production, markets) which precipitate crises (chronic unemployment, realization crises, etc.) with the eventual result of a shift in the accumulation process to a higher plane (new social wants, new markets, etc.). Newly "rational" locational patterns and improvements in transportation and communication are an inevitable, necessary part of capital accumulation. But there is a spatial aspect to contradiction: in overcoming spatial barriers and "annihilating space with time," spatial structures are created which ultimately act as barriers to further accumulation. This is particularly the case when capitalism comes to rely on immobile, fixed capital (i.e. means of production fixed in space) rather than more mobile variable capital (labor). For capital then has to negotiate a path between preserving the value of past investments in the built environment (the urban landscape, for example) and destroying these investments to make new room for accumulation. The virtue of Marx's location theory, dispersed though it may be in textual fragments, lies in the way space can be integrated into "fundamental insights into the production of value and the dynamics of accumulation" (Harvey 1975: 13).

A series of theorists in the Marxist tradition connect capitalism's internal contradictions with its external "solutions" of the violent penetration of pre-capitalist societies (Lenin 1975; Luxembourg 1951) and the production of a center–periphery spatial organization in the resulting global economy (Baran 1957; Frank 1969). For Harvey, imperialism is the main geographical necessity deriving from the expansionary dynamic of accumulation; the specific economic form of imperialism (whether it is mainly a search for markets, places to invest surplus capital, or new sources of raw materials, etc.) varies over time and is a matter for empirical, historical analysis. In terms of geographic theory, this dynamic theory of contradictions contrasts with bourgeois location theory's equilibrium analysis of optimal spatial configurations:

> The Marxian theory ... commences with the dynamics of accumulation and seeks to derive out of this analysis certain necessities with respect to geographical structures. The landscape which capitalism creates is also seen as the locus of contradiction and tension, rather than as an expression of harmonious equilibrium ... The Marxian theory teaches

us how to relate theoretically, accumulation and the transformation of spatial structures and ultimately . . . the reciprocal relationships between geography and history. (Harvey 1975: 13)

Thus, the internal and external dimensions of space are linked with each other and with capital accumulation. Revolutions in the productive forces, increasing scale of production, and the concentration and centralization of capital are paralleled by urban agglomeration in a widening international capitalist space.

The culminating triumph in a series of creative exegeses came with Harvey's *The Limits to Capital* (1982), a reading of Marx's *Capital* organized around three "cuts" at a general theory of capitalist crisis. The first cut sees crises of over-accumulation – more capital produced than opportunities for using it – resolved through violent episodes of the destruction of value, times when capitalists turn on each other but workers end up paying the social costs (Harvey 1982: 190–203). The second cut examines the expression of productive crises in money and finance, speculative booms and busts which require the intervention of the state: in an internationalized economy, crises take the form of inter-state competition over shifting the effects of devaluation, with national policies to export the effects of crises, and imperialism, neo-colonialism, and even war as potential "solutions" (Harvey 1982: 324–9). The third and last cut integrates geographically uneven development: devaluations of capital are systematized into the continuous restructuring of space through interregional competition. Harvey focuses on "switching crises" (in the movement of capital from one place to another) and crises in the hierarchy of capitalist institutions, so that problems which originate in the chaos and confusion of local events build upwards into global crises. For Harvey, the basic rhythm involves regional economies, or more broadly regional class alliances, periodically alleviating internal crises through transformations in external relations in a spatial "fix" which again has imperialism as its integral component – hence, "an interpretation of inter-imperialist wars as constitutive moments in the dynamics of accumulation" (Harvey 1982: 443). What better reason, he asks, could there be for declaring that capitalism's time has passed, and that there is a need for a saner mode of production?

Uneven Development

Neil Smith's ground-breaking *Uneven Development* (1984) served in the (spatial) realm too as a systematizing synthesis of Marxist notions. As we have seen, Smith argued that different conceptions (of space in this case) are produced by different types of human activities (in space); hence, there is a history of theories of space forming part of the history of human experience. The development of second out of first nature, with advance of the forces of production, is the historical–material basis of a theoretical bifurcation of absolute, natural, and physical space (the world of physical and natural phenomena) from relative and social space (the humanly constituted field of social events). For Smith, conventional conceptual divisions like these accept a dualism between space and society. In an equally conventional economic geography, this dualism is no problem – space is the given sub-stratum, society uses it, the two realms interact. But when the "uprisings" of the 1960s provoked an interest in urban social space, criticisms began to appear of the dualism of space and society: hence, humanistic geography saw space not as objective structure but as social experience; and the Marxist tradition saw space and society as dialectically intertwined. For Smith (1981: 190):

> The notion that space and society "interact" or that spatial patterns "reflect" social structure is not just crude and mechanical in its construction, but also prohibits further insights concerning geographical space; at root this . . . view of the relation between space and society remains tied to the absolute conception of space. Two things can only interact or reflect each other if they are defined in the first place as separate.

Smith substitutes the "production of space" as means of demonstrating this unity so that "human practice and space are integrated at the level of the concept of space 'itself'" (Smith 1984: 77). Here, Smith's discussion repeats the analytical methods developed earlier in his discussion of the production of nature, outlining instead the logic of spatially uneven development.

For Smith, the development of the forces of production transforms absolute (natural) space into relative (social) space in a contradictory movement. Development emancipates society from the constraints of natural space, leading towards "equalization" but only by sinking capital into certain spaces, producing "differentiation" and a relativized space. These contradictory movements determine the specific forms of capitalist space as synthetic outcome: "Space is neither levelled out of existence nor infinitely differentiated. Rather the pattern which results is one of *uneven development*" (Smith 1984: 90). Integrating the geographical notion of "scales" (urban, national, global) as levels of specificity, with temporal notions of rhythms, cycles, and long waves, Smith proposes a "see-saw" theory of uneven development: "capital attempts to see-saw from a developed to an underdeveloped area, then at a later point back to the first area which is by now underdeveloped" (Smith 1984: 149). Surprisingly (and probably incorrectly), Smith finds see-sawing to have a higher propensity to occur at the urban level, where mobile capital destroys, then gentrifies, inner-city neighborhoods. He finds see-sawing less apparent at the national scale, where the return of capital to abandoned regions is limited. Amazingly, he finds the see-saw hardly occurring at all at the global scale (but what about the return of manufacturing to northern England, this time under Japanese control?). For Smith, the real resolution between equalization and differentiation can be achieved only by global political cooperation among working-class peoples.

Everyday Life

Underlying much of this discussion of uneven development in the Anglo-American tradition is the pioneering work of the French sociologist–philosopher Henri Lefebvre (1901–91) on urbanism, everyday life, and the production of space. Lefebvre wrote on these topics throughout the 1930s, 1940s, 1950s, and 1960s, but, while introductions by him to dialectics and materialism (Lefebvre 1968, 1969) were translated, the parts of his work most directly related to geography only gradually became known in the Anglo-American world in the 1970s through brief introductory summaries (Lefebvre 1976) and oblique references (Harvey 1973; Soja 1980). Indeed, only with the translation of *The Production of Space* (1991) were his ideas widely available in English, when they produced a kind of Lefebvrean revival (see chapter 6). Nevertheless, Lefebvre represents the best of the Marxist work on space and we present his ideas here as the culmination, the finest product of the Marxian conception of space.

Lefebvre's life work was a passionate polemic against Stalinist, economist, and other non-dialectical Marxisms prevalent in postwar France, against conventional science and philosophy obviously, but also against structuralism (Lévi-Strauss, Althusser, etc.) and what became known as poststructural philosophy (Derrida, Foucault, Barthes, etc.). Lefebvre proposed a new "reading" of Marx which, he thought, better recalled the original by stressing the dialectical movements of truth and reality, the active nature of social relations, and the significance of the concept "praxis." That is, while Hegel made history culminate in the present as a kind of "end of history" or final equilibrium, thereby paralyzing hopes for social and political action, Marx found historical time characterized not only by quantitative but also qualitative or transformative change. And while Hegel distinguished civil society (families, occupations, towns) from political society (states, governments, bureaucracies), Marx turned "civil society" into *praxis*, practical, sensuous activity which *creates* towns, landscapes, objects common and rare. For Marx, humans are first beings of need, individual and social, which is the practical basis of subjectivity, reason, and rationality. Human need is an activity in dialectical relation with nature and other people, while work begins as a means to satisfy need but ends as a need in itself. Thus, all praxis rests on a dual foundation, the sensuous and the creative: "Every praxis has two historical co-ordinates: one denotes the past, that which has been accomplished, the other the future onto which praxis opens and which it will create" (Lefebvre 1969: 55). Instead of interpreting praxis merely as economic activity, or breaking it into "levels" of base, structure, and superstructure (cf. Althusser), Lefebvre extends praxis to culture and politics. There are three moments of praxis, the repetitive, the mimetic or imitative, and the creative or revolutionary which makes possible the "going beyond" or "overcoming" which is Marx's fundamental difference from Hegel's synthesis.

Lefebvre himself takes Marx's concept of praxis in his own creative direction. He tries to move philosophy (contemplation, speculation) away from its traditional objectives (abstraction which produces truth without reality) towards an analysis of everyday life (the *quotidien*), which he sees as a repository of mysteries and wonders which bewilder people. That is, *praxis*, now redefined to involve mainly inter-human relations, and *poiesis*, involving human relations with nature, do not take place in the "higher" spheres of society (state, scholarship, culture) but in the recurrences and repetitions of everyday existence. Here, the Marxist emphasis on production is rethought as reproduction of the conditions of production, with recurrence intercepted by creativity or "becoming" – "is not the fabric of the imaginary woven from threads of remembrance and therefore of recurrence?" (Lefebvre 1968: 18).

Lefebvre contrasts the tedious misery of everyday life, which he thinks weighs heaviest on women, with the power to create "from its solids and spaces." He compares also the "style" which gave concrete significance to objects, activities, and gestures in an older society, with the "culture" of modern society, with its estrangement from nature, its absence of rhythms, its substitution of signs for significance, its dispersal of community and loss of unity.

The rise of what Lefebvre calls the "Bureaucratic Society of Controlled Consumption" in France in the 1950s did not so much destroy everyday life as convert it into a screen onto which rationalized institutions project their structures and power; everyday life in an urban setting ("urbanism") is for him part of a global process of Americanization. Yet such a society contains its own self-criticism, felt generally as a sense of unrest and dissatisfaction, a slump in ideas, a terrible lack of significance. For Lefebvre, the end, objective, and meaning of industrialization is urbanization, and thus crisis in this society of consumption and rationalization takes an urban form. This urban-focused crisis Lefebvre explores not primarily in conventionally economic ways, but as the linkages between the ever-increasing consumption of signs, the resulting craving for make-believe, and its inevitable disappointment. Lefebvre believes in resurrecting a new everyday life through a cultural revolution with political and economic implications.

The Production of Space

The themes of praxis and everyday life, urbanism and space, which pervade Lefebvre's sociology lead eventually to his main work of interest here, *The Production of Space* (1991), originally published in French in 1974. This is a fascinating, complex book full of philosophical and historical speculations, yet drawing too on a detailed empirical knowledge especially of Italian cities. The book is impossible to summarize effectively and should be read intensively; we therefore present only a few of its categories and themes.

Space, Lefebvre argues, has become a "mental thing," deeply separated from physical or social reality, in mathematics and philosophy, but also in the semiology (Barthes) and grammatology (Derrida) ascending the French intellectual scene in the early 1970s. For Lefebvre, the resulting discourses on space express the dominant, ruling-class ideology, often disguised as politically disinterested knowledge, and substitute descriptions and endless fragmentation for a science which should unify the various fields of space, whether physical (nature, the Cosmos), mental (logical and formal abstraction), or social (the space of everyday life). For Lefebvre, a unitary theory of space like this cannot be derived from analogies with physics, even a physics which sees space as the product of energy, because physical and social energies are fundamentally dissimilar. Nor can a unitary theory be derived from philosophy, which helped bring about the schism between mental and physical space in the first place. This leaves only universal notions, seemingly belonging to philosophy, but existing more exactly as Hegel's "concrete universal" or Marx's concept of production. Hence, Lefebvre proposes an analysis of the actual production of space to bring the various kinds of space and the modalities of their genesis within a single theory. Furthermore, while Lefebvre does not accede to the priority of language, believing that material activity probably precedes it, he thinks that space can be "read" or "decoded," for space implies a process of signification as well as material practice – codes are spatial languages, parts of practical relationships between subjects and their surroundings.

For Lefebvre, an earlier search for this unified theory of space had been abandoned. In Hegel, historical time is solidified within the rationality immanent to an immobile space (i.e. space as the locus of Reason, space as organized by Reason's agent – for Hegel this being the state). Reacting to this fetishization of space in the service of the state, Marx reinstates history as revolutionary time, while Lukács (1971) sees space as defining reification and false consciousness. Only Nietzsche (1968) maintains the primordial nature of space, not as a residue of time, but as the absolute space of energy and forces. Lefebvre sees the contemporary period very much in terms of the state rationally organizing society, crushing time by reducing difference to repetition. In this same space, however, the very rationality of the state provokes opposition as a "tragic negativity which manifests itself as incessant violence" (Lefebvre 1991: 23). Yet philosophy is split, as time is broken into types (social time, mental time, etc.) and an epistemology of an abstract, mental space prevails.

Lefebvre aims at exploding this sorry state of affairs with the thesis, simply put, that (social) space is a (social) product. Every society, every mode of production, produces its own space. But the production of social space is not like the production of commodities, because space subsumes many different things, is both outcome and means (of fresh action), and is both product (made by repetitious labor) and work (i.e. something unique and original). It consists of objects (natural and social) and their relations (networks and pathways). Space contains things yet is not a material object; it is a set of relations between things. Hence, we are confronted with many, interpenetrated social spaces superimposed one on the other, a "hypercomplexity" in which each fragment of space masks not one social relationship but many. For Lefebvre, the "problematic" of space has displaced that of industrialization. He therefore proposes an analysis of space itself to uncover the social relations embedded in it using a triad of spatial concepts:

1 *Spatial practice* – production and reproduction secrete a society's space, forming the particular locations and spatial sets (the perceived space) characteristic of each social formation. Spatial practice ensures continuity and some degree of cohesion for social formations and guarantees a level of competence and performance to people as actors. (Social) spatial practice, for Lefebvre, is practical (material reproduction), employs accumulated knowledge, and involves also signifying processes.

2 *Representations of space* – abstract conceptions of space using a system of verbal and graphic signs, the celestial sphere in antiquity, maps and plans in the modern period. Representations of space, shot through with knowledge (a mixture of understanding and ideology), always relative and changing, subordinate people to a logic and play a dominant role in social and political (spatial) practice.

3 *Representational space* – space as directly lived through associated images and symbols by inhabitants and users but also writers and artists who describe it.

Representational space overlays physical space, making symbolic use of natural objects. Representational space tends towards systems of non-verbal symbols and signs; it obeys no rules of consistency or cohesiveness. Redolent with imaginary and symbolic elements, it has its source in the history of a people, and is therefore studied by ethnologists, anthropologists, and psychoanalysts. Representational space has an affective center of everyday life (ego, bedroom, house); it embraces the loci of passion, action, lived situations, and thus implies time. It may be qualified in various ways, as directional, situational, or relational, because it is essentially qualitative, fluid, and dynamic.

The three moments of the triad, perceived, conceived, and lived, are held together by dialectical relationships. The triad contributes to the production of space in different combinations according to the mode of production and the historical period. Relations between the three moments are never simple or stable, nor are they entirely conscious.

For Lefebvre, applying this triadic distinction means looking at history in a new light, studying not only the history of space as spatial practice, but the history of representations of space, their interrelations and relations with practices and ideologies. Representations of space play a substantial influencing role by way of the project or architecture embedded in a spatial context. While the producers of space have probably always acted in accordance with representations, the users of space experience whatever is imposed on them. So, for the production of space the concept of ideology might be useful – ideology describes a space, uses its vocabulary, and embodies its code. Ideology achieves consistency by intervening in social space and thus taking on body. Indeed, ideology per se might be said to consist primarily of a discourse on social space. So, for Lefebvre, representations combining ideology and knowledge within socio-spatial practice supplant the Marxist concept of ideology alone, and become the most appropriate tool for analyzing space.

For Lefebvre, nothing disappears completely in social space. Earlier characteristics and effects underpin later ones, so that even "primary nature" persists, in an acquired and false way, within the second nature of altered space. This persistence, evoked by terms like strata, periods, and sedimentary layers, Lefebvre analyses through what he calls *spatial architectronics*. The term is employed in a radical way, with Lefebvre attempting to return to the body's original creation of space in the sense that each living body (deployment of energy) is, and has, space. Thus, Lefebvre visits (theoretically, speculatively) an original "biologico-spatial reality," inquiring into the genesis of the individual organism in the opposition between an internal milieu and an external space, and the accumulation and expenditure of energy by the organism in altering that space. He follows this with an anthropological inquiry, when symbolic and practical activity in networks of places result in various kinds of social space – places of abode, accessible spaces, boundaries, junctions, etc. Here, the spatial body serves as point of departure, the body which smells, listens, and enacts before a long learning process produces abstraction and representational space. Lefebvre poses such long-term changes in terms of a movement from what he calls "absolute space" to "abstract space." By *absolute space* Lefebvre means fragments of nature at sites chosen for their intrinsic qualities, which were assigned magical and cosmic qualities thereby becoming religious and political. Natural space might be populated by political or religious forces, as when architecture transforms a site by means of symbols, the gods and goddesses in Greek temples for example, retaining aspects of naturalness in modified form. Through such processes the original natural space, while still in the background, disappears and will soon be lost to thought – "nature is resistant, and infinite in its depth, but it has been defeated, and now waits for its ultimate violence and destruction" (Lefebvre 1991: 31). He sees the beginning of *abstract space* in the medieval towns of western Europe, with an added impetus occurring in the sixteenth century, when town overtook country in terms of social importance and representations of space were applied to the conceptualization of cities and their plans. From this came the relativized and historical space of the capitalist accumulation of wealth and resources. Here, abstract labor produces an abstract space as a set of things/signs and their merely formal, quantitative relations, which erase (absolute) distinctions derived from nature, time and body. The dominant form of space – centers of wealth and power – endeavors to mould dominated spaces – peripheries – by violent means, while representations of space, in thrall to knowledge and power, give narrow leeway to representational spaces whose contents barely achieve symbolic force. Humanity, he thinks, suffers in this abstract space, for people cannot discern their own reality in it:

> Abstract space is not defined only by the disappearance of trees, or by the receding of nature; nor merely by the great empty spaces of the state and the military – plazas that resemble parade grounds; nor even by commercial centres packed tight with commodities, money and cars. It is not in fact defined on the basis of what is perceived. Its abstraction has nothing simple about it: it is not transparent and cannot be reduced either to a logic or a strategy. Coinciding neither with the abstraction of the sign, nor with that of the concept, it operates negatively to that which perceives and underpins it – namely, the historical and politico-religious spheres. It also relates negatively to something which it carries within itself and which seeks to emerge from it: a differential space–time. It has nothing of a "subject" about it, yet it acts like a subject in that it transports and maintains specific social relations, dissolves others and stands opposed to yet others. It functions positively vis-a-vis its own implications: technology, applied sciences, and knowledge bound to power. Abstract space may even be described as at once, and inseparably, the locus, medium and tool of this "positivity". (Lefebvre 1991: 50)

Abstract space incorporates, dissolves, and replaces former "subjects" (villages and towns) in becoming a pseudo-subject, the abstract "one" of modern social space concealing the real subject, state political power. Given that abstract space is buttressed by a non-critical, positive knowledge, and is backed by violence and maintained by bureaucracy, is it that final stability forecasted by Hegel to which the only possible response would be spasms of what Bataille calls the acephal (i.e. headless or irrational actions)? For Lefebvre, in contrast, abstract space harbors contradictions, some modified from those of the past, others new, which he sees in spatial terms: the reproduction of social relations obeys two tendencies, dissolution of the old, generation of the new, so that a tendency towards homogenization in abstract space carries the seeds of a new kind of space, differential space, as distinctions are also generated. So while the pre-existence of space conditions the subject's presence, action, and discourse, these also negate this space. Changing society means changing space.

Lefebvre favors a strategic political project embodying spatial practices and actions as part of an effort to transform the mode of production. Theoretical and practical questions concerning space, he says, are becoming more important, tending to resituate earlier concepts related to biological reproduction and the production of commodities. Marx argues that a mode of production does not disappear until it has realized its full potential. But when, for Lefebvre, the productive forces leap forward but the relations of production remain intact, the production of *space* replaces, or is superimposed upon, the production of *things in space*. At the present time, a surge in the forces of production, with an inadequate control of markets, produces spatial chaos which, he thinks, might be the capitalist system's Achilles' heel. In brief, Lefebvre wants to modify the left's monocentric political strategy (revolution by a single class from a single center) with a manifold and multiform strategy, more polycentric in shape, of peasants, marginal social elements, and the working class, in both the underdeveloped and industrialized countries, the basic principle of which is "the mobilization of differences" (Lefebvre 1991; cf. Soja 1996).

Socio-Spatial Dialectics

We hear echoes of these Lefebvrian positions in the Anglo-American literature of the 1970s and early 1980s. In *Social Justice and the City* (1973), Harvey criticizes Lefebvre for placing excessive causal emphasis on spatial relations. Edward Soja (1980; Soja and Hadjimichalis 1979), a geographer in the School of Architecture and Urban Planning at the University of California, Los Angeles, counter-argues that, like Harvey, Lefebvre was interested in explaining the survival of capitalism through attenuation of its internal contradictions through the production of space. Soja compares this with the work of the Belgian Marxist Ernest Mandel (1976), who argues that the unequal development of regions is just as fundamental to capitalism as the direct exploitation of labor power. Mandel's basic point is that the historical survival of capitalism depends on the differentiation of space into over- and underdeveloped regions, the principal role of underdevelopment being to furnish reserves of labor and compensatory markets to relieve pressures in a spasmodic, contradictory capitalist development (Mandel 1976: 43). This global capitalist system is maintained and intensified by the geographical transfer of value through the extraction of super-profits, in competitive industrial capitalism from rural peripheries, and under imperialism from colonial and semi-colonial countries to First World urban centers. Unequal development, conventionally thought of in non-spatial terms as the vertical differentiation of economic sectors, branches, and firms, is also "horizontal" or inherently spatial (Mandel 1976; 1978, chapter 3).

Soja places Lefebvre and Mandel at one extreme in a Marxist debate on space: they give the structure of spatial relations a transformational capability comparable with class struggle. At the other extreme lies the conventional Marxist approach centered on traditional class analysis. In between, Soja says, are those like Harvey who seem to adopt the Lefebvre–Mandel position but, when pushed to make an explicit choice, maintain the pre-eminence of aspatial class definitions. This is part of a wider syndrome within Marxist analyses of space, what Soja calls a rigidifying pattern that weakens analysis because it incorporates "an unnecessarily limited and inappropriate conceptualization of space and spatial relations in an effort to escape spatial fetishism" (Soja 1980: 208). This is ironic, for the primary source of misunderstanding is a failure of Marxist analysis to appreciate the dialectical character of social–spatial relations. What Soja calls the "socio-spatial dialectic" fits neither alternative posed by Lefebvre or Harvey:

> The structure of organized space is not a separate structure with its own autonomous laws of construction and transformation, nor is it simply an expression of the class structure emerging from the social (i.e. aspatial) relations of production. It represents, instead, a dialectically defined component of the general relations of production, relations which are simultaneously social and spatial. (Soja 1980: 208)

For Soja, an homology (correspondence) exists between class and spatial relations in the division of organized space into dominant centers and subordinate peripheries, a structure captured by the concept of geographically uneven development. The two sets of relations are not only homologous, in that both arise from the same origins in the mode of production, but also are dialectically intertwined. This dialectical homology was suggested by Marx and Engels, but a hundred years of scholarship failed to develop it, as western Marxism evolved without a strong spatial perspective. For Soja, a flurry of debate over a new urban sociology, new geography, etc., actually signifies something broader, a dialectical materialism simultaneously historical and spatial.

Distinguishing between "contextual space" as an objective form of the existence of matter and the "created space" of social organization and production, Soja argues that discussions of the absolute or relative properties of contextual space, its character as a "container" of human life, its objectifiable geometry and phenomenological essence, are an appropriate foundation for analyzing human spatiality. Space itself may be primordially given, but, as with second nature (i.e. altered natural environments), its organization, use, and meaning are products of social transformation. Once it is recognized that space is socially organized there is no longer a question of its being a separate structure with rules of transformation independent of the wider social framework. What becomes important is the dialectical relationship between created space and society (the structures of a given mode of production). The social–spatial dialectic calls, therefore, for the inclusion of socially produced space in Marxist analysis as something more than an epiphenomenon. Soja takes the argument one step further by suggesting (with Lefebvre) that the social and the spatial are dialectically linked "in that each shapes and is simultaneously shaped by the other in a complex innerrelationship which may vary in different social formations and at different historical conjunctures" (Soja 1980: 225). For Soja, the interplay between the social and the spatial should be a central issue in concrete Marxist analysis.

Criticizing Marxism

These were some of the positions taken by Marxist geographers in the 1970s and early 1980s. Many of these positions survive into the present. But already, by the middle 1970s, while Marxism remained at the frontier of geographic interest and adherence by progressive intellectuals, significant criticisms appeared of Marx's original thought and of Marxist geography as derivation. These critiques centered on what was seen to be Marx's functional, mechanical, and economistic understanding of history and geography, as well as the totalitarian, repressive nature of the supposedly Marxist-inspired "communist" countries. We recount some of these at the end of chapter 4. Here, we give a brief account of one of the more informed critiques, by Anthony Giddens, a professor of sociology at Cambridge University.

A Structurationist Critique of Historical Materialism

For Anthony Giddens (1981: 2), there is much in Marx that is "mistaken, ambiguous or inconsistent . . . in many respects Marx's writings exemplify features of nineteenth century thought which are plainly defective when looked at from the perspective of our century." Basically, his position is that historical materialism, understood as the progressive growth of the forces of production, as the history of class struggle, or as a schema of historical evolution, should be rejected, leaving only the more abstract elements of a theory of human practice. For in Marx, he says, the question of exploitation is bound up with a certain characterization of class systems – classes come into existence with an expansion of the forces of production such that surplus is generated and appropriated by an elite. For Giddens, by comparison, exploitation existed before, and extends beyond, class domination.

Giddens's first sustained criticism concerns Marx's schema of social evolution – the idea that societies pass through stages, with the movement of historical change founded in the dialectic of forces and relations of production and culminating in the "ascendancy of human kind to control over its own destiny" (Giddens 1981: 74). Marx, he says, sees capitalism as the summation of history thus far, yet as a society which, in maximizing human self-alienation, opens the way for a new social order. For Giddens, rather than being the summation of history, capitalism as a distinctively class-ridden society is fundamentally discontinuous with previous history. Giddens objects to the whole notion of a progressive evolutionary process in Marx. However, as he points out, Lefort (1978) distinguishes two versions of history in Marx's (1973: 471–512) *Grundrisse*, a continuist (evolutionary) version and a discontinuous perspective which places the whole evolutionary argument in question. Whereas Marx (1970) argues that societal transformation occurs when advances in the productive forces can no longer be contained within the existing relations of production, in *Grundrisse* Marx (1973) finds pre-capitalist production subordinated to social relations connecting nature, individual, and community, with primacy accorded to ecological factors in the stimulation of social transformation.

Giddens rejects evolutionary models, including that he finds in Marx, as incorporating two connected theses: the measure of development of a society is its capacity to control the material environment by developing the productive forces; and social development is a "mechanically adaptive" process. He proposes instead that societal transformation occurs through episodes which are not mechanically inevitable, while different kinds of society coexist along "time–space edges." Focusing on relations between tribal and class-divided societies, Giddens argues that there is no immanent logic to surplus production, and there is no "scarcity principle" in many so-called "subsistence societies" – the dynamic of hunting and gathering societies is influenced more by ritual and ceremony than material imperatives. For Giddens, this suggests in general that, prior to capitalism, the development of the forces of production (as Marx suggests) does not underlie major episodic changes. Similarly, he finds Marx's analysis of Oriental societies (organized by the "Asiatic mode of production") to be illuminating but seriously flawed in terms of its Eurocentrism, its evaluation of Asian societies as stagnant, its thesis of connection between irrigation and the state, and its problematic extension of an "Asian" mode to the Near East, South America, and Africa. In general, Giddens (1981: 88) rejects Marx's argument for the primacy of production over other aspects of social life: "It certainly does not follow that, because material production is necessary to sustain human existence, the social organization of production is more fundamental to explaining either the persistence of, or change in, societies than any other institutional forms."

Conclusion

Radical and Marxist geography responded to the political events of the 1960s and early 1970s in ways which transformed the discipline. There was a growing intolerance to the topical coverage of academic geography, a feeling that it was either an irrelevant gentlemanly pastime concerned with esoterica like tourism, wine regions, or barn types, or it was an equally irrelevant "science" using quantitative methods to analyze spatial trivia like shopping patterns or telephone calls, when geography should be a working interest in ghettos, poverty, global capitalism, and imperialism. The radical geography of the late 1960s and early 1970s, characterized by social relevance and intense political activism, thus attempted to change the arena of topical coverage. But the very success of this effort proved contradictory: a change in topic revealed weaknesses in theory and technique. Led by David Harvey's seminal *Social Justice and the City*, radical geography underwent a further metamorphosis into Marxist geography in the middle 1970s, a period of re-education, painstaking exegesis, and the gradual emergence of a creative science of environmental space. Here, the critique of conventional geography centered not so much on its irrelevant topics, but on its spatial fetishism – that is, geography's restriction of causality to the spatial realm. Marxism's essential role was to link the spatial and environmental with the social and economic. An over-emphasis on the spatial had isolated an irrelevant but conservative geography; the link with the social through Marxism made geography part of a radical social science of totalities.

Marxism centers on the creative potential of labor in the production of existence. Its strength lies in the conceptions brought to the analysis of production – dialectics, social relations, consciousness, and so on. In the materialist dialectic, which Marx rescues from Hegel's compelling but ultimately wrong idealism (wrong because neither spirit nor God exists), the dynamic of history results from the contradictions within and between all social phenomena. Hence, the relations between people and between society and nature produce instability even as they form the characteristics of these phenomena. This lends social reality its quality of structured coherence tempered by an ever-present tendency to transformation. Hence, production, the application of force to nature under the direction of social relations, is both formative of the structures of existence, yet also the main source of the generation of new forms of life. Thus, in the fully materialist conception (after God is removed entirely as a cause of events) history has coherence and elements of directionality, but is not determined, and is certainly not teleologically directed.

Yet the materialist dialectic offers even more to geographical understanding than to the historical imagination. In its earth tradition, geography could not conceptualize natural causation without resorting to a mechanical version of environmental determinism, because it lacked the notion of the dialectic of inner relations between natural elements and it lacked too the mediation of production as the main focus of nature–society relations. In its space tradition, geography was caught between two related deficiencies: fetishization of the spatial into an all-consuming causal interest, yet simultaneously the trivialization of the aspects of space the discipline chose to focus on. Reeling from criticisms of environmental determinism, lost for years in the by-ways of regional description, geographers in the "quantitative revolution" rushed into a spatial "science" which discovered an increasingly significant dimension of life (space) only to fail to link it with other, equally important aspects of existence. This failure of linkage produced continued (if ameliorated) intellectual and theoretical isolation for the discipline of geography. So, for all its supposed deficiencies, Marxism saved geography from extinction, irrelevance or, worse still, becoming a poor relative of regional science. The central Marxist notions of the social production of nature and space, even though exaggerated (social *transformation* would be a better term), with the production process understood dialectically, linked geography to society and combined the two traditions of geography into aspects of a single understanding. Human geography was finally linked into social science, as one of its more critical components, drawing on the full range of social scientific concepts, while adding to them sophisticated notions of environmental space. From being good persons to have around while doing a crossword puzzle, geographers moved to center stage in explaining environmental catastrophe and the globalization of economies and cultures.

Marxism thus proved a powerful, persuasive argument. As a result, the discipline changed again, in terms of political tenor, obviously, but also in the quality of its writing (from description and statistics to philosophy and social theory), the degree of its interaction with social theory (from isolation to immersion), the type of students it attracted (from memorizers to analyzers), and the charged atmosphere of its conferences (from the goldfish industry to multinational corporations) – although it was remarkable how quickly yesterday's socialists became today's elite! By the end of the 1970s, Marxism had an almost hegemonic position, not necessarily in the discipline as a whole, where the teaching of "geographic facts" continued largely unabated for many years, and graduate students were still made to slave over "quantitative techniques," but in those leading sectors where new ideas are formed and discussed on a daily basis. Indeed, Marxist geography itself was ripe for an anti-hegemonic critique by the early 1980s. But before we discuss this, we move to the strange tale of the structuralist incursion into social theory and, for a brief but intoxicating while, even into geography, where it too has left more than a trace that shows its passage.

Chapter 4

Structuralism and Structural Marxist Geography

Structural and structural Marxist ideas sweeping through France in the 1950s, 1960s, and early 1970s did not have a pronounced effect on Anglo-American geography until the middle to late 1970s. There are structural aspects, derived from Piaget, in Harvey's (1973) *Social Justice and the City*. More importantly, structural work on cities and urban planning (Preteceille 1976; Pickvance 1976) began to appear in English in the middle 1970s. Latin American scholars more attuned to developments in France (Santos 1977; Corragio 1977) spread structural notions. Most importantly, a translation of Manuel Castells's (1977) structuralist work on cities, *The Urban Question*, had a profound effect, especially on urban geography. Early Marxist geography had entailed mainly the direct interpretation of the Marxian classics. Structural ideas tended to be introduced indirectly via works in anthropology (Godelier 1978), semiotics (Greimas 1966), and the state (Poulantzas 1978), rather than through a direct reading of Saussure, Lévi-Strauss, or Althusser (but see Gregory 1978). Structuralism produced a different kind of Marxist geography, stressing certain analytical categories, like mode of production and social formation, and emphasizing interrelations among elements in signifying chains. The move towards structuralism, never complete in geographical thought, represented a search for greater theoretical coherence and rigor. It is also the most misrepresented and under-appreciated period in social and geographic thought.

Structuralism

We can approach the development of structuralism in French social thought by bringing up to date earlier developments in existential phenomenology – structuralists like Claude Lévi-Strauss and Louis Althusser developed their ideas in vehement opposition to Sartre and the humanist tradition of the 1950s and early 1960s.

Sartre's Marxist Humanism

It might be expected that Sartre's existentialism, eloquently if obscurely displayed in *Being and Nothingness* (1966), would be criticized by some historical materialists as subjective, idealist, and even irrational (Poster 1975: 109–60). But the critique of Sartre came exactly when he was changing his position from existential phenomenology towards an existential Marxism. Written in the late 1950s, Sartre's *Critique of Dialectical Reason* (1976) and the more accessible *Search for a Method* (1968) tried to synthesize existential phenomenology with a humanist Marxism in a kind of existential anthropology, a philosophical science of the human being. In this synthesis, Sartre accepts the Marxian dictum that the mode of production of material life determines the social, political, and intellectual life process. Marx tried to generate knowledge dialectically, rising progressively from the broadest determinations to the most precise, from the abstract to the concrete and, for Sartre, individual human beings are the most concrete entities, but Marxism lacks a hierarchy of mediations which would allow it to grasp the process which produces a person in a class, within a society, at a given historical moment. Existentialism, he says, "intends, without being unfaithful to Marxist principles, to find mediations which allow the individual concrete – the particular life, the real and dated conflict, the person – to emerge from the background of the general contradictions of productive forces and relations of production" (Sartre 1968: 57). Mediations such as the psychological structure of the individual and the (usually local) residential or work group to which the individual belongs, have to be allowed a relative autonomy and power of mediation. Also, the temptation in Marxism to simplify productive forces into productive techniques, or to consider social relations as conditioned entirely by technology, has to be avoided.

Sartre accepts the Marxist thesis that humans make history in a conditioning environment. But how, he asks, are we to understand that people make history at the same time as history is making them? An "idealist" Marxism takes the easy course of making people into passive products, sums of conditioned reflexes, determined by prior circumstances, in which case there is no difference between the human agent and machine. In a fully complex Marxism, however, humans are indeed products of history, but are also agents whose praxis both conserves, and goes beyond, their formative conditions. However, people may not grasp the real measure of their actions, may objectify themselves and be alienated from history. In this sense, history appears as a foreign, uncontrollable force in so far as people do not recognize the meaning of their endeavors in the total result. The objective of Marxism, Sartre (1968: 89) believes, is to give history a meaning – by becoming self-conscious, the proletariat recognizes itself in history and becomes its subject.

For Sartre, human activity is conditioned by the "practico-inert" – the existing material environments and human structures. Material conditions, such as the presence of environmental resources, impose factual necessities. But these act through mediations: "as Marx has often insisted, the geographical givens (or any other kind) can act only within the compass of a given society, in conformity with its structures, its economic regime, the institutions which it has given itself" (Sartre 1968: 164). Yet, for Sartre, humans are characterized not only by their (geographical) conditioning, but above all by their ability to go beyond the given situation. The origins of this "going beyond" he now finds in need: scarcity expresses a given situation but also contains an effort to go beyond it. Thus, human behavior is determined in relation to the real factors which condition it and in relation to that which it is trying to bring into being – what Sartre calls "the project." In relation to the given, praxis is negativity; in relation to the future, praxis is positivity, that which opens onto the "nonexistent," that which has not yet been: "A flight and a leap ahead, at once a refusal and a realization, the project retains and unveils the surpassed reality which is refused by the very movement which surpasses it" (Sartre 1968: 92). This surpassing is conceivable only as a relation of the existent to its possibles: to say what people are is also to say what they can be. By transcending the given towards the field of possibles, and by realizing one possible from among others, the individual, by means of work and action, objectifies him or herself and contributes to making history.

From Existentialism to Structuralism

Yet exactly as Sartre criticized the materialist dialectic with a project of existential Marxism in mind, circumstances changed and his ideas were relegated to the sidelines, as Marxism, along with other modes of social thought, shifted dramatically in a direction opposite to existentialism. As opposed to the humanist idea that history is created by human praxis, structuralism argues that social (and other) structures have no agents and cannot be understood through studying individual human beings or empirical events. Indeed, the father of French structuralism, Claude Lévi-Strauss (1966: 62), an anthropologist at the College de France, found existentialism to be the exact opposite of true thought by reason of its "indulgent attitude toward the illusions of subjectivity. To promote private preoccupations to the rank of philosophical problems is dangerous, and may end in a kind of shop-girl's philosophy." In a savage critique, Lévi-Strauss (1966: 250) found that Sartre "retreats into individualism and empiricism and is lost in the blind alleys of social psychology." In opposition to Sartre's anti-reductionism, Lévi-Strauss proposed scientific reductionism. In his own field of anthropology, a model of such a reduction would be that ethnographic analysis (observing and analyzing discrete human groups) tries to arrive at the invariants of a general humanity, from which an attempt is made at reintegrating culture into nature and, beyond that, life into all its physico-chemical conditions. Lévi-Strauss adds that the "reductions" he envisages are legitimate only if the studied phenomena are not impoverished in the process (i.e. their distinctive richness and originality are preserved) and the scientist is ready to overturn preconceived notions of things discovered through reduction. Scientific explanation does not consist of moving from the complex to the simple, but in replacing a less intelligible complexity by one that is more so. In contrast to Sartre, Lévi-Strauss (1966 247) believes the ultimate goal of the human sciences is "not to constitute, but to dissolve man."

Lévi-Strauss's epistemology hypothesizes the existence of an unconscious meaning in culture. He rejects immediate, spontaneous evidence as criterion of truth, questions the empiricist method's claim to reach reality through sensory perceptions, and jettisons phenomenology and existentialism as philosophies of meaning. His own approach is "geological" (yet drawn from Marx, Freud, and Saussure) in the sense of reducing the apparent surface of reality to its hidden dimensions through a process of decoding and constructing models through which empirical reality can be interpreted to discover its unconscious infrastructure (Rossi 1974). Lévi-Strauss reached this position through a study of structural linguistics, especially the work of Roman Jakobson (1962). Linguistics, Lévi-Strauss says, occupies a special place among the social sciences in that it alone can truly claim to be a science. Structural linguistics moves from the study of conscious linguistic phenomena to their unconscious infrastructures; it does not treat linguistic terms as independent entities but takes the relations between terms as the basis of analysis; it sees language as a hierarchy of corresponding structures of sound, grammar, and meaning; it introduces the concept of system; and it aims at discovering general laws. For the first time, a social science is able to formulate necessary relations. Lévi-Strauss thought that structural linguistics would play "the same renovating role with respect to the social sciences that nuclear physics, for example, has played for the physical sciences" (Lévi-Strauss 1977: 33).

Structural Linguistics

In the early twentieth century, the innovative work of the Swiss linguist Ferdinand de Saussure caused what has been described as a "Copernican revolution" in linguistics, indeed, in the study of humanity in general. In the view of Harris (1986), translator of *Cours de Linguistique Generale*, after Saussure, words would no longer remain peripheral to the understanding of reality; instead, understanding comes to be seen as revolving around the social use of verbal signs. That is, words are not vocal labels attached to things given in advance by nature, or grasped independently by the human mind; rather, languages supply the essential conceptual frameworks for the analysis of reality and, at the same time, the verbal equipment for describing it.

In opposition to the prevailing evolutionary (or diachronic) linguistics, Saussure proposed giving priority to the present user's point of view, seeing language as a complex system of differences or contrasts between sounds implicitly recognized by a given community of speakers, a static (or synchronic) linguistics. Whereas previously emphasis had been given to mental images, concepts, or meanings (signifieds), Saussure emphasized instead the sound patterns (signifiers) used to designate these. The link between signifier and signified (twin aspects of the sign) is arbitrary, a matter of social convention – there is no internal connection between an idea and the sequence of sounds which acts as its signal in communicating with others. Therefore, Saussure thought that the linguist should concentrate on the (social) codes linking communicators, the language system (*langue*) rather than the particular utterances of speakers (*parole*).

Saussure's structural linguistics thus emphasizes the supra-individual and social character of language systems in a synchronic analysis. This has great importance for understanding other aspects of society, culture, and thought. Social and cultural phenomena may be interpreted as signs (Eco 1973). Such phenomena do not have essences, but are defined by networks of relations, and, if they have meaning, it is the underlying social system of conventions which makes such meaning possible. Thus, the cultural meaning of any particular object or act is determined by the social system of constitutive rules. These rules create the possibility of particular forms of human behavior. In this sense, a culture is a symbolic system (Saussure 1986; Lyons 1973; Culler 1973).

Structural Anthropology

This last idea can be explicated by summarizing some of the leading structuralists in social and cultural theory. Lévi-Strauss (1977) extends Jakobson's linguistics and Saussure's analysis of the sign to a wide range of social practices (ceremonies, kinship relations, cooking methods) seeing these as a kind of language which permits communication between individuals. Just as in language, where meaning is communicated by oppositions between sounds, so other cultural elements, such as myths, carry meaning through binary oppositions, raw and cooked, earth and sky, etc.; relations between the opposing terms, rather than the symbolism of the terms themselves, give culture its meaning. Thus, for Lévi-Strauss, the various constituents of cultural behavior are to be seen not as intrinsic entities but in terms of their contrastive relations, as parts of systems, or as partial expressions of a total culture ultimately conceived as a single language. His purpose is not only to ask whether the different aspects of social life can be studied with the help of linguistic concepts, but "whether they do not constitute phenomena whose in-most nature is the same as language" (Lévi-Strauss 1977: 62; Hawkes 1977: 32–58). That is, Lévi-Strauss proposes expressing the different features of social life (e.g. kinship systems, myths) as a set of general terms, a "sort of general language," which could be compared with actual languages. The object would be to ascertain whether different types of communication systems (kinship, myth, language) are caused by identical unconscious structures. "Should this be the case," he concludes in a classic piece of understatement, "we could be assured of having reached a truly fundamental formulation" (Lévi-Strauss 1977: 62). In other words, supporting the notion that "anthropology draws its originality from the unconscious nature of collective phenomena," he believes it possible to discover, behind the chaos of rules and customs displayed by a multitude of societies, a single structural scheme operating in different spatial and temporal contexts: he wants to find "the unconscious structure underlying each institution and each custom" (Lévi-Strauss 1977: 18, 21).

Lévi-Strauss's argument is that natural conditions are defined and given meaning in concepts organized into a system with logical rather than natural order. The human mind mediates between praxis and culture by elaborating a conceptual system between facts and ideas – in this system facts are turned into signs with which people communicate. Yet Lévi-Strauss proposes a dialectical explanation which consists of rethinking social phenomena in their unconscious rather than their conscious logical order, believing that the unconscious origin of cultural phenomena is more genuine than conscious explanations given for them (cf. Freud, Marx, Mauss, Boas, etc.) – that is, conscious representations are rationalizations of unconscious categories. The primary appeal, then, is to the unconscious linguistic structures of Jakobson and others of the Prague school; Lévi-Strauss believes that language is structured at the phonological, grammatical, lexical, and perhaps the discursive levels. Laws of language determine humans' way of communicating and therefore their way of thinking (Rossi 1974).

Lévi-Strauss's scientific endeavor, his vision of total understanding, inaugurated a period of intense intellectual excitement over structuralism and its potential which lasted in France for most of the 1960s and continued, in Britain and America, until the late 1970s, when various poststructural tendencies came to the fore. We can gain some notion of the influence of structuralism by briefly examining some of the ideas of other leading intellectual figures of the time, people like Lacan, Barthes, Foucault, and Althusser, although none were as profoundly influenced by structural ideas as Lévi-Strauss; indeed, many of these same writers were later to be major contributors to poststructuralism.

An Unconscious Structured Like a Language

For French psychoanalyst Jacques Lacan (1968; 1977; 1981), as opposed to Freud, the mental scientist attends to cultural rather than natural forces, the human order rather than biology. For Freud, the mind is a wordless interplay of pressures and intensities which provide the hidden meanings behind speech. For Lacan, by comparison, even the unconscious is structured like a language, an idea he derives from Jakobson and Saussure via Lévi-Strauss. Lacan thinks that Freud's account can be restated using linguistic concepts; he undertakes a sequence of two-way "mappings" in which the unconscious plays on language (language may have been created in the partial image of the unconscious) and language reveals the unconscious (the unconscious is available only in linguistically mediated forms) – Lacan himself inclines to the side of language creating the unconscious. Thus, rather than seeing the unconscious as a primordial, instinctual mental realm behind or beneath speech, for Lacan, the "vertical" dependencies of the signifying chain extend into the hidden worlds of mental processes. In acquiring speech, the subject submits his or her free instinctual energies to the systemic pressures of the existing symbolic order. Using Saussure's idea of the bonding that occurs between segments of the thought-realm (signifieds) and of the sound-realm (signifier) once their (originally accidental) relationship is established, Lacan argues that attempts at locating and delimiting the signified in pure form are frivolous; for him, language *constitutes* thought. Psychoanalysis should thus focus on the signifying chain. For Lacan, relations between signifiers take precedence over relations between signifiers and signifieds – indeed, the signifier colonizes the signified. Lacan uses this as a way of destabilizing psychoanalytic theory (Bowie 1979).

For Lacan, the ego (conscious self) is schismatic. The infant's "mirror stage" (when the child sees its behavior reflected in the imitative gestures of an other – discovers "that is me") is deceptive, for the mirror, seemingly reassuring, is in fact a decoy, a producer of mirages rather than images. Hence, the process of ego construction is an alienated process and the individual permanently discordant with itself. Into the original act of the construction of the ego is woven destruction, the only escape being further alienation. Lacan extends this to the structure of all knowledge which, like the ego, is typified by a will to alienation. For Lacan, the encounter between the desirous subject and the Other (whether defined singularly or alterity as a general condition) is mediated by language. In this system of relations:

> the other-infested subject can have no other destiny than that of successive disappearance and return, entity and non-entity, sense and nonsense, concentration and dispersal, being there and being gone. The subject's language is not a late-coming and accidental vehicle for this rhythm: for language was there from the beginning, as the condition of the individual's subjecthood, and supplies the underlying vacillatory pattern for all his adventures in being ... language [in the form of speech] becomes a "third locus," the endless mobile space in which the Subject and its Other are made, dissolved and remade. (Bowie 1991: 82)

Lacan positions the individual in a force-field via a tripartite system of "orders" – the Symbolic, the Imaginary, and the Real. The Imaginary is the order of mirror images in which the individual repeats its original, alienated ego-identificatory procedures in relation to an external world of people and objects. The Symbolic is the realm of language, the unconscious, and otherness. Yet for Lacan (as for the semiotician Peirce), there is a world outside the signifying dimension in the mental and material worlds, which he calls the Real. For Lacan, the three orders together "comprise a complex topological space" in which the disorderly motions of mind can be plotted (Bowie 1991: 98–9).

Cultures as Signifying Chains

Roland Barthes (1967) uses structuralist methods to launch a critique of contemporary literary criticism as ahistorical, psychologically naive, positivistic, and obsessed with the notion of the single meaning of a text. Mystification endows historical or cultural phenomena with the appearance of being natural, the idea being that the existing society is the product of god or nature. In *Mythologies*, Barthes (1972) undertakes to demystify apparently innocent cultural phenomena (like guidebooks or astrology) to uncover their ideological base. His method derives from his experience as a mythographer and from semiotics, the study of signs. Hence, in a simple case, a magazine illustration of a black soldier saluting the French flag (the signifier) is uncovered as an argument for French imperialism (the signified). Furthermore, a writing style does not innocently reflect reality but instead shapes reality, acting as an institutionalized carrier or encoder of a way of life and its values. Responding to such writing involves acceding to its implicit values and reinforcing the way of life it supports. When that way of life disintegrates, so does the style supporting it and supported by it. The literary transaction between writer and reader, then, involves a complex structure of codes which modify, determine, and generate meanings. Likewise, even ordinary buildings organize space to signify society's priorities, assumptions concerning human nature, and politics. Semiotics is thus expanded to (un)cover all aspects of social and cultural life – Barthes's favorite target being fashion and fashion magazines (Hawkes 1977; Sturrock 1979b).

Archaeology

Michel Foucault, in his structural (archaeological) period, attempts to elucidate the epistemological field, or "episteme," in which human knowledge is grounded. The episteme defines the basic configurations within the space of knowledge that give rise to diverse forms of empirical science. Within the episteme of western culture, Foucault's "archaeological method" discovers discontinuities explainable not in terms of intentional creativity but more as sudden structural transformations. Hence, in the European Renaissance (up to the end of the sixteenth century) the resemblance between things was the organizing principle of knowledge. The Classical Age (from the mid-seventeenth to the early nineteenth centuries) attempted to construct a universal method of analysis which would yield perfect certainty by ordering representations and signs to mirror the ordering of the world. Then, after a sudden epistemic shift at the end of the eighteenth century, modern people sought to understand not only objects but themselves as subjects. For Foucault, it is not humans who constitute the modern sciences but, rather:

> the general arrangement of the "episteme" that provides them with a site, summons them, and establishes them – thus enabling them to constitute man as their object . . . a "human science" exists, not wherever man is in question, but wherever there is analysis – within the dimension proper to the unconscious – of norms, rules, and signifying totalities which unveil to consciousness the conditions of its forms and contents. To speak of "sciences of man" in any other case is simply an abuse of language. (Foucault 1973: 364–5)

Any science questioned at the archaeological level thus reveals the epistemological configuration that made it possible. It is in the sense of particular thought patterns being captured by deeper structural movements that Foucault (1973: xiv), while denying that he uses any of the "methods, concepts, or key terms that characterize structural analysis" can be termed at least a "quasi-structuralist" (Dreyfus and Rabinow 1983: 43).

Semiotics of Space

Structuralist ideas about linguistics and semiotics were most directly transferred into the study of space via social semiotics or the study of signs. Defined by Saussure as composed of a signifier and a signified, the sign is part of the recognition by the individual of the social and natural environment and of his/her internal world. In spatial semiotics, material objects (the elements of space) are the main vehicles of signification, although analyses can be extended to include codes of property ownership, written texts of planning, etc. *Socio*-semiotics (Greimas 1966) links signifying systems with their social contexts through the study of the ideology incorporated in signs. The two writers most involved in translating social semiotics into a study of space, sociologists Mark Gottdiener and Alexandros Lagopoulos (1986: 5), extend this linkage back to the material, social processes accounting for systems of signification. Hence, for Gottdiener and Lagopoulos, connotative codes are social products produced by groups and classes involved in spatial practices; they see space not as a text but a "pseudo-text" because it is produced by non-semiotic ("exo-semiotic") as well as semiotic processes. Explanation of semiotic systems requires specification of how they are constructed socially: it is this articulation between semiotic and exo-semiotic processes which differentiates the socio-semiotic from the semiotic approach (Gottdiener and Lagopoulos 1986; Lagopoulos and Boklund-Lagopoulou 1992: 35; Gottdiener 1995).

Structural Marxism

However, structuralism entered geography, as with most of the social sciences, mainly through structural Marxism. Given the eventual critique of structuralism as a kind of Stalinist determinism, it is important that we accurately represent structural Marxism's political and intellectual origins. The orthodox tradition of Marxist philosophy sees nature, human history, and thought as ultimately material with dynamics which follow dialectical laws. In the Stalinist conception of the "iron laws" of history, social progress comes from advances in the forces of production (hence, the Soviet fetish of steelworks and machine-tool plants) and revolutionary change is inevitably caused by contradiction between advancing forces and relatively static relations of production. As Sartre points out, this interpretation of Marx denies a creative, directing, meaning-bestowing role for human subjects. Hence, Stalinism was opposed in postwar France by the phenomenological movement. Thus, with Merleau-Ponty, Husserl's conception of consciousness as intentional (necessarily of something) becomes a concept of historical practice as bestowing meaning on, and transforming, its object; for Merleau-Ponty there are no iron laws and the history made by humans is always fragile and contingent. Similarly, Sartre rejects scientific and deterministic Marxism while emphasizing the free and creative making of history by human beings. Yet, as we have seen, French philosophy shifted dramatically in the late 1950s and early 1960s with the structuralist critique of phenomenology and existentialism (Lévi-Strauss especially). The British Marxist historian E. J. Hobsbawm (1994: 4) sees Louis Althusser rising meteorically to fame as an ideological hardliner, challenging the political and intellectual softening of the Sartrean left, as part of a new generation of rebels in France – although this is a controversial interpretation (the "hardliner" part). Influenced by structuralism, Althusser (1969) undertook a major revision of the basic Marxist analytical categories, with the aim of differentiating between Marx's "prescientific" humanist ideas and the mature, "scientific" ideas of Marx's *Capital*. Yet Althusser was critical of Stalin's economism and technological determinism and saw himself as providing a third way in Marxism, which was neither Stalinist nor humanist.

In establishing this position, Althusser drew on the broad sweep of twentieth-century French philosophy, especially ideas in conventionalism and historical epistemology. As opposed to classical philosophies of science (rationalism and empiricism), conventionalism argues that scientific theory is underdetermined by the available empirical evidence or the formal reasoning which constructs its ideas. Instead, a set of concepts and laws is adopted by convention rather than as a result of the persuasive force of definitive proof. In conventionalism, ethical and aesthetic values, along with other "extrinsic" conditions, enter the making of scientific theory. Hence, the sciences are historical phenomena, subject to transformations, and locked into relationships with other social practices. This "historical dimension" to epistemology distinguishes French from other forms of the philosophy of science.

For Marx

In *For Marx*, Althusser (1969) launches a critique of humanist interpretations of Marx, arguing that these are derived from empiricist readings in which Marx's texts have only to be read to be understood, or more generally derived from an empiricist epistemology in which the real is immediately present in phenomena and is readily accessible through a properly informed "gaze." Althusser counter-poses to this empiricism a sharp separation between real-objects, which theory seeks to explain, and distinct "thought-objects" making up science, which knowledge works on, and through which we come to know reality. Thought-objects are the pre-existing concepts and theories which science continually transforms. Science is thus an historical (changing) practice.

Althusser's discussion of the dialectic begins with the metaphor of Marx's inversion of Hegel (see chapter 3). In both Hegel and Marx, the dialectic sees history moved by internal contradictions. For Althusser, however, altering the (social) object of the dialectic changes its nature. In Hegel, all the instances of an "expressive" totality reflect a basic contradiction, for history is the expression of a spiritual essence. By contrast, Althusser interprets Marx as believing that history is the result of causal relations between distinct social "instances," none of which is reducible to one basic instance (or basic cause) such as economy. Even so, in Althusser's conception of Marx, social totalities have structures, and contradiction between the forces and relations of production determines the character of the social totality. But this contradiction does so by determining which of the other instances is "dominant": social totalities are structures in dominance. So, for example, under feudalism, ideology (religion) and the (local) state are dominant, whereas under capitalism, economy is both determinant and dominant. The various instances of a totality (economic, political, ideological) possess a certain hierarchical order, organized by determination of the economic, yet also enjoy a relative autonomy. Althusser's notion of "overdetermination" sums up this conception of the Marxist dialectic: in the complex, structured unity of the social totality, the way the different contradictions are articulated on each other determines the particular direction taken by the whole. The whole is a unity of instances developing unevenly at different timescales – the term "conjuncture" expresses the specific complex of unevenness at any time. The unity of the social totality is that of a complex of instances at uneven stages of development. This conception of totality is greatly different from both Hegel and the mechanistic Marxism of the Bolsheviks and Stalin: Althusser's conception opposes reductionism, whether to spiritual essence or to the economy. Far from being epiphenomena of the economy, the other instances are its conditions of existence. Pure (last instance) determination by the economic never happens: "From the first moment to the last, the lonely hour of the 'last instance' never comes" (Althusser 1969: 43; Callinicos 1976).

Ideology and Ideological State Apparatus

To summarize: for Althusser, Marx's social totalities are different from Hegel's in that each society is constituted by "levels" or "instances" articulated by specific determinations: the level of "infrastructure" or economic base (unity of two instances, forces and relations of production); and the level of "superstructure" containing two instances, the politico-legal (state and legal system) and ideology (religion, ethics, law, etc.). This representation of society employs the spatial metaphor of a topography (i.e. a definite space with sites occupied by several realities) in which the visible upper floors (superstructure) are supported by the base (infrastructure). The effect of the spatial metaphor is to endow the base with effectiveness: determination in the last instance of what happens in the upper floor by what happens in the base (see again figure 3.1). For Althusser, the great advantage of the base–superstructure metaphor in the Marxist tradition is that "determination in the last instance" is thought of as: (1) the relative autonomy of the superstructure with respect to the base; and (2) reciprocal action of the superstructure on the base. The great disadvantage of the topographical metaphor is that it remains descriptive. Althusser goes on to look at the superstructure from the point of view of an analytic of reproduction.

Social formations must reproduce their conditions of production as they are (simple reproduction) or at an extended scale (expanded reproduction or development). In terms of the forces of production (the first instance of the economic base), this means replacing used up physical means of production (machines, buildings, etc.) and reproducing labor power (through wages which support families). Reproducing labor power entails education in techniques and practical knowledges (skills), but also people learn rules of good behavior involving morality and conscience which, for Althusser (1971: 132–3), ultimately entails submission to the "rules of the order established by class domination"; workers submit to the ruling ideology (e.g. learned at school) and the agents of repression reproduce their manipulative abilities (e.g. learned at universities) so they can dominate "in words." In the Marxist tradition, the state is conceived as a machine of repression with the basic function of enabling ruling-class domination through the violent repressive state apparatus (RSA) of police, courts, prisons, the army, and so on. But Althusser proposes going beyond this political terrain. As with Gramsci's (1971) distinction between state institutions and repressive institutions in civil society, Althusser employs the term "ideological state apparatus" (ISA) to refer to those institutions, like churches, families, trade unions, communications, and cultural media, often private but operating in the interest of the state, which function in cultural and ideological reproduction primarily through ideology and only secondarily, often symbolically, through violent repression. Thus, in terms of the reproduction of the relations of production (the second instance of the economic base), capitalist social formations primarily use ideology and especially, in mature ("democratic") systems, the "educational ideological apparatus comprising a school–family couple." While each institution of the ISA has a specialized role (hence, the communications media cram people with "daily doses of nationalism, chauvinism, liberalism, moralism"), the school has the main role of drumming into children knowhow wrapped in ruling ideologies. It should be clear that Althusser extends ideology to the whole symbolic cultural order and that he sees ideological institutions as sites of class struggle.

By ideology Marx meant "the system of ideas and representations" that dominate people's minds. In *For Marx*, Althusser (1969, 231–6) sees ideologies as systems of representations (images, myths, ideas) which are organic parts of all social totalities – "human societies secrete ideology as the very element and atmosphere indispensable to their historical respiration" (Althusser 1969: 232). People live their actions through ideology – that is, the lived relation between people and world passes through, or rather *is*, ideology. For Althusser (1969: 233), people's lived relations to world are "relations between relations" or "second degree relations" or "imaginary 'lived' relations" in which are expressed will, hope, and nostalgia. In this complex overdetermination of the real by the imaginary and the imaginary by the real, ideology is active in reinforcing the relation between people and their conditions of existence. Even those using ideology in the belief they are its masters are caught up by it. Hence, the bourgeoisie *lives* its real relation to the conditions of existence (a liberal capitalist economy with free entrepreneurship) but invests this with an imaginary relation (that all people are free as they are) thereby mystifying themselves as well as the working class – "the bourgeoisie has to believe in its own myth before it can convince others" (Althusser 1971: 234). Althusser's central (and compelling) structural thesis, therefore, is that ideology has the central function of "constituting" individuals, that it "interpolates" (i.e. recruits, transforms, and subjects) people so they can work by themselves and submit "freely" to exploitation. For Althusser, people are subjected beings stripped of all freedom except that of freely accepting their submission. He thus places ideology within his more general philosophy, which opposes Sartrean humanism with the view that:

> History is an immense *natural–human* system in movement, and the motor of history is class struggle. History is a process, and a *process without a subject*. The question about how "*man* makes history" disappears altogether. Marxist theory rejects it once and for all; it sends it back to its birthplace: bourgeois ideology. (Althusser 1976: 83–4)

Althusser could not resolve the obvious objection to this pronouncement – that he has just portrayed the struggling working class as caught in the same ideology as the ruling class – how then does class struggle "drive" (or even "motor") history?

Critics were to say that this was a functionalist conception of ideology as a thing to which people are passively subject and which they cannot change. There is little validity to this criticism. Althusser sees ideology as the main site of struggle and contention, with Marxism being a science capable of demystifying the social process. We might therefore put it this way: Althusser points to the compelling power of ideology in the modern world, sees people as its victims, but offers a way of analyzing history which enables oppositional consciousness.

Structural Marxist Geography

Structural Marxism emphasizes relations between aspects of social life conceived as a totality, theorizing this through the levels or instances of modes of production. The outstanding contribution of Althusser, now forgotten or grossly misunderstood, consists of seeing economy as indirectly determinant of politics, ideology, and culture. "Determination in the last instance" implies the relative autonomy of the superstructure with respect to the base and reciprocal action of the superstructure on the base: determination is reconceptualized as overdetermination. Economy is not some "essence" conceptualized via a vertical or depth analysis but is more part of a "horizontal" signifying dimension which gives order to ideologies, social forms of consciousness, and the practices of the state. We need also to recollect that Althusser saw causality in terms of the relations between structures which are hidden and effects which conceal while manifesting structures – stating this geographically, (social) structures consist in their (spatial) effects – "essence" is a structure dispersed among its (geographic) elements.

When notions like these appeared in geography, structural Marxism became involved in the ongoing debate on the relations between society and space (outlined in chapter 3). Just as Althusser tried to clarify relations between instances of totalities, structural Marxist geographers tried, with some success, to clarify relations between modes of production and space; that is, space is seen as a "level" or "instance" in a totality of existence. Each aspect of social life has a relation with environmental space; each mode of production creates certain spatial arrangements; successions of modes of production create and alter landscapes. While this forms part of Marxist geography in general, the structural approach is distinct and has left permanent reminders in the present geographical positions of many who would not call themselves structuralists. In many ways, subsequent critiques of structural Marxist geography have missed the mark, creating a monster out of what was instead a careful attempt at specification. But then each generation of intellectuals has to diminish its predecessors, the more to exaggerate (if only to itself) its own innovative accomplishments.

The Urban Question

In *Social Justice and the City*, Harvey uses a version of structuralism, derived via Piaget, in an interpretation of urbanism and space. But he makes no attempt at systematically reading Lévi-Strauss or Althusser, does not consciously incorporate their work into Marxist geography, and indeed was definitely not an Althusserian structuralist. By comparison, the sociologist Manuel Castells (1977: ix), subsequently a professor of urban planning at the University of California at Berkeley, whose work, initially published in France, became highly influential in Anglo-American geography in the middle 1970s, *formally* proposed adapting Marxist concepts to the urban sphere using Althusserian reasoning. The theoretical questions he posed are: what is the process of the social production of the (urban) spatial forms of society; conversely, what are the relations between urban space and structural transformations in society?

Castells reasons that the idea of the city as the projection of society on space is both an indispensable starting point and yet too elementary an approach. For it runs the risk of imagining space as a white page on which actions are inscribed without encountering obstacles other than the landscape traces of past generations. This is tantamount to conceiving nature as fashioned entirely by culture, whereas the whole social problematic is born from the union of the two terms through the dialectical process by which humans as a particular biological species in struggling for life transform the environment. As part of this struggle, humans enter into particular social relations which give to space a form, function, and social signification. Space, then, is a concrete expression of each historical ensemble in which society is specified. This means there is no theory of space that is not an integral part of a general social theory. For Castells, any social form, like space, may be understood in terms of the historical articulation of several modes of production – by modes of production Castells means the particular matrix of combinations of the fundamental instances (systems of practices) of the social structure: essentially the economic, politico-institutional, and the ideological, with the economic determining, in the last instance, the laws of the entire mode of production. Analyzing space as an expression of the social structure thus amounts to studying its shaping by elements of the economic, political, and ideological systems, their combinations, and the social practices derived from them. In effect, one can "read" space according to the economic, political, and ideological systems which form it.

Each system is composed of a few interdependent fundamental elements. An economic reading concentrates on the spatial expressions, or "realizations," of production (factories, offices, etc.), consumption (housing, socio-cultural institutions), and a derived element, exchange (means of circulating goods and ideas). In a society where the capitalist mode of production is dominant, the economic element is the basis of the organization of space. This does not mean that economic activities like industry simply shape space according to logics like profit maximization, for there are a number of tendencies within production. But economy sets the conditions under which the other instances of society systematically shape space. Hence, the *politico-juridical* system structures institutional space according to processes of integration, repression, domination, and regulation emanating from the state apparatus – for example, space is divided into locally based collectivities, each with a certain capacity for direct decision making (integration), organized into a hierarchy vertically linked with centralized decision making (repression). Under the *ideological* system, space is charged with meaning, its forms and arrangements being articulated one with another in a symbolic structure. (Expanding this a little, given the previous discussion of Althusser's conception of ideology, this instance not only places ideological structures in space – from churches to movie theaters – but also is the medium through which space is experienced and conceptualized.) In general, for Castells (1977: 127), the social organization of space can be understood in terms of the determination of spatial forms by each of the elements of the three instances (economic, politico-juridical, ideological), by the structural combination of the three (with economy determining which instance is dominant in shaping space), but also empirically by the persistence of spatial forms created by earlier social structures, articulated with the new forms in ever more specific, concrete situations, and by the specific actions of individuals and social groups in interaction with their environments (this last being an important "concession" to individuality and agency for a structuralist!). Does space have a return effect on social relations? For Castells (1977: 442), there is a spatial determination of the social. However, space as such does not have a return effect; rather, social activity expressed in spatial forms reproduces structures.

Thus, in Castells's structuralism, each mode of production, and each stage in a mode, even each instance of a mode, implies a different organization of space: in advanced capitalism, elements concerned with the administration of the labor process and the circulation of capital are characterized by delocalization, or movement on a world scale, the tendency being to eliminate space as a source of specificity; the means of production are organized at the regional scale; and the spatial organization of the reproduction of labor power is organized at the local scale in urban areas – cities can be analyzed as "units of the collective reproduction of labour power in the capitalist mode of production" (Castells 1977: 445). This leads Castells to questions of the urban, urban problems, urban politics and planning, and urban social movements as central issues of advanced capitalism – that is, space as urbanism indeed has a "return effect" on society. As he puts it in *City, Class and Power* (Castells 1978), "the urban question refers to the organization of the means of collective consumption as the basis of the daily life of all social groups: housing, education, health, culture, commerce, transport, etc." This sector is in a state of deepening crisis at the same time as popular protest demands amelioration of the collective means of daily existence. In an attempt at resolving the contradictions and resulting conflicts, the state intervenes in the city and the reproductive crisis is politicized. The urban question and the linked issues of ecology and environment thus outline a "new axis of social and political change in advanced capitalism" (Castells 1978: 4).

Spatial Structures

A view quite similar to Castells's "structuring of space" was outlined at about the same time by the French economist Alain Lipietz (1980). For Lipietz, space is the material form of the socio-economic relations which structure social formations. Concrete socio-economic space can thus be analyzed in terms of the articulation of the "spatialities" of the different instances of the modes of production present in any social formation; hence, there are economic, legal, and other spatialities. Presence/absence in geographical space is specified by participation/exclusion in the underlying structure. While space is a reflection of social relations, it also constrains the redeployment of these relations. Society, Lipietz thinks, recreates its space on the basis of spaces established in the past.

Subsequently, structural Marxist geography further elaborated two themes raised by Castells, Lipietz, and other European structuralists (see also Carney, Hudson, and Lewis 1980): the structuring of space by the instances of modes of production; and the spatial relations between social components "implanted" into space (spatial dialectics). This work responded to radical criticisms of "spatial fetishism" in positivist geographic thought, but more constructively began to carefully compose an alternate view of the *social* construction of space. Criticized as "economic determinism" even as it was forming, this structural Marxist school proved important in shaping subsequent work, particularly the "new industrial geography" of the 1980s and 1990s (see also Corragio 1977; Buch-Hanson and Nielson 1977; Dunford and Perrons 1983).

The work of the Brazilian geographer Milton Santos, then living in exile but subsequently at the University of São Paulo, derives from this structural tradition but also shows distinct differences – Santos's work is a kind of dialectical–existential structuralism which integrates time and dynamics into the structuring of space and employs Sartre's "project" even in functional analyses. Santos (1977: 5) argues that modes of production become concrete on historically determined territorial bases: spatial forms thus constitute a "language" of modes of production. He proposes a genetic study of the social formations affiliated with modes of production; mode of production is the genus and social formation the species, or mode of production the possibility and social formation the realized possibility in the form of an historically determined society. This process of "realization" cannot occur without reference to space. Differences between places are the result of the spatial ordering of particular modes of production. This is often stated in strictly functional terms, as with the notion of social formations obtaining from nature elements required for satisfying society's needs. But then Santos argues that every aspect of social life is relevant by itself, none has primacy, and each is constantly being revalued by changes in the social totality. Also, no society has permanent functions, or a fixed level of forces of production, or definite, fixed forms of social relations. So too with the effectivity of space. While space results from crystallizations of social processes, it is also an active dimension of existence in a number of ways: (1) location in space is the result of the interaction between the "external" forces of presently hegemonic modes of production and factors internal to social formations (local social relations, natural factors, built forms from the past, etc.); (2) space is a selective medium so that any general force derived from a hegemonic mode of production appears differently in different localities; (3) places are endowed with particular meanings at each historical moment. Into this dialectical functionalism, Santos weaves Sartre's notion of project and intention, so that space is not just a question of *practico-inerte* but of *inertia dynamica*; praxis is both conditioned by space and is the active force recreating space. Hence: "Modes of production write history in time; social formations write it in space" (Santos 1977: 5).

Spatial Dialectics

A somewhat different view, aimed at moving beyond the structural notion that production creates space, was proposed by Peet (1978; 1981). This involved extending Althusser's relative autonomy to space and spatial relations in a structuralist version of Marxist geography. For Peet, the concept of a Marxist geography has validity in structural terms in that while Marxism is a science of totalities, the various specialisms within Marxist science study the various instances, or relations between instances, of the societal whole. As each instance has relative autonomy, so does each part of science, while remaining within a holistic knowledge. Marxist geography thus specializes in studying two fundamental relations: the dialectical relation between social formations and the natural world; and the dialectical relations between formations embedded in different environments; taken together these make up the "environmental relations" of social formations. The basic reason for studying these specific instances is to concretize the highly generalized insights of historical materialism, especially because differing natural conditions of existence influence the form and development of modes of production, while external spatial relations between environmentally embedded formations modify, and even transform, their (internal) contents. Thus, the geography of capitalism is composed of unevenly and differently developing specificities (social formations). As social contradictions build internally in any social formation, its external socio-spatial relations also change, with various effects being transmitted elsewhere or antidotal solutions imported. This may slow down or redirect the build up of contradiction in one social formation but may qualitatively change social formations elsewhere in space where, in interaction with local (class-dominated) processes, new hybrid social formations come into existence. The complex interplay across space between the social formations of a global system may be called "spatial dialectics." "World history is understandable in terms of the dialectics of the whole, the geographical instances of the whole, and the relations across space between these instances. The essential contribution of Marxist geography in this formulation is an understanding of the uneven development of contradictions in space, the forms in which contradictions appear as complexes of crises, and the (spatial) relations between these complexes" (Peet 1981: 109).

Thus, most of the work carried out in geography under the structural understanding spelt out the implications of the aspects and totalities of social existence for the shaping of space and the return influences of structured space on the reproduction of social existence. Yet the kinds of detailed work called for by empirical structuralists, a project of spatially and environmentally specifying modes of production, never took place (but see Lapple and van Hoogerstraten 1980). Structuralism of the Althusserian variety had barely taken hold in geography (from about 1976 to 1981) when it was criticized and abandoned in its pure form; elaborations of structural themes mainly occurred indirectly, usually in interaction with ideas derived from alternate viewpoints, for example in the new industrial geography of the 1980s and 1990s. Within Marxist thought a critical encounter and productive interaction occurred between structuralism and notions of hegemony derived from the Italian Marxist Antonio Gramsci, which produced the "neo-structural" tendency known as the French regulation school. We thus turn to examinations of Gramsci and the regulation school.

The Regulation School

Antonio Gramsci was active in the Turin working-class movement and the Italian Socialist and Communist parties before being confined to prison by Mussolini (1926–37). His *Prison Notebooks* were published posthumously in Italian between 1948 and 1951 and selections were later translated into English (Gramsci 1971). Gramsci's ideas were derived from the Hegelian–Marxist writings of Benedetto Croce and Antonio Labriola, which opposed positivistic, scientific, and mechanistic Marxism and wanted to fuse materialism and dialectical idealism in a new understanding of praxis. Gramsci himself thought that an adequate theory of revolution could not rest on materialist foundations alone, nor be worked out from the laws of capitalist development, but required an active practical knowledge of human needs, objectives, and historical consciousness expressed through creative subjectivity. While wishing to retain the notion of mode of production shaping historical development, Gramsci found this deterministic idea not very useful for explaining the diverse interplay of forces operating during "conjunctural periods" of social transformation. He found the relationship between economic base and political and ideological superstructure to be reciprocal, complex, and changing – politics, ideas, culture could have overriding powers. For him, beliefs, attitudes, superstitions, and myths are real or material as catalysts activating objective contradictions; that is, contradictions do not explode themselves but are seized upon by thinking people.

Gramscian Marxism

Gramsci's key notion for theorizing the relation between base and superstructure is "ideological hegemony," a concept derived from Croce's "ethico-political" themes of history. Gramsci compared the idea of domination (direct physical coercion in political society) with that of hegemony (ideological control through consent in civil society). Hegemony implied the permeation through agencies like unions, schools, churches, and families of an entire system of values, beliefs, and morality supportive of the established order and its dominating classes: hegemony is a world view diffused through agencies of socialization into every area of daily life which, when internalized, becomes part of "common sense." Hegemony mystifies power relations, public issues, and events, encourages fatalism and political passivity, and justifies system-serving sacrifice and deprivation. Hegemony works to induce the oppressed to consent to their exploitation and misery. Revolutionary political transformation, Gramsci says, is not possible without a crisis of ideological hegemony in civil society. A crisis of the modern state occurs when the ruling class is stripped of its spiritual prestige and power and reduced to its obvious economic–corporate forms. Therefore, socialist movements must, Gramsci concluded, create a "counter-hegemony" to break the existing ideological bonds and penetrate the false world of established appearances as prelude to the making of a new universe of ideas and values for human liberation (Gramsci 1971; Boggs 1976: 21–44). In "Americanism and Fordism," Gramsci (1971: 279–318) asks whether Americanism is a new form of civilization and Fordism the ultimate phase of industrialization? Europeans were fascinated with the prospect of a United States free from feudal restraints such as landowning nobles and divine-right kings. Hence, Gramsci thought that the prerequisite for Americanism was a "rational demographic composition" – that is, a lack of parasitic classes (civil service, clergy, landowners, etc.) found in abundance in post-feudal Europe as in India and China. Without the "leaden burden" of the "sedimentations of idle and useless masses living on 'their ancestral patrimony'" the United States economy was able to accumulate formidable amounts of capital while allowing superior living conditions to its "popular classes" (Gramsci 1971: 281, 285). Hence, in Fordist America:

> Since these preliminary conditions existed, already rendered rational by historical evolution, it was relatively easy to rationalize production and labour by a skillful combination of force (destruction of working class trade unionism on a territorial basis) and persuasion (high wages, various social benefits, extremely subtle ideological and political propaganda) and thus succeed in making the whole life of the nation revolve around production. Hegemony here is born in the factory and requires for its exercise only a minute quantity of professional political and ideological intermediaries. The phenomenon of the "masses" ... is nothing but the form taken by this "rationalized" society in which the "structure" dominates the superstructures more immediately and in which the latter are also "rationalized" (simplified and reduced in number). (Gramsci 1971: 285–6)

In the United States, rationalization elaborates (through psychophysical manipulation) a new type of human suited to the new industrial techniques introduced by Henry Ford: the use of "Taylorist" methods involving the mechanization of the worker's movements and actions and the use of semi-automatic assembly lines. American industrialists, Gramsci says, are concerned to maintain the continuity of the physical and muscular–nervous efficiency of the worker and prevent the collapse of workers exhausted by the new methods. The interest lies in a stable, skilled, machine-like workforce. Whereas in the Soviet Union, military models of coercion were used to create worker discipline and the adaptation of customs to the necessities of work, the monopoly given to United States industry by the new techniques enabled "coercion" to be achieved through high wages, at least for an aristocracy of skilled workers. Gramsci thought this would be a temporary phenomenon because the new methods would spread to other countries and the new type of worker would become universalized. While he did not find in it a new form of civilization, as an ideology and a new culture the spread of Americanism hastened the decomposition of old strata in countries like Italy, already in the grip of social dissolution. In essence, Gramsci discussed alternate ways of regulating working populations in the new realities of the twentieth century. These ideas were elaborated by what came to be known as the French regulation school.

Regulation Theory

Regulationist ideas were first formulated by de Bernis discussing the norms and adjustment mechanisms of capitalist economies as part of a more general critique of neoclassical theories of economic equilibrium (Boyer 1986; Dunford 1990). This line of thought intersected with an increasingly critical reaction to Althusserian structural Marxism in the 1970s. A generation of French Marxists coming to intellectual maturity in the 1960s had been profoundly affected by Althusser. One of these, Michel Aglietta, wrote a thesis (completed in 1974) examining how systemic reproduction could occur in a capitalist system where social relations divide individuals and social groups (Dunford 1990). His answer was that codifications of social relations, called modes of regulation, mediate, normalize, and regulate contradictions. Aglietta (1979: 19–20) uses the term "structural forms" for the "complex social relations, organized in institutions, that are the historical products of the class struggle," sees these as constituting "morphologies" or unevenly developed spaces, and theorizes that the determinate relationships reproduced in these particular structures assure integrity and cohesion to the entire socio-economico-political system. Weak spots appear in these relationships where corrective, regulative mechanisms may break down, threatening the system, which reacts as a totality by modifying its regulatory forms; a change of regime takes place in a morphological transformation that may be considerable in scope, with such ruptures marked by crises of intense social creativity. Here, Althusser's notions of uneven development and overdetermination are reworked into a neo-structuralist but also intermediate-level theory of social regulation.

Such a critical continuity with structuralism is evident also in the work of the economist Alain Lipietz, active in the regulation school from the late 1970s onwards. Lipietz acknowledges his debt to Althusser – indeed, as we have seen, his early work on space bears the direct imprint of the strict Althusserian style (what Calvinism is to Protestantism, Althusserianism is to Marxism!). Lipietz was active in French politics, as a left critic of the "neo-liberal" policies of the ruling socialist party, and as theoretician, activist, and candidate for the Green Party. As a result of this practice he became critical of economists, Marxists and otherwise, who reduced historical change to a "quantitative evolution which conforms to the 'overall logic of the system'" (Lipietz 1992a: ix) – history is more complex, contingent, and fluid. He became critical too of Althusser's conception of the reproduction of society, with its denial that social totalities are made and remade via the agency of human subjects. This led Lipietz away from an Althusserian functionalist interpretation of reproduction towards an interest in the contradictions reproduced in otherwise coherent structures, an analysis of the resulting crises, and thus Aglietta's problem of how to "regulate" a society full of contradiction and conflict. The idea was to replace transhistorical mechanisms of coherent social reproduction with historically and geographically specific *modes* of regulation by which economies and societies are actively, institutionally regulated (Lipietz 1993). Hence, a series of intermediate concepts (intermediate between the general–abstract and the specific–empirical) theorized socio-economic processes exhibiting significant spatial and historical variation. The basic concepts were elaborated in detail by a group of Parisian researchers (CEPREMAP), including R. Boyer, working on the long-run economic history of France. In the early 1980s, regulationist ideas were taken up in Germany, for example by Joachim Hirsch (1984) in the "state derivation" debate – that is, the derivation of the form of the state from the social relations of capitalist production. In the early 1980s, regulation theory entered British geography (Dunford and Perrons 1983) and in the middle 1980s became more widely known in United States geography (Scott and Storper 1986a). Regulation theory is now highly influential, if not hegemonic at least on the left, as a line of thought employing structuralist yet intermediate-level and quasi-empirical concepts to theorize phases of capitalist development and associated territorial structures.

The basic position of the regulation school is that the overall societal framework of capitalism is quite stable over long periods of time. Yet the system periodically bursts into struggles, wars, and even revolutions – periods of intense change occurred at the end of the nineteenth century, in the 1930s–1950s, and in the period since the end of the 1960s. Lipietz and the regulation school theorize this dynamic in terms of equilibriums (development models) and their transformations. Models or patterns of development are analyzable, they say, from several perspectives: as *technological paradigms* in terms of the general principles which govern the social organization of labor; as *regimes of accumulation*, that is, in terms of the macroeconomic principles describing long-term compatibilities between production conditions and uses of the social product (i.e. production–consumption relationships) – extensive accumulation occurs through investing more inputs, intensive accumulation through increasing the efficiency of input use; and as *modes of regulation*, combinations of adjustments in the contradictory behavior of individual agents with the collective principles of the regime of accumulation – that is, cultural habits and institutional rules. This last aspect is sometimes elaborated as a *societal paradigm* or world view which permeates an era and shapes people's conceptions of what is moral, normal, and desirable. The regulation school sees the world as divided into a hierarchical system of nation states, with national modes of regulation; but a number of countries coexisting within the same pattern yields a *world configuration* (Leborgne and Lipietz 1988; Lipietz 1986; 1992a).

Fordism

Following Gramsci (and Henri de Man), the hegemonic development model of the postwar period is called "Fordism." Let it be said immediately that this is a confusing usage in that other developmental models are not named for individuals. Also, the personal emphasis on Henry Ford as origin of an entire system is misplaced because, while he perhaps understood that mass production had to be balanced by mass consumption (Gramsci's high wages), Lipietz and the regulation school actually place more causal emphasis on worker struggles forcing a "grand compromise" on capital that came to resemble Ford's personal vision of the "American way of life" (i.e. "Fordism"). The principles of the technological paradigm of Fordism, prevalent in the 1940s, 1950s, and 1960s, are standardization of production and separation of conception, organization, and control from manual work. In terms of regime of regulation, these produce a rapid rise in the volume of goods produced per person. This expansion is counterbalanced by an equally massive growth in consumption, first by unionized wage earners, then by all sectors of the population. In the Fordist mode of regulation, the competitive adjustment mechanisms of the nineteenth century decline in favor of compulsory agreements between capital and labor (collective bargaining), the hegemony of large companies, and state control through Keynesian macro-economic policies. In regulation theory, crises may be internal (e.g. the build up of tensions between aspects of the system and the exhaustion of development models) or external (e.g. natural disasters). In the break up of Fordism, internal crisis began in the technological paradigm, when a decrease in the growth of productivity and a fall in profitability in the late 1960s produced a more general economic crisis in the 1970s, characterized by the internationalization of production, state austerity programs, unemployment, and eventually a crisis of demand (underconsumption crisis). All these resulted in a move to a new accumulative regime of "flexible accumulation" from the middle 1970s to the present (Leborgne and Lipietz 1988). There is a suggestion also that regimes of accumulation may have environmental implications. Hence, Lipietz finds the "logic" of systems based on intensive growth and mass production to lie in maximizing production and stimulating consumption. Yet production involves transformation of the natural and social environments, neither of which has to be paid for by individual firms, Hence, the "natural" tendency is to deplete these or overwhelm them with waste. During Fordism, Lipietz argues, Keynesian regulation by the state did not extend to environment; only when social movements exerted force did the state institute ecological laws and regulations. He finds the (perverse) "logic" of Fordism to be implacable – better to repair damage to the environment, thereby boosting consumption, than not to pollute in the first place! For Lipietz, environmental crisis is an integral part of a post-Fordist development model.

Regulationist Geography

These regulationist ideas first appeared prominently in geography in Michael Dunford and Dianne Perrons's *The Arena of Capital* (1983), which carried an account of changes in the space economy accompanying the development of capitalism. For Dunford and Perrons, space is composed of the structures and forms produced by modes of production in historical sequences. In these sequences, the nature and space modified by one mode forms the "inherited circumstances" faced by the next. By using this more social and historical conception, they reconstruct geographical theory to look more like classical political economy, before locational analysis was separated into an independent study.

The central notion is that the development of the capitalist mode of production takes the form of a broad succession of phases, regimes of accumulation characterized by particular forms of production (especially labor processes) but also, more interestingly, by the way of life (mode of consumption) of wage earners, patterns of social and economic behavior and institutional forms, and forms of territorial development and systems of international relations. Dunford and Perrons outline four regimes of accumulation corresponding to Krondatieff long waves (i.e. expansion and decline) or Mandel's (1980) theory of economic waves linked to the rise and fall of revolutionary technologies. Generally, the idea is that surplus value can be increased and the accumulation of capital speeded up, either by "capital widening," that is, using more capital and labor in a given ratio (extensive accumulation), or by capital deepening, changing the ratio by using more capital (as machines) and increasing labor efficiency through disciplining the workforce (intensive accumulation). The two methods are combined in proportions which favored the second (intensive accumulation) as West European society moved from manufacture through machinofacture to scientific management, Fordism, and beyond.

In the regulation school, they point out, the production of commodities is matched with a distribution of incomes and set of consumption abilities and styles which clears the market: that is, production, consumption, distribution, and exchange are integrated. In such systems, institutional forms and social practices must be developed so that individuals and social groups act in ways consistent with the functioning of the system – this produces the collection of structural forms called the mode of regulation. Their perspective on space is that the "arena of capital" is made up from layers of human social activity each shaped by earlier layers, which are erased at the same time as they exert influences; each layer is organized by a new logic of development, or way of organizing social reproduction as a whole. Dunford and Perrons emphasize the functional and spatial differentiation of social reproduction systems – that is, the tendency for capitalism to reproduce social and spatial inequalities in new forms. Their emphasis lies on the overpowering weight of structural necessity rather than the creative power of human agency.

Meso-Level Analysis

Regulation theory's greatest influence lies in the new industrial geography revitalized by the realist–structuration–locality notions of theorists like Doreen Massey but typified more by neo-structuralist notions derived from Lipietz. (Here, the discussion merges with the structure–agency debate and other themes outlined in chapter 5.) In an edited book, Allen Scott and Michael Storper, both at the University of California, Los Angeles, draw on structuralism by criticizing it in regulationist terms; structuralism, they argue, cannot handle the new complexities of advanced capitalism, Hence, under the new realities of capitalism, especially internationalization of economy and society, research should focus on the exact strategies organizing investment, production, and work rather than "some independent and abstract structural imperative" (Storper and Scott 1986: 4). Conventional theories, they think, miss or underestimate the dynamic potential for new industrial complexes to grow in new places, while (structural) Marxism cannot anticipate capital's technical dynamism and social creativity. So the new realities have to be assessed through theories of corporate behavior embedded in organizational webs of production, or through ideas of labor market segmentation, technical change, and the long-run potentials of capitalist development, all non-teleological conceptions in which contingency plays a significant role. Such theorization backs away from the (structural) notion of predetermined development paths, and pays attention instead to the details of class relations, technical change, and political struggle as the concrete, contingent determinants of history. They think that the historical dynamics of socio-economic systems can be comprehended only in geographical context because spatially specific circumstances limit the possibilities of human actions. Yet territorial analysis is not a science in itself since the basic forces of locational activity are expressions of wider systems of social relations. This conceptual maneuvering leads Storper and Scott to the position that while a viable analysis of capitalist development must include macro- and micro-levels, the interactions of the two in a *meso-level* of analysis should be kept at the forefront:

> Territorial analysis is intrinsically such a case where, as we move from the dynamics of the mode of production down to the specifics of community and place (and back again), it is necessary to invoke a complex series of intermediate variables dealing with such issues as industrial organization, the division of labor, technology, labor market processes, international capital flows, and all the rest. This is also ... a domain that is especially strongly touched by contingency and open-endedness so that as we move analytically through this domain to the micro-level we arrive at an extremely varied and often quite unexpected set of outcomes, however stable and uniform the generalized structures we may start out with. (Storper and Scott 1986: 14)

Hence, capitalism takes the form of a varied mosaic of socio-spatial relationships and these, when "retotalized," create the more dynamic and differentiated capitalist system which otherwise eludes theory. Even so, their basic approach to space remains broadly structural (reminiscent sometimes even of Lévi-Strauss): "territory (i.e. humanly differentiated geographical space) is a creature of those forces that underlie the material reproduction of social life ... any discourse about the modern space economy is most effective when rooted in the problem of the expressive effects of the commodity production system as it is organized in space" (Scott and Storper 1986b: 301). This reminiscent structuralism is especially evident when by "commodity production system" they mean a logic of productive activity (capital accumulation) or a dynamic structure in which social and geographical realities unfold. This logic, they add, is "primary" in constituting the driving dynamic of social existence, but does not simply "fix" patterns of life, to understand which we have to turn to "secondary" forms of knowledge – hence, their meso-level analytics. So why, they ask, is the landscape of capitalism structurally marked by unevenness and disparities? In part, because of the irregular distribution of basic resources. Also, it is "preordained" to developmental disparities as capital and labor necessarily concentrate at privileged sites; from this, potent territorial effects emerge, for example as geographically specific technical changes. Yet also, diseconomies of concentration shift units of production to decentralized locations. Hence, a "restless system of territorial processes creates and recreates the geographical anatomy of industrial capitalism" (Scott and Storper 1986b: 302). This sets up a social-theoretic framework (a kind of neo-structuralism concentrated at the "meso-level") similar to many subsequent regulationist studies.

A Sympathetic Critique of Regulationist Geography

Given the importance of this line of thought – the leading school of economic-geographical thought in the late 1980s – let us carry the discussion through some of the criticisms of regulation which began to appear in the early 1990s (e.g. Jessop 1990; Hirst and Zeitlin 1991). In a series of articles, Adam Tickell and Jamie Peck, geographers respectively at the Universities of Manchester and Southampton, in England, survey the range of ideas using this approach. They provide a basically sympathetic critique which they say restores a regulationist framework to a geography showing increasing signs of eclecticism (Tickell and Peck 1992: 191). They are particularly interested in regulation theory's troublesome relation between the two main parts of societal structures, the regime of accumulation and the mode of regulation. Lipietz, they say, oscillates between the position that regulation is compatible with accumulation (in a kind of economic determination in the last instance – Jessop 1990: 199) and the position that the coupling between the two results from chance discovery. This oscillation reflects the insecurity generated by a movement out of Lipietz's earlier (Althusserian) structuralism (Peet 1989b), but also the complexities of a real world whose subtleties constantly confound theoretical generalization. Tickell and Peck argue constructively that stabilization between accumulation and regulation occurs in multiple geographical forms mainly at the level of the nation state – hence, under Fordism a variety of "subcouplings" exist, while the new industrial spaces of the post-Fordist flexible accumulation exhibit vastly different regulatory environments, ranging from neo-conservative deregulationism to radical collectivism. Hence, they find missing links in the regulationist project. The nature and function of regulation in flexible accumulation is not well theorized, so that many contemporary developments (Thatcherism in Britain, Reaganism in the United States, for instance) may be short-term strategies to cope with immediate crises rather than durable structures. Conceptualizing transition from one regime to another stresses contingency, so that it cannot provide a systematic account of change.

Tickell and Peck are most critically innovative in their third missing link, dealing with spatial scales of analysis. Regulation theory, they say, is sensitive to space in two ways: a stress on national specificity appreciates that different regions respond to the same process in different ways; and successive regimes have different spatial structures, nationally and internationally. Even at its height, vast areas of the North American–West European heartland hardly encountered Fordism, while in the present flexible regime Fordist structures continue to exist. What accounts for such spatial paradoxes? For Tickell and Peck, nationally hegemonic modes of social regulation may be mediated at the subnational scale, creating local regulatory modes in distinct production cultures; they find this specificity of regulation important for many of the new industrial spaces whose conditions may not be reproducible, let alone transferable, to other regions – localities desperate for jobs cannot simply copy apparently successful models from elsewhere. Also, national modes of regulation can be hegemonic if they provide conditions for accumulation in core areas of economies, which disengages peripheral systems and leads to the effective presence of "two nations" within a given state (e.g. northern and southern England, Rust Belt and Sun Belt in the United States). Subsequently, accumulation in core areas may depend on the exploitation of these peripheries. Hence, regulation theory begins to merge with theories of uneven development, regional and even local modes of social regulation being embedded within national and international modes. As Tickell and Peck (1995) later point out, regulation theory posits that regimes break down in crises provoked by internal contradictions manifested differently in different nation states. That these national systems are made up of different regional structures elaborates the notion of structural crisis as a series of "geographical contradictions of the regime of accumulation" (Tickell and Peck 1995: 374). They contrast a shift towards regional state structures with a growing internationalization, suggesting that the privileged role of the nation state (as under Fordism) is no longer assured; nation states are "hollowed out" by a combination of localization and internationalization ("glocalization"). And they find the tensions in core–periphery relations a crucial regulatory problem which neo-liberal strategies cannot accommodate – hence, the region as site of geographical contradiction. There is no mechanism for regulating uneven development in global capitalism even with supra-national institutions like the World Bank or the IMF, hence, constant instabilities and geographies of crisis.

Arguments in Structural Marxist Geography

From this discussion we can see how broad notions of structure have gradually been refined towards theories of uneven development and local specificity under conditions where the "geographic" is increasingly of real significance in contemporary capitalism. This changing theoretical position, from structuralism in the late 1970s to regulation theory in the late 1980s, responded to various critiques, especially in the "structure–agency" debate. Some of the main positions in what subsequently became known as the structure–agency debate were established in a particularly sharp critique of Althusser by E. P. Thompson, champion of the creative potential of human agency as opposed to the weight of structural necessity; counter-positions were established by Perry Anderson, reluctant defender of Althusserian structuralism. Other positions reflecting poststructural notions were established in a critique of Althusser by Ernesto Laclau and Chantel Mouffe. In both cases, the critique of structuralism set the stage for later, important developments in social theory. Many of these arguments were paralleled by corresponding arguments in human geography, particularly a critique of structural Marxist geography by James Duncan and David Ley. From these criticisms stemmed numerous positions retaining certain aspects of structuralism, dismissing others – for example, the anti-essential Marxism of Graham (1990; 1992) and Resnick and Wolff (1987; 1992).

The Poverty of Theory

Edward Thompson, perhaps the leading British Marxist historian of the postwar period (Thompson 1966), published a scathing attack on Althusser in a book entitled *The Poverty of Theory*, written from the perspective of an empirical and agent-centered Marxism (Thompson 1978). His first criticism concerns the nature of historiography. In the English-speaking world, Thompson says, historical materialism has an empirical idiom of discourse, whereas for Althusser, empiricism is bourgeois ideology and the empiricist project an illusion. For Thompson, Althusser offers instead only an ahistorical theoreticism which discloses itself, on closer examination, to be an idealism with attributes of theology. Furthermore, Althusser's epistemology is said to derive from an isolated academic learning process indifferent towards primary data (what Althusser calls Generalities I) and their origins in experience, an isolation that finds scientific theories (Althusser's Generalities II) producing their own "facts" without external appeal to experience, with the result that no genuinely new knowledge can emerge from a closed, purely mental system (Althusser's Generalities III). For the historian Thompson, such an idealist method cannot handle human experience (social being's impingement on social consciousness) and falsifies the dialogue with empirical evidence in the production of knowledge.

Thompson's second critical theme concerns structure, process, and agency. Althusserian structuralism reminds Thompson of the conservative structural functionalism of Talcott Parsons (1949; 1951) and Neil Smelser (1963) and Stalin's equally conservative caricature of Marxism in which superstructure serves base. For Thompson, both schools of thought see history as a process without a subject, evicting human agency, and presenting consciousness and practice as self-motivated things. Althusser's structuralism, he says, works like a clockwork model, its terms (economy, ideology, class struggle) are categories of stasis, its crucial concepts, like economic determination in the last instance, remain unexamined. Thompson's own empirical research does not suggest that "superstructural" elements (like law) keep to one level, but instead occur at every level, being simultaneously imbricated in production relations and present in philosophy. Nor does he think that economy determines only in the last instance. Speaking of his own research into the making of the English working class, he says sarcastically that "on several occasions, while I was actually watching, the lonely hour of the last instance actually came. The last instance like an unholy ghost actually grabbed hold of law, throttled it, and forced it to change its language and to will into existence forms appropriate to the mode of production" (Thompson 1978: 96). He finds Althusser's constructions not only actively misleading, but anti-human: "all these instances and levels are in fact human activities, institutions, and ideas. We are talking about men and women in their material life, in their determinate relations, in their experience of these, and in their self-consciousness of this experience" (Thompson 1978: 97). For Althusser, structures rather than classes are the subject of history. For Thompson (1978: 106), by comparison, class formations arise "at the intersection of determination and self activity: the working class 'made itself as much as it was made.'" Working people, not structures, he says, are the agents of history.

Thompson's passionate critique and advocacy of an empirical and agent-full history drew an equally elegant response, not from Althusser (by this time incapacitated by mental illness), but from Perry Anderson, also an English historian and social theorist. Anderson finds the apparently simple term "agent" in Thompson's writing to be deceptive, signifying at once active initiator and passive instrument. Thompson, he says, identifies historical agency with the expression of will or aspiration, forgetting the material compulsions of scarcity that also force actions. Likewise with Thompson's "experience," which again may mean occurrence, as lived by participants, or may refer to subsequent learning, which modifies ensuing actions. For Anderson, experience need bring no necessary illumination. In Thompson's work, the idea is that collective experience is converted into social consciousness; the working class owes as much to agency as to conditioning; and it makes itself as much as it is made. For Anderson, the parity between agency and conditioning is a postulate never tested. Thompson's definition of class in terms of common consciousness he finds voluntaristic and subjective. The central theoretical difficulty is the place of "will" in history. What, Anderson (1980: 51) asks, explains the ordered nature of wills? Why does the intersection of wills not produce "the random chaos of an arbitrary, destructured log jam?" Talcott Parsons (1949; Parsons and Shils 1964) postulates common norms and values informing individual acts, whereas Sartre (1976), refusing to invoke hyper-organicist values, is unable to demonstrate how struggle generates an ultimate structural unity. Confronted by the same issue, Althusser phrases social unity in terms of the reproduction of the relations of production secured by the coercive and cultural machineries of the state (RSA, ISA), especially the massive inculcation of ideology (Althusser 1971). For Anderson, therefore, the problem of social order cannot be resolved at the level of individual intentions. Instead, the dominant mode of production confers unity on a social formation, allocating objective positions to classes, distributing agents within classes, and resulting in an objective process of class struggle regulated by political power. For Anderson, too, crises are not just confrontations between classes but overlap with systemic contradictions. "Thus in both reproduction and transformation – maintenance and subversion – of social order, mode of production and class struggle are always at work. But the second must be activated by the first to achieve its determinate effects, which on either ground will find their maximum point of concentration in the political structure of the State" (Anderson 1980: 56). While Thompson (1978) approaches acknowledging this basic duality in historical determination, arguing for a rule-governed structuration within which people remain the subjects of history, he uses the analogy of society as a game whose rules are learned by players. For Anderson, by comparison, no one "learns" the rules of social relations, there is no equality of initial position among players, and there is no common goal, specified by rules, for which they compete. Althusser's position is that "immediate experience is the universe of illusion" with a (related) stress on the overpowering weight of structural necessity; Thompson's position is that experience is the medium in which consciousness awakens and creative response stirs; for Anderson (1980: 58), by comparison, the "classical equipoise of the founders of historical materialism is some distance from both."

A Post-Marxist Critique

Rather than criticizing from within western Marxism (as with the Thompson–Anderson debate) Laclau and Mouffe (1985: 4) want to establish a "post-Marxist terrain" which develops certain intuitions of Marxism and eliminates others as part of a struggle for a radical, libertarian, and plural democracy. For Laclau and Mouffe, Althusser tried to differentiate his conception of society as a complex structured whole from the Hegelian notion of totality. In Hegel, social complexity is always the plurality of moments in a single process of the self-unfolding of the Idea. Althusserian complexity, by comparison, is a process of overdetermination. Laclau and Mouffe note that the concept of overdetermination derives from psychoanalysis – for Freud, it is no ordinary fusion or merger (as in the physical world) but entails a symbolic dimension and a plurality of meanings. Hence, for Laclau and Mouffe (1985: 97–8), Althusser's statement that the social is overdetermined asserts that "the social constitutes itself as a symbolic order" and therefore society and social agents lack any (objective) essence. This analysis, they say, seems to open a new (symbolic, discursive) concept of "articulation," but instead a new variant of essentialism is reinstated. Althusser conceptualized determination in the last instance by the economy as a truth valid for every society, an a priori necessity, something defined independently of any specific type of society. Yet, they add, Althusser begins by denying the need to hypostatize the abstract, for there is no reality that is not overdetermined. Thus, Althusser lapses into the defect he criticizes by saying that there is an abstract, universal object, the "economy," which produces concrete effects. This means, for Laclau and Mouffe, that we are faced by a simple, one-directional determination, and overdetermination is extremely limited to the field of contingent variation.

Laclau and Mouffe outline instead a different conception of articulation (Freud's symbolic aspect) which results in a structured totality they refer to as "discourse." They reject the distinction between discursive and non-discursive practices. Instead, every object is constituted as an object of discourse. According to Laclau and Mouffe, this "has nothing to do with" the independent existence of real objects external to thought, but is an assertion that objects "constitute themselves" inside discourse. That is, discourse has a material rather than a purely mental character or, rather, "the practice of articulation ... pierce[s] the entire material density of the multifarious institutions, rituals and practices ... discourse is a real force which contributes to the moulding and constitution of social relations" (Laclau and Mouffe 1985: 109–10). This is part of an abandonment of the thought/reality opposition – their position stems from a "post-Marxism" profoundly influenced by poststructural and postmodern ideas (chapter 6).

A Geographical Critique of Structural Marxism

The late 1970s and early 1980s also saw a sudden escalation in the ongoing dialogue between humanistic and Marxist geography. From the side of humanistic geography came a critique apparently of structural Marxism, but actually of the whole Marxist enterprise in geography and social science, written by James Duncan and David Ley, professors of geography at Syracuse University and the University of British Columbia respectively. Duncan and Ley (1982: 30) critically assess the "ambitious radical tradition [in human geography] derived from structural Marxism." Their critique finds Marxian analysis in geography inclined towards mystification and theoretical stasis; indeed, they think that the Marxist movement in geography foundered when theory encountered geographical circumstance. For them, this impasse derives from a philosophy of holism, totality, and essence, derived originally from Hegel, but present too in Marx, which frustrates empirical analysis. Their critical focus, therefore, is on the "problematic relations" between philosophical holism and geographical reality.

Holism argues that large-scale social events are "emergent and unrelated to the conscious actions of the individuals who participate in them" (Duncan and Ley 1982: 32). Typically, they say, a supra-individual entity with its own logic or properties is portrayed as active, while human individuals are its passive victims. Of many kinds of holism, organicism has most adherents. Organicist holism essentially maintains that the whole is more than the sum of the dynamically related parts it determines. For Duncan and Ley, by comparison, wholes are not active forces, having no inner logic or causal properties of their own, and, while individuals are not free to transcend their social context, neither are they passive agents of such larger entities as the logic of capitalism or the mode of production.

For Duncan and Ley, holistic Marxism and Marxist geography emerged from Hegel's idealist notions of *Geist* (World Spirit) and Reason. Hegel, they maintain, considered *Geist* a comprehensive, vital force acting in, and through, all objects in the world, especially human beings: using the Aristotelian distinction between efficient and formal causation, Hegel argued that *Geist* is the formal cause and humans the efficient cause through which *Geist* drives towards its own rational ends. Marx, they say, apparently broke with Hegel over the question of idealism (i.e. *Geist* as original cause) yet frequently lapsed into transcendental idealist thinking, as when entities such as "capital" are endowed with an inexorable, mysterious power over people: in Marx, then, World Spirit was simply replaced by Capitalism in a still-holist analysis. For Duncan and Ley, Marx retained from Hegel a teleological perspective on history, with humans moving inexorably through stages until they reach perfection in communist society. For Duncan and Ley, Althusser and the French structural Marxists further developed the Hegelian view while claiming to be doing the opposite: Althusser's "structures" are as transcendental as Hegel's *Geist*. And finally, in explicitly supporting the holistic claims of structural Marxism, many Marxist geographers preserve this link with Hegelian idealism, as can be seen from their language, replete with terms like totality, wholes, and parts.

For Duncan and Ley (1982: 35–6), holism usually involves reification (the "fallacy by which mental constructions or abstractions are seen as having substance and causal efficacy"), which takes on organismic (living) qualities – for example, capitalism "needing" to multiply, modes of production "writing" history, etc. Such reification obscures the underlying processes by which the actions of individuals produce structural conditions; in addition, other important explanatory factors are precluded from the analysis. Reified categories have a purpose, or telos, in their sets of internal laws, with people as means of implementing the dictates of a structural telos according to a "black-box" stimulus–response model which relies on ideology as main mode of habituation. Here, Marxist geographers are said, by Duncan and Ley, to support an over-socialized view of humans and have a diminished concept of consciousness, or no concept at all: Marxism's unwillingness to deal with empirical questions of the relations between consciousness and structure stems from the ontological status attributed to structures. Duncan and Ley criticize what they see as the strong connections between Marxism and Parsons' structural functionalism in terms of the tautological nature of functional explanation (in which functions exist because they are functional) and the teleological nature of these functional explanations (which imply some systemic rationality guiding events towards a preordained goal). This furthers Duncan and Ley's (1982: 44) view that "the philosophy of structural Marxism is . . . a mere verbal transformation of Hegel's claim that the Idea guides the course of history."

The errors of an underlying holistic philosophy are said, by Duncan and Ley, to be transmitted into Marxist political-economic empirical work. There, claims to break with conventional social science (often by theorists previously trained in positivistic geography) turn out to be less than complete; and a further claim to a universal set of insights is not only invalid, but is made at the cost of economic reductionism. The pre-eminence of a priori theoretical categories in structuralist methodology leads to ossification (hardening), so that categories (like class) are either imposed on events or defined imprecisely. This weakness is an instance of a more general tension between structural theory and empirical investigation in which, lacking openness to historical phenomena, the theoretician uses historical reality only to illustrate theory. Such shortcomings become critical when theory makes claims of practical or political efficacy, while additionally ideas are granted privileged status over empirical circumstances. In structural Marxist geography, pronouncements of objectivity obscure the fact that theories may be subject to political rather than scientific validation – that is, theories are justified merely because they produce social change of a certain kind.

For Duncan and Ley (1982: 55–6), therefore, the integrity of structural Marxism is predicated on "theoretical overspecification" while its holistic arguments are characterized by "determinacy and closure." The thesis of structural Marxism can be sustained only through mystification and the neglect of empirical study, for attention to historical or geographical circumstances might challenge the integrity of theory. The intention behind structural Marxism is less explanation of the real world and more the preservation of an abstract model – "the fundamental objective then becomes idealistic, the defense of the mental categories of the author" (Duncan and Ley 1982: 55).

God in *Geist*

Clearly, this was a sophisticated, well-argued critique, qualitatively different from complaints about "all this Marxism ruining geography as we knew it" by the old guard of the discipline, exactly because these critics turned on the very radical tradition that had nurtured their social-theoretic argumentative abilities. The immediately published replies to the Duncan and Ley bombshell were muted and overly concessionary. Thus, Chouinard and Fincher (1983) found that Duncan and Ley had failed to make a convincing critique of Marxist geographical work, mainly because a variety of approaches had developed in Marxist research, many of which were neither excessively structural, as with Althusser's theoreticism, nor voluntaristic, in the sense of historian Thompson's extreme disavowal of structural Marxist theory. But this reply only conceded the central ground of the Duncan and Ley critique – that is, its characterization of structuralism as telos. Instead, let us give some elements of another reply.

Duncan and Ley present a certain "reading" of structural and Marxist ideas which might fruitfully be compared with the presentations in the previous two chapters of this book. Compare, for example, Duncan and Ley's version of holism with Ollman's ontology of internal relations. Far from seeing totalities as active creators of their dependent parts, in a simple update of Hegel, the internal relations thesis places emphasis instead on the active nature of individual elements – the human's capacity for creative labor, for example – integrated through relations into totalities which shift and change with movements of the parts. Similarly, Duncan and Ley interpret Althusser as saying that an overwhelming unitary structural force (mode of production) makes people correspond with its "will" in an analysis which unwittingly continues Hegel's idealist theory of *Geist* or spirit. Yet what Althusser really says is that structures are overdetermined by multiple interacting forces, including classes struggling against each other, in a system which is not random but, in the last instance, economically determined. Essentially then, the Marxist reply is that Duncan and Ley engage in caricature assassination, criticizing not structural Marxism but an Hegelian figment of their own imaginations.

Commenting on this, Peet (1989b) found that Duncan and Ley take one aspect of Marxism, the tendency to theorize in systemic ways, and exaggerate it beyond all proportion. Marx's connections with Hegel are misinterpreted because the fundamental difference between materialist and idealist dialectics cannot be known by Duncan and Ley, who themselves are (religious) idealists. In a materialist (and therefore atheist) dialectics, there can be no end point latent in the movement of history, for there is no grand force directing history, but only struggles and interactions among factors, institutions, and agents. The religious mystic, by comparison, the fundamentalist Christian for whom "faith" in God is substituted for empirical facts, finds such a force directing history, believing that there is an end point already decided by God's intent. The religious mind is inherently prone to finding teleologies where none exist: for that is the very nature of religious understanding, its methodology, so to speak. Archetypically exemplifying religious mysticism, in an earlier article Ley (1974: 67, 71) found the urban landscape "reflective of a greater truth, a deeper structure" revealed by evangelical Christian analysis to be "the evil of the city, but more fundamentally the evil of man. The analysis is timeless, and this is the fundamental structure, the bottom-most level of explanation for the urban alienations." In Ley's mythical analysis, historical events result from the contest between Good and Evil, deified as God and the Devil (the one letter difference in both sets of words being no accident), with the faithful believing that Good (God) will eventually prevail over Evil (Devil). The religious mind finds mysterious intentions prevailing despite the contrary wishes of agents. With minds infested by ghostly, spiritual imaginaries, Duncan and Ley fundamentally misunderstand structural Marxism. Hence, their statements that Marx retained the essence of *Geist* while believing he was criticizing that notion literally out of existence; their finding Althusser developing the Hegelian elements in Marx while claiming to despise them; and so on, in an argument reminiscent of Hegel's "cunning of Reason" (restated, "God moves in mysterious ways"). In other words, Duncan and Ley confuse their own (religiously and mystically based) idealist misreading of concepts like holism and determination with a structural Marxism which in reality is overdeterminist, materialist (i.e. atheist), dialectical, and non-teleological. Duncan and Ley merely criticize their own simplistic, religious, mystical misunderstanding (Peet 1989b).

Nevertheless, the Duncan–Ley critique, read superficially (i.e. positively), had sufficient content that it contributed to the fragmentation of the Marxist project – indeed, undercut the entire radical project in geography. For the critique came at a time when Marxism was being questioned for conservative political reasons; this coincided, as external critiques often do, with internal disarray over Althusser and structuralism (e.g. the Thompson–Anderson debate). As the 1970s turned into the 1980s, criticisms of structuralism in the Anglo-American intellectual world mainly concerned the efficacy of human agency in the face of structural necessity (chapter 5). In France, the critique of structuralism led more in the direction of poststructuralist and postmodern notions (chapter 6).

Conclusion

What then is this structuralist approach? Structuralism attempts to build a science of human existence by delimiting and ordering its components. It accepts the basic notion of "determination," meaning that the elements and events of life are linked by discernible, knowable causal relations, but is dissatisfied with: unicausal explanations, in which prior change in a single cause triggers change in an effect; and with mechanical versions of causality, in which the linkages between causes and effects are direct and automatic. Instead, historico-geographical events are "overdetermined" by multiple "causes" (i.e. webs of related elements) to which they are directly and indirectly related – "indirect" in the sense of relations passing through several mediations. Yet structuralism does not understand multiple, indirect, and interdependent causality as chaotic, random, or unique (i.e. always structurally different) – there are still structures to existence which exert pressures, even if the particular form of these pressures varies between cases.

Structuralism and Necessity

For many theorists, Marxism is inherently structural; "structure" is an order of necessity; and necessity is interpreted in reproductive terms; in the end, "necessity" is that set of social practices performed for the sake of human survival. Marxism is conceived as a science for the emancipation of the working class, often by theorists from working-class backgrounds, who know well the press of necessity on human actions. Academic critics from middle-class backgrounds, now safely established in prestigious professions, tend to forget that the vast majority of the world's people live in circumstances where economic necessity impinges on every decision and action, where the "last instance" of economic determination is always directly present in the first outcome of how to eat today – hence, critics of Marxism have the liberty to call reproductive necessity a "biological metaphor" (Barnes 1992) when there is nothing "metaphorical" about it. (Try telling a hungry child her belly pains are only metaphorical!)

However, Althusserian structuralism theorizes Marxism not as the constant presence of the compulsion of necessity in a vertical (depth) analysis moving from nature through production to consciousness, but more like linguistic structuralism, as a horizontal analysis of interdependencies and pressures. That is, economy (social relations and productive activity) determines the necessary combinations of the various aspects of the social totality, gives these orders of priority, in social and cultural forms characteristic of each historical era or geographical circumstance. In other words, structuralism attempts a complex, dialectical, overdeterministic, scientific theory of social totalities and their dynamics and instances. Let it be admitted that, for structuralists, science (conceptualized structurally rather than empirically) takes the place of religion, in the sense that explanation gives meaning to life activities (such as politics) rather than just representing them formally. In the critical scientific attitude, exactly because the causes of action are knowable (i.e. do not derive from god, spirit, energy, or random chaos), people are responsible for their actions (exactly as Sartre said), and societies (especially their elites) are accountable for what they have done and show every sign of continuing to do. From this we can see that structuralism's great mistake lay in pronouncing the death of the human subject, rather than its ongoing life in a structured context, a mistake copied by many poststructuralist theorists (chapter 6). This overly dramatic pronouncement has to be seen, in terms of the history of dominant ideas in social philosophy, as an overreaction to the dominance of existentialism in postwar leftist intellectual circles. Instead, structuralism is at its best when human agency is placed in the context of social conditions. People are responsible for changing the structures which create them.

Structure and Territory

Structuralism produced a variant of Marxist geography with distinct characteristics. Just as Althusserian structuralism became (overly) engrossed in working out the relations between the aspects of existence in theoretical terms of the instances and levels of modes of production, structural Marxist geography emphasized the imprinting of these aspects and instances within a space too often conceived as passive surface. The intention behind this was to create a science of the making and changing of space; that is, understanding the structural order of the forces and relations which impinge on space – not how economy is reflected in space, but how economy arranges the political, cultural, and social organization of space or, in a more sophisticated statement, how economy is its spatial instances. Hence, each instance of a social totality shapes space in a certain way, while instances combined by economy into specific arrangements articulate overall spatial patterns (regions, cities, landscapes). This theorization enables a careful, specific analysis of territorial structures or spatialities, the structuralist terms for spatial ensembles corresponding to social formations.

It was probably the case that such a science of space was possible only because the pronouncement of the "death of the subject" enabled a high level of theoretical abstraction. Yet it is true also that this kind of scientific abstraction sometimes gave structuralist work a quality of unreality, as though the contents of space are laid down by driverless social machines passing over it, like a road-laying machine only with whole landscapes rather than just tarmac left behind! Also, the "return effects" (itself a clumsy term) of space on society are minimal and mechanical in some structuralist approaches. Basically, the approach lacks most the active mediation of human agency, people as individuals and organized by social relations into families, classes, institutions, and other groupings, who are formed by space and recreate it anew.

Neo-structuralist regulation theory responds to this by positing the structural question at the more immediate (institutional) level. Regulationist geography then continues specification by outlining the spatial forms of regimes of accumulation and modes of regulation and, more importantly, seeing contradiction as intensely, increasingly geographical. Structural Marxism, in its pure Althusserian form, was short-lived in geography and the environmental and spatial sciences; yet it was highly productive of insights into the social creation of space; it left its mark in numerous neo- and quasi-structuralist approaches which partly rectified structuralism's numerous problems and which continue to be the leading approaches in much of the economic and even the social and cultural areas of human geography. But structuralism was vulnerable to critique, from existentialism and humanistic positions as we have seen, and from anti-essentialist Marxism as we have also seen, but from structurationism too, various poststructuralisms, and from feminism – these are discussed in the following chapters.

Chapter 5

Structuration, Realism, and Locality Studies

Social theory is still reeling from structuralism's claims to be a true science of the totality of existence. After all, structuralism in many ways was the critical modernist culmination to the Enlightenment's project of using knowledge for the emancipation of humanity. This is hardly the worst of human endeavors. Nor is it a project which has ended. But there definitely was at least a pause, if not a breakdown, in structural–theoretical confidence during the 1970s in France and in the early 1980s in the Anglo-American world, which splintered the structuralist project into post- quasi- and neo-structural fragments. We spend much of the remainder of this book following the trajectories of some of these fragments, spiralling off the disintegration of structuralism like neutrons in an atom smasher. In this chapter, we look at some of the immediate results of this fragmentation. Structuralism's obvious, and often intentional, overstatement of the power of reproductive necessity in forming, rather than framing, the intentions of agents was challenged, even corrected, during debates in the early to middle 1980s on structure, agency, and their synthesis in structuration theory. More complexly, certain problems of Marxist epistemology and ontology were rethought, from the perspective of realism, itself a version of structuralism in that it poses the question of causation in terms of the powers of objects related into structures. In a spatial parallel, structural Marxism's overemphasis on grand systems operating at the global scale brought about re-emphasis on locality studies in geography. In the 1980s, the radical politics which had dominated social theoretical and the more advanced sectors of geographical thought were not abandoned, but were reformulated in diverse theoretical ways. We turn to a consideration of some of these.

Further Arguments within Human Geography

As we have seen, two streams of critical thought dominated human geography in the 1970s: phenomenology, existentialism, and humanistic geography; radicalism, structuralism, and Marxist geography. These were different protests against the prevailing disciplinary orthodoxy which offered competing propositions for alternative approaches. The two positions were critical one of the other, but usually coexisted in what was still a single project. However, the whole notion of a political project collapsed as the "long decade" of the radical 1960s finally came to an end in the late 1970s. This was part of a more general political transformation, a change in mood which eventually brought Ronald Reagan to the United States' presidency and Margaret Thatcher to be British prime minister, among many other signs of a shift to the right in political attitudes. The shift back to conservatism was as dramatic, and perhaps even more far-reaching, than the political radicalization of the 1960s had been. The period since the end of the 1970s has seen dissolution of a coherent radical project, a change in the role of the scholar–activist (from committed member of a project to individual committed primarily to his/her status and reputation), yet also several interrelated but still critical tendencies have emerged. In geography, a sequence of critiques and counter-critiques was initiated, a quest for different modes of understanding began, while a series of disintegrations and temporary reintegrations occurred at the political and philosophical levels which continue to the present day. These changes have produced a vibrant, controversial, and multifaceted geography. Yet this writer mourns the passing of the radical movement in geography.

Structure and Agency in Human Geography

The themes of the debate initiated by E. P. Thompson within Marxist theory, or by Duncan and Ley within geography, reverberate through Anglo-American geography in the 1980s. A key spokesperson for a Thompsonite position in geography is Derek Gregory, then a professor of geography at Cambridge University, and later at the University of British Columbia. Gregory (1981) used the publication of Ley and Samuels's *Humanistic Geography* (1978a) as a vantage point for looking at the resurgence of humanism in modern geography – "resurgence" because many humanistic geographers claim descent from the earlier *geographie humaine* of Vidal de la Blache and, similar to humanism, want a geography distinguished by what Ley (1980) calls "a central and active role for man." Gregory (1981: 2) was critical of such retrospective reconstructions of Vidalian geography. These may stem from a desire for a philosophically sound yet active understanding of human existence beyond positive science, but their neo-romanticism, he thought, invites withdrawal from the world, rather than engagement with it, whereas parallel projects in sociology and social history moved beyond celebrating the existential freedom of the human being to admit the "boundedness" of human life.

Gregory (1981) suggests that the problems raised by humanistic geography can better be stated in terms of the relations between action and structure. Hence, the argument for the centrality of space in human affairs could be translated into the language of agency and the bounded contingency of practical life reconceptualized through structures capable of defining a "matrix of contingency." Marxist humanism already clarifies the relation between human agency and structural transformation which ought to lie at the heart of human geography – for Gregory (1981: 5), "any such geography must restore human beings to their worlds in such a way that they can take part in the collective transformation of their own human geographies." Yet the problem is to find a model which allows autonomy to social consciousness within a context determined, in the final analysis, by social being, one in which history is neither willed not fortuitous, and neither lawed nor illogical.

Gregory wants to bridge humanism and Marxism: the materiality of social life is weakly developed in modern humanism; structuralist versions of Marxism have an attenuated conception of human agency which cannot encompass intentionality and consciousness. Thus, for Gregory, a return to "the original Vidalian prospectus" might indeed be fruitful, not to resurrect the determinism–possibilism debate in geography, but to reconstruct it in explicating the material grounding of practical life which lies at the root of both *genre de vie* and mode of production.

Reconstituting Regional Geography

A similar argument, also pointing to structuration as middle ground between structure and human agency, came from Nigel Thrift, a British geographer at Bristol University, and active in founding the new journal *Society and Space*, which rapidly became the sounding-board for many such ideas in geography. In an article prominently displayed in the first issue of the journal, Thrift (1983) found human geography increasingly involved with social theory. This ranged from the extreme determinism of some structural Marxist approaches, which try to "read off" the specifics of place from the general laws of capitalism, to the extreme voluntarism of most humanistic geography, which hopes to capture the features of place through the specifics of human interaction. For Thrift, the problem of translation between structure and agency provokes four responses: empiricists and humanists find too much ground ceded to structural social theory; certain (mercifully unnamed!) "jumbo Marxists" trumpet that social theory was never meant to be applied to the unique; some human geographers favor a structurationist problematic; and Thrift's own solution, that general knowledge about unique events can be produced through the interpenetration of structurationist concerns and Marxist social theory, specifically the latter's strong notion of determination.

Thrift and Gregory both turn to the theory of structuration, first suggested by Berger and Luckmann (1966), but reaching maturity with Giddens (1979b; 1981), Bhaskar (1979), and Bourdieu (1977) among others. In this view, human agency must be seen contextually as a continuous flow of conduct situated in time and space, yet with the places of activity resulting from institutions (home, work, school) which reflect structure. Thrift outlines some components of an historically specific, non-fragmented contextual theory of human action stressing practical reason and concrete interaction in time and space. This is part of an argument for a reconstructed *regional geography*, building on the traditional, but having theoretical and emancipatory aims. The social activities in a region (which, Thrift says, is lived through, and not in) take place as a continuous "discourse" rooted in shared material-situations, with cultures having both limiting and active capabilities. A reconstituted regional geography might start conventionally with a compositional account of the regional setting, followed by the organization of production, class formation, and structure, the sexual division of labor, and the local form of the state. But since the concern of this new regional geography is to develop a contextual theory of social actions that interpenetrate (and change) the (spatial) context, it is necessary to go further. This means constituting the region as setting for interaction, or in Giddens's (1979b; 1981) terms, a locale: that is, a region provides the constraints and opportunities for action, the base for what is known about the world, and the materials for changing it. In the particular pattern of locales punctuating a landscape, certain locales (home–reproduction or work–production) are dominant because they are main sites of class formation. In Thrift's geographical reformulation, dominant locales structure people's life paths in space and time, place constraints on their interaction possibilities, provide the main arenas of interaction (and thus are sites of conflict), provide the activity structure of daily routines, are major sites of social-ization processes, and so on. Dominant locales are interrelated with other institutional locales, dependent on them for existence, and have counter-institutional aspects which emerge as reactions. A considerable body of work studies the effect of institutional locales on people's life paths. Time–space convergence means that *locales* increasingly do not have to be *local*, but, for Thrift, this does not mean that the region, as a particular intersection of locales, has lost its coherence. The emphasis of this new regional geography, then, is the region as basis for social action.

For Thrift, the analysis of social actions as a discourse through, and in, a region is a goal rather than an achievement, needing a concentrated program of theoretically informed empirical research to back it up. Among the most pressing aspects of a research program are the historical and geographical study of human personality, the availability and penetration of knowledge (Thrift stresses several types of "un-knowing" that can exist in a locale or region), and how sociability, the sense of community or place, promotes or inhibits understanding. Thrift sees these aspects of social action coming together to form the capacity of particular groups to carry on class and other forms of conflict. He therefore finds it possible:

> to conjoin a theory about social action, that of Marx, to the structurationist analysis of social action, utilizing the richness and the importance of what Marx called the "active life process" as it must take place in space and time, but retaining the crucial element of determination. (Thrift 1983: 49)

Lack of such a theory of social action made Marxism emancipatory yet oppressive. But it is increasingly rare for social action in space and time to be treated by social theorists as simply an afterthought or as an autonomous realm of existence.

Time-Geography

Taking this position for a new regional geography, Thrift was profoundly influenced by the time-geography developed in Sweden by Torsten Hagerstrand (Thrift and Parkes 1980). Indeed, Hagerstrand's notion of time-geography was a significant component of the entire structurationist position developed conjointly by sociologists and geographers. We look briefly at two statements of position by Hagerstrand, an early article in 1970 stressing the *time–space constraints* on human activity, and a later version published in 1982 displaying influences from humanistic geography in a more sophisticated conception of the social agent's *purpose*.

In his initial statement, Hagerstrand (1970) criticized models of large aggregates, such as those in regional science, for lack of attention to the micro-level at which the individual acts. For Hagerstrand, macro-generalities should be founded on individuals, identities, and the micro-level, rather than on populations treated as a mass of freely interchangeable particles, people as "dividuals" rather than "individuals," as he puts it. Yet individual biographies are the province of the historian, rather than the geographer, so Hagerstrand proposes that geography explore the twilight zone between biographies and large aggregates. For Hagerstrand, a location has time and space coordinates: the individual existing somewhere now is always tied to being somewhere a moment earlier. Time has critical importance when people and things fit together for functioning in socio-economic systems. Hagerstrand (1970: 10) therefore proposes a kind of socio-economic web model showing "what sorts of web patterns are attainable if the threads in the web (i.e. individuals) may not be stretched beyond agreed levels of 'livability.'" In time–space, the individual has a life path stretching between the points of birth and death. This can be broken into day path, week path, yearly path, etc., and shown graphically. At

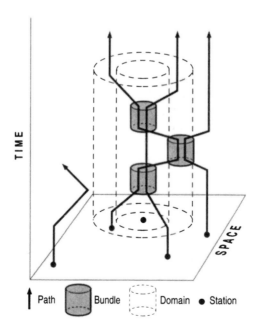

Figure 5.1   Hagerstrand's model of time-geography.
This is a web model (derived from demography) in which space and time are resources drawn on by individuals realizing projects.
Source: Redrawn from Johnston, Gregory, and Smith (1994: 625)

this stage, Hagerstrand simply posits continued survival as the motivation of individuals. Sets of possible actions are restricted by the presence of other people and a maze of cultural and legal rules. Hence, life paths are captured within nets of (spatial–structural) constraints, some imposed by physiological and physical necessity, others by private and common decisions. Even when constraints are formulated generally as absolute rules of behavior they can be given physical shape in terms of location in space, areal extension, and duration in time (figure 5.1).

Hagerstrand proposes three aggregations of constraints on individuals. *Capability constraints* limit the activities of the individual because of his/her biological constitution. Some have predominantly time orientation – sleeping and eating. Others are predominantly distance oriented and enable the time–space of the individual to be divided into a set of concentric tubes or rings of potential accessibility: an inner ring of immediate accessibility; an intermediate ring; and a daily life area around the home base of the individual, which expands with improved transport technology – because time is involved this resembles a prism rather than a tube or ring. Paths inside these daily prisms of potentiality are ruled by *coupling constraints* defining where, and for how long, the individual has to join other people, tools, materials in order to produce, consume, transact – a grouping of several paths is called a "bundle." *Authority constraints* occur in the form of a hierarchy of domains, time–space entities under the control of individuals or groups, with accessibility protected by the exercise of power. The three aggregations of constraint – capability, coupling, and authority – interact in various ways. For Hagerstrand, societies are institutionalized power and authority systems consciously or habitually composing long-term domains and bundles with no particular regard for the individuals entering the system. Under the driving power of technology, domains and bundles change positions in time–space as new units are born and existing ones grow, dwindle, or die. Viewed from a time–space perspective, two diverse systems interact: the predominantly time-directed warp of individual life paths; and the more space-oriented set of imposed constraints of domains and bundles. This interaction links the micro and macro realms (Hagerstrand 1970).

Later, in "Diorama, Path and Project," Hagerstrand (1982) reconceptualizes the concept of path or trajectory to better appreciate continuity in a sequence of situations constrained by physicality. The intentions of the living subject influence these sequences:

> The fact that a human path in the time-geographic notation seems to represent nothing more than a point on the move should not lead us to forget that at its tip – as it were – in the persistent present stands a living body subject, endowed with memories, feelings, knowledge, imagination, and goals – in other words capabilities too rich for any conceivable kind of symbolic representation but decisive for the direction of paths. People are not paths, but they cannot avoid drawing them in space–time. (Hagerstrand 1982: 323–4)

Hagerstrand introduces the (existential–phenomenological) concept of "project" to help geographers rise from the flat map of static patterns and relate events to the strivings for purpose and meaning hidden behind them. Project ties together all the "cuts" in evolving situations an actor must secure to reach a goal. But for Hagerstrand as practical (even positivist) researcher, projects have to be specified as observable practical realizations more than underlying intentions. Hagerstrand stresses also the notion that projects can be seen as "objective constructions of the human mind" (Popper and Eccles 1977): "we are bound to take out projects from the blue-print library more or less in the same way as a pianist picks out ready-made tones from his instrument" (Hagerstrand 1982: 324). Hence, projects are understood as both rooted in the flow of life and as ready-made entities preserved in the storehouse of culture, whereas the situations which projects deal with are not creations of the human mind but emerge from the historically given (created by many actors' projects and naturally caused). For Hagerstrand, there is a reflexive relation between project and situation: a situation is undetermined until a project defines it; yet the situation only permits certain events to occur. Hagerstrand adds another level of reality to the interplay between project and situation: "Nothing can become part of a project or of a situation without first being *there* as an idea, a feeling, an organism or a thing" (Hagerstrand 1982: 325) and these existents are finite in number and have definite locations. Moving projects forward involves holding back competing claims, stepping in gaps, and mobilizing substitutes, and for these strategies location is crucial. In geography, the best approximation of momentary "thereness" and relative location of continuants is landscape; landscape defines the grand situation which conditions the actions involved in fulfilling projects. Landscapes stretch from the interiors of houses to the clouds and include intangibles like rules and regulations: this enriched version of landscape Hagerstrand terms "diorama." Hence, there are paths, projects, and dioramas: in the fine-grained structure of the diorama lies a key to subsequent transformation.

Hagerstrand's time-geography thus contained the two central elements of structure (constraints in spatial form, landscape as conditioning human actions) and agent (the purposeful individual imbued with projects, moving through space–time) theorized in synthetic form (daily, weekly, and life paths) along with a system of graphic notation displaying the innumerable versions of this synthesis. This highly original formulation spatialized the conceptualization of structure and agency in the theory of structuration.

Structuration Theory

Thus, structural Marxism was criticized as overly abstract, a totalizing and deterministic conception of human existence which left little room for the autonomy of consciousness or the actions of individuals. As a result, theoretical attention turned not to humanistic geography, but towards a middle ground of social theory, especially various conceptions of a more active process of structuration which incorporated time and space (Gregory, Thrift, Hagerstrand) into a new kind of regional human geography. Here again, Anglo-American geography derived social theory from French and German philosophy developing in the 1970s. There was a proliferation of concepts and positions each grappling with that huge range of institutions, practices, and experiences lying between determining structures and active individual agency – these ranged from social psychological through sociological to social geographic conceptions. To give some indications of the range of positions, Castoriadis (1991) finds that humans organize their worlds, including their economic worlds, through *social imaginary significations* which invest everything with meaning – this underlies Touraine's (1988) notion of social struggles in the self-production of society. Habermas (1984–7) stresses *communicative action* and rationality, tracing the conflicts between system (the sphere of material reproduction) and lifeworld (the symbolic space of collectively shared background connections). Bourdieu (1977) thinks that *habitus* is "the process of socialization whereby the dominant modes of thought and experience inherent in the social and physical worlds (both of which are symbolically constructed) are internalized by social agents"; habitus is "the mechanism by which meanings of the cosmos are internalized and incorporated," or more simply became "cultivated dispositions to act" (Robbins 1991: 84, 109). There were many other notions, merely in the area of the social and cultural making of the human subject.

In the end, however, there prevailed a version of structuration put forward by Anthony Giddens as the dominant "bridging notion" between structure and agency. Giddens's structuration theory wants to end the "empire-building endeavors" of the imperialisms of subject (the individual) and object (society) by proposing instead that the basic domain of the social science is made up of social practices ordered across space and time. Human social activities, he says, are "recursive" in the sense of being continually recreated by social actors, just as many processes in nature are self-reproducing. But the sort of "knowledgeability" displayed in nature (coded programs) is distant from the cognitive skills of human agents displayed in their (recursive) reproductive actions, and here Giddens (1984: 3) draws on interpretative sociology and, indeed, accepts "a hermeneutic starting point" for his overall position.

Action, Agency, and Power

For Giddens, the recursive ordering of social practices involves a specifically reflexive form of human knowledgeability, "reflexivity" being understood not merely as "self-consciousness" but as the mental monitoring of the flow of social life (i.e. watching and learning from actions). Humans are purposive agents with reasons for acting that can be discursively elaborated (i.e. spoken about, elaborated symbolically). But terms like "purpose" have to be treated with caution since they are often associated with hermeneutic voluntarism and with the isolation of human activity from its time–space contextuality (i.e. the view that people just think, have their own intentions, and then act on them). For Giddens, human action and cognition occur as a *duree*, or continuous flow, and purpose is not separate intention or reason, but rather intentionality is a process, a routine feature of human conduct, the implication being that actors may not have definite goals consciously in mind as they act. However, the reflexive monitoring of action involves rationalization, or the capability of actors to give reasons for their conduct. In Giddens's "stratification model" of the acting self (figure 5.2), reflexive monitoring, rationalization, and the motivation of action are treated as embedded processes. Actors continuously monitor both the flow of their activities, expecting others to do the same, and the social and physical (spatial) contexts of their actions. By rationalization, then, is meant the practical maintenance of a continuing theoretical understanding of the grounds of activity. Motives are somewhat different, supplying overall plans or "projects" (in Schutz's sense of the term), although much day-to-day conduct is not directly motivated. Thus, the phenomenological and ethno-methodological notion of "practical consciousness" is fundamental to structuration theory, whereas this is missing in structuralism. For Giddens (1979a), the line between discursive and practical consciousness is fluctuating and permeable, but there are barriers (repression) between discursive consciousness and the unconscious.

Concepts like these refer to the human agent. But what of agency? The duree of day-to-day life, occurring as a flow of intentional actions, has *unintended consequences*, which systematically feed back as the unacknowledged conditions of further acts (figure 5.2 again); for example, speaking unintentionally reproduces language which limits and enables speaking. Frequently, human agency is defined only in terms of intentions, other forms of behavior being merely reactive responses. For Giddens, *agency* refers to capabilities people have of doing things – agency implies power. Intentionality characterizes acts which agents believe will have a particular outcome, where knowledge is used to achieve this outcome. What is done by an agent is separated from what is intended, as are unintentional doings and the unintended consequences of doings. The unintentional consequences of intentional conduct are vital to the social sciences, but unintended consequences have usually been linked with functional analysis (Merton 1968), which Giddens rejects: in such analysis, unintended consequences ("latent functions" in Merton's terminology) smuggle in "society's reasons" for the existence of a needed practice, whereas for Giddens, actors make things happen, although they can behave in cognizance of what they take to be social needs. The influence of unintended consequences can be analyzed in terms of the cumulation of patterns of unintended consequences initiated by a single event; or as a complex of individual activities in terms of the regularized but unintended consequences of activities in time–space contexts which influence the further conditions of action in the original context.

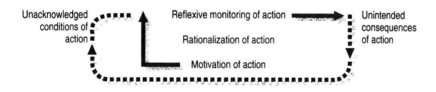

Figure 5.2 Giddens's stratification model of the human agent.
The reflexive monitoring of activity involves the individual and aspects of the social and physical contexts.
Source: Redrawn from Giddens (1984: 5)

This brings Giddens to the connections between action and power. For Giddens, "having no choice" should not be equated with the dissolution of action into reaction, which he associates with objectivism and structural–functional sociology. Action involves power in the sense of transformative capacity – in this sense "power is logically prior to subjectivity" (Giddens 1984: 15). The "duality of structure" in power relations refers to the drawing on and reproduction of resources as structured properties of social systems by knowledgeable agents. For Giddens, structures of domination built into social institutions do not grind out docile individuals who behave automatically, as suggested by objectivist social science; in the "dialectic of control" all forms of dependence offer some resources for the subordinate to influence their superiors.

The Duality of Structure

At the core of Giddens's theory of structuration lie the concepts "structure," "system," and "duality of structure." Explaining these in turn: structure in functionalist writing is some kind of patterning of social relations or phenomena, as in analogies of the skeleton or morphology of an organism – here, structure appears external to human action, as a constraint on free initiative. In structuralist writing of the French school (Lévi-Strauss et al.), by comparison, structure is more interestingly thought of as an intersection of presence and absence, underlying codes being inferred from surface manifestations. For Giddens, structure can best be analyzed as "sets of rules and resources." "Rules" imply "methodological procedures" of social interaction relating to the constitution of meaning on the one hand (signification) and the sanctioning of social conduct on the other (legitimation) – any given social practice involves an overlapping, loosely connected set of such rules. "Resources" refer to the facilities or bases of power to which an agent has access in the course of interaction with others:

> Authoritative resources are capabilities that generate command over persons (life-chances, spatio-temporal positioning, organization and relations between human beings). Allocative resources are capabilities that generate command over material aspects (raw materials, means of production, produced goods). (Cohen 1989: 28)

For Giddens, "structure" has only a "virtual existence" in the reproduced social practices of social systems and memory traces orientating social conduct. By contrast, "systems" have concrete existence as "interconnected or articulated series of institutionalized modes of interaction reproduced in spatially distinct social settings over a determinate period of history" (Cohen 1989: 89). So by the "duality of structure" structuration theory proposes that recursive social practices both draw on structural rules and resources and reconstitute them: "Structure enters simultaneously into the constitution of the agent and social practices, and 'exists' as the generating moments of this constitution" (Giddens 1979b: 5). Structure is what gives systemic form to social practices across time and space. Human interaction involves the communication of meaning, the operation of power (use of resources), and normative modes of sanctioning (including physical violence). In the production/reproduction of interaction, agents draw on corresponding structural elements of social systems: signification (meaning), domination (power), and legitimation (sanctions).

The two "levels" (system and structure) are connected by three structuration "modalities" (figure 5.3). As Gregory (1982: 16) summarizes:

> Giddens argues that relations between actors (that is, interactions) are organized as systems of communication, power and sanction; that they routinely draw upon the semantic rules, resources and moral rules – the interpretative schemes, facilities and norms – made available by structures of signification, domination and legitimation; and that they do so in such a way that their successive and simultaneous engagements necessarily reconstitute these structures.

For example, the use of power involves the application of facilities enabling agents to secure specific outcomes; these facilities can be analyzed as resources which comprise structures of domination. For Giddens, furthermore, institutions are clusters of regularized practices, structured by rules and resources, which are "deeply layered" in time and space (that is, "stretch" through time and space). Institutions can be classified according to the modality central to their structuration.

Giddens theorizes systemic change in a similar manner to Marx in that the structural principles, which operate in relation one with another, also contravene

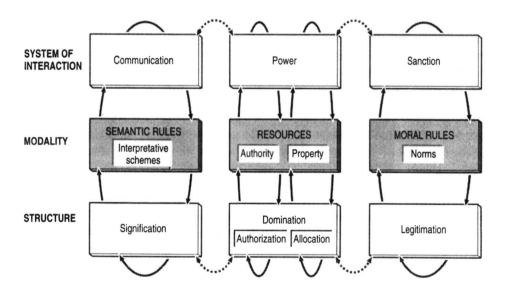

Figure 5.3   The duality of structure in Giddens's ontology.
In replacing the conventional dualism between agency and structure with a "duality" Giddens distinguishes social systems, involving situated activities of human subjects, from agentless structures; these are bound together by rules and resources instituted by knowledgeable, capable subjects.
Source: Redrawn from Johnston, Gregory, and Smith (1994: 600)

each other. Primary contradictions are thus oppositions or disjunctions of structural principles fundamentally involved in the system of reproduction of a society; secondary contradictions are brought about as a result of primary contradictions; and conflict is linked to contradiction with an area of contingency between the two (Giddens 1979b: 141). However, contrary to an "evolutionary reading" of Marx, contradiction can stimulate retrograde movements of historical change. And as well as the basically Marxist notion of "structural contradiction" there is in Giddens a geographic conception of "existential contradiction" in the generic relations between humans and their organic conditions: there is "an antagonism of opposites at the very heart of the human condition, in the sense that life is predicated upon nature, yet is not of nature and is set off against it. Human beings emerge from the 'nothingness' of inorganic nature and disappear back into that alien state of the inorganic" (Giddens 1984: 193).

Time and Space

The appeal of Giddens's structuration theory for geographers came mainly with *Central Problems in Social Theory* (1979b: 202), which proposed that "most forms of social theory have failed to take seriously enough not only the temporality of social conduct but also its spatial attributes." With this, the theory of structuration begins to portray time–space relations as constitutive (i.e. formative) features of social systems. For Giddens (1981: 30–4), the philosophical basis for this view was pioneered by Heidegger's discussion of being and time (also relevant are analyses of time–space developed in post-Newtonian physics). As we saw in chapter 2, for Heidegger (1962), philosophy must return to the question of being, rediscovered through the "primordial horizon" of time. In this sense, being exists in the coming-to-be of presence in time and space (Heidegger's later writings reject the priority given earlier to time). Heidegger thus characterizes being as "presencing." Giddens (1981: 37) similarly sees the movements of individuals through time–space as "processes of presencing/absencing." That is, individuals interact with others who are physically co-present in situated contexts – here Giddens (1984) draws on Merleau-Ponty's (1962) discussion of the human body as the center of action and awareness, and Erving Goffman's (1963; 1972; 1974) themes of the body in situations of co-presence and the primacy of the human face as medium of expression and communication, to explicate elementary categories of human encounters – seriality, positioning, etc.

In showing how the psychological qualities of the agent and the interactions of agents in situations of co-presence relate to the broader aspects of social systems, Giddens turns to the "situatedness" of interaction in time–space. Giddens (1984: 110; 1985) says that a remarkable convergence has occurred between geography and the other social sciences, as a result of which geographers, drawing upon the various established traditions of social theory, made contributions to social thought of "some significance." He has in mind (by this gracious/gratuitous remark) the concept of time-geography developed by Hagerstrand, which stresses the routinized character of daily life connected with the basic features of the human body, its mobility and means of communication, path through the life-cycle, the human's biographical project, and so on. According to Giddens, Hagerstrand (1975) identifies sources of constraint over human activity given by the nature of the body and the physical contexts of activity which provide boundaries limiting behaviour across time–space. However, Giddens (1984: 116–18) expresses reservations about Hagerstrand's time-geography: he thinks that it operates with a naive and defective conception of the human agent; it recapitulates the dualism of action and structure; it focuses on constraint but does not see this also as opportunity; and it has a weakly developed theory of power.

Developing time-geography's ideas in the light of structuration theory involves, for Giddens, reconceptualizing the notion of "place" to mean more than point in space. Giddens (1984: 118) therefore substitutes the term "locale" to refer to the "use of space to provide the settings of interaction," these being essential to specifying the "contextuality" of interaction and the "fixity" underlying institutions. Locales can be designated in terms of their physical properties (natural and human) and the properties specified by their modes of human utilization. Ranging in size from a room in a house to the territory of a nation state, locales are internally regionalized, with regions being critically important as contexts of interaction. For Giddens (1984: 119), regionalization extends beyond localization in space to refer to "the zoning of time–space in relation to routinized social practices." This leads Giddens to classify modes of regionalization (form, character, duration, span), differentiating "front and back" regions, distinguishing centers from peripheries, and so on. The point of all this is to specify a set of spatial categories which correspond to the theory of structuration.

Time–Space and Power

Giddens's more innovative work on space involves connecting the time–space constitution of social systems with the generation of power. The idea basically is that certain types of locale permit a concentration of allocative and authoritative resources which generate power. For Giddens, as opposed to Marx, the concentration of allocative resources (command over means of production) depends on factors creating authoritative resources (command over people). These latter include the possibility of surveillance that various settings allow; the possibility of assembling large numbers of people who do not spend most of their daily activity involved in material production; facilitating the scope and intensity of sanctions (at first in the city, later in the nation state); and the creation of conditions that influence the formation of ideology (Giddens 1985: 13–17). For Giddens (1981: 5), "storage capacity is a fundamental element in the generation of power through the extension of time–space distanciation" – that is, through the "stretching" of societies across time and space. Typically, in this non-Marxist theorization, storage of authoritative resources is considered more important than storage of allocative resources. Giddens's argument essentially is that information-storage devices, like writing, are simultaneously part of the generation of power and means of extending social control in time–space, an extension which involves increasingly elaborate devices of societal integration.

To give some examples: the time–space organization of tribal societies is characterized by a high degree of presence, or presence–availability, with societal
integration depending on immediate interaction – this Giddens (1981: 160) terms the
"fusion of social and system integration." In tribal societies, there are no separate
agencies of either political administration or legal sanctioning. By comparison, class-
divided societies are stretched over longer spans of time and space, are characterized
by distinctions between city and countryside, with the city as locus of the mechanisms producing system integration. And the structural characteristics of class
society (capitalism) are decisively different in terms of time–space distanciation (the
world capitalist economy) and the major importance of surveillance as a pervasive
element in societal interaction, a phenomenon bound up with the formation of the
nation state (Giddens 1987). In essence, this amounts to a power–space theory of
history.

Criticisms of Giddens

This is actually a brief and simple exposition of Giddens's ideas. Giddens's theory is
validly criticized on several grounds (Held and Thompson 1989). His notions of
structure, rules, and resources are found to be vague, while there are similar problems
with the various levels and modalities of structuration – that is, "structure" refers to
that which "gives form and shape to social life, but ... is not itself that form and
shape" (Giddens 1989: 256): so what, therefore, is it? Likewise, Giddens elaborates
Marx's aphorism that "humans make history, but not in circumstances of their own
choosing," yet rejects Marx's materialist conception of history. Marxists defend their
position against Giddens's critique of functionalism, evolutionism, and the class basis
of divisions in capitalist societies (Wright 1989; Jessop 1989). Giddens's geographic
ideas on time–space are criticized by Saunders (1989) in terms of being "added on"
lately to the theory of structuration. Giddens is said to focus on local routine and
thus social stability at the expense of change (Gregory 1989). Giddens is criticized
also for not attending to questions of gender (Murgatroyd 1989). And finally, Thrift
(1985) finds the relationship between structuration theory and empirical
investigation "deeply disappointing" while Gregson (1989: 240) similarly finds
Giddens's theory "lacking the degree of specification required for empirical work."
Even so, structuration theories of the Giddens variety became perhaps the leading
theme in much critical geographic writing in the early to middle 1980s and left their
mark in subsequent theorizations (Gregory and Urry 1985).

From critical appreciations of Giddens's work come a series of research endeavors.
Bruno Werlen, a professor of geography at the University of Zurich, thinks that
"space" does not refer to any specific conception of material objects but is only a
formal, classificatory concept. In *Society, Action and Space*, Werlen (1993) advocates
discarding space as a starting point for geography, and beginning anew with the
perspective of an "action-oriented geography ... that focuses on the embodied
subject, the corporeality of the actor, in the context of specific socio-cultural,
subjective and material conditions." That is, the geographic emphasis should be on
subjective agency as source of action and change, together with the social world

shaping the action which produces it: in this, actions rather than space are constitutive, and "space" only provides a pattern of reference for the entities bearing on actions.

Structurationist Geography

Yet the influence of such ideas on geography is best evaluated through a critical examination of empirical works. Here, we look at two books employing versions of structuration theory. Dereck Gregory's *Regional Transformation* (1982) rejects both the structuralist view of humans as *trager* (bearers of social relations) and Schutz's view of the intentional agent. Gregory turns to E. P. Thompson's view of history as an existential struggle, as "unmastered practice"; rephrasing Thompson in structurationist terms, historical actors display some knowledge of the rules and resources made available by structures which are not mere constraints on action but are essentially involved in the production of social life, while actions in turn reproduce social structures. This opens a space for the return of "conscious knowledgeable agency" whose bounds are not constant but are "beaten out by the changing modalities of 'experience'" through which "structure is transmuted into process" and the subject re-enters history – thus, it is by practice that production is sustained. Gregory (1982: 10) interprets this in structurationist terms to mean that the "production and reproduction of social life is a *skilled* accomplishment, that all actors have some degree of 'penetration' of the rules and resources made available by their societies (even if this is imperfect and impermanent), and that in so far as this is not incidental then the 'curve of knowledgeability' is an indispensable part of an authentic history." In this vein, for Gregory, all geography is historical and the locus of motion, the recurrent intersection of system and structure, is social practice. Gregory's position is that English working-class political consciousness (an essential part of the factory system) developed unevenly and in somewhat different ways under regionally specific transitional circumstances, as a set of responses and formative actions in particular sequences of historical experiences. In criticism, we could say that Gregory does not manage to connect historical experiences with specific elements of emerging working-class consciousness and thus definite forms of agency in the new factory structure coming into existence. The basic bridging device between structured experience and causal agency – structuration theory – proves far more difficult to demonstrate in practice than it is to elaborate in theory.

Somewhat similar arguments recur in Allan Pred's *Place, Practice and Structure*. For Pred (1986), a professor of geography at the University of California at Berkeley, traditional human geography portrays places and regions as little more than frozen local scenes of human activity. For Pred, by comparison, place involves an appropriation of space and nature inseparable from the reproduction and transformation of society; place is characterized by the flux of human practice in time and space. Pred proposes a theoretical synthesis which accounts for the material continuities of people and the natural and human-made objects employed in time–space-specific practices. Participating individuals are regarded as integrated human beings, at once objects and subjects, whose thoughts and actions, experiences and ascriptions of meaning, are constantly "becoming" through involvement in the workings of society. Pred's empirical work is strongest in elucidating the multiple agencies and processes mediating between large-scale processes and local outcomes (in the enclosure movement in the villages of southern Sweden). But the return flow of influences from the local to the global ("what contributes to history"), the practices by which people make not only village life but also world history, is not dealt with in any detail. Forces from elsewhere (the international economy, the state, etc.) are the structural causes of events, while local agency only modifies and perhaps redirects these events. So the "intermeshing" of local with more extensive structuring processes favors, in practice, the global and the national as causal arenas, with the local merely as modifier of broader structural tendencies. In effect, only one spatial aspect of the structurationist dialectic of reproduction is explored, that passing from structure to agent, or from global changes to local transformation. But surely the whole point of Thompson-type Marxism, Giddens's structurationist theory, Gregory's Marxist humanism, or Pred's becoming of place, is to show not just how (global, structural) history makes people, but how (local, active) people make history, albeit under conditions not of their choosing (cf. Pred 1986: 198). If people's lives are determined by global forces, then structuration theory must ask, must demonstrate, where these forces come from – that is, who makes the global forces which make people? Structurationist geography is bound to answer that global forces are accretions of local forces which, as they form into structural complexes, achieve their own consistency and dynamic. In other words, studies of the becoming of places must also show how place-based actions contribute to the becoming of regional, national, and international socio-spatial structures. This is a very tall order indeed! But it is the inescapable consequence of the structurationist-geographic argument. Lacking an answer, the structurationist "approach" remains a theoretical device proven or demonstrated only in part, the less important part, basically the same aspect (global to local) already theorized by structuralism.

Birds in Egg/Eggs in Bird

An alternative conception of "structure and agency" rich in implications for the poststructural/postmodern arguments discussed in chapter 6 came from the Swedish geographer Gunnar Olsson (1980). Here, we follow a reading of Olsson by Philo (1984). As Philo (1984) says, Olsson put down his logical positivist tools in the early 1970s, and began to behave more as poet or jester. At the core of this new endeavor is an investigation into two languages: that of social science associated with a Galilean tradition focusing on the rule-governed external world and translated into geography in a positivist and functionalist science of location; and that of human action associated with an Aristotelian tradition emerging as a focus on the internal worlds of human agents in behavioral and humanistic geography. For Olsson, Galilean–positivist social science pursuing certainty imposes an unrealistic, static, and "thingifying" linguistic straitjacket on its "object matter": Philo extends this to positivistic geography's locational patterns, simple structures of existing objects which thingify agents into dots on maps and lead to over-simplistic assumptions about identities of objects (places for instance). The language of action, shaped by a schema of political reasoning and teleological understanding, is not interrogated with the same level of critique, although many criticize humanistic geography's experiments for failing to provide adequate validation procedures. Olsson's investigations into language center, Philo says, on Wittgenstein's observation that the "limits of my language mean the limits of my world" or Nietzsche's expression that we are destined to dwell in the "prison-house of language" – that is, unable to distinguish between reality and the language used to portray it. Olsson agrees that theorists will always be prisoners of language but thinks that better forms of expression can be found. Olsson begins experiments in search of a new dialectical language, pursuing certainty and ambiguity together "as keys ... that fit the lock of the gates of creativity." For Philo, this leans more towards ambiguity than certainty, hence, turns to poetry and surrealism.

Olsson passionately champions human agency, in particular the individual locked into itself, although defined also in terms of Others which it lacks, with an emphasis also on personal emancipation. For Philo, Olsson's conception of agency and structure are locked in the internal worlds of human agents – in terms of agency as unique individuality, in the case of structure as collectivities or collective unconscious (Jung) – whereas most structure–agency theorists focus on the external world. Philo finds the two approaches (internal/external) to be complementary. There is in Olsson's work a rudimentary version of society–individual relations: this is a hypothetical space where individuals and society *internally* confront one another recursively:

> Olsson ... evidently pictures his "mandela of thought-and-action" as a hypothetical space where thinking and "being" *individual* human agents confront the "collective unconscious," which for him is comprised of "archetypes" (or "deep neurostructures") submerged in the minds of human agents in *collectivities*. Moreover, he equates the "collective unconscious" with his own appreciation of society. In short, therefore, Olsson's "mandela" witnesses the primarily *internal* clashing of his conceptions of agency and structure. (Philo 1984: 223)

Olsson thinks this is a universal schema that tries to capture the fundamental interplay of individual and society. Olsson portrays the "thunderbolt world" of the collective unconscious influencing individual consciousness, and the "wombworld" of individual consciousness influencing the collective unconscious. For Philo, Olsson goes further than time-geographers like Pred or Thrift in that he sees individuals as countering the thunderbolts of certainty emanating from structures with counter-bolts of ambiguity; for Olsson, the thoughts and beings of individual human agents are only partly determined by the collective unconscious. In brief, Olsson complements the more external focus of the structure–agency model with a highly internal focus on the individual–society relation. In his later work, Olsson (1991) strives to escape the "flatland" in which social thought is entrenched to a "spaceland" which allows other truths to be understood about the connections between the abstract (immaterial) and the concrete (material); for Philo (1994), however, Olsson's new conceptual geometry carries problems not so different from those bedevilling spatial science.

Realist Structuration Theory

The central difficulty encountered by empirical geographic studies employing structuration theory, the problem of the making of structures through human agency, is a main preoccupation of realist approaches. Here, we briefly outline one such argument which serves as a comment on the previous discussion and a bridge to the next section. From a realist perspective, Bhaskar (1979) agrees with Marx that societies consist not of individuals but the sum of the relations between them, and that scientific theory should move from the manifest phenomena of social life, as conceptualized in the experiences of social agents, to the essential relations which necessitate these phenomena yet remain hidden from agents. Bhaskar argues against "methodological individualism" – the notion that societies can be explained solely in terms of individuals – on the grounds that human individuals are always social. In Weberian sociology, society–individual relations are conceptualized in terms of the social object being constituted by individuals through intentional, meaningful behaviour. In the Durkheim tradition, societies have a life of their own and coerce individuals. In the Berger model (Berger and Luckmann 1966), society forms the individuals who form society in a continuous dialectical movement – social structure is not characterizable as a thing apart from the human activity producing it, yet once created is encountered by the individual as an alien facticity and a coercive instrumentality. Despite its obvious structurationist appeal, Bhaskar finds this last model misleading: for him, people and society are not related dialectically, as two moments of the same process, but are greatly different kinds of things. For Bhaskar, the fact that society pre-exists the individual suggests a radically different conception of social activity than that typically informing the society–person connection. It suggests an Aristotelian "transformational model" of social activity:

> Society is both the ever-present *condition* (material cause) and the continually reproduced *outcome* of human agency. And praxis is both work, that is conscious *production*, and (normally unconscious) *reproduction* of the conditions of production, that is society. One could refer to the former as the *duality of structure*, and the latter as the *duality of praxis*. (Bhaskar 1979: 43–4)

For Bhaskar, the properties possessed by social forms are fundamentally different from those possessed by individuals: "purposefulness, intentionality and sometimes self-consciousness characterize human actions but not transformations in social structure" (Bhaskar 1979: 44) – that is, people in their conscious activity *unconsciously* reproduce, and occasionally transform, the structures governing their activities. This, for Bhaskar, preserves the status of human agency while dismissing the myth of creation, and allows that necessity in social life operates, in the end, via intentional human activity. For Bhaskar, such a model can sustain a general concept of change and generate a clear criterion of the historical significance of events (i.e.

those leading to transformations in social forms). From it comes a conception of a *non*-alienating society, with the difference (from the present) that people self-consciously transform their social conditions of existence to maximize the possibilities for the exercise of their natural (species) powers.

The basic difference here, between neo-Weberian structuration theory and Marxist realism, is Bhaskar's separation of the duality of structure from the duality of praxis, especially the notion of limitations on human (social) reproductive and transformational activity. We can comment that Bhaskar's notion of intentionality characterizing daily human activity, but not transformations in, or even reproduction of, social structures, gives some indication why most structuration theory remains within a broadly structural problematic. But this means also that it encounters extreme difficulty in showing how agency creates structure. It simply is the case that all forms of structuration theory fail, in the end, when it comes to an adequate theorization of the relations between structures which, once made, constrain but also project human agency, and agents created by structures who act intentionally, reproduce structures with only a partial realization that they are doing so, yet also, occasionally, in conditions of structural crisis, transform the conditions of their existence. The structure–agency relation is a theoretical and (especially!) an empirical problem encountered repeatedly in a series of theories from Marxism to postmodernism. Indeed, it is perhaps the central theoretical issue of our time, redolent with political implications – how can structures be democratically controlled if we do not know where they come from nor how local actions change them?

Realism

The argument presented here is that structuration theory does not solve the structure–agency crisis arising particularly from structuralist understanding. Basic epistemological and ontological questions remain unresolved, and empirical work does not raise important questions of the creation of structures. Searching for clarifying ideas, an increasing number of critical geographers, particularly in Britain, turned to realist philosophy for answers. Realism was often seen as a radical alternative to a "discredited" Althusserian structuralism (e.g. Saunders and Williams 1986).

Scientific Realism

An updated version of the "scientific realism" of the nineteenth century was elaborated during the 1960s and 1970s by the philosopher Rom Harre (1970; 1972; Harre and Secord 1972; Harre and Madden 1975). Harre argues that most philosophers and scientists accept the existence of two kinds of knowledge, facts and theories. Particularly at times of crisis in science, the idea may arise that theories are fictional rather than factual; the search for truth is then abandoned. The ideal theoretical knowledge becomes merely the best fictional tale, the neatest, shortest, and most elegant story. For Harre, the main motive for treating theories in this storytelling way stems from difficulties in determining which theories are true and which false.

Realism, by comparison, accepts that the entities a theory refers to actually exist, or may exist when they are hypothetically postulated, and believes that statements about them might, with great difficulty, be designated true or false ("true" meaning practically adequate rather than completely accurate). When a hypothetical entity is indicated by a (convincing) act of demonstration, that entity may be said to exist. Realists see science as fundamental knowledge of the constitutions and nature of things, from which emerges laws of the behavior of things. Realism has a generative theory of cause; events would not happen without a certain, knowable cause. This theory basically states that things have causal powers, which can be evoked under certain circumstances; things are also interrelated through causal mechanisms. Indeed, the qualities and powers of things should be defined, for scientific purposes, as structural relations among elementary units so that the presence of a certain mode of organization, rather than the character of an individual entity, is preferred as the main form of description and causal explanation. In "microexplanation," the properties and powers of individual things are seen as resulting from their "fine structures" – that is, the dispositions and interactions of their parts. But the characteristics of a group or aggregate are not just additions of these individual properties and powers. "Emergent" properties are to be explained by structural relations and the total ensemble of relations among things, rather than individual characteristics. Thus, in "macroexplanation," by comparison, the nature and structure of the parts of a thing are explained in terms of the characteristics of the whole. For example, in functionalist anthropology social phenomena are explained in terms of the functions they perform in the life of a society. Harre (1970: 163) concludes that there is no "purely objective knowledge" in the sense of a knowledge in which metaphysics and theories of science play no part. The legitimate ideals of objectivity are not achieved by denying the a priori elements in scientific description, but in recognizing, changing, and improving them.

Transcendental Realism

Drawing on this initial formulation, the British philosopher Roy Bhaskar (1978) attempts to resolve what he calls the central paradox in the philosophy of science, that humans in their social activity produce knowledge of things which are not their own creation. The physical and natural "objects of knowledge" (real things and structures, mechanisms and processes, events and possibilities) which do not depend on human activity for their existence or continuation he calls "intransitive," while the artificial objects made into knowledge by the science of the day (antecedently established facts, theories, models, techniques, etc.) are "transitive." In the scientific endeavor, "social products, antecedently established knowledges capable of functioning as the transitive objects of new knowledges, are used to explore the unknown (but knowable) intransitive structure of the world ... science ... is a social activity whose aim is the production of the knowledge of the kinds and ways of acting of independently existing and active things" (Bhaskar 1978: 23–4).

Bhaskar compares this with two previous positions in the philosophy of science. *Classical empiricism* (Hume and his heirs) sees the ultimate objects of knowledge as atomistic events, represented in theory as given facts. In this conception, science is an automatic response to the stimulus of given facts and their conjunctions: science becomes a kind of epiphenomenon of nature. *Transcendental idealism* (Kant and subsequent philosophers) sees knowledge in terms of models, ideals of natural order, etc., artificial constructs which, while they may be independent of particular people, are not independent of human activity in general. The objects of knowledge do not exist independently of human activity or, when there are things that are independent (things in themselves), no scientific knowledge can be obtained. In this philosophy, the natural world becomes a construction of the human mind or, in the modern version, a construction of the scientific community. *Transcendental realism* is a third position advanced by Bhaskar (1978: 25):

> It regards the objects of knowledge as the structures and mechanisms that generate phenomena; and the knowledge as produced in the social activity of science. These objects are neither phenomena (empiricism) nor human constraints imposed upon phenomena (idealism) but real structures which endure and operate independently of our knowledge, our experience and the conditions which allow us access to them. Against empiricism, the objects of knowledge are structures, not events; against idealism, they are intransitive (in the sense defined). On this conception, a constant conjunction of events is no more a necessary than it is a sufficient condition for the operation of a causal law.

To ascribe a law one needs a theory containing a conception of a causal link. At the core of a theory is a picture of the mechanism or structure at work. Some postulated mechanisms can be established as real; they form the objective basis of ascriptions of natural necessity. Real structures (causal mechanisms) exist independently of the actual patterns of events, and are often out of phase with them, while, similarly, actual events occur independently of experiences, and experiences are often out of phase with events. Hence, in transcendental realism the domains of the real, the actual, and the empirical are distinct. Yet the real basis of causal laws are provided by the generative mechanisms of nature and these are nothing more than the ways of acting of things. Hence, causal laws must be analyzed as tendencies, the powers (or liabilities) of a thing which may be exercised without being manifest in any particular outcome. Hence, in Lovering's (1987: 289) terms, this results in transcendental materialist realism: "transcendental in that an analysis is employed to show that if certain phenomena exist certain conditions must precede them; materialist in that these are conditions of the world rather than of some universal mind; and realist in that the world is regarded as stratified such that there is an ontological distinction between causal laws and patterns of events."

In a further argument of particular interest to geography, Bhaskar (1979) asks whether nature and society can be studied in the same way. A naturalist tradition posits that the sciences can be unified in accord with positivist principles, while an anti-naturalist, hermeneutical tradition posits difference in methods grounded in difference in subject matter, with the social sciences elucidating the *meaning* of objects. For Bhaskar, both err in accepting an essentially positive account of the natural sciences phrased in terms of an empiricist ontology. But recent developments in the philosophy of science (especially transcendental realism) permit a reconsideration of the possibility of naturalism – the thesis of an essential unity of method between the natural and social sciences. In both cases, the objects of scientific inquiry are real structures and the method of science, from a transcendental realist view, entails moving from a knowledge of manifest phenomena to the structures that generate them. There are indeed limits to this common naturalism imposed by real differences in the subject matters – hence, social structures (unlike natural structures) do not exist independently of the activities they govern or the agents' conceptions of their activities. Yet, Bhaskar maintains, there is a unity of scientific method in terms of the form taken by social and natural scientific knowledge, the reasoning by which it is produced, and the concepts which theorize its production.

In later writings, Bhaskar (1986; 1989) emphasizes the critical (political) dimension to scientific transcendental realism. Realism, he says, entails a view of the world as structured, differentiated, and changing. It argues for an understanding of the relationship between social structures and human agency based on a transformational conception of social activity – the social world is reproduced or transformed in daily life. All social structures depend on social relations and realism directs attention to these. Paying attention to basic structures is both the explanatory key to understanding social events and the focus of activity aimed at the self-emancipation of exploited and oppressed people: "transforming society towards socialism depends upon knowledge of these underlying structures. The world cannot be rationally changed unless it is adequately interpreted" (Bhaskar 1989: 5).

Realism as Social Scientific Method

These notions form the basis of a leftist critical realism particularly important in British social theory. The crucial work introducing realist philosophy into geographic theory, however, was Andrew Sayer's *Method in Social Science* (1984) – Sayer was a lecturer in social science at Sussex University in England and subsequently at the University of Lancaster. This work tries to resolve, from a realist view, central philosophical issues of abstraction, structure, and causation. Sayer (1984: 80) argues that knowledge must consciously devise methods for "individuating objects, their attributes and relationships." That is, to be practically adequate, science must abstract from the many conditions of an object to focus on those which have significant effect. From the many methods of abstraction Sayer chooses a method similar to that of Marx. That is, abstraction means isolating in thought a one-sided or partial aspect of a concrete object constituted by many aspects, elements, and forces. The idea behind this is to consider each concrete determination abstractly, to form concepts about them, before returning to the concrete armed with a rich array of theoretical understandings. Sayer (1991a: 290–1) later adds that there is a continuum rather than a dichotomy between abstract and concrete, that there are abstract and concrete concepts, that both are different from their real referents, and that concrete objects vary in scale from the very large (multinational corporations) to the small (the corner shop and even more minute phenomena). In any case, abstractions, for Sayer, try to distinguish the essential from a maze of incidental characteristics.

Objects are embedded in relations which Sayer differentiates into external or contingent (the relation between an individual and a "lump of earth" is external in that either can exist without the other) and internal or necessary (as between master and slave, or landlord and tenant, where what an object is depends on the other). Sets of internally related objects or practices Sayer terms "structures." Durable social structures have positions associated with roles independent of the individuals occupying them (figure 5.4); together with associated resources, constraints, or rules, reproduced social structures determine events. Structures may, however, be invisible to commonsense thinking. Similar to Bhaskar, Sayer thinks that while structures (e.g. language) are reproduced only by people's actions (e.g. speech), these rarely have reproductive intention. Yet enduring structures are transformed only through the skilled accomplishments of actors employing practical knowledges – Sayer (1984: 88) finds forms of structuralism in which conditions do the acting (and people are their dupes) to be "dehumanizing social science."

For Sayer, the synchronic notion of abstraction allows only indirect reference to diachronic processes of change. The latter require causal analysis, a contentious area of philosophy. The cause of something is what makes it happen, what produces or determines it. In the realist view, causality is not a relationship between discrete

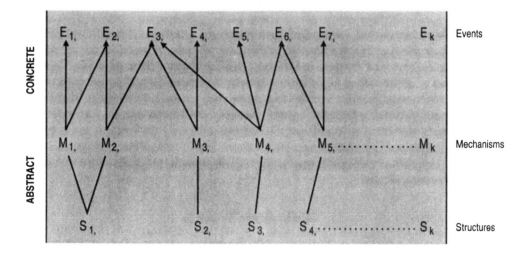

Figure 5.4 Structures, mechanisms, and events in realist theory.
Abstract theory analyses constitutive structures, concrete research looks at the events resulting from their combinations.
Source: Redrawn from Sayer (1984: 107)

causes and effects, is not about explaining patterns of events, but concerns instead the causal powers (or liabilities) of objects, their ways of acting, or mechanisms. The nature of an object and its causal powers are internally (necessarily) related, but whether powers are activated, and their effects when they are, depends on conditions whose configuration is contingent ("conditions" are caused by different mechanisms among objects with their own powers). Hence, the juxtaposition of necessity and contingency is complex. Rephrasing this in terms of abstract and concrete analysis:

> Abstract theory analyses objects in terms of their constitutive structures, as parts of wider structures and in terms of their causal powers. Concrete research looks at what happens when these combine. (Sayer 1984: 107)

Sayer also argues that objects have emergent powers which cannot be reduced to their constituents – hence, the world is stratified as well as differentiated. Emergent powers are created or modified within structures of internally related objects.

In realism, the discovery of empirical regularities (as with positivist research) only begins a series of further questions into causal systems. For regularities to be produced: the object possessing causal power must operate consistently, what Sayer terms the "intrinsic" condition; relations between causal mechanisms and external conditions must be constant, the "extrinsic" condition; hence, no new causal powers develop in the system. Where both conditions are met, a "closed system" produces empirical regularities – for example, experiments in natural science artificially create closed systems. But most systems violate these conditions and are "open." The social sciences deal with such open systems if only because humans interpret conditions, respond, and modify the configuration of a system. Whereas conventionally scientific laws are confirmed statements about empirical regularities, in the realist view laws refer to necessary causal mechanisms and not to the contingent conditions in which mechanisms produce regularities: in realism, causal laws concern necessity and not regularity or, for that matter, prediction. Realist science tries to make "rational abstractions" which isolate significant elements having unity and autonomous force, as with structures. Theories in this view make their strongest claims at the abstract level about internal relations, causal powers, and necessity in the world. By comparison, the form of contingent relations must always remain an empirical question, answered by observing actual cases. The implications for space of this position (on abstract and contingent analyses) are considerable – these are developed in the following section

Realism and Space

Critical realist philosophy self-consciously develops a theory of space and time. As we have seen, Harre sees science as consisting fundamentally of knowledge of the existence of things, their constitutions and natures, from which follow laws of behavior. The totality of possible references to existing things, he says, makes up space – that is, space is the totality of places where things can exist at a given time. If the minimal thing is a point, then space is the totality of points each of which exists at a place. How, Harre asks, is the system of places organized? One can begin with a simple relation of "betweenness." Three things, A, B, and C, mark three points related by the relation of betweenness. But the places can be considered in abstraction from the particular things occupying them. This system of points related by betweenness is space. Sayer (1985: 52) later claims that space in this explanation can exist only in and through objects but is independent of the types of objects present.

Similarly, events and processes do not just happen but take time. Saying that an event is in time means that it is changing, from one state to another. The totality of such changes is time. Time differs from space in that while there can be empty spaces, there cannot be empty time. By referring things to space their relations can be expressed as the relation between places, and by referring things to time their relations can be expressed by reference to some standard process, like a clock. In these ways, structure can be expressed: the spatio-temporal system provides a way of expressing facts of structure in terms of a universal, abstract system of relations.

The generative view of causation (outlined earlier) sees things as having causal powers which can be evoked in suitable circumstances. For Harre, it is an important feature of this concept of causality, and of time and space, that changes in the spatial relations of things can never be causes, but only effects. If some (first) thing is changed when it is moved, we must look to some other (second) thing nearby which could effect the change by coming to be differently related to the first. Likewise, the temporal order is completely immune from causality, changes in time, in this case, being neither causes nor effects.

Realism, Space, Geography

However, the most direct and significant use of realist thought to look at geographic issues, especially the question of space, again comes from the writings of Sayer (1984; 1985). As we have seen, Sayer (1984) carefully outlines his version of a realist methodology before embarking on geographical analysis. To repeat, knowledge must abstract from particular conditions excluding the irrelevant to concentrate on conditions with significant effects. For Sayer (1984: 80), abstraction "isolates in thought a one-sided or partial aspect of an object." Abstract theory can recognize causal powers as necessary properties of objects but can make only conditional statements about what happens in concrete circumstances – to explain these, concrete research is needed of the actual (contingent) conditions in which the causal mechanisms are located.

In an article titled "The Difference that Space Makes," Sayer (1985: 51) uses this distinction to argue that while social theorists have largely been justified in giving space little attention in their abstract theoretical work, the position with regard to concrete research is quite different. The usual discussions of space in geography distinguish an abstract concept, in which space is empty, and a relative concept, in which space exists only where it is constituted by matter. While the absolute view of space is implicit in common sense it is incoherent because what is empty is nothing, and what is nothing cannot be (Blaut 1961; 1962). In the relative concept, space is constituted by matter (objects have spatial extension). For Sayer, the important, but overlooked, position established by Harre is that while space is constituted by objects it is not reducible to them and is independent of the types of object present – this gives the notion of absolute space a certain plausibility. Given that "space as such" is a contentless abstraction, for Sayer, there can be no "science of space" in the positivist geographic tradition. Thus, while it is common to separate space and substance, and speak of space as though it were a thing, for Sayer this is merely shorthand, so that "distance" is really a surrogate for the energy and time spent travelling or exchanging information.

If space cannot be abstracted from its content, can content be abstracted from form to yield an aspatial science? The answer, for Sayer (1984: 132–5; 1985: 50–7), depends on the kind of research, abstract or concrete. Similar conclusions about space were reached by John Urry (1985; 1987), a professor of sociology at Lancaster University. Sociology, he thinks, pays too little attention to the spatial patterning of social practices, a relationship particularly important because major changes in contemporary capitalist relations undermine the coherence of individual societies. Arguing against a "container" view of space (space separate from the objects located within it), Urry sees space as the relations between social objects. Hence, spatial patterns do not interact, only the social objects within them; hence, it is incorrect ("spatially fetishistic") to speak of one region exploiting another, the center exploiting the periphery, and so on. Similarly fetishistic is the notion of spatial structure determining patterns of social organization. Hence, for Urry, it is impossible to develop a general science of the spatial in the sense of a distinct set of laws – space as such has no general effects. Instead, objects have causal powers which may manifest themselves in empirical events depending on relationships with other objects in time–space.

Realism: A Critique

The critical (transcendental) realism which entered geography in the early 1980s makes a careful attempt at elucidating the connections between manifest phenomena and generative structures. It sees social objects with causal powers embedded into structures of relations, and finds the purpose of science to be the discovery and theorization of these fundamental elements of social existence. Yet it also has a sophisticated perspective on the contingent, the specific, and the efficacy of knowledgeable agents. Realism should be appreciated for its politics of emancipation and, most of all, for its attempt (best demonstrated by Sayer's work) to specify with exactitude a methodology which can guide careful social research. Realism appealed particularly to a new school of left-leaning geographers and sociologists, critical of Althusserian versions of structuralism, yet wishing to retain strong notions of necessity as well as contingency and agency, critical too of overly generalized theory and wishing also to buttress abstraction with the careful results of empirical research.

Realism drew an overly critical reaction from some structuralists adhering more closely to what they found to be Marx's own method. For Smith (1987b: 379), realism's initial attempt at codifying Marxist epistemology eventually became a theoretical justification for believing that there can be no general theory of geographical space which belongs instead to the realm of contingent, not necessary discourse: "Realism has become a means of premature closure concerning the geography of capitalism." Similarly, commenting on the "myth" that the abstractions of Marxist theory cannot explain historical specificity nor geographical particularity, Harvey (1987: 373) says:

> Sayer proposes a realist philosophy that combines wide-ranging contingency with an understanding of general processes (judged relevant because inherently connected with the events in question) ... The problem with this superficially attractive method is that there is nothing within it, apart from the judgement of individual researchers, as to what constitutes a special instance to which special processes inhere or as to what contingencies (out of a potentially infinite number) ought to be taken seriously. There is nothing, in short, to guard against the collapse of scientific understandings into a mass of contingencies exhibiting relations and processes special to each unique event.

This argument mischaracterizes critical realism which (as the previous discussion amply illustrates) is an attempt to build a theory of the relations between structural necessity and contingent conditions: it is not primarily a theory of contingency. A better critical review, from the urban sociologist Mark Gottdiener (1987), finds realism contributing to the formation of a precise language about space. Gottdiener agrees with Sayer's basic position that the analysis of space is a matter for concrete rather than abstract research, but claims that realism has no specific theory to guide that work. Realism, Gottdiener says, is an epistemology clarifying thinking about analytical constructs; it does not explicitly provide a theory of social process or socio-spatial organization, although such a theory is often implicitly assumed – hence, Urry (1985) simply grafts realism onto Marxian political economy in a weak analysis which manages to say nothing new about space. Gottdiener (1985; 1987) counterposes his own Marxian theory of space, asserting: first, that one cannot speak of social relations articulating with space because they are about space – Gottdiener finds this similar to the realist position; second, that space is part of the forces of production and thus fundamental to the capitalist process. For Gottdiener, space enters, and is intimately involved with, the relations of production, through commodified land for instance, an area slighted by realists, yet a middle-range level of analysis that could guide empirical research. In general, Gottdiener (1987: 414–15) concludes:

> Realists have little to say about the action of space in the abstract, in keeping with their emphasis on the analysis of open systems through empirical research. Analysis of the concrete, however, tends to be very ordinary and relatively uninformed by theories of social organization or eclectic in the use of such theories. At the deepest level of social structure, however, space belongs to the forces of production. As such it possesses causal powers in the abstract sense, and a theory of the way space as a causal power articulates with other forces of production can help guide concrete research. Such a "middle range" approach improves upon the realist perspective without negating its important conceptual advances.

In other words, Gottdiener establishes an uneasy relationship between a Marxist political economy of space, in which space is fundamental and causal, and realism, where space may be fundamental, depending on the situation, but is not causal. There seems to be some confusion here.

This confusion might be cleared up by examining more closely and critically the basic positions realism establishes about space and research. Critical realism does have certain problems which become practically important for the empirical research favored by this school of thought. These problems center on the distinction realism draws between abstract and concrete research and continue into the related issue of whether space can be theorized abstractly. Realism differentiates between the internal, or necessary, powers of objects, and external, or contingent, conditions, claiming that abstract theory can only consider objects in their constitutive structures, while the contingent is analyzed concretely. As Harvey too briefly alludes, the problem comes in differentiating between the "constitutive structure" of an object (especially the system of relations with other objects which generates the emergent powers of the object) and "contingent conditions" (the system of relations which forms the conditions under which causal powers may or may not be activated). Realism grants to "abstraction" the awesome power of differentiating aspects and conditions of an object which endow causal powers from those which merely activate these powers. Structures of objects are said by realism to definitely exist, but in a realm beyond our (everyday, commonsense) knowledge, a precarious formulation which gives theory the ability to penetrate beneath and beyond the obvious. Yet there is no social ontology of structures (as with Marx's mode of production) to guide the abstraction of the necessary from a web of contingencies – Gottdiener seems to allude to this. Factors constitutive of the powers of an object at one time may be conditional to their exercise at another – for example, the environment of natural phenomena is the origin of social objects (gives them their powers), yet later, many aspects of nature condition the objects they once created. Does this make nature subject to abstract, concrete, or some mixture of abstract–concrete research? There is a need to link realism as philosophy with an historical theory of social structures which can guide abstraction in the different phases of social existence. One might indeed say that realism has a metaphysics of object powers – objects are just made powerful by their fine structures and necessary relations. Exactly when realism needs to be concrete, it is instead metaphysical! Hence, realism's distinction between abstract and concrete research is arbitrary, as Sayer, for example, seems to realize with the (later) notion of a continuum between abstract and concrete. To abstract or not comes down to the theorist's choice.

The problem for geography with the metaphysical arbitrariness of this notion of abstraction is its implication for space and spatial research. In realism, abstract social theory need consider space only as far as the necessary properties of objects are concerned. But realism abstracts from the many qualities of space to produce a one-sided, but unrealistic, definition of it. Space for Harre is a relation of betweenness (or linearity, or convexity, etc.) independent of particular objects. Space for Urry is the relations between social objects. Similarly, space for Sayer is the spatial form of the relations between powerful objects. Realism criticizes positivistic views of abstract space as the empty stretches between things. It appears at some points to argue that space is "constituted by" objects. Yet it too quickly accepts Harre's problematic claim that while space is "constituted by" objects it is "not reducible" to them, but is instead the residual "betweenness" between object positions. This is a precarious argument, fraught with problems, especially in that while objects are said to create space, they subsequently disappear (theoretically) from the space created. The resulting notion of an abstract betweenness, or spatial relations divorced from objects, resembles the positivist view of container space. Employing this definition, realism considers space to be a contingent factor which activates (but does not create or alter) the powers of objects. Yet earth space is never, in reality, just in-betweenness (as with the white space separating letters on a page). It is the stretch of socially altered natural environment between things, in which they are embedded, and of which they are a related part. It is impossible to separate things from the relations in which they exist. Space consists of *objects in their relations across stretches of environment* and not the artificially separated (alienated) relations alone. Environment is made up of matter of various kinds which constitutes objects and gives them their powers: for example, air supplies oxygen to living things which then act. The contingent space of mere betweenness or alienated relations is therefore a figment of the "realist" imagination. It is a left-over (via Harre's scientific but not social conception of space) from the impoverished imagination of positivist science.

Let us therefore pose a counter-view of space more realist than that used by critical realism. Suppose earth space is theorized not as an abstract betweenness but as *what it always really is*, stretches of socially altered natural environment (i.e. assemblages of socio-natural objects) similar to Lefebvre's (1991) social space. Instead of abstracting space from objects we might abstract about objects in, or rather as, space. What difference would this real conception of space make? The powers of objects would not exist separately from the (socio-natural) spaces in which they are embedded. Indeed, following the philosophy of internal relations, outlined in chapter 3, an object is composed from its relations with other objects, *is* its relations with other objects, and as these relations diminish with distance (i.e. greater stretches of environment) space is a factor *formative* of particular causal powers rather than just conditional of their activation. Hence, space as environment of objects would be one essential component, sometimes *the* essential aspect, of what realism calls abstract social theory, for it can be the very origin of an object's powers. To repeat, space does not merely allow independently existing causal powers to act or not; space as environmental objects causes those powers to be there in the first place and is one main source of variations in the powers possessed by objects located in different places. In brief, socio-natural space is a central component of what realism calls abstract research. What a difference *the definition* of space makes!

The argument is that realism encounters problems in the excruciatingly difficult process of elaborating methods of social scientific analysis especially as applied to space. Problems such as those suggested here are not unresolvable, nor do they invalidate the realist approach. They are exactly the kind of difficulty we would expect in formulating definitions to make philosophies methodologically precise (see also Yeung 1997). But these particular issues had a significant effect on realism's view of geography and space, especially on locality studies, a school of empirical research emerging particularly in Britain in the 1980s. On the one hand, theorists of locality find space to be increasingly significant; on the other hand, in persistently appealing to realism as method of analysis, they find space "in itself" (whatever, wherever that is) not to have causal powers. The quandary created by this dichotomy provides an interesting lens through which to read the "locality debate." We enter locality studies through a significant, influential work on the effects of industrial restructuring on British cities and regions by Doreen Massey which argues (surely to the contrary of realism) that "geography matters."

Locality Studies

The themes surveyed in this chapter, structuration and the new regional geography, realism and the contingent analysis of space, the critique of structural Marxism and a renewed emphasis on specificity and the local, resulted in part from an intra-theoretical dynamic of proposal, criticism, and theoretical reformation. Yet this theoretical movement converged also with a growing sense that geography and space were becoming more significant in the sense that global restructuring has powerful, sometimes devastating effects on the old regions of industrial capitalism, a transformative effect on the new industrial countries, and in general that space is a weapon of power. This convergence between theory and reality was particularly strong in Britain. During the 1970s it became increasingly evident that British economy and society were shifting from manufacturing to services, resulting in a permanent increase in unemployment, changes in the occupational structure and so on. These changes took the particular form of a spatial restructuring of economy, occupations, and employment. People's experiences and hence their political beliefs varied greatly from one place to another, the London suburbs versus the North of England for instance. It became politically important to know how national and international changes impacted on different parts of the country. In this context, significant work was conducted on the spatial division of labor and, based on this, a series of "locality studies" inquiring into the effects of economic restructuring on a series of places in Britain (Massey 1991). The key text initiating a new realm of interest and then directly stimulating the locality studies program was written by Doreen Massey, a professor of geography at the Open University in England.

Spatial Divisions of Labor

Massey's earlier critique of neoclassical economics and location theory (see chapter 3), her increasingly critical attitude towards (Althusserian) structural forms of Marxism which she formerly adhered to (Massey 1974), her personal formation of a number of ideas similar to, rather than drawn from, structuration and realism, and her new concern for the local were combined in a series of publications written in the late 1970s and early 1980s, dealing with the changing social and industrial geography of the United Kingdom. In a seminal article in *Capital and Class*, Massey (1978: 116) argued that "the social and economic structure of any given local area will be a complex result of the combination of that area's succession of roles within the series of wider, national and international, spatial divisions of labor." Continuing this theme in *Spatial Divisions of Labour*, Massey (1984) finds the increasing importance of large, multi-plant firms forcing an awareness of spatial organization and the social process of production. This raises the issue of the relations between the social and the spatial, which Massey examines within the Marxist tradition – that is, exploring the geography of industry by interpreting the spatial organization of social relations. Yet she is critical of a (structural) Marxism of predetermined and economistic laws and tendencies which leave little scope for real conflict and struggle, let alone surprise and setback, which dichotomize formal models from empirical description, and which has problems with particularity, unevenness, difference, place, and locality. Massey favors another mode of explanation, with similarities to realism, which recognizes underlying causal processes but does not see these operating in isolation, for precisely their varying combinations produce variety and uniqueness – spatial variations in economic activity are products of many determinations, and differences should not be normalized or treated as mere deviations from a tendency, but understood and appreciated for their effects. In brief, for Massey, both the general and the specific are essential to analysis and action.

Massey employs this perspective in an industrial geography of the spatial organization of production and its effects – for instance industrial organization and the geography of occupational structure – which incorporates not just economic phenomena but social, political, and ideological relations, shifts in national politics, varieties of social forms of capital, gender relations, and so on. Spatial structures of production, or spatial organizations of capitalist relations of production, develop through social, conflictual processes. Hence, the geography of industry and its technical and organizational characteristics are not structurally produced by "capital's requirements" but are objects of social struggles. From these struggles come spatial patternings of society, an overall spatial division of labor, changes which represent new sets of relations between activities in different places, new geographies of social organization, new dimensions of inequality and relations of dominance and dependence.

Massey criticizes traditional geographic methods such as comparing two maps, one representing cause and the other effect, for even clear spatial regularities, she thinks, cannot be assumed to have geographical causes. Stepping back from the geographical means looking at production in terms of wider forces. Yet when this was first attempted Marxist geographers saw capital as mechanistically responding to abstract, immanent tendencies in the mode of production, whereas in fact the way an actor (firm in this case) copes with structural pressures depends on the kinds of capital and labor involved and the battle between them in the context of broader social processes inside and outside the firm (Massey and Meegan 1982). This means conceptualizing the firm, or whatever institution is being analyzed, in a way that enables it to be related to broader structures of society – that is, for Massey, in Marxist terms of social relations between capital and labor. Yet social relations vary greatly from region to region even within capitalism, while there are intra-class and non-class divisions and conflicts as well – hence, analysis must also be spatial and geographical. How then is the structure of capitalist ownership to be defined so that links can be made between different realms, such as politics, investment, and locational decisions? Massey rejects categories like industries (iron and steel for example), place in the economic structure, or phases in the labor process (Fordism etc.), in favor of the organizational structure of capital with its wide range of economic and social characteristics.

Massey's basic argument is that while geographical studies of location have not been related to wider social relations, the academic division of labor has, in return, also harmed economics and sociology which proceed as though society exists on the head of a pin. This is important:

> For geography matters. The fact that processes take place over space, the facts of distance or closeness, of geographical variation between areas, of the individual character and meaning of specific places and regions – all these are essential to the operation of social processes themselves. Just as there are no purely spatial processes, neither are there any non-spatial social processes. Nothing much happens, bar angels dancing, on the head of a pin. (Massey 1984: 52)

By this she does not mean that space alters social processes, which merely reposits separation between space and process, but that social processes are necessarily spatial. So, for example, production change and locational change may be alternative ways capital can achieve the same economic ends:

> It is not, then, just a question of mapping social relations (economic, sociological or whatever) *on to* space. The fact that these relations *occur over* space matters. It is not just that "space is socially constructed" – a fact with which geographers have for a while been coming to terms – but that social processes are constructed over space. (Massey 1984: 56)

Hence, the order of analysis should not be first the aspatial or aggregate and then the distribution over space (i.e. production and then location). Rather, geography should be part of the specification of problems from the beginning. Space conditions the reproduction of social structure. Social relations and structures vary dramatically, not only in terms of the uneven distribution of classes, but also in that the constitution of social groups occurs spatially, in places. For example, place-based relations between work and community form part of structural class capacities (Wright 1978), influence local class characters, and are fundamental parts of social antagonisms. Yet also geography itself may be a self-consciously defining characteristic of people as political subjects – community groups, regional issues, etc.

However, for Massey, spatial patterns can also be conceptualized in terms of social processes. Hence, the geography of employment should not be interpreted in a two-dimensional way, as a (spatial) surface pattern, but as the outcome of socio-economic processes operating over space. The geography of jobs reflects the way production is organized over space in Massey's "spatial structures of production," a term which connotes space not as a passive surface on which social relations are mapped, nor as a negative constraint (as with distance to be crossed), but as an active and integral condition of production. Massey elaborates three (of many possible) forms or archetypes of the spatial organization of production relations: autonomous single-region firms with locationally concentrated spatial structures; headquarters–branch-plant structures employing the "cloning" of multiple branch-plants; and multi-locational companies using part-process spatial structures (figure 5.5). Each is subject to change, each contains great variation. Spatial structures are not simply imposed by structural necessities, like the demands of capital, but are established, reinforced, and changed through political and economic strategies and battles on the parts of managers, workers, and political representatives.

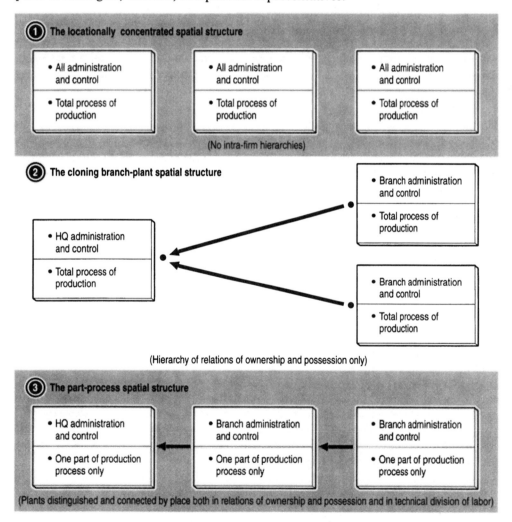

Figure 5.5   Some spatial structures in production.
Three simple cases illustrating how the relations of production can be spatially organized.
Source: Redrawn from Massey (1984: 77)

example?

Why does this matter? Because each (spatial structure) implies a distinct form of geographical differentiation and inequality. Different regions are allocated different bundles of functions (organization, research, production, etc.), with different kinds of interregional relations of dominance and subordination between them. Massey particularly has in mind the infamous "branch-plant economy" subject to external ownership and control (from headquarters regions). But she warns that politically compelling geographical notions like a "loss of local control" or "being at the mercy of external forces" disguise the fact that workers never had control in the first place: "control" lies in managerial response to wider competitive and market forces. Her main point, however, is that each spatial structure of production is associated with a pattern of social differentiation, as with the characteristics of groups performing different functions, this providing a link with regional and local class formations.

For Massey, no two places are alike, and spatial differences matter. Most people still live local lives with consciousnesses formed in distinct places. Place-variety is significantly based on spatially differentiated patterns of production and the resulting geographical variation in social structures and class relations. But local areas rarely bear the marks of only one form of economic structure:

> They are products of long and varied histories. Different economic activities and forms of social organization have come and gone, established their dominance, lingered on, and later died away. Viewed more analytically, and concentrating for the moment on the economic, the structure of local economies can be seen as a product of the combination of "layers," of the successive imposition over the years of new rounds of investment, new forms of activity ... each related to a wider setting. Spatial structures of different kinds can be viewed historically (and very schematically) as emerging in a succession in which each is superimposed upon, and combined with, the effects of spatial structures which came before. (Massey 1984: 117–18)

Each layer brings new economic bases of social organization, new structural capacities, and a new position in a broader geographical division of labor. Yet also the incorporation of a new division of labor into a local area causes changes whose degree and type depend on the existing character of the area, itself the product of a complex history – local areas are not simply passive recipients of changes handed down from a higher level. Also, the layers of history sedimented over time contain cultural, political, and ideological strata, each with its own local specificity. Hence, for Massey, it is time to reinstate regional and local particularities as central foci in geographical thinking, not as a return to "good old-fashioned regional description" but as a way of understanding relations between the general and the particular, specifically how local areas fit into wider schemes of capitalist production. This, for her, is the new regional geography.

The Locality Debate

Massey's work reinvigorated the field of industrial geography, which had lapsed during the 1970s, descending from a previous position of dominant interest in positivistic location theory into a backwater of unending case studies. Massey's ideas had an equally stimulating effect on the study of localities in the context of industrial restructuring: Massey's book was the theoretical inspiration for the entire localities studies project. Massey's notion that a given locality should be investigated in terms of its place within various spatial divisions of labor was the theoretical basis for a "locality study" of Lancaster, in northern England in 1980–1: with portent for the debate to come, this study concluded that the problems of local analysis are "fairly complex," especially how different forms of social experience are sedimented in particular places and how these combine to produce varied outcomes over time (Urry 1986).

Massey was also instrumental in proposing that the Economic and Social Research Council, an organization set up by royal charter in Britain to promote social scientific research, conduct an intensive program of locality studies. Along with two other programs, the Council established the Changing Urban and Regional Systems (CURS) research program, directed by Philip Cooke, a geographer at the University of Wales, to conduct intensive studies (between 1984 and 1987) of localities with differing experiences of national and international change. The objectives were to explore the impact of economic restructuring at the national and local levels and to assess central and local government policies dealing with these processes. But the CURS research also looked at the conceptual status of the idea of "locality" in terms of a whole range of social scientific research (Cooke 1989a), and it is this latter aspect that we emphasize here.

Given that people's lives are mainly circumscribed by the localities in which they live and work, the CURS project asks whether local people can influence the fate of these places when their destinies are increasingly controlled by global forces. In trying to answer this, the CURS research looks at how seven different localities in Britain cope with long-term industrial decline or rapid economic change. This raises the issue of the meaning of the term "locality." Giddens's cognate concept of locale (space as providing the setting of social interaction) is found by Cooke to be loose, unspecific, and too passive a term (as only the context for action rather than a constituting element in it). A better conceptualization (Savage et al. 1987) sees localities as products of the interactions of supra-local structures. But, for Cooke, this too has problems in that it reduces locality to an outcome of structural determinations and has a blind spot with respect to the potentially effective power of the active practices of local people. Cooke's (1986; 1989a) eventual position is that such initiatives are illustrations of local mobilizations by individuals and groups taking advantage of their proactive capacities, the rights that come with citizenship in the modern nation state. As the space in which people conduct their lives, locality is the base for much individual and social mobilization which activates, extends, and defends citizen rights, not only in the economic sphere, but more generally in cultural, economic, and social life. Subjects can exercise their capacity for proactivity by making effective interventions within and beyond the base provided by locality. However, for Cooke, a significant measure of the context for exercising local proactivity is provided by structural factors defining the composition of locality (hence the divisions in Britain between the North and West, and London and its suburbs); variations between similarly endowed localities can be understood in terms of the interactions between external and internal processes spurred, in capitalist societies, by the imperatives of collective and individual competition and the quest for innovation. Hence, for Cooke, the stress of this work is not on localities as recipients of fortune or fate from above, but localities as actively involved in their own transformation, although not necessarily as masters of their own destinies. "Localities are not simply places or even communities: they are the sum of social energy and agency resulting from the clustering of diverse individuals, groups and social interests in space. They are not passive or residual but, in varying ways and degrees, centres of collective consciousness. They are bases for intervention in the internal workings of not only individual and collective daily lives but also events on a broader canvas affecting local interests" (Cooke 1989a: 296).

Clearly, this is an innovative statement which incorporates the promise, rather than the empirical reality, of structurationist-type locality theory into the quest for control over local destiny in a globalizing environment. Such a position did not go uncontested. Indeed, a debate on locality erupted even as the CURS project was being carried out. This debate, which extended over a five-year period in the late 1980s, centered on two key issues: the turn towards empirical research signified by the study of a series of places undergoing restructuring ("empiricism"); and the thorny question of the difference space makes (the locality issue more directly).

In terms mainly of the first issue, locality studies were criticized from the beginning by Marxist theorists of urban and regional restructuring. For Neil Smith (1987a), the main problem for studies of industrial restructuring is to link Marxist theory, which gives an explanation of the general outcomes of historical change, with the specifics of changing patterns on the ground. The starting point for such work is usually Marxist theory, with empirical patterns of urban and regional change being selectively analyzed to support or illustrate theory. But a critique of Marxism, emphasizing its supposed conceptual rigidity, more specifically its overly structural perspective on social change, shifts the primary analytical focus to empirical research in the study of localities: hence, the CURS program. This, for Smith, walks a knife-edge path between the abyss of abstract theory and the chasm of empiricism, between structure and agency, and between other polarized excesses. For Smith, the purpose of the CURS initiative, to look at the complex effects of international restructuring on localities, contains the evident danger of yielding a morass of statistical information about local areas in and of themselves. Smith finds the view that complexity defies generalization tending towards a local form of empiricism which repeats the mistakes of an earlier generation of geographers (the examination of places for their own sakes). A second related concern for Smith involves the question of scale, basically the issue of choosing localities which are meaningful (e.g. an entire urban area versus a sector of a larger urban mass). Transformations in the scale of economic activity alter the scale at which regions are constituted; yet an adequate language or theory of the development of geographic scale does not exist. More generally, these criticisms are comments on the retreat from Marxist theory and the rediscovery of the uniqueness of place. He finds structurationist attempts to incorporate space equally disappointing: "Structuration has functioned as an elaborate theoretical edifice legitimating the focus on individual and institutional agents and local causes, albeit situated in their social context" (Smith 1987a: 66). Smith does not advocate a return to abstract Marxist theory, agreeing that empirical research has much to offer, but appeals against going too far in the opposite (local, empirical) direction, foreclosing the possibility of a theoretical middle ground. Elsewhere, Smith (1987b: 380-1) calls the Massey–Cooke position a "virtual stampede back to the unique and up the 'cul-de-sac of complexity,'" and locality research a limiting localism, precisely what is not needed in a racist society – he thinks that an "ideological resistance" to theorizing is crippling in a global context. For Smith, localities research ought not to be localist, but suffused with global implications.

In a reply to Smith, Cooke (1987) found researchers disaffected by structural Marxism, in particular its tendency to discourage empirical testing in favor of illuminating theoretical insights. This led to an interest in industrial restructuring as part of a desire to further knowledge rather than reconfirm existing theory – hence, the CURS initiative on localities, which deploys theory diagnostically rather than dogmatically. Cooke wants geography to develop its own theories by analyzing its own object of interest, which he specifies as unequal development across space. The empirical research undertaken by CURS is not a case of throwing information into a "statistical casserole and waiting for tasty morsels to materialise from the resulting mess" (Cooke 1987: 74), appetizing though this may sound, but involves interrogating the local through "master concepts" (e.g. the theory of economic restructuring) that have explanatory intent. In the process of interrogation, a new thought on restructuring may emerge – for example its dependence on the particular characteristics of specific places.

How might specifically derived information be more generally theorized? One approach (Williams 1981) is to provisionally extend the content of locally derived knowledge beyond its unique sources. Another is "clinical inference" (Geertz 1973) – that is, taking a theoretical advance from one subfield and applying it to another; for Cooke, this means generalizing not across but within cases, an approach relevant to locality studies. That is, locality research might generalize within cases and compare these with generalizations drawn within other cases, adding to existing theoretical constructions addressing processes operating on an inter-case basis. Thus, in terms of the scale problem raised by Smith, Cooke argues that some processes are primarily local, others organized internationally – hence, an understanding of "objective scale distinctions" contributes to geographic theory.

The "locality debate," as it came to be called, was carried into a second phase, dealing more interestingly with "the difference space makes," by an article authored by Simon Duncan and Mike Savage (1989). This challenged the basic view underlying locality studies, the position that "space matters," from a realist perspective. For Duncan and Savage (1989: 179), social theory's renewed stress on the importance of spatial variations has a problem: "space does not actually exist in the sense of being an object that can have effects on other objects; in other words, spatial determinism is an incorrect mode of explanation." How then, Duncan and Savage ask, is it possible to reconcile two crucial observations: that spatial variations matter, but space itself does nothing? This leads them into a pretty complex analytical schema, drawn mainly from realist philosophy and methodology, which tries to allow a recognition of the importance of spatial patterning without regarding space as a thing with causal powers. Arguing that space "makes a difference, although it does not determine," Duncan and Savage (1989: 194) see locality as a mediating concept in empirical research: social phenomena vary because places (localities) are different. But locality is a confused concept, taken as self-evident, remaining unlinked with spatial variation. Also, the local is confused with the concrete or particular, yet "concrete" in realist terms refers to level of analysis rather than spatial scale. Hence, the concern emerging in the 1980s for more concrete and empirically based research (in response to structuralism) does not necessarily entail the study of localities, nor does the study of particular places mean atheoretical research. Duncan and Savage set out to remedy these neglects.

For these authors, a long road separates a general recognition of the spatiality of social life from the use of specific spatial concepts such as locality. Duncan and Savage want to specify how space affects social processes in a way that avoids the terminology of locality. They adopt a relativist view of space in which things create spatial relations between themselves; absolute space does not exist, nor therefore can it have independent effects. Yet for them the argument does not follow that spatial variation is unimportant – social relations take place in a spatial arena and institutions develop spatial patterns which achieve physical fixity (the built environment, for example). Relations between social objects in space ("spatial relations") take a variety of forms. These cannot be predicted from abstract analyses of social institutions, but may (contingently) affect how an institution actually works. In this realist formulation, "contingency" does not signify lack of importance. It says only that spatial effects cannot be deduced at the abstract level but only by empirical, concrete research. Duncan and Savage catalogue neglected effects of spatial relations – spatial boundary effects and the uneven development of social institutions – the latter seen as "caused by the routine workings of the institutions of capitalism" and in this case, they add, abstract research does need to consider the uneven development mechanism of various social processes.

What do these arguments about space entail for locality research? According to Duncan and Savage, locality is operationalized in two ways: the concept of locale; and the definition of local labor markets. They find Giddens's concept of locale nebulous. Giddens does not, for them, specify how a setting actually determines interaction or influences human action, nor does he discuss the relevant boundaries specifying the size or scale of a locale. By contrast, theorizing locality in terms of local labor markets (e.g. Urry 1986) appears to solve the boundary problem (in that a labor market can be specified as an urban center and its commuting field) and links locality into wider social processes (production, labor, etc.). Yet there remains a basic problem: for Duncan and Savage, there is no such thing as a local labor market, but only a series of segmented labor markets each with its own spatial boundary. Hence, for Duncan and Savage, the concept of locality cannot be used in the sense of local labor markets. Indeed, they find locality difficult to define as a concept at all. It might even be dangerous, in that implicit notions of spatial determinism are smuggled into urban and regional studies; better therefore to use terms like case study area or, more simply, spatial variation (Duncan 1989). In particular, they find Cooke's notion of the proactivity of localities spatially deterministic in that it is people who act, not localities. Cooke's related notion of citizenship fails, for Duncan and Savage, in that birth within the boundaries of a nation state confers citizenship and, in any case, citizenship is a weak basis for seeing locality as a basic social process. In other words, they find no grounds for agreeing with Cooke that locality is a socio-spatial construct around which gathers significant social dynamism driving the development of modern society. Instead, they think explanations should construct abstractions "appropriate to the causal chain under examination, including spatial specifications if and when relevant," but that it is not appropriate "to base explanation or abstraction on spatial differentiation ... locality is no longer needed as a conceptual gap-filler because the role of spatial variation is now better understood" (Duncan and Savage 1989: 203).

Cooke's (1989b) reply to Duncan and Savage explores the genealogy of their position in an "aspatial structural determinism" and a sociological antipathy towards geographical theorization found in most extreme form in the work of a collaborator of Duncan and Savage, the British urban sociologist Peter Saunders. (This argues against the importance granted to space by Giddens's structuration theory, agrees with Urry that space in itself has no general effects, and concludes that urban sociology needs freeing from the "anachronistic, restrictive and ultimately futile preoccupation with spatial forms which ... choke[s] new theoretical initiatives" – Saunders 1985: 86.) Cooke finds Duncan and Savage's spatial variation, case study, and similar "place" alternatives to locality lacking precision and defends the notion of local labor markets. Cooke interprets Duncan and Savage's argument on space as saying that while spatial variation matters socially, it stems from exogenous "top-down" structural forces which refuse to allow scope for "bottom-up" influences except, perhaps, as secondary effects. Instead, for Cooke, citizens organizing around locality (local trade unions, business organizations, chambers of commerce, etc.) are an alternative base of collective identification to the more widely recognized nation state. In general, Cooke maintains a guarded sympathy with the realist philosophy underlying Duncan and Savage's position, but thinks that it must go beyond its present simple level to tackle problems of far greater complexity. "'Locality' can be seen to be a fascinating, complex concept of considerable value to geographical theory and empirical research" (Cooke: 1989b: 272).

As this (increasingly acrimonious) locality debate went on, an intermediate realist position was established by Kevin Cox and Andrew Mair (1989), both associated with the geography department at Ohio State University. Their view is that the dichotomy between abstract and concrete research, and the equation of the geographical and the local with the concrete, are key problems in the debate. Instead of what they term Sayer's (1984) originally "rigid" dichotomy between abstract and concrete, there is a continuum from the most highly abstract to the most concrete ideas, a hierarchy of levels of abstraction (cf. Gibson and Horvath 1984). Furthermore, necessary relationships can be identified at each level which incorporate greater geographical variability at the lower levels. These authors favor intermediate levels of analysis such as those employed by regulation theory.

Let us, however, give the final word to Cooke. In *Back to the Future*, Cooke (1990) rephrases his argument in terms of the increased significance given to the local by the postmodern critique of modernist theory (see chapter 6). There is, he says, a remarkable unanimity among postmodern thinkers such as Foucault, Lyotard, and Rorty that the local dimension is neglected by an overly centralized, dominating modern culture. Contemporary social innovation shifts "the pivot of creativity" from a top-down direction to a bottom-up process. Cooke argues that economic changes erode the will and capacity of the modern nation state to solve widespread problems, placing a greater responsibility (if not always greater power) on the locality. The CURS program, he says, finds that local social innovation plays an important part in enabling fortuitously located places to anticipate and prepare for change and to enable dislocated communities in coming to terms with crisis. But the element of local capacity, especially its proactive disposition, varies widely. Proactivity seldom draws on older traditions of authority; rather "it arises from the struggles by individuals and organizations, both formal and informal, to press local claims for justice and prosperity" (Cooke 1990: 120). Even in the most socially dislocated localities, social innovation survives as a struggle to limit the worst effects of decline. Hence, the CURS research suggests that locality retains significance and social meaning even when the state, multinational corporations, and the mass media have all but effaced the older social solidarities of the community. Cooke (1990: 180) finds an emergent trend towards a revival of localism in economy, initiatives to employment, and the recovery of local identity: localism may yet be a key agent.

Critique of Locality Studies

Locality studies responded to the economic restructuring of old industrial regions under advanced, global capitalism. But, as we have seen, the geographic study of the effects of global forces on particular places raises difficult questions of philosophy, theory, and methodology. For a long time, these questions were postponed, rather than resolved, by an effective confinement of theorization to the understanding of broad structural processes: theory and macro-structure seemed to go together, with particular places usually being described rather than analyzed. Where analysis is attempted, places get their characteristics from the layered effects of broader structural processes which, at best, recombine in "unique" ways in localities. Even so, the places which began to fascinate geographers anew in the 1980s were no longer those of the earlier idiographic tradition of Hartshorne's regional geography, nor were they centers of meaning, as in humanistic geography. They were places in context, places as localities emersed in external relations. The burning question thus became how to reconcile theories of global structure with the theorization of particular places.

The basic issue is whether, indeed, places (locales, localities, etc.) can be theorized and, if so, what theoretical language is adequate to the task? For much of the 1980s in Britain, locality was theorized in critical realist terms. As we have seen, realism outlines a quite precise methodology, buttressed by philosophical justification, for the concrete rather than abstract analysis of space. Despite persistent contrary readings, realism does not argue that space be addressed purely in empirical terms, but rather that it be theorized in concrete rather than abstract terms – concrete being quite different from empirical. Again, despite contrary readings, realism does not say that space is unimportant in determining events, but rather that space is conditional rather than constitutive and causal. Even so, the question remains whether this is a productive formulation, and whether realism provides an appropriate language for locality studies. We make two critical comments on this.

Critical realism emerged into prominence at the same time that locality reappeared as a central issue in geography – the convergence between the two being particularly pronounced in Britain. While this convergence produced a theoretical and methodological debate on space and place far superior to the earlier idiographic/nomothetic distinction, it also served to confine this debate within one school of thought; with the exception of structural Marxist critics of the entire endeavor, all the active participants in the locality debate claimed to be realists of one kind or another. There was little questioning of the basic notions of the realist theory of space by these locality theorists. The intellectual productivity, not to say its empirical and political output, would be greater and, more simply, the entire debate more interesting, were it conducted between adherents to a variety of philosophies with their associated social-theoretic views – for example a classically Marxist theory of locality, a regulationist theory, a more empirically oriented structurationist theory of locale, even a reinvigorated (economic) humanistic version of place. The conceptualization of locale should be situated at the crossroads of a number of theoretical tendencies rather than swept along a single current of thought.

This, however, is merely polite prelude to the more controversial question of the appropriateness of critical realism for the analysis of localities. The CURS initiative inquired into the power of local people to intervene in the broader processes of social and economic change drastically affecting their lives; yet realism sees space as conditional and localities primarily as modifiers of causal processes. In the realist view, local intervention in broad processes of change is therefore limited. Thus, the central paradox of realist locality studies – Duncan and Savage's "space makes a difference but does not determine" – proves incapable of theoretical or empirical resolution (although it was productive of elegant if evasive theorization) and, more importantly, incapable of guiding research into anything resembling Cooke's "local proactivity"; indeed, despite Cooke's broad claims, the CURS empirical research focuses exclusively on the policies of the local state ("local authorities" in British parlance), rather than the whole series of social movements which together make up local initiative (Cooke 1989a: 297). What gives these movements local proactivity? Space makes a difference in two ways. First, as distance (set of intermediating objects) between centers of structuring influence and local places it preserves differences from a past when locality had more significance – for example, such differences in language and dialect even within the confines of the British Isles that people can scarcely understand each other. Second, difference is continually recreated by the assemblage of objects surrounding actors in localities. These enable localities, as local collectivities of people and institutions, to counter structural influences with initiatives in part their own. Indeed, space as differences is a main source of innovation. Because of its artificially restricted definition of space as in-betweenness (or other abstract spatial characteristics) or alienated relations, realism is exactly the wrong philosophy for locality research, given the CURS objective of inquiring into local initiative. Clearly, this was an important debate. But the conclusion we must reach, based on the critique of realism's limited conceptualization of space outlined previously, the limited range of ideas discussed interminably but without resolution during the locality debate, and the restriction of proactivity to the reactions of the local state, is that realism is not a theoretical language adequate to the task, and that the convergence between realism as approach, and locality as focal topic, limits this fascinating area of geographical inquiry.

Materialism, Locality, Post-Enlightenment Marxism

These debates about structural Marxism were brought to a head in a cathartic exchange in the journal *Society and Space* in 1987. David Harvey (1987: 367; cf. Saunders and Williams 1986) argues that "the time has never been more appropriate for the application of Marx's conceptual apparatus to understanding processes of capitalist development . . . I believe the claim of Marxian analysis to provide the surest guide to the construction of radical theory and radicalizing practices still stands." This responds to a strategic withdrawal from Marxism in urban analysis. For Harvey, three myths underlie this withdrawal. First, that Marxist geography of the Harvey type was a structuralist enterprise in the Althusserian tradition – "I, for one was never an Althusserian" (Harvey 1987: 369). Second, that the abstractions of Marxian theory cannot explain the specificities of history nor the particularities of geography – here Harvey sees a revival of the idiographic/nomothetic debate and a holier-than-thou claim of greater respect for individuals. For Harvey, Marx talked of processes (rather than events) and suggested abstraction as method of uncovering laws of motion, rather than imposing abstractions on situations. That is, Marx analysed processes in empirical detail to arrive at the "concrete abstractions," like money or the working day, to which individuals respond – "it is the processes of capital accumulation that do the abstracting." Marx explores these abstractions dialectically to derive other kinds of necessities, yet always with historical-geographical materials as substance. Hence, Marxism in urban studies always seeks to forge abstractions from materialist analysis of historical and geographical circumstance (e.g. Harvey 1985a; Harvey 1985b). Harvey is critical of transcendental realism's notion of contingency (Sayer 1984) and Massey's (1984) depiction of general theory as external to specificity. Third, the myth is that Marxism, with its talk of "totalities," can never enter a "never-never land of non-totalizing discourses" (cf. Lyotard 1984). For Harvey, there is nothing more totalizing than the penetration of capitalist social relations and the commodity calculus into every niche of contemporary life. Arguments like Lyotard's (see chapter 6), that totalities cannot be thought, or metatheories constructed, are contradicted by reams of studies of how localities are caught up in universal processes:

Postmodernist philosophy tells us not only to accept but even to revel in the fragmentations and the cacophony of voices through which the dilemmas of the modern world are understood. It has us accepting the reifications and partitionings, actually celebrating the fetishisms of locality, place, or social pressure group without recognizing that history, geography, community etc. are being dominated, penetrated, and then recuperated under contemporary capitalism as pastiche ... This rhetoric is dangerous for it avoids confronting the realities of political economy and the circumstances of global power. (Harvey 1987: 375)

For Harvey, countering these realities necessitates a discourse of political freedom and justice which makes metatheoretical claims. So, for Harvey, there may be good reason to resist totalizing discourses that claim omniscience and omnipotence, but not theories which seek understanding of the intricate mesh of forces at work in the totality of the contemporary world – and here Harvey finds dialectical thought extraordinarily open-ended. Thus, historical materialism is best thought of as historical-geographical materialism with historical geography as its method of theorizing (see also Archer 1987). The version proposed a few years earlier (Harvey 1984: 9–10) takes the form of a "people's geography" built around five theses:

1 A popular geography free from prejudice but reflective of real conflicts and contradictions which can open new channels of communication and common understanding.
2 A people's geography not beholden to narrow or powerful special interests, but instead broadly democratic.
3 A dual methodological commitment to scientific integrity and non-neutrality.
4 Geographical sensitivities integrated into general social theories from the historical materialist tradition
5 A political project that sees the transition from capitalism to socialism in historico-geographical terms.

Harvey's passionate defence of Marxism, his dismissive attitude towards structurationist modifications, and his early critique of postmodern notions of difference (see also chapter 6), did not bode well for relations between the various components of the left in geography – Marxists, realists, structurationists, and a growing camp of postmodernists – who from this time on began to regard each other with a growing hostility. The journal *Society and Space*, which carries much of the new work, became increasingly differentiated from *Antipode*, which remains largely Marxist in orientation; indeed, *Society and Space* refuses to carry Marxist articles. In this case, Harvey's statement was "balanced" by a series of counter-statements, some sympathetic (Smith 1987b; Archer 1987), some defending realism (Sayer 1987), others critical, of which we give two examples. Nigel Thrift (1987), an active participant in the formation of the new versions of left scholarship, finds Marxism of only limited utility in illuminating the notion of structure and agency – Marx's idea, that is, that people make history but not under conditions of their own choosing. In the Marxist tradition, Thrift says, the individual is "radically social," structured in a context of interaction. But, for Thrift, this only begins an understanding of "subjectification" – that is, how people are made by an interacting set of institutions, a process in which space is important as a strategy in the system of institutional discipline (Foucault 1979a) and as a local context, while also there are operational problems. Moral issues and ethical questions of respect for individuals and political matters of attaining not "socialism" (unattractive to many people) but "popular hegemony" and a politics of culture, experience, and the body also concern him. For Thrift (1987: 404), too, the notion of Marxism as totalizing discourse has a long history – by "totalizing" he means a kind of holism which sees society as an integrated system of universal processes which can be apprehended from a total vantage point, such as that of the working class. This kind of totalizing discourse, Thrift finds, comes under question within and outside Marxism. Hence, societies are only partly integrated, being predicated on universal tendencies and differences in how these are worked out – hence, structuration theory and realism. By comparison theory of the Harvey type "overtotalizes" society as capital is theorized as an overwhelming process reaching all aspects of social life: "Harvey's materialist theory is the transcendental mirror of this vision of Capital. It can reach everywhere ... a searchlight flooding every nook and cranny of society with light" (Thrift 1987: 405). Thrift differs in judging processes of subjectification more important. He proposes instead a theoretical and empirical research agenda of subjectification/subjection, the formation of personalities and communities, without which only part of the geography of capitalism can be explained.

Michael Storper (1987) finds a new kind of post-Fordist industrial capitalism in the making of which is needed a post-Enlightenment Marxism. Marx, he says, was a product of the Enlightenment in terms of his metanarrative of human history based on faith about the progressive universalization of reason. This is linked with a modernist microtheory of the structures of human action – hence, Marx's totalistic picture of capitalism. For Storper, this project could be strengthened through modification. First, Storper differentiates totalization in history from totalization in theory, with its myth of expressive totality ("underneath it's all capitalism"), so that all phenomena are expressions of underlying forces. This view cannot generate specific historical and geographical observations. For Storper, too, the jump often made in Marxism, from observing that societies are thoroughly capitalistic to claiming that capitalism is the main route of explanation for all their characteristics, is illogical. Capitalism is structured by societies, including their non-capitalist dimensions – in this sense the local makes the global, so that the nature of Japanese capitalism derives not just from capital but from Japanese civil society:

> The local ultimately becomes global because it forecloses other possibilities in a wide variety of other localities. Capital is not just revealed but made: its essence is changed. The now structurally ensconced practices supervene other phenomena; they are truly social. (Storper 1987: 420–1)

Hence, the historical geography of capitalism should create the theory of capital and not simply be used as a backdrop to reveal facets of a phenomenon we think we already know. This suggests to Storper a different kind of theoretical totalization which rejects Marxism's vertical metaphors of causality (i.e. concrete realities result from causal iterations from the most general down to the more particular). Instead, the architecture of explanation, for Storper, must be horizontal, where forces are not sequential or hierarchical but simultaneous. Storper wants a form of Marxism which is not (dialectical, materialist) science but critical reason, using meso-level theoretical constructs (see also chapter 4). Hence, a post-Enlightenment Marxism must be concerned with the micro-physics of power, the details and poetics of material, social life. For Storper (1987: 425):

> The significant substantive advance of post-Enlightenment theory is to put civil society on an equal footing with political economy in the theorization of capital and the explanation of history and geography, while not insisting on subjecting them all to a dialectical totalization.

We might add that this is exactly what Harvey proposed, and that from this time on debate on the left increasingly became a dialogue of the deaf. We might note also that structure and agency died out as a controversial issue in the late 1980s, to be replaced by similar discussions posed in the poststructural (postmodern) and feminist terms of difference.

Conclusion

From this debate we pass to a critical assessment of the entire range of related ideas presented in this chapter – structuration, realism, locality studies. These tendencies in social theorizing respond to the changing political temper of the times in direct and indirect ways. Directly, there was, beginning in the late 1970s and lasting through most of the 1980s, a crisis of confidence on the left, marked by the abandonment of an earlier revolutionary sentiment by many previously committed intellectuals, and the passing of political activism to the "revolutionary" right, the coming to power of conservatives, and the saturation of popular ideology by neo-liberalism. The thesis here is that the passing of revolutionary impetus from the left to the right underlies a second crisis on the left, an apparent crisis of confidence in structural thinking, particularly the growing critique of an almost deliberately misunderstood "structural Marxism." However, the connections between politics, philosophy, and social theory are never that simple. Each of these relates to, and is formed by, the other (to say the obvious), and each has its own momentum generated (again obviously) by its own internal relations. This autonomy of movement means that old ideas never die but only fade away, often to reappear in new guises. Indirectly, the consequence for geographical thought of broader changes in politics and theory was not the abandonment but the realignment of critical structural thinking; that is, the transition from structural Marxist geography to structurationist thinking, the structure–agency relationship, the attempt by realism to more carefully specify the connections between structures, mechanisms, and events, locality studies' scepticism about global structuring yet its retention of the metaphor (derived from Massey) of the layering of local spaces by restructuring. "Continuity in change" only begins to understand the complex interactions between the tendency to project thought into new realms yet the employment of existing categories in this projection, hence, the drag of an already structured imagination on concepts which supposedly replace the old.

In geography, matters of politics emerge often as questions of scale. The critique of structural Marxist geography, formulated (by Duncan and Ley) in terms of its supposed holistic, teleological, and structural certainty, interacted with the humanistic conception of intentional agency to produce a series of social theories dealing with structuration and a new regional geography emphasizing the local and the specific (Pudup 1988). Places are conceptualized as the (structured) settings for human action (agency). How is this phrased? Structures are seen as having local effects which, in interaction and achieving partial autonomy, create people whose actions reform structures. What this misses is the active role of (relatively autonomous) local structures in creating different kinds of agents who live (partly) local lives which may alter the frameworks and trajectories of broader structures, indeed create and recreate them – act locally, create globally. There is a consistent tendency to pass over, or be unable to specify, local creativity – indeed, this is persistently misinterpreted merely as local modifications. In geography, this is a deliberate blindness, for place specificity is interpreted as idiographic description, and many think that "idiographic" describes the writing of idiots! But it means also that geography proved incapable of playing, at least to the full, the significant role assigned to it by social theory: explaining where new structural elements come from – that is, from contextualized, local practices.

Thus, we can see in these discussions a pervasive avoidance, a complex refusal, layered with all kinds of philosophical excuses, to come to grips with geography's preoccupying, persisting, and pre-eminent position. Let us phrase this in structural terms for, despite criticism, the broad phrases of structuralism remain the language intellectuals (sometimes only secretly) enjoy. Where do structures come from? In terms of scale, do structures emerge from changes in general among massive forces, or from the accretion of changes in particular among a variety of local tendencies? And to the extent that local agencies form global structures, what is it about locality that produces causal efficacy? All these are geographical questions, but the last, the eruption of the local into the global, the making of structures by locally based agents, is spatial geography's particular area of contribution to this kind of knowledge (cf. Storper 1987). Structuration theory, realism, locality studies, new regional geography, all try to formulate some kind of approach, all provide insights, yet all eventually fail. Structuration employs locale as its scalar thinking device in trying to wed agency to structure. Yet Hagerstrand's daily life paths, even when they intersect, are only vague indications on a far more complex map. Giddens's locale may be the setting for action in the making of structure, but how does a setting formed by one structure, and recreated through unintended consequences, achieve the necessary autonomy to condition differently the agents creating the next structure? In leading representations of structurationist geography, as with Gregory or Pred, "structures from nowhere" encounter only local modifications – that is, locale remains the source of variations in structures rather than the origin of their new elements. And, for Olsson, structure is some unreachable collective unconscious which interacts with individual consciousness through the prison house of language – there are too many unconsciousnesses colliding here and too much glorification of the ambiguous, as though ambiguity is the free house where truth resides. Critical realism, equally problematically, sees space only as conditionally activating the powers metaphysically residing in objects. Hence, realist locality studies can only begin to counterpose local proactivity to global structuring. All these tendencies eventually founder on the truly fundamental problems of imagination and specification in the straits connecting structure with agency in social theory and the global with the local in geographic theory. Why is this?

The easy reason is that local creativity is inordinately difficult to understand. It is not just a question of local research into the sources of particular innovative actions, how the characteristics of localities bind into agents as difference, how different agents collect in localities of innovation, but also a question of the elaboration of the local into the regional, the national, and the global – that is, how local initiatives combine into, and interact with, broader tendencies. The more difficult reason may be that structural thinking, including structuration, realism, and locality studies (the last of which, after all, examine the effects of industrial *restructuring*), as well as the now dreaded Althusserianism, cannot or will not imagine local creativity except as a (largely determined) response to structural forces. In this sense, structuralism is the enemy of the unique; globalism coopts localism; agents only modify structures. These are the kinds of realizations which begin (reluctantly) to dawn as the structural experience in its many (dis)guises is subjected to contemplative reassessment. These are some of the materials from which the next, even more complicated, chapter in geographic thought is constructed: poststructuralism, postmodernism, and difference.

Chapter 6

Poststructuralism, Postmodernism, and Postmodern Geographies

Structuralism, structuration, realism – these are philosophies which believe, in various ways, and to different degrees, in the promise of modernity, especially the liberatory potential of modern scientific understanding: evidence, fact, truth shall set us free! Scientific liberation breaks the constraints of nature on human life. Liberation also means applying knowledge to the rationalization of society, freeing it from the mysticisms and injustices of the past. Liberation may be meant too in the more radical sense of an escape from human nature as it has been. In the modern world, that European space-time following the feudal middle ages, especially since the Enlightenment of the eighteenth century, progress and liberation are seen to be founded in reason, logic, and scientific thought. Reason advances knowledge; knowledge enables science; and science serves the liberatory aims of society. In enlightenment thinking, ethics can be based on the crystallized lessons of human experience, mediated or interpreted by rational inspection, rather than having a divine source. In this, human reasoning about experience replaces God as moral authority, and the rational individual becomes self-guiding, and possibly self-governing, rather than slave to (religious and civil) authority. The modern aspiration is that all people sharing a similar ethical rationality might agree on a system of norms to guide the operation of society. Self-disciplined by ethical reason, individuals might voluntarily adhere to decisions reached through rational democratic means, rather than constantly be disciplined by laws. The benefits of science could thus be shared by all in a just, egalitarian, ethical, and technologically advanced modern society. Even more, with a universal scientific method "there can be nothing so remote that we cannot reach to it, nor so recondite that we cannot discover it" (Descartes 1968: 92). Thus, the sense of limitless, self-directed progress embedded in modernism.

These modern beliefs, found to different degrees in virtually all liberal and radical modern political thought, have been questioned several times since their inception. They were questioned at the turn of the nineteenth century, but have never been scrutinized more than recently, with the postmodern turn in philosophy and social theory. Poststructuralism and postmodernism in their theoretical guises are very much the direct products of events in France. In May 1968, a Parisian alliance of student agitators and working-class militants rose in spontaneous revolutionary upheaval. It seemed for a short while that the dreams of radical modernism were about to be realized in their ultimately radical, social-anarchistic form (worker self-management, participatory democracy ...). But the eventual, eternal return of bourgeois rational normalcy to Paris began a period of contemplative reaction on the left. This turned against structuralism and Marxism immediately, hence, a series of *post*structural and *post*-Marxist ideas. But thinkers began also to react once more against the aspirations of modernism as a whole, hence, the postmodern aspect to poststructural philosophy. There was a revival of interest in anti-modern philosophies, Nietzsche and Heidegger in particular, together with an intensification of interest in the critically modern writings of the Frankfurt school Marxists. Notions of a post-industrial society (Touraine 1971; Bell 1973) were merged with cultural critiques of modern aesthetics (Burger 1984) in a series of new philosophies and social theories (Crook 1991; Best and Kellner 1991).

Poststructural thinking, especially in its postmodern forms, emphasizes that other side of rational modernity, its peasant, female, and colonized victims, its disciplinary institutions (schools, prisons, psychiatric clinics), and, more generally, the sacrifice of spontaneity and pleasure entailed by rational control – the idea that modern people suffer by continually scrutinizing the emotional upsurge of pleasurable, free behavior through the lenses of logic, thought, and rationalized ethics. In postmodern philosophy, modern reason is reinterpreted critically as a mode of social control which acts openly through disciplinary institutions, in more disguised forms through rationalized socialization and, most subtly, through rational self-discipline. In *modernity*, reason legitimates its interventions into the open arena of public order, and into the most personal reaches of the private mind through an appeal to truth. That is, reason produces truth, and truth guides good social practice – reasoned practices are true practices. By comparison, in the *poststructural* view (Foucault especially), modern philosophy's claim to universal truth is interpreted as a claim to universal power. Here, the critique focuses on modern philosophy as guardian and adjudicator of truth. The poststructural philosopher Richard Rorty, for example, criticizes modern theories of representational truth, in which systems of symbols (statements, theories, models) accurately reflect ("mirror") the structures of events and practices of a separate reality. In poststructural thinking, by comparison, representational theories of truth at best provide perspectives from the view of particular thinkers. For poststructural philosophy, especially Derrida, the relations between reality and mind are not direct, and therefore objectively accurate ("truthful"), but instead are linguistically mediated and historically specific.

Some *postmodern* theorists, Deleuze and Guattari, but also Baudrillard at times, go beyond this critique of truth to reject modern assumptions of coherence and causality entirely, arguing instead for fragmentation, multiplicity, and indeterminacy. These critics of modern humanism call for a philosophical revolution in which affirming or denying subjectivity would no longer be relevant. The new philosophy would not necessarily produce better forms of knowledge, only different ones. The enlightenment belief in historical progress is abandoned, including the notion of the accumulation of greater truth, while history is seen as "ending" in the sense of a loss of faith in progress. The rational, unified subject of modern theory becomes the decentered, fragmented, emotional, multi-identitied being of postmodern theory – conscious subjectivity becomes multiple, socially constructed identities. An understandable structured world which consciousness may endow with meaning (as in existential phenomenology) becomes the spontaneous eruption of fragmentary events beyond systematic understanding, with no meaning, inherent, endowed, or even interpreted, except that we are here, and even presence is defined in relation to absences! Postmodern philosophy, therefore, is more than a critique of reason, it is a critique of modern humanity, a critique of the existing human ideals, a critique of ways of knowing and being taken for granted since the eighteenth century.

Virtually all poststructural theorists use spatial metaphors, if not geographical concepts, as media of expression. Yet geography came late onto the poststructural scene and, it could be argued, has never fully entered a postmodernist phase. While poststructural theories were developing into a full-blown postmodernism in the 1970s and early 1980s, critical human geography was still preoccupied with Marxism, humanism, and various spin-offs from the critique of structuralism, like structuration theory. Yet the main route of diffusion of poststructural ideas into Anglo-American geography passed through Marxism, rather than directly through geographical readings even of the more obvious, spatialized versions of the originals. Such was the dominance of Marxism and its offshoots in critical human geography that many ideas in what is supposedly poststructural and even postmodern geography turn out as hybrids derived from blending these with historical materialist notions. Additionally, the years which saw the spreading influence of poststructural ideas were also noticeable for the growth of a feminist movement in and around the discipline. Many postmodernists are also feminists, feminist geography has materialist (socialist feminist) and postmodern strains, the postmodern/feminist politics of difference draws from all schools of thought (see chapter 7). This confluence of ideas produces a "postmodern" period in contemporary geographical thought that is often little more than a series of exegeses, "readings through other authors," critiques and counter-critiques. Postmodern geography may have its philosophical elite (successfully) vying for disciplinary power, especially in Britain, but it cannot claim exclusiveness, for behind stands a notion which is mongrel through and through.

This chapter first outlines some of the attitudes (Bataille) and ideas (Nietzsche) which recent poststructural thinkers draw upon – we previously discussed Heidegger (chapter 2), important for all the writings mentioned here, especially the deconstructionists. Foucault, Derrida, and Rorty are discussed in turn, as poststructural philosophers, followed by discussions of Lyotard, Deleuze, and Guattari, and Baudrillard as postmodern social theorists. The chapter then moves through Jameson and the introduction of postmodern ideas into geography by Dear, Soja, and Harvey, before eclectically surveying a range of subsequent postmodern positions in the discipline. It concludes with a brief critique of the postmodern movement which draws particularly on the writings of Habermas and the counter-notion of radical (modernist) humanism.

Poststructural Philosophy

The notion that modernism represents the victory of the rational over the irrational, and that rationality is an inherent human potential, an inherent logic awaiting discovery in every mind, gives to intellectual histories of modernity an air of inevitability and invincibility. Modernity is the culmination of history or, in some (conservative) versions, liberal democracy is the end of history (Fukuyama 1989). Yet modern, rational thinking, and the secular beliefs and attitudes that come with it, continually encounter multiple, popular resistances. These began as modernist rationality was initially forming. Thus, Giovanni Battista Vico (1668–1744) opposed the radical rationalism of the French *philosophes* in the name of the irrational forces creating human nature and the irrational common senses in societies (Vico 1984; Lilla 1993). Thus, it cannot be assumed that modern rationalism is so clearly the final, superior form of thought that everyone subjected to logical persuasion ("mental awakening") immediately succumbs to its obvious charms. Nor should the finest product of rationality, the plenitude of modern life, with its high mass consumption, its ability to meet even the slightest (consumptive) whim, be seen as satisfying all with its seductive, sedative appeal. Here, we give two examples of resistance to the normalcy of bourgeois taste and the boredom of modern life: the first (Georges Bataille) a cry of revulsion against the spread of cultural normalcy; the second (Friedrich Nietzsche) an attempt to retheorize life in terms not of disciplined rationality, but of power, will, and affect. Nietzsche then forms an entry point directly into poststructural thought.

Visions of Excess

Georges Bataille (1897–1962) was a lapsed Catholic, a librarian, and a rebel surrealist. Bataille's writings, collected into *Visions of Excess* (1985), dwell obsessively on unspeakable objects – excrement, flies, ruptured eyes, a rotten sun – in place of the previous ideals – spirit, mind, vision, the sun of reason. He intends by this disgusting diatribe not to replace one system of thought with a better, but to establish a new attitude towards thinking, in which there can be no hierarchies, but also in which a primary stratum does not "cause" other secondary phenomena. In his essay "The Use Value of D. A. F. de Sade," Bataille (1985) outlines the principles of a "practical heterology" (i.e. discourse on difference) which attacks conventional morality as merely the ethical disguise for bourgeois profit making. For Bataille, the Marxist theory of exploitation should be expanded into a critique of capitalist morality. When people no longer crush each other under the yoke of morality, he said, they acquire (again) the capacity to be violent and excited, to be entranced with heterogeneous elements. Bataille's "heterology" thus discovers revolutionary potential in urges usually taken to be antisocial. He wants "the submerged masses, doomed to an obscure and impotent life" to violently liberate their energies and forces and spend their strength freely (Bataille 1985: 100). Revolutionaries must discover their profound complicity with natural forces, violent death, gushing blood, catastrophe, horrible cries of pain, the terrifying rupture of what once seemed immutable, the fall of that which was elevated into stinking filth ... and so on!

In "The Notion of Expenditure," Bataille (1985) attacks classical (materialist) utilitarianism as flat, untenable, the moralizing conception of a boring human existence. Utilitarianism reduces life to productive activity, pleasure being relegated to subsidiary diversion. Modern humanity, Bataille says, recognizes rights to acquire, conserve, and consume rationally, but excludes non-productive expenditure on principle. Bataille reverses the order of this dualism – now production becomes secondary to expenditure. For Bataille, life cannot be limited to the closed systems of reasonable convention. Instead, life is recklessness, discharge, and upheaval. Order and social reserve, he says, have meaning only for those ultimate moments when people are liberated to lose themselves in unaccountable ends, for spectacular moments of excess, for insubordinate free expenditure. Bataille wants these moments to become life itself.

The Will to Power

Bataille was a cultural terrorist passionately disrupting the morality of modern normalcy. Friedrich Nietzsche (1844–1900) was a poet–philosopher disrupting the rational basis of modern thought. In the conventional view, Nietzsche was a proto-Nazi (his notion of the superman). In more generous appraisals, he was a naturalistic philosopher of passionately desiring human being (Kaufmann 1974). More recently, Nietzsche is read for his critique of truth and his conception of power. For Nietzsche (1979: 84), "truths are illusions we have forgotten are illusions" or "truth is the kind of error without which a certain kind of being could not live" (Nietzsche 1968: 493). Modern life is compelled to found itself on the unquestioned principles of spirit, progress, and truth. Yet the modern world entails, for Nietzsche, an impoverishment of experience, so that people no longer find in it meaning or truth. Postmodern theory is one long explication of Nietzsche's claim that truth, like God, is dead (Clark 1990: 1–3; Strong 1988).

Nietzsche's ideas were introduced most powerfully into recent French philosophy by Giles Deleuze's *Nietzsche and Philosophy* (1983; Bogue 1989: 15–34). In Deleuze's reading, Nietzsche developed a philosophy of becoming and affirmation by employing notions of the will to power and eternal return. For Deleuze, Nietzsche employs evaluation and interpretation in an affirmative, new image of thought, which counteracts negative, reactive western philosophy. Beneath the modern search for truth Nietzsche finds moral, nihilistic will. This he wishes to transform into creative will, so that thinking can invent new possibilities. In this new conception of interpretation: truth is replaced by value and meaning; stupidity replaces error as the main enemy (for Nietzsche, there are imbecile thoughts made up entirely of truths); and method is less important than the force necessary to make thinking active. Deleuze reads Nietzsche: as an interpreter–physician reading modern symptoms of negativity; as an evaluator–artist creating a new image of thought; and as a poet inventing new forms of expressive articulation (aphorisms). Continual reinterpretation Deleuze calls "eternal return," and that which interprets he calls the "will to power."

In Deleuze's Nietzsche, the will to power is approached via a physical/

psychological conception of force and body. Nietzsche sees the world in terms of a series of unstable identities. Nature is a multiplicity of dominating and dominated forces within which the body is constituted. Nietzsche distinguishes dominant and dominated quantities of force. Active (affirming) and reactive (negating) qualities are determined by the relationship of forces. Internal to force is the will to power. This is not a universal will, nor is it an individual will. It is a plastic will to become, inseparable from each case in which it is determined. The primordial qualities of the will to power, affirmative (becoming active) or negative (becoming reactive), are served by forces which are linked (spatially and temporally) into lines of development. The will to power manifests itself as a human capacity for being affected. Power is a feeling with affectivity, sensation, and emotion. Hence, the will to power is essentially creative and giving (Deleuze 1983: 40–86; Bogue 1989: 20–4).

Complicating this already complex account is Nietzsche's belief that reactive forces win over active forces. Hence, the history of the west is reactionary nihilism triumphant. Victory is achieved by the developed reactive forces separating active forces from what they can do, turning active force against itself, making it reactive. Humans are constituted by a multiplicity of these active and reactive forces, with the active precipitating and the reactive inhibiting action, the two responding also to a field of external forces. Deleuze interprets Nietzsche's *On the Genealogy of Morals* (1967) in terms of the stages by which the reactive forces achieve dominance over the active through a series of negative imaginary fictions, mainly the fiction of god in contradiction to life. Nietzsche's genealogy reveals nihilism (the will to nothingness) to be the motor of the reactive forces. For Nietzsche, human history is a universal tendency for the reaction of forces. People can become affirmative only through return to the "Overman" – return not in a cyclical sense, nor in the sense of the return of the Same but, argues Deleuze, as the return of becoming and difference. Eternal return means participating in becoming, affirming becoming, recognizing that all moments are instances of becoming – return is the being of becoming itself. For Deleuze, Nietzsche's world of becoming is all chance and chaos. Becoming entails affirmation of all the possible combinations involved in effort, and affirmation too of their specific outcomes. Humans (in Deleuze's opinion) count on a large number of attempts to get what they want, rather than chancing all in a single venture and accepting the necessary outcome. Nietzsche expresses an active love of fate which forces one to will whatever happens as the necessary manifestation of chance. In Deleuze's understanding of Nietzsche, active forces alone affirm becoming and have true being in a world of becoming. Ultimately, the possibility of overcoming humanity and realizing true affirmation opens a (second) stage of (reactive) nihilism in which the negative will, separated from the reactive forces, inspires in people the inclination to destroy all known values. This inaugurates the transvaluation of values, establishing a new active way of life for the creation of values – the eternal return (Deleuze 1983; Bogue 1989).

In this reading, Deleuze elaborates his own thoughts and beliefs as much as those of Nietzsche. For Deleuze, philosophy affirms difference as the chaotic multiplicity of becoming in the world; thought, he says, must be directed against reason without ceasing to be thought; thought must interpret, evaluate, and create new possibilities of life; thought must explore the body's powers of activity and affectivity. Deleuze (1983; Bogue 1989: 32–3) follows Nietzsche in seeking a philosophy of difference, a bridge to French poststructural philosophy. Deleuze finds in Nietzsche an alternative (or at least supplement) to Marx and Freud. Nietzsche is used to replace consciousness with affective will and to disrupt modern patterns of similarity with the affirmation of difference. This attempt at massive disruption is replicated, perhaps even exaggerated, by the work of the greatest of poststructural philosophers, Michel Foucault (1926–84), one time professor of the history of systems of thought at the College de France.

Knowledge, Truth, Power

Foucault shares with Nietzsche a fascination with the power–truth–knowledge complex and emphasizes with Bataille topics previously relegated to the margins. In the modern world, Foucault says, reason saturates life, rationality intrudes into every corner, science classifies and thereby regulates all forms of experience. Like Nietzsche, Foucault maintains a hostile position towards modernity, what he finds to be its repressive, totalizing modes of thought. Foucault launches two levels of attack on the philosophy of modern humanism. First, he says that it metaphysically grounds an image of universal humanity, such as the Cartesian conception of universal rationality, on traits that are culturally specific. Second, the values and emancipatory ideals of the Enlightenment (autonomy, freedom, human rights) are ideological bases for a normalizing discipline which imposes an "appropriate" identity on modern people. This notion of reason as despotic western enlightenment may be seen in relation to the history of European colonialism, as its "finest hour" (Young 1990: 9). In place of western enlightenment, Hegelian or Marxist dialectics, Foucault favors difference, fragmentation, and discontinuity, multiple forms of analysis rather than single truths, microanalyses interwoven with macroanalyses, pure opinion mixed with exact historical studies. Foucault tries to detotalize history as a whole unified by a telos or essence, and to decenter the subject as a constituted rather than a constitutive consciousness. Foucault sees history as a non-evolutionary, fragmented field of disconnected knowledges and society as a dispersed regularity of unevenly developing discourses and practices. Foucault wants to respect differences and specificities, to rethink power as originating at multiple sites, flowing through many channels, to promote a micropolitics in opposition to the existing macropolitics (Best and Kellner 1991: 34–75).

Foucault's writings are usually divided into three distinct periods:

1   an archaeology of knowledge (1960–72) in which he wrote *Madness and Civilization* (1967), *The Birth of the Clinic* (1978), *The Order of Things* (1966; trans. 1973), and *The Archaeology of Knowledge* (1972);
2   a genealogy of knowledge and power (1975–80) in which appeared *Discipline and Punish* (1979a) and *The History of Sexuality*, volume 1 (1979b);
3   an ethics of the self (1981–84) in which his last books were written – *The History of Sexuality*, volumes 2 and 3 (1986c; 1988).

Interests.and methods developed in one period (e.g. archaeology) appear in others (e.g. genealogy). Foucault's work appears as a series of linked phases.

Archaeology

Foucault's archaeology of knowledge emerges from French historical epistemology – that is, the study of science as a rule-governed mode of discourse. Whereas Gaston Bachelard (1938) was concerned with the history of physics and chemistry, and Georges Cangelheim (1943; 1988) with biology, anatomy, and physiology, Foucault's archaeology, or archaeological history, is concerned with the history of the "human sciences" over the last 400 years (Machado 1992). Foucault's archaeology might be located within the triangle formed by structuralism, phenomenology, and hermeneutics (Dreyfus and Rabinow 1983). Structuralism tries to discover the basic elements of human activity and the rules by which these are combined, dispensing with the subject and meaning, while phenomenology proposes interpreting through hermeneutics the meanings embodied in everyday practices. But Foucault is not interested in the human's unnoticed everyday self-interpretation, and does not think that a hidden deep truth is the cause of profound misinterpretation. Instead, Foucault proposes moving beyond all three alternatives in the archaeological study of human beings.

Foucault's early works (*Madness and Civilization, The Birth of the Clinic*) center on historically situated systems of institutions and their discursive practices. By *discourse* Foucault means not so much everyday speech but the serious speech acts of experts in the human sciences. Counterpoised against hermeneutics (an attempt to systematize the deepest reaches of the human experience) Foucault's archaeology uses a structural (or semi-structural) approach to medical and other discourses to show that they have (social, institutional) systematic forms. Dreyfus and Rabinow (1983) interpret this as Foucault avoiding a futile search for deep ontological meanings by emphasizing instead the conditions of possibility of more discrete, reachable expert discourses. In *The Order of Things* (1973), Foucault inquires into the defined regularities of the empirical knowledges, asking whether the practice of science obeys the laws of a "code" or "positive unconscious." The archaeologist, Foucault says, tries to rediscover the basis, or conditions of possibility, of organized knowledge and theory – that is:

> within what space of order knowledge was constituted; on the basis of what historical *a priori*, and in the element of what positivity, ideas could appear, sciences be established, experience be reflected in philosophies, rationalities be formed ... archaeology, addressing itself to the general space of knowledge, to its configurations, and to the mode of being of the things that appear in it, defines systems of simultaneity, as well as the series of mutations necessary and sufficient to circumscribe the threshold of a new positivity. (Foucault 1973: xxii–xxiii)

Foucault calls the setting which decides whether statements count as knowledge the epistemological field, or *episteme*. So by episteme he means the set of relations between discursive practices in a given period that create formalized systems of knowledge (Foucault 1973: 191). Archaeological inquiry reveals two epistemic breaks within western culture: the first, between the Renaissance and the "Classical" period, occurred in the middle seventeenth century; the second, between the Classical and Modern periods, occurred in the late eighteenth and early nineteenth centuries. In the latter epistemic break, "man enters ... for the first time, the field of Western knowledge" (Foucault 1973: xxiii).

In *The Archaeology of Knowledge* (1972), Foucault purifies his earlier analysis of discourse to treat the human sciences as autonomous, rule-governed systems of discourse. Foucault claims to discover a domain centered on a previously unnoticed type of linguistic function, the statement, what Dreyfus and Rabinow (1983: 45–47) call the "serious speech act" (cf. Searle 1969), by which is meant statements with validation procedures made within communities of experts. Foucault is interested in types of speech acts, the regularities exhibited by their interrelations (discursive formations), and the transformations these undergo. In doubly bracketing the truth and meaning claims of serious speech acts, Foucault claims to leave behind transcendental and existential phenomenology in a pure description of discursive events and the logical spaces in which they occur. The discursive relations between serious speech acts are related to institutions, techniques, social forms, etc., and to the ways practicing subjects reflectively define their behavior, but discursive practices now have priority because they establish the relations between the other practices. That is, discourse unifies social, economic, and political factors into coherent unities. Discursive formations have internal systems of rules determining what gets said about which objects. The trouble with this, according to Dreyfus and Rabinow (1983: 79–100), is that descriptive rules are given causal, prescriptive efficacy by Foucault:

> The result is the strange notion of regularities which regulate themselves. Since the regularity of discursive practices seem to be the result of their being governed, determined, and controlled, while they are assumed to be autonomous, the archaeologist must attribute causal efficacy to the very rules which describe these practices' systematicity. (Dreyfus and Rabinow 1983: 85)

This problem is compounded by Foucault's claim that archaeology speaks from a blank space outside any horizon of intelligibility or meaning. Yet, to be taken seriously, Foucault must claim some meaning and truth for his own discourse. For Dreyfus and Rabinow, it is no coincidence that Foucault's *Archaeology* is followed by a self-imposed silence broken by two books in which the author, while still using archaeological techniques, no longer claims their phenomenological detachment.

Genealogy

In works published in the 1970s, Foucault gives priority to genealogy over archaeology, sees greater importance in practice as compared with theory, and recognizes his involvement in the social practices he studies. The interpretative analytics of genealogy involves diagnosing relations of power, knowledge, and the body in modern society. Genealogy is opposed to traditional historical methods of inquiry in that it claims to recognize no fixed essences or underlying laws, seeks discontinuities, avoids searching for depth, and records the past to undermine the notion of the modern march of progress. The genealogist finds hidden meanings, heights of truth, and depths of consciousness alike to be shams: instead, genealogy's truth is that things have no essence. Whenever genealogy hears of original truths it looks for the play of wills; when talk is of meaning, value, goodness, or virtue the genealogist looks for strategies of domination; instead of explicit human intentionality, the genealogist finds force relations worked out in specific events. For the genealogist there is no subject moving history. The play of forces in any situation is made possible by the space which defines them – it is the field or clearing that is primary. In archaeology, Foucault thought that the space in which we encounter objects and speak about them is governed by a system of rules. In genealogy, this field is understood to be the space in which social practices occur, when subjects engage in the repeated play of dominations. History is not the progress of universal reason but, rather, humanity moving from one domination to another.

In genealogical understanding, the body is an essential focus for the operation of modern power relations – the body is the place where, for Foucault, the most minute and local practices are linked with the large-scale organizations of power. Foucault's reading of Nietzsche suggests that the body can be experienced in many ways, desires can be changed by cultural interpretations, and every aspect of the body modified given the appropriate techniques. The task of genealogy is to show that the body is involved in a political field, that power relations make and train it, this process being deeply connected with the economic system's demand for productive, subjected people. Foucault calls the knowledge of the body and the mastering of its forces "political technology." In *Discipline and Punish* (1979a), Foucault writes a history of the appearance, articulation, and spread of power at a different level than the institutional. That is, Foucault claims to isolate the mechanisms by which power operates (its rituals), the way it is localized (political technology of the body), and the dynamics of how it works (microphysics of power).

For Foucault, modern knowledge is enmeshed in the clash of dominations. Knowledge did not detach itself from its practical, empirical roots to become pure speculation, subject only to the demands of reason. Rather, for him, power and knowledge operate in mutually generative ways:

> it is not the activity of the subject of knowledge, useful or resistant to power, but power/knowledge, the processes and struggles that traverse it and of which it is made up, that determines the forms and possible domains of knowledge. (Foucault 1979a: 28)

What, then, distinguishes science or serious knowledge in this power-ridden domain? Foucault argues that the history and place of science in the larger context of power needs to be examined in order to evaluate knowledge's claim to describe reality. Archaeology is a technique for isolating this place in a discursive formation; genealogy adds another level, the historical and political role played by a science. Thus, for Foucault:

Truth is not outside of power ... Each society has its own regime of truth, its general politics of truth ... There is a combat for the truth, or at least around the truth, as long as we understand by the truth not those true things which are waiting to be discovered but rather the ensemble of rules according to which we distinguish the true from the false, and attach special effects of power to "the truth". (Foucault 1980: 131)

In *The History of Sexuality*, volume 1, Foucault argues that modern "bio-power" emerged in the seventeenth century as a coherent political technology when the fostering of life and the growth and care of populations became central concerns of the state. Systematic empirical investigation of historical, geographical, and demographic conditions engendered the modern human sciences, which continue to be connected with technologies of bio-power. Their aim is to produce docile but productive bodies in advance, rather than as a consequence, of capitalism (Dreyfus and Rabinow 1983).

Two lectures given in 1976 (Foucault 1980: 78–108) stress aspects of genealogy particularly interesting to geography. Foucault counterposes "the efficacy of dispersed and discontinuous offensives" to the inhibiting effects of global, totalitarian theories, including psychoanalysis and Marxism. For Foucault, thinking in terms of totality and striving for theoretical unity curtail and caricature local research. Instead, he favors an autonomous, non-centralized theoretical production whose validity does not depend on approval from established regimes of thought. Hence, local criticisms proceed by means of a "return of knowledge," or an insurrection of subjugated knowledges, by which he means blocs of historical knowledge disguised by functionalist and systematizing theory, knowledges usually disqualified as inadequate, naive, beneath the required level of scientificity. By resurrecting a history of struggles, and through these subjugated knowledges, Foucault thinks that critical discourse may discover a new essential force. In this sense, genealogy undertakes the painstaking rediscovery of struggles, a reconstruction which would not be possible unless the tyranny of globalizing discourses were eliminated. So by genealogy, Foucault (1980: 83) also means "the union of erudite knowledge and local memories which allows us to establish a historical knowledge of struggles and to make use of this knowledge tactically today." Genealogies, then, are anti-sciences, opposed not necessarily to the contents, methods, or concepts of science, but to the effects of the centralizing powers linked to organized scientific discourse – "it is really against the effects of the power of a discourse that is considered to be scientific that the genealogy must wage its struggle" (Foucault 1980: 84).

Foucault's project also examines relations of domination. These are not solid and global kinds of domination, one large group of people over others, but manifold forms of domination exercised within society in multiple forms. Looking at power relations genealogically involves a number of methodological precautions:

1 analysis should not concern itself with forms of power in their central locations, but with power at its extremities, in its more regional and local forms and institutions;

2 analysis should not concern itself also with power at the level of conscious intention or decision, but where intention, if there is one, is completely invested in real and effective practices;

3 power should not be taken as a phenomenon of the domination of one individual or one class over others, but as something which circulates or only functions in the form of a chain;

4 rather than starting from the center of power and discovering the extent to which it permeates the base, one must conduct an ascending analysis of power, starting from its infinitesimal mechanisms, each with their own history, trajectory, technique, and tactics, and see how these mechanisms are colonized by ever more general mechanisms and by forms of global domination;

5 while it is quite possible that the major mechanisms of power are accompanied by ideological productions, they are much more and much less than ideology, in that power is exercised through the production of effective instruments for the formation and accumulation of knowledge.

This then is the methodological course Foucault believes the genealogy of power should follow.

Ethics of the Self

Foucault's last works, published in the 1980s, shift attention to technologies of the self, using as empirical material a history of sexuality in Greek, Roman, and early Christian cultures. As Foucault (1983: 237) puts it, three domains of genealogy (or historical ontologies) are possible: the self in relation to truth through which people constitute themselves as subjects of knowledge; the self in relation to fields of power through which people constitute themselves as subjects acting on others; the self in relation to ethics through which the subject constitutes itself as a moral agent. Foucault's *History of Sexuality* is about morals, or rather behavior in relation to imposed moral codes. But, for Foucault, there is another side to moral prescription, the kinds of relationship people have with themselves, or ethics, which also determines how the individual constitutes itself as a moral subject. In turn, this (latter) relationship has four aspects: the aspect of self or behavior (ethical substance) concerned with moral conduct (desire for Christians, feelings for the modern subject); the mode of subjection by which people are made to recognize their moral obligations (divine law, natural law, rational rules); the means by which the person elaborates itself to become an ethical subject (moderation, eradication of desires, asceticism); and the kind of moral being people aspire to, or telos (pure, immortal, free, master of self). For Foucault, these four independent and related aspects make a framework that can be applied to historical forms of ethics. Hence, for the Greeks the telos was a beautiful life, the ethical substance was pleasure/desire, and the technical means self-mastery. For Foucault, the Greek ethical system was an aesthetic of existence in the sense that acts could be performed without being grounded in norms underwritten by religion, law, or science. Yet the Greek system, founded in inequality, is no solution to the modern problem of an ethical life. Foucault finds hardly any remnant left of the principle that the main work of art for the individual is one's own life. His own ethical politics apparently consist of the liberation of the individual from the state's mode of individuation: "We have to promote new forms of subjectivity through the refusal of this kind of individuality which has been imposed on us for several centuries" (Dreyfus and Rabinow 1983: 216; Rabinow 1984). This seems to involve a shift in ethical substance from desire to pleasure, a change in telos from autonomy to an aesthetics of existence, and a self that constitutes itself as an autonomous, self-governing being.

Deconstruction

Complementing Foucault's analysis of the relations between truth and knowledge is Jacques Derrida's deconstruction of the very possibility of telling coherent truths. Deconstruction, in Derrida's use of the term, means reading a text in such a way that its conceptual distinctions can be shown to fail because of their inconsistent and paradoxical employment – the text is shown to fail by its own criteria. Philosophy claims that its statements are structured by logic, reason, and truth and not by the rhetoric of the language in which they are expressed. What Derrida terms "logocentrism" orients philosophy towards an order of meaning (thought, truth, etc.) conceived as existing in itself, as a foundation and an origin, beyond which we need not go. Furthermore, fundamentals are conventionally designated in terms of the constancy of a presence – that is, the presence of an object to sight, presence as existence or essence – this serves as a centering, grounding force or principle, leading to what Derrida terms a "metaphysics of presence" (cf. chapter 2). For Derrida, almost all philosophy assumes this immediately available arena of certainty. Further, in oppositions such as nature/culture, positive/negative, meaning/form, the first (superior) term belongs to the logos; the second is a complication, negation, manifestation, or disruption of the first. Philosophical analysis is an attempt to return to an origin of certainty and primacy, a pure standard, one counterposed to derivations, complications, and accidents. "This is not just *one* metaphysical gesture among others; it is the metaphysical exigency, the most constant, profound and potent procedure" (Derrida 1978: 236). Philosophy tries to maintain presence by giving priority to speech (as immediate capturing) over writing – this priority Derrida calls "phonocentrism"; furthermore the internal dialogue within consciousness is prioritized as the high point of pure presence. But, for Derrida, even here, in the presence of consciousness to itself, there is non-presence or absence. For Derrida, the problem is that presences turn out to be complex products. While we may think of the real as that present in any given instant, we must also think of the present as difference. Events (such as the meanings of words) are determined by prior structures (such as languages) which themselves are produced by prior events. We find only non-originary origins in such retrogressions, a shuffling back and forth (e.g. between words and language) which never leads to synthesis – hence, Derrida's term *différance*, referring to this alternation, means both differ and defer. Différance (different and deferred) is his antidote to the stress on presence. Any feature of experience requires other, absent features of experience to make sense. Presence, then, is not, for Derrida, an absolute matrix form of being, but is a particularization and effect within a system of différance. Thus, in Saussure's linguistics, signs are not positive entities pointing to objects, but are effects of differences (between signs).

Derrida finds in this a powerful critique of western logocentrism. Theories grounded on presence undo themselves as the supposed foundation proves to be the product of differentiation and deferral; theories are thereby deprived of authority. But Derrida's deconstruction of logocentric theories does not lead to a new theory setting things straight. Rather, theory may permanently be condemned to structural inconsistency. Deconstruction, then, shows the difficulties in theories defining meaning in a universal way (Lawson 1985; Culler 1982; Derrida 1974; 1978; 1981).

The Mirror of Nature

The philosopher Richard Rorty, professor of humanities at the University of Virginia, reaches similar conclusions, but draws on the American tradition of pragmatism rather than the French traditions of semiotics and structuralism. Rorty's *Philosophy and the Mirror of Nature* (1979) criticizes modern philosophy as the adjudicator of truth claims. In modern philosophy, knowing means accurately representing a reality outside the mind. Since the seventeenth century, philosophy has aimed at being a general theory of representation which can divide culture into accurate and less accurate components. Protests against the conception that culture needs "grounding" and queries about philosophy's pretensions to perform such a service, by Nietzsche, or the pragmatist William James, as two instances, went largely unnoticed until the supreme position of philosophy as guardian against superstition was undermined by the triumph of the secular over the claims of religion. Deprived of its task, philosophy became isolated, its pretensions now seeming absurd.

For Rorty, the three most important philosophers of the twentieth century – Wittgenstein, Heidegger, and Dewey – tried in their early years to find a new ultimate context for thought, only to see these efforts as self-deception. Hence, their later work is therapeutic rather than reconstructive, designed to make people question their motives for philosophizing rather than supplying a new philosophical program. In particular, all three think that the notion of knowledge as accurate representation should be abandoned. Rorty surveys recent developments in analytical philosophy from the point of view of this anti-Cartesian, anti-Kantian revolution, arguing that the philosophies of Wilfred Sellars and W. V. O. Quine, when extended in a certain way, allow a view of truth as "what is better for us to believe" rather than "the accurate representation of reality" (Rorty 1979: 10). Rorty interprets the distinction between theory's search for objective knowledge and other less privileged areas of activity as merely the difference between "normal" discourse (i.e. employing agreed-upon criteria for reaching agreement) and "abnormal" discourses (those without such criteria). He finds philosophy's attempt at explicating "rationality" and "objectivity" in terms of accurate representation to be self-deceptive efforts at eternalizing the normal discourse of the day. Rorty (1979: 357) says:

> The notion that our chief task is to mirror accurately, in our own Glassy Essence, the universe around us is the complement of the notion ... that the universe is made up of very simple, clearly and distinctly knowable things, knowledge of whose essence provides the master-vocabulary which permits commensuration of all discourses. This

classic picture of human beings must be set aside before epistemologically centered philosophy can be set aside.

Thus, Rorty favors an edifying philosophy over a systematic philosophy, one which refuses to claim objective truth, philosophy as a continuing conversation rather than a method. In his later essays, Rorty (1991) claims that whatever good philosophy's notions of objectivity and transcendence may have done for modern culture could be attained equally well by (Dewey's) idea of a democratic, pluralist community that strives for intersubjective agreement and novelty. Like Dewey, Rorty favors a political position in the socio-political culture of liberalism. Unlike Foucault and other poststructuralists, Rorty finds opportunities for self-criticism and reform in the present liberal society. Rorty therefore calls himself, only partly ironically, a "postmodern bourgeois liberal."

In summary, we can say that for poststructural theories the social projection of rational consciousness results in universal and totali*zing* forms of knowledge that also are dominating and totalit*arian*, in that the whole of existence, and its very essence, supposedly opens to the contemplative thinker. The rational One can sit in Paris, London, or New York and "think the world," playing the mind's eye across global surfaces and societies never seen, penetrating into the consciousnesses of people never met, discovering the secrets of cultures never lived. Yet theory is still post*structural* in that all its theories, to some extent, fit events into wider contexts which conceptualization attempts to characterize in some systematic way. (Derrida is something of an exception to this.) Tensions between non-totalization and systematization produces theories phrased in the language of space rather than time. Also theorists recast the role of thinking so that it is no longer an instrument for penetrating into essence, nor is it armchair explorer of realms and lands never physically entered, but instead theory is a categorizing play on surface, spatial appearances which, when it enters into the relations between things, tries to understand in non-causal, non-hierarchical, self-deprecating, ironic yet still systematizing ways.

Postmodern Philosophy

There are no sharp differences between poststructural and postmodern philosophies. Generally, however, poststructural philosophy criticizes the certainties of modern knowledge, as with its claims to coherence, neutrality, and truth, while postmodern philosophy carries this further into an alternative discourse based on oppositional modes of understanding. Postmodernism proposes new ways of being a person which involve, on the one hand (with Deleuze and Guattari, and, in some phases, Lyotard), the liberation of desire, yet on the other (Baudrillard), utter cynicism or nihilistic "resistance" to the forces of modernity. We take postmodern philosophy, therefore, to be a more extreme form of philosophical skepticism than poststructuralism. This section begins with Lyotard's deconstruction of postmodern forms of knowledge and then surveys the excesses of Deleuze, Guattari, and Baudrillard.

The Postmodern Condition

Jean-François Lyotard is often thought to be *the* postmodern philosopher. His book *The Postmodern Condition* (1984) introduced the term "postmodern" firmly into philosophical discourse, while with his work on theory, ethics, politics, and aesthetics Lyotard tries to break fundamentally with the modern and adopt postmodern positions. Like Foucault, Lyotard criticizes totalizing and universalizing theories and methods and favors difference and plurality. Previously linked domains, such as the theoretical, the practical, and the aesthetic, have their own autonomies, rules, and criteria. Universal and foundational theories and claims that one method or set of concepts has privileged status are rejected: indeed, these are deemed terroristic and totalitarian theorizations.

In his early work, Lyotard is a kind of Nietzschean romantic. Books such as *Discours, figure* (1971), criticize semiotic approaches which privilege texts and discourses over sensual experience. Lyotard's polemic is directed also against unity and coherence in theoretical discourses, against the language of dialectics ("infinite and useless") and the left's project of critique in general. Lyotard (1974) adopts instead a Nietzschean affirmative discourse in a politics and philosophy of desire. His position is a kind of Nietzschean vitalism (showing influences from Bataille) affirming the free flow of life energies. Thus, the objective of "libidinal economy" is to describe the flows, intensities, and territorializations of desire, liberate the flows of desire, unleash desire in its full and glorious varieties and intensities. In the mid-1970s, Lyotard broke with this early position; *Economie libidinale*, he came to believe, was a failed attempt to develop a philosophy of desiring forces. Lyotard turns instead to the philosophy of language for insights into (a re-evaluated) politics of justice. In *Just Gaming* (just in the sense of justice), Lyotard and Thebaud (1985) attack the Enlightenment belief in absolute criteria for judgment, preferring a situation in which one judges without criteria, in which justice is local, multiple, provisional, and subject to contestation and transformation. Discourses are theorized as moves in language games (cf. Wittgenstein 1968) and "just" moves are tactical and contextual.

The Postmodern Condition (Lyotard 1984) is a sustained critical evaluation of modern science and an outline of the conditions of postmodern knowledge. Lyotard uses the term "modern" to designate any science legitimated by appeal to metadiscourses, such as dialectics of spirit, hermeneutics of meaning, and emancipation of the rational subject or the working class. The postmodern, by comparison, is defined as "incredulity towards metanarratives" (Lyotard 1984: xxiv), the underlying sentiment being that all metanarratives are now obsolete. Postmodern knowledge, Lyotard says, redefines a sensitivity to differences and reinforces an ability to tolerate the incommensurable. Its principle is not the expert's homology (correspondence, sameness) but the inventor's paralogy (difference). Lyotard emphasizes that science is not the only form of knowledge. Science conflicts with another kind of knowledge, which he calls "narrative." The narrative form, preeminent in traditional (prescientific) knowledges, provides its own immediate legitimation in terms of determining criteria of competence and defining what has a right to be said and done in the culture in question. Lyotard compares this with scientific knowledge which, he argues, is separated from society and must presuppose its own validity unless it appeals to narrative, which it dismisses as no knowledge at all. Modern science must instead find validity in a practical subject – humanity and its emancipation. Here, the important thing becomes not only legitimating utterances as true, but legitimating prescriptive statements as just. Positive knowledge in this context can only inform the practical subject about the reality within which the prescription is to be inscribed; there is nothing to prove that because a statement is true, a prescription based on it will be just. Lyotard makes such arguments to show that science is merely one more language game with no special calling to supervise praxis. Here, Lyotard employs Wittgenstein's (1968) notion that types of utterances are language games, defined in terms of rules specifying properties, uses, etc., which are the object of contracts between players

By comparison, in postmodern culture, Lyotard argues, we no longer have recourse to grand narratives, the dialectic of spirit or the emancipation of humanity, as validations for postmodern scientific discourse. Instead, little narratives are the quintessential form of imaginative invention, particularly in science. Legitimation can only spring from people's own practice and communicational interaction. The heteromorphous nature of language games implies renouncing the "terror" which tries to make them isomorphic. It means also that any consensus on the rules defining a game must be local – that is, agreed on by the present players and subject to cancellation. This favors a multiplicity of "fine meta-arguments," by which Lyotard means argumentation concerning metaprescriptives which is limited in time and space. Hence:

> The postmodern would be that which . . . searches for new presentations, not in order to enjoy them but in order to impart a stronger sense of the unpresentable . . . it is our business not to supply reality but to invent allusions to the conceivable which cannot be presented. (Lyotard 1984: 81)

Postmodern knowledge is thus against metanarratives and foundationalism, avoids grand schemes of legitimation, is for heterogeneity, plurality, constant innovation, and the pragmatic construction of local rules and prescriptives agreed upon by participants (and thus for micropolitics). In brief, the new conditions of knowledge demand a new epistemology (Lyotard 1984; 1988; Best and Kellner 1991).

Schizoanalysis

Giles Deleuze (1925–95), a philosopher, and Felix Guattari, a psychoanalyst, combine Marx, Freud, Nietzsche, Kafka, a critique of Lacan, Barthes, and others, a reading of Wilhelm Reich and Henry Miller, and an appreciation for psychotics, in a series of works titled *Capitalism and Schizophrenia* (Deleuze and Guattari 1983; 1987). As we have seen, Deleuze (1983; 1984; 1988) wrote a series of studies in the history of philosophy, most importantly interpretations of Kant, Nietzsche, and Foucault. Guattari was active inside and then outside the French Communist Party, trained in (but later rejecting) Lacanian psychoanalysis, and worked on a theory of the social and political unconscious. Deleuze and Guattari's first collaborative work, the *Anti-Oedipus* (1983), is immediately an attack on Lacan's psychoanalysis and an attempt to replace it with "schizo-analysis." More generally, the book is a critique of modernity, especially capitalism and the family as institutions which channel, repress, and redirect desire (hence the *Anti*-Oedipus of the title). Deleuze and Guattari replace the negative conception of desire, in Lacan's terms, as the lack which emerges between need and demand, with a Nietzschean conception of desire as a positive, primary force, a free-floating energy, immanent and unconscious, uniting nature with humans conceptualized as "desiring-machines" rather than subjectivities. Desire is a dynamic machine ("desiring-production"), producing things, running in discontinuous flows, making connections with objects (or partial-objects) and other desiring machines (parts of the human body). The idea is to break with modern theories of the conscious subject; one can, in Deleuze and Guattari's (1983: 20) terms, dimly perceive a subject, but with no fixed identity, a spare part adjacent to the desiring machine. Likewise, this position rejects modern rationalist schemes of representation and interpretation as repressive impositions fixing and stabilizing desiring flows and damming creative energies. Instead, Deleuze and Guattari want direct contact between desire and flows of energy (material/semiotic fluxes). In the words of Brian Massami (1992), Deleuze and Guattari criticize "state philosophy" (the representational thinking which has dominated western thought since Plato) and substitute nomad thought, moving freely, riding difference, changing things by throwing brick-concepts through the windows of the court of reason:

> The space of nomad thought is qualitatively different from State space. Air against earth. State space is "striated," or gridded. Movement in it is confined as by gravity to a horizontal plane, and limited by the order of that plane to preset paths between fixed and identifiable points. Nomad space is "smooth," or open-ended. One can rise up at any point and move to any other. Its mode of distribution is the *nomos*; arraying oneself in an open space (hold the street), as opposed to the logos of entrenching oneself in a closed space (hold the fort). (Massami 1992: 6)

Deleuze and Guattari attempt to construct such a smooth space of thought. Theirs is a politics of desire rather than a rational appeal (Deleuze and Guattari 1983; Best and Kellner 1991).

A Thousand Plateaus (Deleuze and Guattari 1987) employs "rhizomatics" to interpret reality as dynamic, heterogeneous, and non-dichotomous. Biological, geographical, and geological metaphors abound, as also in the chapter on geophilosophy in Deleuze and Guattari's (1994) last collaboration *What is Philosophy?* One can vaguely see the remnants of the concept of structure, called "strata" in *A Thousand Plateaus*: Deleuze and Guattari distinguish three major strata, physicochemical, organic, and anthropomorphic. Each stratum presents diverse forms and substances and a variety of codes and milieux, yet retains a unity of composition. The strata are mobile, one stratum may always serve as substratum of another, and one may collide with another independently of any evolutionary order. Between the strata are machinic assemblages composed of: arborescent multiplicities that are molar in the sense of being organizable, unifiable, and conscious; and rhizomatic multiplicities that are molecular, intensive, composed of particles that do not divide without changing character. In as much as they are territorial, assemblages belong to the strata, but assemblages are also constituted by lines of deterritorialization, some opening to other assemblages, others opening onto a land that is eccentric, immemorial, or yet to come. Strata and assemblages are complexes of lines: some lines are molar, forming a segmentary, arborescent system; others are molecular of the rhizome type, where the line passes between things; a third kind is made up of lines of flight or deterritorialized movements. Indeed, the strata are defined by their speeds of relative deterritorialization, the anthropomorphic being more deterritorialized than the organic, and that more than the physicochemical. In addition, absolutely deterritorialized matter forms a plane of consistency. Individuated entities are inscribed on this plane of consistency but they are not persons or substances, but "haecceities" whose bodies include heterogeneous things and whose duration may be brief or extended. How far this leads postmodern theory from the philosophy of the subject is shown by Deleuze and Guattari's (1987: 162) statement that:

> Flows of intensity, their fluids, their fibers, their continuums and conjunctions of effects, the wind, fine segmentation, micro perceptions, have replaced the world of the subject. Becomings, becomings-animal, becomings-molecular, have replaced history, individual or general.

This is an utterly anarchic work which disrupts its more coherent statements before it makes them, disturbs the few conventional readers who might hesitantly venture into its pages with phrases like "God is a lobster" and in general (if generality is possible here) is a Nietzschean geography of forces and intensities taken beyond all limits.

Hyperreality/Cyberblitz/Simulacra

Jean Baudrillard is a sociologist critic of Marxian, Freudian, and structuralist positions as well as a poststructuralist and postmodernist critic of life under capitalism. A student of Lefebvre's, and originally an anarcho-situationist and participant in the events of May 1968 (Smith 1997), Baudrillard initially used structuralism and semiology to recast Marxian theory. His first published works explore the "system of objects" of a "consumer society." In Le Système des objects, Baudrillard (1968, trans. 1996) sees the human subject facing a modern world of objects which fascinate and control perception, thought, and behavior. Baudrillard argues that consumption is not a passive absorption of things in contrast to the active process of production, but instead consumption is an active relationship to objects which founds the entire cultural system. Consumption, he says, is no longer a material practice, but instead is the organization of things into a signifying fabric. To be an object of consumption, the product must become a sign, deriving consistency and meaning from an abstract, systematic relationship to all other sign objects. Hence, the commodity is consumed not in its materiality, but in its (signifying) difference. Further, Baudrillard argues, the conversion of the object to the systematic status of the sign implies the simultaneous transformation of the human relationship into one of consuming and being consumed, with the sign as mediation of consumption and consummation. For Baudrillard (1996: 203), consumption can be defined as a "total idealist practice" in that the "objects of consumption constitute an idealist lexicon of signs wherein the will to live itself is discernible in an ever-receding materiality." To explore this world of consumption, Baudrillard proposes a semiology of the environment and everyday practices, in which objects refer to a social logic which keeps people in their places. Such a semiology of consumption would analyze domestic spaces and the distribution of objects within them as well as a vertical analysis of the hierarchical scale of objects in the social universe; he proposes a rhetorical and syntactic analysis of the environment which would examine hierarchies of goods as well as the organization and social use of objects.

From the mid-1970s on, Baudrillard's reflections on political economy and the consumer society are replaced by simulation, media, and new technologies, which together result in the "implosion" and "hyperreality" of the postmodern world. In *Simulations*, Baudrillard (1983) argues that a shift has occurred from the primacy of the mode of production to that of the code of production (i.e. signs and codes are the primary constituents of social life). We live in a hyperreality of simulations in which images, spectacles, and the play of signs replace the logic of production. This informational era of simulations, governed by models, codes, and a system of "general economy," has social domination as its overarching goal. In it, the boundary between representation and reality implodes: the experience of the real disappears, to be superseded by total relativity, simulation in which signs exchange without interacting with the real, where the sign is emancipated from its archaic obligation to designate something, where signs and codes now constitute the "real." Whereas production ("metallurgy") determined modern society, Baudrillard's postmodern society is characterized by radical "semiurgy," a proliferation of signs, an implosion of distinctions and with them the binary oppositions maintained by modern philosophy.

For Baudrillard, the broadcast media, especially television, create a hyperreality more real than real. In the postmodern "mediascape," the private sphere is exteriorized as the most intimate life processes became the feeding ground of the camera intrusive, while inversely the universe explodes on the domestic television screen, saturating people with information, images, and ecstasies. People enter a new "subjectivity" in which the person is switching center for networks of influence. In Baudrillard's concept of "cyberblitz," individuals, objects, and society are the effects of cybernetic codes, models, modulations, and social steering systems. "Simulacra" (representations of objects or events) emerge in "orders of simulacra" – that is, orders of appearance in their relations with the "real." In the feudal era, with its fixed social hierarchy, signs were transparent and "obligatory." In the modern order, the counterfeit is the paradigmatic mode of representation initiating a new order of simulacra: early modernity had a natural law of value in which simulacra represented nature or embodied natural rights; during the industrial revolution infinite reproducibility took the form of the industrial simulacra or series (exact replicas turned out in series); today we are in a third order of simulation proper, in which simulation devours representation and models take precedence over things. For

Baudrillard, as distinct from Lefebvre, simulations rather than representations, structure space. The society of simulations limits the individual's choice of behavior in a "radically indeterminist" model of social control. In the triumph of cybernetics, a self-reproducing system rules out radical change. Disneyland presents itself as an imaginary space to conceal the fact that "all of 'real' America ... is Disneyland" (Baudrillard 1983: 25), the hyperreal being that which is always already reproduced. With the victory of simulation over the reality principle, determination is both total and totally indeterminate. In hyperconformity, the masses concern themselves solely with the next opportunity to consume spectacle. In such a world, previous social theories are obsolete if they posit individuals or classes capable of social action. For the social has imploded into "the masses," indifference is true practice, mass and media are a single process. Baudrillard suggests that mass apathy can be seen as strategic resistance, a refusal of meaning.

In *Forget Foucault*, Baudrillard (1987) argues that Foucault's theory of power is obsolete in a society of simulations. Power no longer resides in institutions, nor in the economy, but resides in codes, simulations, and media. Power becomes increasingly abstract. There is an intense fascination with power because it has changed into signs of dead power, with simulations replacing the real exercise of power. Thus, Baudrillard argues, Foucault's theory of power refers to an earlier stage when power was actively visible. Similarly, for Baudrillard, sexuality no longer exists in the forms described by Foucault and psychoanalysis (that is, as a localized domain of erotic practices surrounded by recognized prohibitions) but instead sexuality is manifest throughout society, no longer a private activity, but instead socially mandated: everything is sexuality, yet nothing is sexual. Discourses of liberation, whether of labor or sexuality (as with the "micropolitics of desire"), only reproduce capitalist rationalization: the radical alternative to *product*ivist sexuality is *seduc*tion. Thus, Baudrillard's *De la seduction* (1979) interprets seduction not in the sense of enticement for sexual intercourse, but as a game at the level of appearance, surface, and signs, something fundamentally artificial, something quite unlike the "natural" pursuit of sexual pleasure. Baudrillard defends artificial over natural beauty and praises the sexual object. Women, he says, were never dominated, but were always dominant. More generally, in the society of media, simulations, and information, film stars exert a cool seduction through all areas of social experience and the masses "respond" with simulated response or "enigmatic belief."

Baudrillard argues for predestination in a "spiral of the worst," where catastrophes reveal the tendencies of objects and nature to exceed themselves, delighting people with their spectacular excesses. Baudrillard concludes that we should submit to the supremacy of the object and follow the spiral of the worst until, in a version of Nietzsche's eternal return, metamorphosis perhaps gives the subject a second chance (Kellner 1989).

Poststructural/Postmodern Theory Reconsidered

In their excellent survey of postmodern theory, Steven Best and Douglas Kellner (1991: 2) say that "there is no unified postmodern theory, or even a coherent set of positions. Rather, one is struck by the diversities between theories often lumped together as 'postmodern.'" Reading these poststructural–postmodern ideas one is struck by the diverse intensity of what are often outrageous ideas, especially at the postmodern end of the spectrum. Contrary to Best and Kellner, however, there are a number of "positions" which recur. These are theories critical of modern philosophy because it shares the rationalism of modern life. Poststructural theory draws from nihilism and existentialism to find philosophy narrow, exclusive, and complicit with the very problem found prevalent in modern society, its rationalism – overbearing in the sense that rationality cripples the modern subject ("mind over body" is exactly the problem, not the solution). For most poststructural theorists representational theories of truth are both impossible, in terms of the available guarantees of accuracy, and inadequate, in that even accurate description only begins to approach the nebulous realm of truth. For some, like Derrida, speaking theoretically involves erasing one's assertions before they are made; others, like Baudrillard, delight in the shock-value of outrageous, unprovable but definite statements. Poststructural theories, especially those at the postmodern end of the spectrum, are declarative rather than rational, systematic in a fragmentary way rather than totalizing, and, while they cannot avoid representing (words are representations), do not claim truth in terms of representational accuracy – often, indeed, the point of theoretical writing seems to be taking ideas to their limit, convincing through the wear and tear of perpetual exaggeration, rather than through resolute claims for the exact replication of reality by truthful ideas.

Postmodern theories derive from the tradition of critical thinking: this generation of theorists matured in a leftist culture which took Marxism for granted as the political language of intelligent people. These are theorists often critical of the present form of society; but the objects of social criticism differ from those of Marxism. As opposed to Marxian class analysis, poststructural theories appeal to Nietzschean notions of power, while postmodern variants are founded on desire as basic category. In modern society, knowledge is developed in the service of power yet power is immanent in all relations rather than exercised by a ruling class. Modern society uses power to repress desire rather than ensure profit. As opposed to Marx's productivism, postmodern theory emphasizes consumption, and rather than being materialist in terms of the production of objects, it emphasizes instead the rule of objects and the dominance of signs.

Postmodernism has a politics, but it is anti-modern rather than anti-capitalist, and nihilistic rather than radical, although nihilism is sometimes thought a revolutionary position. Poststructural theory understands modern society to be a system of power and expresses extreme skepticism about totalitarian politics, be they capitalist or communist. Poststructural theory instead takes the side of marginal groups, values difference over sameness, and has an identity rather than a class politics, conceiving identity as body rather than consciousness, as differentiated, mobile, and socially constructed rather than inherent or, for that matter, rooted firmly in definable places (cf. Harvey 1996). Postmodern politics is often expressed in terms of unleashing the creative power of desire, breaking the chains of repression imposed on humans by the constraints of rationalism. It is anarchistic rather than socialistic, unorganized rather than disciplined, and can thus be considered naive relative to the awesome power of the very megasystems it exposes. It confronts Marxism with an unnecessary ferocity, explainable largely through the cynicism of middle age, which turns on its own youth with a vengeance born of bitter revolutionary disappointment and a complexity driven by personal regard for individual reputation. While suggestive of a politics of difference, postmodernism is inherently and deliberately incapable of producing the necessary alliance or network of organizational ideas or institutions. In the end, therefore, its revolutionary nihilism is more simply just negatively nihilistic in the sense of revelling in the consumption of signs and hedonistically delighting in the intensification of desire.

Towards Postmodern Geography

Such poststructural and postmodern philosophical notions, developed during the 1970s, diffused slowly into Anglo-American geography during the 1980s. Most early ventures into postmodern theory in geography were not pure statements of a new position, but resulted from interactions between earlier Marxist work and certain of the "safer" postmodern positions. The main "carrier" of postmodern notions into geography was an article in the *New Left Review* by the Marxist literary critic Frederic Jameson. Subsequently, Marxist critiques of postmodern ideas, or reactions by Marxists to postmodernity as an historical period, remained for years the best-known and most influential postmodern geographies. However, this began to change in the early 1990s when other postmodern writers, especially those coming from the intersection of post-colonial or feminist positions and poststructural and postmodern notions, began to be more widely read. Here, we first outline Jameson's ideas as basis for the central "postmodern" notions of Dear, Harvey, and Soja. The section then concludes with a sampling of other postmodern ideas in geography, culminating in one of the few extreme statements of "pure" postmodernist geographical position made so far.

The Cultural Logic of Late Capitalism

Frederic Jameson (1984), a professor of comparative literature at Duke University, argues that around 1960 high modernism in art, literature, and philosophy were exhausted and a new era of postmodernism, most dramatically visible in architecture, came into being, as with Robert Venturi's *Learning from Las Vegas* (1972). For Jameson, postmodernism does not represent the hegemony of a new overall style; rather the postmodern is a cultural dominant (a dominant cultural logic or hegemonic norm) which allows for the coexistence of a range of different yet subordinate features – indeed, many features of the postmodern can be found in high modernism. For the Marxist Jameson (1984: 57), postmodern culture is a superstructural expression of American military and economic domination in the world ("the underside of culture is blood, torture, death and horror"). In the postmodern era, Jameson says, aesthetic production becomes integrated into commodity production generally and subject therefore to its waves of novel-seeming goods and ideas.

What are the constitutive features of the postmodern? Comparing interpretations of Van Gogh's (modern) painting of peasant shoes with Andy Warhol's (postmodern) *Diamond Dust Shoes*, Jameson finds: in the first an inert obectal form taken as a symptom for some vaster (and more truthful) reality; whereas the latter is a random collection of dead objects shorn of their lifeworld origins, hence deprived of hermeneutical gesture. In the postmodern, there is a new kind of depthlessness or superficiality, symbolic of a fundamental mutation in the object world (now becoming a set of texts or simulacra) and in the disposition of the subject. For Jameson, too, the postmodern brings a waning of affect, feeling, emotion, and subjectivity. The artistic expression of modernist notions of alienation, anomie, or social fragmentation in what used to be called "the age of anxiety" presupposed some separation within the subject and a metaphysics of inside and outside, all of which have vanished in postmodernism – indeed, the poststructural critique of the hermeneutic is a significant (philosophical) symptom of postmodern culture. In the postmodern era, the depth sought by modern philosophies is replaced by surfaces and intertextuality. Anxiety, alienation, and the experiences to which they correspond, are no longer appropriate in the postmodern world. In the context of literary criticism, the waning of affect might also be characterized as the disappearance of the high modernist thematics of time and temporality. With this, Jameson (1984: 64) thinks that "our daily life, our psychic experience, our cultural languages, are today dominated by categories of space rather than by categories of time."

The disappearance of subject and style in the postmodern engender a cultural practice of pastiche rather than parody (pastiche being blank parody). With the collapse of style, cultural producers have nowhere to turn but the imaginary museum of the past, or what architectural historians call "historicism," by which is actually meant random cannibalization, the play of random stylistic allusion or (in Lefebvre's words) the increasing primacy of the "neo." The culture of the simulacrum comes to "life" in a society where exchange value effaces the memory of use value or, in Guy Debord's (1983) situationist terms, the image becomes the final form of commodity reification. The new spatial logic turns what used to be historical time into a vast collection of contemporaneous images. Conforming to poststructural linguistic theory, the past as referent is bracketed and then effaced, leaving nothing but texts. Loss of the subject's capacity to organize the past and the future into coherent experience means that cultural production becomes dominated by a spatial "logic" of fragments and a randomly heterogeneous practice. The postmodern city, Jameson thinks, involves a mutation of built space with which human subjects, raised in the space of high modernism, cannot cope – his example is the Bonaventure Hotel in downtown Los Angeles. Jameson's conclusion from this is that postmodern hyperspace transcends the capacity of the individual to locate itself, to perceptually organize its surroundings, or cognitively map its position in a mappable external world, this being a microcosm of an incapacity to map the global multinational communications network in which the subject is caught. Distance in general, and critical distance in particular, has been abolished in the new space of postmodernism

– "our postmodern bodies are bereft of spatial coordinates and practically (let alone theoretically) incapable of distantiation" (Jameson 1984: 87). For Jameson, global space demands the invention of a (left, political) internationalism, a cultural politics of a radically new type in which spatial issues are fundamental organizing concerns. The aesthetic of this spatial politics Jameson terms *cognitive mapping*. This draws on Kevin Lynch's notion of mental maps in *The Image of the City* (1968) and the idea that disalienation entails the practical reconquest of a sense of place. Jameson reads this in terms of Althusserian and Lacanian redefinitions of ideology as the representation of the subject's imaginary relation to its conditions of existence, so that specialized geographical and cartographic issues are rethought in the broader terms of social space – in this case, social relations to the international context, which his analysis shows exactly to be the problem in postmodernism. An aesthetic of cognitive mapping will have to respect a complex representational dialectic of codes and media as well as experience and knowledge. For Jameson, the world space of multinational capital needs an as yet unimaginable new mode of representation within which we may again begin to grasp our positioning as individual and collective subjects and regain our capacity to act and struggle – the (critical) politics of postmodernism will have to invent a global cognitive mapping on a social as well as a spatial scale.

The Postmodern Challenge to Human Geography

Jameson's article and subsequent books (e.g. Jameson 1991), phrased often in spatial terms, positioning space as the privileged realm of the postmodern, had particular appeal to geography. Reading postmodern social theory in the 1980s, geographers began to think again about the place of geography and space in social theory. One such set of statements, important particularly because its author was editor of the new journal *Society and Space*, which carried much of the new postmodern geography, came from Michael Dear (1986; 1988), professor of geography at the University of Southern California. Dear essentially argues that postmodernism makes geography an offer it cannot afford to refuse. For Dear, this means that there can be no grand theory of human geography; yet he is "unhappy with the extremes of deconstructive relativism" (Dear 1988: 267). It is from this paradoxical position, enticed by postmodernism, worried by its anarchy, remaining modern, that Dear wants to reconstruct human geography.

Later, Dear (1994) calls postmodern social thought a "tidal wave" sweeping through human geography, provoking active hostility, incomprehension, indifference, yet intense interest. Postmodernity, Dear thinks, involves a style (as in architecture), an epoch (in terms of a radical break with the past), and a method (revolt against the rationality of modernism). For Dear, postmodern geography first emerged in 1986 with publications on postmodern urbanism and planning (Dear 1986) and on deconstructing Los Angeles (Soja 1986), both coming from a decade or more of geographical engagements with social theory. Postmodern consciousness in human geography derives from diverse perspectives – debates on social theory, work on the cultural landscapes of modernity, and the notion of flexible specialization. For Dear, postmodernism most influences geography in the following areas:

1 cultural landscapes and place making;
2 the economic landscapes of post-Fordism;
3 philosophical and theoretical disputes related to space and problems of language;
4 problems of representation in geographical writing and cartography;
5 politics of postmodernity, feminist geography's discontent with postmodernism, questions of post-colonialism;
6 the construction of the individual and boundaries of the self (i.e. the issue of identity);
7 reassertions of natural and environmental issues.

In such areas, Dear thinks that postmodernism enfranchises and empowers those outside the traditional centers of scholastic authority, legitimizes difference, undermines the hegemony of existing power systems. Postmodernity is liberating but is attacked for its loss of rationality and its essential conservatism. For Dear, postmodernism intensifies the revolution which brought theoretical and philosophical human geography into mainstream social science. We might say, however, that, with slight changes in terminology and context, this could be a statement made in 1959 about quantitative, theoretical geography's difference with regional description.

The Condition of Postmodernity

In *The Condition of Postmodernity* (1989), Harvey too sees postmodernism as a configuration of new sentiments and thoughts which defines the trajectory of social and political development. Hence, Jonathan Raban's book *Soft City* (1974) was a cultural marker, he says, evidence of a shift in the conceptualization of urbanism from the city as rationalized system to the city as producer of signs and images, the city as maniacal scrapbook filled with people of soft, fluid identities, endlessly open to the exercise of will and imagination. Harvey recounts his reactions to an exhibition of Cindy Sherman's postmodern photographs, seemingly of different women, but (he realizes with a certain shock) actually all of the same person, the photographer herself – here he finds a striking parallel with Raban's insistence on the "plasticity of human personality through the malleability of appearances and surfaces" as also with the "self-referential positioning of the authors to themselves as subjects" (Harvey 1989: 7). Harvey interprets modernism itself as a movement in contention. The unity of the Enlightenment reason was challenged by socialism; counter-cultural and anti-modernist movements arose in the 1960s; postmodernism emerged between 1968 and 1972 as a semi-coherent movement in architecture and planning, and in literature and philosophy. Hence, postmodern architecture eclectically mixes pieces from the past, while the postmodern artist Rauschenberg uses images from Velazquez's *Rokeby Venus* and Rubens's *Venus at her Toilet*, silk-screening photographic originals onto a surface containing a mirror (from which the naked Venus looks out at the viewer), piles of plates, trucks, helicopters, car keys, etc.

While equally critical, perhaps even more so, of postmodern theory (he finds it totally accepting of ephemerality, fragmentation, discontinuity, and chaos, as if that is all there is), Harvey's analysis of postmodernism delves more than Jameson's into the political-economic production of postmodernism as an historical condition. That is, Harvey sees cultural and economic logics as intertwined more directly, and explains late capitalism more specifically in regulationist terms of a shift from Fordism to flexible accumulation. Harvey's specific contribution is a closer examination of the experience of space and time as an important mediating link between the dynamics of capitalism's historical-geographical development and the complex processes of cultural production. For Harvey, conceptions of space and time are created by material processes of the reproduction of social life. Since capitalism is a revolutionary mode of production, the objective qualities and the meanings of space and time change equally dramatically, with severe consequences for the ordering of daily life. In particular, the shift from Fordism to flexible accumulation in the late 1960s and early 1970s corresponds with an intense phase of "time–space compression" which has a disorienting and disruptive effect on social and cultural life similar to disruptions occurring at the turn of the nineteenth century. Harvey argues that the transition to flexible accumulation occurred through rapid deployment of new organizational forms and technologies (vertical disintegration, just-in-time delivery systems, labor deskilling and reskilling, improved systems of communication, etc.) which sped up the turnover time of capital and the circulation of commodities. Consumption likewise changed through the mobilization of fashion in mass markets and a shift towards using more services. This general speed up accentuates volatility and ephemerality – of fashions, techniques, labor processes, ideas, values, and practices – in Berman's (1983) sense that "all that is solid melts into air." In commodity production, the primary effect of speed up is to emphasize instantaneity and disposability; this extends to values, lifestyles, relationships, buildings, and people. Sensory overload brings psychological responses, the blocking out of stimuli, blasé attitudes, excessive simplification. Short-term gains come to be preferred over long-term planning. The production of volatility entails manipulating taste and opinion particularly through the construction of new sign systems and imagery (advertising and media). Yet also images of permanence and power remain necessary (respectability, quality, prestige). His main point is that we have witnessed "another fierce round in that process of annihilation of space through time that has always lain at the center of capitalism's dynamic" (Harvey 1989: 293). The collapse of spatial barriers does not mean that the significance of space decreases. Heightened competition forces corporations to pay closer attention to relative locational advantages, especially in conditions of labor control – qualities of places are emphasized in the midst of an increasing abstraction of space. Thus, capitalism's historic tension between centralization and decentralization is worked out in new ways.

Harvey's study of postmodernism thus places new emphasis on the cultural effects of political-economic transformation. The world's geographical complexity, reduced nightly to a series of television images, he says, is experienced vicariously as a simulacrum. As with Baudrillard, simulacra become reality in the construction of buildings and places. In the postmodern era, dazed and distracted characters wander through eclectic, anarchic landscapes. There seem to be two reactions in daily thought and action: taking full advantage of all the divergent possibilities; and the opposite, searching for personal or collective identity, for secure moorings in a shifting world. Among social movements, the latter emphasizes connections between place and social identity ("Think globally, act locally"), with places and their meanings constructed qualitatively and aesthetically. Harvey, however, finds this meshing well with the notion of spatial differentiation as a lure for peripatetic capital. Postmodernism, he thinks, tends to disengage urban space from its dependence on functions, to see it as autonomous, to liberate spatial imagery from social determination, and so on. Is there any way out if we have lost the modernist faith in becoming, Harvey (1989: 305) asks, except via the "reactionary politics of an aestheticized spatiality"? For Harvey, putting the postmodern condition (ephemerality and fragmentation) into its context as part of a history of successive waves of space–time compressions indeed makes it accessible to analysis. With Harvey, we find a belief still that analysis and theoretical understanding provides a map for political action.

For Harvey, the ideas associated with postmodernism can be deployed to radical ends as part of a liberatory politics. This politics he finds grounded still in historical materialism, but with significant differences from the orthodox Marxian positions:

1 The treatment of difference and otherness should be omnipresent from the beginning in any attempt to grasp the dialectics of social change – hence, the importance of recuperating race, gender, and religion within an historical materialist frame traditionally emphasizing capital, money, and class.
2 Historical materialism has to recognize that the production of images and discourses should be analyzed as part of symbolic orders and that aesthetic and cultural practices matter.
3 Historical materialism should take its geography seriously in terms of the real geographies of social action.
4 Historical-geographical materialism is an open-ended and dialectical mode of enquiry, and metatheory is not a statement of total truth but an attempt to come to terms with historical and geographical truths.

Harvey thus envisages a renewal of historical materialism and the Enlightenment project.

Justice, Nature, and the Geography of Difference

A few years on finds Harvey (1996) laying greater stress on uneven geographical development and difference. Spatial and ecological circumstances which differ radically, Harvey says, are constituted by, and constitute, socio-ecological and political economic processes, including standards of social justice. Harvey employs a relational dialectics similar to the notion of "cultural narratives of relational positionality" (Friedman 1995) in which identities shift with a changing context and are fluid sites, yet different from this in that Harvey recognizes the limits of reducing everything to fluxes and flows and wants to recognize the permanences which also give meaning to life – dialectical argumentation cannot be understood as outside the significance and power of the concrete, material conditions of the world. Harvey argues against the "new idealism" in which thought and discourse are believed to be all that matter in powering historical-geographical change. Harvey still wants to reconstruct Marxian metatheory with space and relations to nature integrated as fundamental elements. This emphasizes not values but processes of valuation, how relatively permanent values are constructed for diverse forms of socio-ecological action, especially the value of social justice, which allows a return to the terrain of *Social Justice and the City* (1973).

Place, like space and time, is a social construct. For Harvey, entities achieve relative stability creating space, permanancies come to exclusively occupy a piece of space for a time, and the process of place formation involves carving out permanancies which turn out to be contingent. Place then has a double meaning, as position, and as entity or permanence constituted within a social process. Place can also be understood as the locus of imaginaries, as institutionalizations, configurations of social relations, material practices, forms of power and elements in discourse:

> it is precisely the way in which all of these moments are caught up in the common flow of the social process that in the end determines the conflictual (and oftentimes internally contradictory) processes of place construction, sustenance, and deconstruction ... it is the only way to attack the rich complexity of social processes of place construction in a coherent way. (Harvey 1996: 316)

Social beings individually and collectively invest places with the permanence necessary for them to become loci of institutionalized social power. Harvey now sees the politics of place construction ranging across material, representational, and symbolic activities. Is this Harvey's third metamorphosis?

Postmodern Geographies

Edward Soja typically makes a bold claim for postmodern geographies in a sustained, theoretical analysis which draws on Lefebvre's Marxism, but also on Foucauldian poststructuralism, as main sources of inspiration. For the past century, Soja (1989) argues, time and history occupied a privileged position in critical social theory; understanding the making of history was the primary source of emancipatory insight. For Soja, such an essentially historical epistemology pervades critical social theory, preserving a privileged place for the historical imagination, but occluding sensitivity to the spatiality of social life: that is, seeing the "lifeworld of being" located not only in the making of history but in the construction of human geographies, the social production of space, and the formation of geographical landscapes. Foucault (1980: 70) says of critical theory: "Space was treated as the dead, the fixed, the undialectical, the immobile. Time, on the contrary, was richness, fecundity, life, dialectic"; and elsewhere (Foucault 1986b: 22) adds:

The present epoch will perhaps be above all the epoch of space. We are in the epoch of simultaneity: we are in the epoch of juxtaposition, the epoch of the near and far, of the side by side, of the dispersed. We are at a moment, I believe, when our experience of the world is less that of a long life developing through time than that of a network that connects points and intersects with its own skein. One could perhaps say that certain ideological conflicts animating present-day polemics oppose the pious descendants of time and the determined inhabitants of space.

Similarly, for Soja, the 1980s began a dramatic shift towards a far-reaching spatialization of the critical imagination. He finds a distinctively postmodern, critical human geography emerging, which reasserts the significance of space or, rather, sees time and space together in a creative commingling as the vertical and horizontal dimensions of being. Associating modern with history, and postmodern with geography, Soja traces the hidden narrative of space in twentieth-century social theory in an attempt at countering an "historicism" that is "an overdeveloped historical contextualization of social life and social theory that actively submerges and peripheralizes the geographical or spatial imagination" (Soja 1989: 15).

A postmodern critical geography is spatially deconstructive, in the sense of exposing the intellectual history of critical social thought, and is spatially reconstructive, in the sense of an emphasis on the struggles of peripheralized, oppressed peoples. Soja compares this with "neo-conservative" deconstructive postmodernism which reduces history and geography to "meaningless whimsy and pastiche," and which celebrates the arrival of postmodern culture as though all the problems of modernity melt into air. Like Jameson, Soja calls for a new cognitive mapping, critical in terms of seeing through both reactionary postmodernism and late modern historicism, and creative in making a politicized spatial consciousness and a radical spatial praxis – the most important postmodern geographies, he says, remain to be produced. In what is probably his best essay, "Reassertions: Towards a Spatialized Ontology," Soja (1989: 118–37) returns to that *fin de siècle* moment when critical theory turned resolutely historicist. Drawing on the (structural) Marxist, Nicos Poulantzsas, as well as on Foucault and Lefebvre, Soja sees three kinds of space overlapping and interacting: physical, mental, and social space. Soja's (1989: 79, 120) focus is on the notion of *spatiality*, "the created space of social organization and production" which "exists in both substantial forms (concrete spatialities) and as a set of relations between individuals and groups, an 'embodiment' and medium of social life itself." The spaces seen at the turn of the century, he argues, were illusive and blurred the capacity to envision the social dynamics of spatialization. There are two sources of such illusion. First, *myopia* distorts spatial theorization through the illusion of opaqueness, a focus on immediate surface appearances, space as a collection of things: this empiricist interpretation dominates post-Enlightenment scientific thought as an objective naturalism. In it, spatiality is understood only as objectively measurable appearances grasped through sensory-based perception, Cartesian mathematical-geometric abstractions, and mechanical materialism. Soja finds theories making spatial organization socially inert as a deadened product of the friction of distance, these theories always masking social conflict and agency (recall the earlier critique of spatial fetishism – chapter 3). Second, *transparency* is the illusion that sees through concrete spatiality into the intuitive realm of the purposeful mind – that is, the production of spatiality is literally represented as cognition and mental design, space being reduced to a mental construct (recall chapter 2). This is the neo-Kantian transcendental spatial idealism which pervades the hermeneutic tradition. Both forms of illusion (myopia, transparency) can be broken, and a spatialized materialism reconstituted, Soja claims, through a socio-spatial dialectics.

Summarizing this, Soja (cf. Giddens 1979b; 1981) says that spatiality is a social product, part of "second nature," simultaneously medium and outcome of social action and relationship; spatio-temporal structuring defines how social action and relationship are made concrete in a process filled with struggle, with contradiction arising primarily from the duality of space as outcome and medium of social activity; concrete spatiality (actual human geography) is a competitive arena for struggles over social reproduction; the temporality of social life is rooted in spatial contingency; and the materialist interpretations of history and geography are inseparably intertwined with no inherent prioritization of one over the other. Taken together, these premises frame a "materialist interpretation of spatiality" (Soja 1989: 130).

Thirdspace

Soja recasts many of his earlier arguments in a series of essays assembled as *Thirdspace: Journeys to Los Angeles and Other Real-and-Imagined Places* (1996), "Thirdspace" being a term derived from the post-colonial literary critic Homi Bhaba (1994). For Bhaba, the act of cultural enunciation is crossed by the difference of writing. That is, interpretation is never a simple act of communication between the I and the You, but rather: "The production of meaning requires that these two places be mobilized in the passage through a Third Space" (Bhaba 1994: 36) representing the general conditions of language and the implication of the utterance in a performative strategy of which it cannot "in itself" be conscious. Soja uses Thirdspace to open up and expand the scope of the imagination about the spatiality of life, a dimension as significant as historicality and sociality. Soja now explicitly approaches this from what he calls a position of *critical postmodernism*, a third path different either from the "smiling mortician's" postmodern celebration of the end of everything and the critical modernist's over-defensive caricaturing of postmodernism as nihilism or new age silliness. Soja wants to set aside either/or choices and contemplate the possibility of a "both/and also" logic which creatively combines postmodernist with modernist perspectives; he sees this as an invitation to enter "a space of extraordinary openness" (Soja 1996: 5) where one can be a Marxist and an idealist at the same time. For this he advocates a critical strategy of "thirding-as-Othering" – that is, injecting an-Other set of choices into binary oppositions, drawing from the two to open new alternatives. Hence, the interjection of a *critical spatial imagination* into the dualism of historical and spatial imaginations, the possibility of an open, combinatorial perspective between modernism and postmodernism. In this specific case, it means building on a Firstspace perspective focused on the "real" material world, and a Secondspace perspective that interprets this reality through imagining representations, to reach a Thirdspace of multiple real-and-imagined places.

For the voyage of discovery to the "outer reaches" of Thirdspace, Soja turns Lefebvre's triple dialectic into "trialectics," a mode of dialectical reasoning inherently more spatial than the dialectics of Hegel or Marx. This clarifies the main themes of Lefebvre's book, the interweaving of perceived (space of material practice), conceived (representations of space), and lived (spaces of representation). On the basis of this formulation, Soja defines Thirdspace as an-Other way of understanding spatiality.

For the last century, he argues, mainstream geographical imagination revolved around a dual mode of thinking: Firstspace fixed on the concrete materiality of spatial forms (things that could be empirically mapped); and Secondspace conceived in ideas about space (representations in cognitive forms) – these are similar to Lefebvre's perceived and conceived spaces. In the late 1960s, Soja says, in the midst of a global crisis, an-Other form of spatial awareness began to emerge, a thirding of the spatial imagination, extending the traditional dualism, simultaneously real, imagined, and more ("real-and-imagined" places). The other spaces of Lefebvre and Foucault remained unexplored or misinterpreted for twenty years, especially in geography, the "master discipline of space," the exception being theorists seriously engaged with critical cultural studies. Thus, bell hooks (1990) recomposes lived spaces of representation as "real-and-imagined," "material-and-metaphysical" meeting grounds for struggles against all forms of oppression and, more generally, radical women of color implant their spatial awareness in the strategic margins of a critically postmodern cultural politics. Soja learns also from spatial feminists like Gillian Rose's (1993 – see chapter 7) rethinking spatiality as polycentric mix, or post-colonial feminists like Gloria Anzaldua (1987), Maria Lugones (1994), or Gayatri Spivak (1988; 1990), and cultural critics like Edward Said (1979) and, as we have seen, Homi Bhaba (1990; 1994). Soja reads Foucault's (1986b) "heterotopias," spaces which draw people out of themselves, as a plea for opening the historical and spatial imaginations to a deeper appreciation of the spatiality of human life – for Soja, this also disrupts historical and sociological thinking, it is a different "geohistory of otherness" (cf. White 1987, 1993; Gregory 1994). Soja sees this explanation of Thirdspace, together with journeys to Los Angeles and other real-and-imagined places, organized around an emancipatory praxis, a search for political solutions to the many forms of inequality and oppression, especially those associated with problems stemming from global restructuring.

Each of these statements about the possibility of a postmodern geography reveals profound ambivalence about the temper of the times and skepticism about the nature and direction of postmodern society. Each at first worries about the penetration of postmodern ideas into geography: in the face of the postmodern onslaught, Dear retreats into structurationism, Soja at first simply repeats his earlier Marxist work on socio-spatial dialectics (although this changes somewhat with his later "trialectics") and Harvey calls for a renewal of historical-geographical materialism with more of a cultural form. These remain statements about postmodernism by predominantly modern geographers, with Marxism or neo-Marxism in their pasts, if not in their presents. Yet these are also some of the main routes through which postmodern ideas became widely known in geography. In the early 1990s, such statements were subject to critique by feminists differently attuned to postmodern theory (see chapter 7) and by non-Marxist postmodern theorists (e.g. Hannah and Strohmeyer 1992; Strohmeyer and Hannah 1992). As the 1990s wore on, a new generation of geographers with no particular background in Marxism, and certainly no stake in socialism, a generation of critical, even "leftist," people who see Marxism as part of the problem rather than the solution, began to assert different kinds of postmodern positions. We turn now to some of these.

Postmodern Geography Achieved

There is a tendency for postmodern geographers to subject famous authors to endless "readings" often through other authors. Take Lefebvre, for instance – a writer, by the way, who clearly appreciated walking real cities rather than reading texts about them. Some interesting notions about power, body, and space come from reading *The Production of Space* (1991) through the authors Lefebvre draws upon. Thus, Andy Merrifield (1995), reading through Nietzsche, says that Lefebvre prioritizes Eros (erotic knowledge) over Logos (logical knowledge), the spatial manifestation of Logos being imposed representations of space which crush lived, sensual representational space of the body, desire, and everyday life (space of the Anti-Logos). Lynn Stewart (1995) emphasizes the bodily generation of space, the body as center in space for example, in Lefebvre. Derek Gregory (1995; see also Blum and Nast 1996) reads Lefebvre through the "grille" of Lacanian psychoanalytic theory. For Gregory, Lefebvre outlines two related histories of space: a history of the social relations between human bodies and spaces in a radicalization of Marx's critique of political economy; and a critique of Lacan's ideas focused on developmental relations between body and space. Kasbarian (1996) calls this a postmodern geography which transforms geographic sensibilities, revamping notions of space and landscape as "inert platforms" to treat them as fluid, dynamic forces produced by, and producing, social relations.

Now, it may be the case that the purview of geography is enlarged through such readings to embrace spaces of a metaphorical, subjective kind acting through cultural production and ideological formation. But representations of representations also amounts to a new kind of fetish, that of representationality. Its utter fascination with texts written about texts may produce a dense intertextuality which precludes contact with the world outside the fetishistic dream. In this sense, the new emphasis on text and reading is a bibliophile's delight. At its best, postmodern geography consists of fragments, flashes of insight into space and environment, or rather their representations, stimulated by experiences almost exclusively in the postmodern world (i.e. since 1972), fragments characterized by sheer brilliance, or rather audacity, of specific insight. At its worst, postmodern geography is a kind of selfish, privileged self-gratification, displayed in essays which meander between personal idiosyncrasy and lazy bits of research, mainly reading works through other works. With one possible exception, Pamela Shurmer-Smith and Kevin Hannam's *Worlds of*

Desire, Realms of Power (1994), there is little attempt at seriously engaging with a postmodern geography of the forces of power and desire proposed by Nietzsche and found in the works of Deleuze, Guattari, and Lyotard among others. Much postmodern geography consists of reading the poststructural literature, arguing interminably over its contents, and making what are actually simple, tentative steps towards the study of space, place, and environment.

Delimiting Human Geography

We can get some idea of postmodern reconceptualizations of human geography by the new generation of literary and cultural intellectuals from a series of discussions held in 1990 and 1991 by the Social and Cultural Study Group of the Institute of British Geographers (Philo 1991a). Summarizing an eclectic series of discussion papers on behalf of the Study Group, Chris Philo (1991b) interestingly argues that human geographers might engage Kant's moral philosophy through their own series of moral geographies. But the moral lens would be different, he says, in that it is concerned with everyday moralities, both the geography *of* moralities, and the geography *in* moralities. In such a (Foucauldian) endeavor, the predominantly economic lens of neoclassical and Marxian geography might constitute "the other," the idea being to gain fresh insight into human-geographical issues whose economic logic is already understood, but whose moral components are as yet invisible. This view is elaborated using several prevalent themes in human geography (see also Sack 1997).

First, in terms of *social differentiation*, geography looks at associations between social groups and particular places but, for Philo, needs also to examine how categories (like gender and class) are invented, how inequalities are reproduced, how they are naturalized. In this, the notion of "culture" is not superstructural, but refers to systems of shared meanings, with local cultures serving as resources which may become oppositional. Here, Philo's statement is prescient of a range of poststructural works appearing on the social construction of place and identity. Much of this work derives from Benedict Anderson's (1983: 13–15) view that nationalisms are cultural artifacts or, more generally, that all communities larger than primordial villages of face-to-face contact are "imagined communities." In the work of geographers like Peter Jackson and Jan Penrose (1993: 12–13), the social constructedness of place contrasts with an earlier (existentialist) "self-indulgent and uncritical humanistic geography" (see also Jackson 1989; Agnew and Duncan 1989). Similarly, in Michael Keith and Steve Pile's (1993: 6) "politics of place" a landscape presents multiple enunciations of distinct forms of space which may be connected to the revisioning and remembering of the spatialities of counter-hegemonic cultural practices. And in *Space and Place: Theories of Identity and Location*, Erica Carter, James Donald, and Judith Squires (1993) argue that the presumed certainties of cultural identity anchored in cohesive communities of shared tradition have increasingly been disrupted so that places no longer provide clear supports for identity even while themes of home continue to resonate through imaginations. These only suggest a literature dealing with differentiation and identity which burgeoned in the 1990s.

Second, Philo argues, in addition to the constitution of social groups, including how groups come to identify themselves and others, explicit consideration needs giving to the *construction and boundaries of the self*, especially how subjectivity is conceptualized in different places. Hence, in psychoanalytic models (Freud, Lacan) the self is fashioned in reciprocal interaction with the Other of the surrounding environment, the self coming to regard itself as bounded, as an entity in space, in the sense of an ecology of the self. Arguments like this lead to re-evaluations of how the subject is conceived in human geography. Thus, Pile (1993; 1996) argues that a truly *human* post-positivist geography cannot exist without psychoanalytic theories of the unknowing self, rather than fully conscious self, one formed in relation to otherness (i.e. socially structured encounters with others in a multilayered, multidimensional world riddled with paradox, ambiguity, and ambivalence).

Third, Philo moves from the individual scale to a recovery of *discourses about globalism* in the sense of westernization, Eurocentrism, Orientalism, global culture, and, we might add, geopolitics. Here, the basic source is Edward Said's (1979: 2; 1993) use of Foucault's notion of discourse in analyzing the political and cultural dimensions of interregional power relations. Said argues that "the Orient" helped define Europe as its contrasting image (i.e. as its Other); Orientalism is a "mode of discourse with supporting institutions, vocabulary, scholarship, imagery, doctrines, even colonial bureaucracies and colonial styles" through which European culture was able to "produce" the Orient (politically, imaginatively) in the post-Enlightenment period. Because the Orientalist discourse limits thought, the Orient was not, and is not, a free subject of thought or action. In this sense, Said finds localities, regions, geographical sectors like Orient and Occident, to be humanly "made." Subsequent work extends this notion of "discourses on the other" to a whole history of the different European conceptions ("science fictions") of "alien cultures" (McGrane 1989; Hulme 1988; Todorov 1984) and indeed to a new approach to culture and post-colonialism (Ashcroft, Griffiths, and Tiffin 1989; Bhaba 1994; Spivak 1988; Turner 1994). Similarly, the political geographer Gearoid O'Tuathail (1996: 7) uses the Foucauldian concept of "geo-power," the functioning of geographical knowledge not as an innocent body of learning, but as a modern ensemble of technologies of power concerned with the production and management of territorial space.

Fourth, Philo finds there to be a need to recapture the ability to speak about questions of environment in terms of the *social construction of nature*. Here, social construction is meant as both human modification and how natural objects are converted into cultural entities as foci of collective and individual systems of meaning so that, for example, the environmental issues chosen as centers of concern result from human evaluations. This links, for Philo, with the theme of "delimiting the human" in terms of western attempts at distinguishing between natural and human, with "human" as white and male, or in terms of human chauvinism towards non-human beings. But there are many ways in which the notion of the social construction of nature is worked out (Gerber 1997). In an innovative rethinking of Marxist theories of nature, Noel Castree (1995; 1996), a geographer at the University of Liverpool, sympathetically criticizes Smith's "production of nature" thesis (see chapter 3) because it loses sight of nature's materiality, ontological existence, and causal efficacy; but also, drawing on cultural studies of the sociology of scientific knowledge, Castree argues that the supposed facts of produced nature never speak for themselves, but are constructs with material and political causes and consequences; in a difficult synthesis, Castree argues that nature is an historically specific discursive product and that the supposed distinction between thought and the real is a distinctive western product. For Castree (1995: 35), this makes Marxism "reflexive *to its very core.*" Alternatively, but similarly, Peet and Watts's (1996) concept of "liberation ecology" integrates critical approaches to political economy with poststructural social theory in a study of society–nature relations. Such a liberatory ecology retains the modern notion of reasoned actions on nature, accepts much of the Marxian and poststructural critique of capitalist rationality, but wishes to substitute in its stead a democratic process of reasoning in a transformed system of social and natural relations. It introduces also the poststructural notion of "environmental imaginaries" derived originally from Lacan via Castoriadis.

In the guise of a "moral geography," therefore, Philo outlines a series of issues different from those usually encountered in social and cultural geography, not, he (generously) says, because the existing work is irrelevant, but more because it already comprises an adequate stock of materials which can be drawn from as other issues are raised. Philo's article did not consciously set an agenda for poststructural geography. But it did reflect the changing interests of the time under the impetus of the new thinking. Much of the subsequent work by geographers influenced by poststructural and postmodern ideas elaborates themes raised in Philo's review. However, his notion of a moral geography was (unfortunately) not subsequently taken up, although some interesting notions of ethics begin to appear (Slater 1997; Smith 1997; Whatmore 1997). Developing such a new position involves exegesis of the geographical aspects of poststructural philosophy, creative explorations within the field, borrowing from parallel movements in cognate areas of thought, statements of poststructural politics of space, and the taking of extreme positions at the daring frontier of what is, in any case, an exercise in re-imagining social and cultural geography. The next sections exemplify each of these tendencies in turn, beginning with exegeses of Foucault's abundant and fertile ideas about space and place.

Foucauldian Geography

An exegesis of Foucault's notions of the spatiality of power forms one obvious entry point into a postmodern geography. In the mid to late 1980s, attempts were made to read Foucault geographically. This reading produced a series of exegeses and discussions, particularly of Foucault's genealogical writings. Felix Driver reads Foucault's *Discipline and Punish* (1979a) as concerned with an historical transformation in the exercise of power and by implication the use of space, for "space has always, in one sense or another, been right at the heart of his concerns" (Driver 1985: 425). Foucault, Driver says, finds power related to forms of knowledge, both being constructed on the basis of concrete, local terrains and technologies. The resulting micropowers shape all relationships and are a condition of existence for centralized or global powers. The geography of these micropowers, which Foucault calls geopolitics, is vital to their exercise. Driver argues that Foucault is interested in space for two reasons: Foucault distrusts histories based on empty abstractions and favors the particular, the local, and their articulation with the whole; and Foucault sees spatial organization as important in social, economic, and political strategies in particular contexts – for example, the division of space is a means for the discipline and surveillance of individuals in the modern era.

These themes are taken up in a second, more satisfactory and nuanced reading of Foucault, again by Philo (1992). In Philo's opinion, too, Foucault's vision of history opens a heightened sensitivity to space and place. In particular, Foucault's attack on "total history" calls forth a geographical view of spaces of dispersion – "spaces where things proliferate in a jumbled-up manner on the same 'level' as one another . . . [where] it can never be decided if 'the essential' has been sighted" (Philo 1992: 139). This reading of Foucault's geography may be unorthodox, relying too much on passages where space is merely a metaphor, but, for Philo, the term "spaces of dispersion" applies also to empirical spaces and places in Foucault's works. Foucault has primarily been interpreted (e.g. Soja 1989) as concerned with the spatial geometry of power. But Philo finds this misleading in terms both of Foucault's geography and his contribution to postmodernism.

Foucault proposes that the phenomena, processes, and structures of history are always fragmented by geography – that is, things turn out differently in different places. For Foucault, total history seeks to reconstitute the main principle behind the overall form of civilization: by supposing that a system of homogenous relations or network of causality exists between events in a well-defined spatio-temporal area; by supposing that the same form of historicity operates in all aspects of life; and by supposing that history can be articulated into great units (stages, phases) each containing a principle of cohesion. All such impositions (of a priori grand historical visions) are suspect to Foucault because they impose a measure of order alien to details and differences and smooth over the confusions, contradictions, and conflicts that form the real stuff of life. For Foucault, by comparison, "nothing is fundamental: that is what is interesting in the analysis of society." Against total history Foucault counterpoises a general history, which overturns grand historical visions and deploys "spaces of dispersion" which insist on the particular, local, and specific. This does not abandon an historical methodology bringing a semblance of order to empirical materials. Instead, it ensures that concepts are not decided in advance but hover responsively above empirical details – hence, in a genealogical approach theoretical statements should gradually materialize as study progresses.

Philo examines Foucault's *Death and the Labyrinth* (1986a), an exegesis of Raymond Roussel, a French poet and novelist, particularly his exasperatingly complete descriptions of uninteresting objects! Here, Foucault finds a demand that the eye preserve the contents of a scene as they are, in a non-hierarchical way, free from the observer's effort to penetrate them. Foucault finds also that Roussel has no privileged point around which to organize a landscape, but rather uses a series of spatial cells placed next to each other in relation not to the whole, but according to a system of directions of proximity – in Roussel's scenic descriptions "time is lost in space" (Foucault 1986a: 110), different things coexist and fuse into each other, and there is a sense, even after minute description, that we remain only at the surface, beyond which silence prevails.

More formally, Philo (1992: 148) says, in *The Archaeology of Knowledge* Foucault (1972) proposes a spatial ontology "which proceeds by imagining a hypothetical space or plane across which all of the events and phenomena relevant to a substantive study are dispersed." The willful muddling, playful juxtaposing of different categories of things, preserving and even accenting details and differences, is a strategy challenging a priori tendencies to totalize historical inquiry. Yet this does not mean that the world is chaotic; rather, Foucault finds order residing in things themselves, an order whose system can only be specified in terms of "local, changing rules" (Dreyfus and Rabinow 1983: 55) which govern, or more simply are, the observable relationships between the many things being studied. Foucault evidently finds there to be an intelligible but momentary geometry enabling the researcher to grasp a measure of order in how thing are connected. Yet while Foucault's sensitivity to spaces of dispersion may appear simply as a conceptual-metaphorical device, Philo (1992: 150) thinks that:

> when Foucault gazes out on the social world of the past, he sees not the order of (say) a mode of production determining the lines of class struggle nor the order of (say) a world view energizing everything from how the economy functions to how the most beautiful mural is painted: rather, he sees the spaces of dispersion through which the things under study are scattered across a landscape and are related one to another simply through their geography, the only order that is here discernible by being near to one another or far away, by being positioned in certain locations or associated with certain types of environment, by being arranged in a certain way or possessed of a certain appearance thanks to their plans and architectures.

Hence, local and changing rules should contain detailed descriptions of substantial spatial relations displayed on the ground, and these should inform any specification of more abstract rules of association and difference.

From this, Philo turns to discussions of Foucault's more substantive spatial maneuvers in his histories of social otherness. First, Foucault shows a finely honed alertness to space, or the way spatial relations are implicated in the complex workings of discourse, knowledge, and power – hence, "histories of power" would amount to histories of "written of spaces" (Foucault 1980: 149). Foucault introduces a geometric turn into histories of social otherness – hence, Baudrillard (1987) connects Foucault to a new naturalism in social thought. This leaves us with an "image of a social world spatially constituted through nodes and channels of power – fixed nodes where power is produced and crisscrossing channels along which power is diffused and collected – and it is for this reason that Foucault might aptly be termed the 'geometer of power.'" In this sense, too, Foucault slides into spatial forms of explanation: hence, Foucault's *Madness and Civilization* (1967) can be read as projecting a simple geometry of inclusion and exclusion onto the history of western madness. Sensitivity to space, in this version, is not so much a challenge to totalization as its geometric complement. Second, Foucault's writings could be said to show little concern for the associations of phenomena with particular material *places*, environments, and landscapes. Hence, Lemart and Gillan (1982) see Foucault following the *Annales* school of history in spatializing time yet not adopting this school's (geohistorical) dialectic of space and time or its notion of necessary relations with material contexts and landscapes. But Philo finds neither of these accounts, of space or place, telling the whole story about Foucault's geography. For as well, Philo argues, Foucault's histories are substantive geographies, full of people, problems, and resistances. Hence, segregation in *Madness and Civilization* recovers the specifics of how particular mad, bad, and sad populations are identified and treated at different times in different places (many not involving segregation), while similarly, in *Discipline and Punish*, the geometric model of Panopticism serves only as a first base in writing an historical geography of prisons. "Foucault therefore arrives at a treatment of space that is not completely beholden to geometry, and he is certainly not labouring with any notion of transcendental spatial laws ... a careful scrutiny of his historical inquiries also unearths a treatment of place that is on occasion more attentive to details of precise location and context," as for example in *Madness and Civilization*, where specific places are more than incidental to events (Philo 1992: 157). So, for Philo, while there is a danger that Foucault's geometric turn might elevate an abstract sense of space above a concrete sense of place, the practice of Foucault's geography has enough content to prevent it becoming an exercise in formal geometry. This notion of patient archaeologist of substantive geographies apparently resonates with Foucault's self-image: "we live inside a set of relations that delineates sites which are irreducible to one another and absolutely not superimposible on one another" (Foucault 1986b: 23). For Philo, Foucault – and Baudrillard too – show the social world as having a disordered geography as a result of the theorists' doubts about the great modern certainties of order, coherence, truth, and reason. Both abandon depth accounts of social life and move to surface accounts, where the things of the world are imagined as lying at the same level, a (spatial) attitude identifiable as postmodern. In Philo's view, Foucault provides a blueprint for a truly postmodern geography:

> in which details and differences, fragmentation and chaos, substance and heterogeneity, humility and respectfulness feature at every turn, and an account of social life which necessarily brings with it a sustained concern for the geography of things rather than a recall for the formal geometries of spatial science. (Philo 1992: 159)

Philo's own research concerns the history and geography of lunatic asylums in Britain. It forms an intermediate position between a still-moral geography and more extreme postmodern positions.

Landscape as Text

If a single tendency characterizes poststructural thought, it is the linguistic turn toward discourse, text, reading, and interpretation. Insights developed in linguistic philosophy and literary theory draw a wide following, especially among those critical of, or disillusioned with, the theoretical claims of historical materialism and the politics of the socialist project. An early critic of structural Marxist geography (Duncan and Ley 1982), James Duncan (formerly a professor of geography at Syracuse University but now at Cambridge University) has been prominent in using poststructural social and literary theory to rejuvenate cultural geography. Working with Trevor Barnes, a professor of geography at the University of British Columbia, Duncan focuses poststructural theory on the traditional geographic concept of landscape. Following literary theorists and cultural anthropologists, Barnes and Duncan (1992) propose expanding the notion of "text" to embrace a range of cultural productions and social, economic, and political institutions as "signifying practices" that can be "read." This expanded view of texts, they say, derives from a broadly postmodern view that sees texts as constituting reality, rather than mimicking it. Barnes and Duncan appeal to Ricoeur (1971) for an argument that the world is indeed like a text: thus, meaning in written discourse is concretized when inscribed or textualized, just as elements of social life take on a similar fixity; texts escape their authors, just as deeds have unintended consequences; written texts and social events are subject to continual reinterpretation; the meaning of a text is unstable and, like social institutions, dependent on a wide range of interpretations from specific textual communities. For Barnes and Duncan, landscapes are characterized by the definitive features of a text: thus "text is also an appropriate trope [figurative use of a word] to use in analyzing landscapes because it conveys the inherent instability of meaning, fragmentation or absence of integrity, lack of authorial control, polyvocality and irresolvable social contradictions that often characterize them" (Barnes and Duncan 1992: 7). In this view, not only are accounts of the world intertextual, but the world itself is intertextual – thus, places are inscribed by practices based in previous texts, while texts in the world act back on the texts that shaped them (Duncan and Duncan 1988; cf. Cosgrove and Daniels 1987).

Duncan (1990) contrasts this (Derridian) position with traditional perspectives in cultural geography. Traditionally, landscapes were recognized as reflections of culture but only rarely as constituent elements in cultural reproduction. Cultural geography paid attention instead to artifacts (house types, fences, landscape ensembles) using methods limited to observation and archival study. The meaning of landscape was addressed only from the interpreter's point of view, with interpretative authority assumed to flow from an unmediated relation between field-work, or archival research, and landscape. Such empiricist landscape interpretation, Duncan claims, is isolated from the self-reflexive disciplines of philosophy and literary theory, as well as from much of social science. Yet descriptions, Duncan insists, are not mirror reflections, but are constructed within the limits of language and the intellectual frameworks of those who write about landscapes. Language is based on shared meanings and socially constructed discourses, while descriptions can have meaning only in a context-bound sense. Furthermore, not everything that is real and has causal power can be observed. For Duncan, resistance to explicit theorizing about such non-observable entities indicates a self-limiting empiricism. Instead, he places landscape interpretation at the center of an interdisciplinary arena where issues like objectification, representation, consciousness, ideology, and their interrelationships are debated. This opens a dialogue between cultural geographers and literary theorists, cultural anthropologists, and others who, in expanding the concept of text, become interested in landscapes.

As an ordered assemblage of objects the landscape (text) acts as a signifying system. Duncan focuses attention on the way landscapes signify power relations in a case study of the precapitalist Kandyan kingdom of Sri Lanka (Duncan 1990). Here, "the landscape is an allegorical narrative of the power of the king and how his power is spatially and temporally contiguous with the power of the gods and the hero-kings of old" (Duncan 1990: 19). The question of how signification takes place raises issues of reading and the role of communication devices in reproducing the social order. The landscape is a concrete visual vehicle of inculcation, an objectifier playing an important part in ideology. Cultural amnesia allows landscape to act as a powerful ideological tool: by becoming part of the everyday, the taken for granted, landscape masks the artifice and ideological nature of its form and content. Textuality and intertextuality are useful also in understanding societies with important textual traditions. Foucault and others argue that control of memory is significant in political struggle as traditions are selectively maintained or invented, particularly when the past is seen as determining the present (as when truth arises from sacred books). In the Kandyan kingdom, Duncan finds narratives of the glorious past incorporated into landscape designs. The term "intertextuality" here conceptualizes relations between historical texts, landscapes, and textualized social practices. Additionally, following Stock (1986), Duncan finds "textual communities" organized around common interpretations of groups of texts involved in contests and struggles, which, he says, may have a basis in real material interests.

The basic position in this school of thought, therefore, is that poststructural theoretical notions drawn from contemporary literary theory can be used to guide the reading of landscapes as text; that is, "how [landscapes] are constructed on the basis of a set of texts, how they are read, and how they act as a mediating influence shaping behavior in the image of the text" (Duncan and Duncan 1988: 120). While landscapes play an important ideological role in the social process by naturalizing dominant assumptions about the way society is organized, when read inattentively or naively this process of ideological inculcation may go unnoticed. But "the ideological aspects of landscapes as texts can be unmasked" and "denaturalization" is proposed as an important task for the critical theorist. This statement links advances in landscape analysis with the dynamic of poststructural and literary theory; and it proposes such a link not for the pure sake of "advancing knowledge," but for the critical purpose of unmasking system-supporting ideologies.

For some Marxists this focuses exclusively on representation, abstracting from the material processes through which people create their worlds and distracting from the social relations of power within which landscapes are produced (Peet 1993). Marxist-geographic analyses, inspired particularly by the cultural materialism of Raymond Williams (1973; 1977; 1981) or the existential Marxism of John Berger (1972), stress instead economy and landscape, with the mediating influence of "structures of feeling" (Williams) or "ways of seeing" (Berger). These are linked far more than for poststructuralists with capitalism and capitalist social relations. Thus, Dennis Cosgrove in *Social Formation and Symbolic Landscape* (1984) sees the idea of landscape arising with capitalism in the Italian Renaissance city, amidst an age when terrestrial space was mapped and rational landscapes constructed:

> Landscape is thus intimately linked with a new way of seeing the world as a rationally ordered, designed, and harmonious creation whose structure and mechanism are accessible to the human mind as well as to the eye, and act as guides to humans in their alteration and improvement of the environment. (Cosgrove 1989: 1221)

With this, the cultural geography of landscape is linked much more effectively (compared with Duncan) with power relations (cf. Daniels 1989). Similarly, Peet (1996) posits the existence of definite power/discourse/landscape systems in a synthesis of discourse and regulation theories using the notion of "discursive regulation." Both versions of "landscape as text" are a far cry from the Berkeley school of cultural geography.

Development as Discourse

Since the middle 1980s, poststructural philosophy has entered the field of development studies. Postmodern skepticism particularly applies to the project of development, modernism's finest hour. Much of the work on this extends Foucault's reconceptualization of power, discourse, and knowledge to western disciplinary and normalizing mechanisms in the Third World (Schuurman 1992; Slater 1992; Peet and Watts 1996; Watts 1993). Foucault's ideas on the appropriation of the mind in the west, it is argued, can be extended to the permeation and appropriation of the Third World by western disciplinary and normalizing power strategies and mechanisms. This literature uses Foucauldian concepts of power, knowledge, and discourse to re-examine development efforts as "uniquely efficient colonizers on behalf of central strategies of power" (DuBois 1991: 19).

The pioneering work, by Arturo Escobar (1984–5; 1988; 1992; 1995), an anthropologist at the University of Massachusetts, sees development discourses as the last insidious chapter of the larger history of the expansion of modern, western reason. Escobar contrasts reason's project of global emancipation with its dark side of domination: i.e. reasoned knowledge using the language of emancipation creates systems of power in a modernized world. Societal background practices, common social meanings, and cultural contents are appropriated through a series of discourses which bring the material conditions of life and the mechanisms of culture into the realm of explicit calculation and subject them to modern forms of power–knowledge. From this perspective, new types of power and knowledge are seen as being deployed in the Third World which insure the conformity of its peoples to First World (especially American) types of economic and cultural behavior. Through this process, the economic, socio-cultural, and political systems of the Third World are permeated and appropriated by those of the "advanced" countries.

Development is one of these emancipatory languages of domination. Escobar sees development as a discourse invented in the First World which "produces," "constructs," or "maps" the Third World, in the sense that it gets people and communities in Asia, Africa, and Latin America to be seen, and to see themselves, as "underdeveloped" – the comparison is with Said's (1979) "Orientalism." Development is anchored in the western economy, understood as an ensemble of production, power, and signification, and this in turn is part of western modernity, understood as a form of knowledge and rationality. While reason, rationality, and democracy have been naturalized through the universalization of European history, an anthropological critique reveals them to be historical practices. A critical study of development should be situated within this anthropology of reason and modernity. Escobar (1995) investigates the formation of this discourse of development, identifying the strategies for dealing with problems of underdevelopment, the practices generated by these strategies, and the mechanisms by which practices operate – in general, the way development enters a nexus of power–knowledge or is put into discourse. In this way, development can be seen not as a matter of scientific knowledge concerned with the achievement of true progress, but as a series of political technologies intended to shape reality in the Third World.

In general, development, for Escobar, has penetrated, integrated, managed, and controlled countries and populations in increasingly detailed ways. It has created a type of underdevelopment which is politically and economically manageable. Its forms of power act not by repression but by normalization, regulated knowledge, the moralization of issues. The new space of the "Third World" constitutes a new field of power dominated by development sciences accepted as positive and true. Yet these political technologies which sought to erase underdevelopment from the face of the earth ended up, instead, multiplying it to infinity. Escobar finds this view of development as a modernist discourse different from the analyses of political economy, modernization, or even alternative development, which propose merely modifying the current regime of development. Such highly critical notions about development intersect with a profound sense of disillusionment about developmental practice (e.g. Edwards 1989) to produce a crisis of confidence in development studies; indeed, perhaps, a crisis in progressive thought in general. Quoting Escobar:

> for some time now, it has been difficult – at times even impossible – to talk about development, protest or revolution with the same confidence and encompassing scope with which intellectuals and activists spoke about these vital matters in our most recent past. It is as if the elegant discourses of the 1960s – the high decade of both development and revolution – had been suspended, caught in mid air as they strove toward their zenith, and, like fragile bubbles, exploded, leaving a scrambled trace of their glorious path behind . . . Hesitantly perhaps, but with a persistence that has to be taken seriously, a new discourse has set in. (Escobar 1992: 20)

Brought on by critical thought's inability to leave behind the imaginary of development, the whole project is said to be sick, dying, gone. Escobar compares this with a powerful social movements discourse which, while unclear about its possible directions, has become a privileged arena for intellectual inquiry and political action.

Escobar tries to bridge the two insights, the critique of development and social movements, believing:

1 that a poststructural critique of the discourse and practice of development can clear the ground for a more radical, collective imagining of alternative futures;
2 that thinking about alternatives to development requires a theoretico-practical transformation which draws on the practices of Third World social movements.

Escobar claims a growing number of scholars in agreement with this prescription who, rather than search for development alternatives, speak about alternatives to development. These scholars share: a critical stance with respect to established science; an interest in local autonomy, culture, and knowledge; and a position defending localized, pluralistic grassroots movements. We could call the tendency, after the title of Escobar's main article, "post-developmentalism" (see also Sachs 1992). Through Escobar's participation in Association of American Geographers conferences, the carrying of his ideas in geographical texts (Crush 1995; Peet and Watts 1996), and the many contacts between geography and the anthropology of development, notions of a poststructural development geography became influential in the field in the 1990s (see, for example, Yapa 1996).

Eroticized Topographies/Queer Landscapes

From positions like these, which retain connection with such traditional themes in geographic research as landscape and development, we move to more extreme statements of postmodern position which began to appear from the fringe of postmodern geography in the 1990s. David Bell and Gill Valentine (1995: 1), geographers at the University of Sheffield in England, want to "read the space of the city as sexed and sexualised." They see urban streets as eroticized topographies, real and imagined, in which sexual identities are made and sexual acts consummated. For them, the straight family home and the pretended family home of lesbians and gays can be read as local sexualized spaces or vernacular erotic geographies. Such landscapes of desire are the focus of a range of theoretical perspectives: geographical work on sexuality in the 1980s dealt with urban gay communities; work in the 1990s, particularly in Britain, is concerned with identity politics. For Bell and Valentine, a body of work literally emerges in geography that explores the way sexual identities are inscribed on the body and the landscape. But mainly they look at poststructural debates outside the discipline and "read these into geography." Thus, a "queer reading" resists the ways geographical knowledge is constituted as masculinist, heteronormative, and disembodied, and proposes doing geography differently – looking at the creative and wild possibilities presented by the elsewhere of decadent urban life, the imagined geographies of the perverse city, queer spaces, and subversive spatial acts (the kiss of two men on a night bus home). What might a geography of sexuality consist of? We can read the contents of Bell and Valentine's collection, which tends to the eclectic and diverse: theorizing maps of identity, or cartographies of sexual identity; the power of landscapes as liberatory or oppressive sites for the performance of sexed selves; the production of sexualized places; or reading resistance as spatial practice. In a review of work on queer geography, Jon Binnie (1997) concludes that space is not naturally, authentically "straight" but is actively (hetero)sexualized. In studying this he finds positivism necessarily heterosexist as a theoretical framework, poststructuralist new cultural geography marked by heterosexism, and therefore suggests the possibility of a "queer epistemology." These are the new topics just beginning to be broached (and bravely too) in a queer reading of geography.

Proverbs for Paranoids

For some, the arguments summarized in this chapter appropriate rather than elucidate postmodernism, deconstruction, difference, and otherness, combining these movements into projects with their own agendas (modernism, Marxism, etc.). Marcus Doel (1993; 1994; 1996), a lecturer in geography at Loughborough University in England, argues that modern human geography, while predicated upon (spatial) difference, knows little, if anything, about its character and movement. For Doel, a truly postmodern human geography entails a completely different conceptualization of difference, not simply as "the spacing between things," but as "a dynamic, affirmative and productive movement, process and articulation" (Doel 1993: 380). The key question, for Doel, is how to gather up concrete differences in a meaningful, coherent way. He sees previous (Marxist) efforts as "dialectical machinations," attempts to "stitch and sew" differences together: "Dialectical accountancy always amounts to (an economy of) the same; difference must be submitted to the authority of that which it differs from" (Doel 1993: 380). This results in badly analyzed composites in a modern human geography he terms "pandemic paranoia," enthralled by what are, for him, nightmares of metaphysics and dialectics. Whereas modern human geography is fixated on discourses of loss and recovery, postmodern human geography should proceed through discourses of retraction, moving through multiple transformations. He thinks that the fate of geography depends on its ability to "descry retraction" (glimpse withdrawal) rather than remain fixated on loss. Doel says that while geographical writing has become cubist in its interlacing of diverse perspectives, the geographical scene eludes representation since it has already withdrawn along lines of flight and deterritorialization (cf. Deleuze and Guattari). Doel is against the dialectic's insatiable appetite for difference, what he calls its false movement of the abstract concept from one opposite to another by means of imprecision, and its attempt to assimilate deconstruction and postmodernism – he sees postmodernism resisting by learning (from Derrida) the tactics of how to avoid speaking and indulging in the ecstasy of indifference (i.e. "an affirmation of the movement in things" or "the intensification of difference" – Doel 1993: 386).

This inability of geography to descry the difference between loss and retraction results, for Doel, in a misunderstanding of postmodern currents which could reinvigorate human geography. Doel (1993: 386) asks: "Does geography speak to you?" For Doel, signs are nomadic (nothing but movement), rhizomatic (without roots), and immersed in things, there is never a meaning, only an unending trace, and a text is only an arrangement of movements. For him, signs, concepts, and theories have nothing to do with representation and geography is semantic incontinence, judgement deranged, demented incomprehension. So, while modern human geography accumulates through the dialectic of slice and stitch, postmodern human geography disaccumulates and retracts through pulling, snagging or ravelling a thread in the joy of obscuration – "an interminable interruption of signification and the deterritorialization of meaning through the relentless hollowing of signs ... retraction is a hollowing movement which accelerates and erodes, leaving nothing but the pores, fractals and colloids of nomadic concepts" (Doel 1993: 388). Or further, on writing geography as a borderless text with nothing to say:

> Pull threads. Release laugh catastrophes. Engage in theoretical terrorism. Stitch pick. Immerse your rigidities in flows. Some have called this strategy postmodernism, deconstruction, schizoanalysis, rhizomatics, quantum philosophy, genealogy and more. I have called it the decompression of geography on hollowed ground. (Doel 1993: 389)

This leaves two questions: how to select a stitch to pick or thread to pull, and what to do with the amassing bits of thread. Neither question can be answered in the abstract, but as only strategic responses to particular contexts – in this context, "all I can say is begin where you are. Pull the thread which chokes, binds or fascinates you the most, even if it is a factious, factitious and fictional one" (Doel 1993: 389). Doel wants to grasp the temptation of indifference and discard the disciplinary defense mechanism whereby destructive critique is acceptable only if coupled with constructive replacement: "a wholly affirmative postmodern geography must be amoral, indifferent and cruel, but it must also activate its latent obscenity ... plunging into the singularity, banality and nullity of the event."

In a second paper, Doel (1994) counters hostile criticisms of postmodernism – its relativism, irrationalism, suicidal nihilism – and again criticizes attempts to capture otherness in "libidinal economies of the Same." Postmodernism and deconstruction work through an "ethical obligation to respond to the call of an-Other, and to wait for the call of an-Other ... who is always to come," what Doel (1994: 1047) calls "telephony" (i.e. postmodernism's placing itself on hold for an-Other). Postmodernism affirms everything which escapes the influence of an economy of the Same, hence, writing difference is both interminable and impossible. Given the singularity and altereity of an-Other, telephony broaches an acategorical theoretical-practice which, for Doel, risks making sense. He sees postmodernism affirming otherness by withdrawing an organizing frame ("incredulity towards metanarratives"), withdrawing the Same into an open multiplicity or affirming that which is out of position in a "socius of deindividuated singularities articulated through complication, experimentation, and invention" (Doel 1994: 1048). Writing difference goes by way of the undecidable, but this undecidability, this affirmation of difference, entails a radical passivity (letting be) that, for Doel, is neither indifferent nor irresponsible. Writing difference "is simply to say 'yes' to the Other" (Doel 1994: 1050). Deconstruction intervenes in the real history of the world in a process of disordering order, although "thankfully" it never provides means for a constructivist or destructivist project to be successfully concluded.

Doel makes an "ethical" argument for passing from deconstructive telephony (remaining on call for an anonymous Other) to picnolepsy (writing otherwise elsewhere). Writing difference moves towards what he calls "liminal materialism" expressed in acategorical terms: "theoretical-practice is obligated by an-Other to risk making sense; it must proceed by way of the acategorical, asignifying, and asubjective in order to affirm and make space for this Other which is not its other. Telephony and picnolepsy respond ethically to the ethics of the event" (Doel 1994: 1053). The method he suggests, *liminal materialism*, is a kind of pure expenditure, writing as a flow among others, interruption, complication, invention, in which there is nothing to interpret or explain. This strips theoretical-practice of its despotic, tyrannical pretensions, plunging it into a surficial ontology:

> The dissolution of representation pertains to the contraction of the simulated distance and depth-of-field between thought on the one hand and the real on the other: now there is only an absolute proximity . . . In the wake of this absolute proximity, a different form of vision is engendered: from one situated within a long-range *optic* space of representation, to one emersed in a close-range *haptic* [touching] space . . . Such is the ethics of the event. (Doel 1994: 1054)

In other words, Doel finds it ethical to be face to face with the nothingness of the event, to be open to the "It happens." That is, theoretical practice is obligated by the singularity of the event to respond without pretext or reserve. Yet it must risk making sense to affirm and make space for the Other: "there is a duty in the deconstructive experiences of telephony, picnolepsy, and liminal materialism. There has to be, if there is such a thing as an Other who is not merely the Same. Interrupt me" (Doel 1994: 1055).

Repressing an intense desire to do exactly that (interrupt), but only for a while, we might add that Doel (1996) draws on Deleuze and Guattari (who he says always speak as geographers) to argue for a fundamental shift in the way space, place, and spacing are configured, a shift which deconstructs the field of geography as we know it:

> This yields a world of continuous variation, becoming, and chance, rather than one of constancy, being, and predictability; and it is populated solely by haecceities [individualities], singularities, and events, strung together through joints, intervals, and folds. Accordingly, a fractal world of infinite disadjustment, destabilization, and disjointure is what is meant by the term "scrumpled geography," and it constitutes the horizon on which one should situate deconstruction, postmodernism and poststructuralism more generally. (Doel 1996: 421)

This "scrumpled geography" follows structural notions of an orderly time–space by only fifteen years. Such are the joys of a geography in flux.

Conclusion

There are several political epistemological positions in what is often taken as poststructural postmodernism. Poststructuralism preserves many aspects of its modernist predecessors. Analysis remains ontologically grounded in immanent forces of desire and power and, in a connected move, a radical politics of marginal groups remains as a vestige of eventual purpose. Postmodernism, by comparison, attempts to produce theory without ontological grounds and politically disengages from the modern project of the perfectibility of humanity – it represents the end point of a metadynamic of disenchantment which moves from religion to groundlessness (cf. figure 1.1). Even so, these are theorists with Marxism in their pasts; even the most extreme postmodernists cannot entirely let go of political radicalism. Thus, Theodor Schatzki (1993), a philosopher and co-director of the committee on social theory at the University of Kentucky, argues that Foucault and Lyotard conceive of social reality as a network of individuals connected by force relations (Foucault) or language games (Lyotard), and for both, politics concerns the nature of these connections. But poststructural politics, Schatzki says, particularly recognizes the pluralization of oppression in western societies. Political activity promotes local struggles concerned with the power of men over women, parents over children, psychiatry over the mentally ill, bureaucracy over people – that is, local variants of power relations. Foucault (1980) is clearly on the side of oppressed people – indeed, genealogy proposes to uncover forgotten ideas and allow unheard voices to surface in an insurrection of subjugated knowledges. Lyotard's (1988) politics consists of watching for wrongs and finding idioms in which they can be expressed. Derrida (1994: 92) says: "Deconstruction has never had any sense or interest, in my view at least, except as a radicalization, which is to say also *in the tradition* of a certain Marxism, in a certain *spirit of Marxism*." Deleuze and Guattari long continued to call themselves Marxists. Even Baudrillard slips from cynical nihilism on occasion to reveal lingering vestiges of leftist commitment. It is clear that the form of left politics which emerges from poststructuralism differs greatly from traditional socialism. Yet there is remarkably little comparative discussion of politics between poststructuralists, postmodernists, and socialists. The camps are separated by fields of difference, mutual suspicion, even hostility. This is not merely a matter of "better communication," as the perpetual liberal solution used to read. Rather, there are real differences of position here, which start with almost deliberate misreadings of each other's theoretical and political stance.

Amoral Geography

Take, for example, Doel's statement, an extreme form of the postmodern position in the discipline of geography, which does manage to lose virtually all connection with any project of emancipatory politics. From the point of view of historical materialism, it begins by mistaking dialectical analysis for an apparatus of the capture of difference, when dialectics distinguishes and relates the two aspects of the event, its sameness and its difference. Events are not "pure difference," but instead combine elements of sameness with elements of difference originating in varying combinations of elements shared with other events as well as in singular movements. Dialectics is a method by which the various aspects of an event can be analyzed, in combination, and individually. Dialectics is also a political method investigating not just the realities of things and events, but their potentialities – that is, what they could possibly become from recombination and the eruption of new aspects. Dialectics is not a deranged analysis but one ranged on the side of oppressed people who have the most to gain from social transformation and are the first to suffer terribly from deranged thinking. In the Doel (1993: 389) version, postmodern political ontology takes the form of "begin where you are. Pull the thread which chokes, binds or fascinates you the most," an invitation to personal indulgence reminiscent of those days of privilege, when academics had triple-barrelled names, and were upper-class dilettantes researching quaint topics of pure esoterica – with this, Philo's moral geography turns into its opposite, Doel's amoral geography. Doel claims some kind of politics – that postmodernism works through affirmation of difference, sides with the unassimilable Other. But this is a passive affirmation, in that telephony waits for an-Other always to come – that is, conveniently never there – so nothing ever needs doing in terms of political practice except criticizing supposed apparatuses of theoretical capture just in case the Other arrives (telephony as "tele-phoney"). Likewise with the ethics of liminal materialism, where ethics is openness to the "It happens" without (political or ethical) pretext. The trouble is that events are never naively pure, spoiled only by interpretation, but rather "(Sh)it happens" and the "pretext" of ethics pre-interprets exactly so that one can respond critically to events, not just accept them in their glorious singularity. Most of all, this extreme version of postmodernism propagated in the name of intellectual anti-terrorism, employs the terroristic device of terminological vagueness, attempting to overpower the unsure reader with indecipherable phrases and a "quotation market" of its own, this time from Derrida, Deleuze, Guattari, and others, that only the privileged can afford to read (because of the preparation needed), and only those trained at the expense of state or private fortune can afford the time to interpret, because of the original vagueness of their exposition, copied and taken to further extremes by lesser writers. Thus, it has a politics, but one of nihilistic terror. Finally, one not so amusing aspect of this exercise is the use by Massami, Doel, and others of Greek and Latin words, and direct derivatives, like haecceity, which are classical signs of oppression by people with a "superior" education. The British Marxist cultural critic Terry Eagleton (1983: 142) says: "Unable to break the structures of state power, post-structuralism found it possible instead to subvert the structures of language." Bryan Palmer (1990: 5) sees the attempt to make systems of signification the main ground constructing human life as a *descent* into discourse: the tendency to reify language, placing it beyond social and political relations, displaces essential structures and formations to the historical sidelines. When discourse is the main enemy and interpretation is advocated as primary political act, postmodernism as discursive idealism degenerates into nihilism at best and a kind of elite academic conservatism at worst.

Modernity as an Unfinished Project

In some of the far reaches of social thought, where postmodern ideas now reign triumphant, it often seems as though the modern project is over and done with. Yet modern humanism has its defenders, even among thinkers well versed in poststructural thought. Philosophers like Richard Bernstein, Ferenc Feher, Jürgen Habermas, and Agnes Heller, for instance, concede that an ethnocentric and oppressively universalistic humanism suppresses difference. Yet Heller and Feher (1991) argue that modern humanism is a restless project, ever enriching its universal ideals of freedom and self-determining autonomy, and not afraid to learn from its mistakes. Similarly, for Habermas (1992), "post-metaphysical" humanism preserves the notion of a self-conscious life and authentic self-realization but disassociates such commitments from the will of a single social subject, believing instead in a radically democratic process of communication and interaction between subjects (Johnson 1994: 7–8).

Perhaps the leading critic of postmodern social theory, Jürgen Habermas, proposes that the main problem of modernity is not too much rationality, but too little. Habermas agrees with his Frankfurt school predecessors, and with Foucault, that the Enlightenment project produces domination, but differs in finding positive potential in rationality and imminent danger in irrationality. Habermas therefore defends certain crucial modern concepts against the postmodern critique. To understand this defense requires that we look at Habermas's ideas in a little more detail.

Habermas's most distinctive claim is that there is a universal core of moral intuition operating at all times with an inherent human interest in emancipation and especially in communication without domination. Ordinary speech has an implicit telos of clear, rational communication and the attaining of consensus; any speech act contains universal validity claims, which can be reconstructed through the method of universal pragmatics. Agreement between people is achieved through the recognition of the validity of these truth claims and in turn their claim to reason. These are the transcendental conditions of understanding or communication which are then historically shaped by working and communicative conditions. Against the corrupted communication systems of late capitalist society, Habermas wants to recover the ideal speech situation whose potential can be seen in the public sphere of early capitalism. This normative vision is contained within a reconstructed Marxian theory of societal evolution in which both production and socialization are crucial components, work being purposive–rational action transforming nature for human purposes (control of outer nature), and interaction being communicative action governed by norms designed to achieve consensus on social issues (control of inner nature). Societies evolve from undifferentiated organic unities to differentiated structures with complex social rules in stages according to advances in the moral–practical learning process – hence, "the fundamental mechanism for social evolution in general is to be found in an automatic inability not to learn" (Habermas 1975: 15).

Habermas wants to rethink critical theory to overcome its pessimistic appraisal of the potential of modernity by returning to Marx's dialectic, which also sees repressive and emancipatory tendencies in modern rationality. Habermas draws also on Weber to interpret modernity as religious disenchantment. But unlike Marx and Weber, Habermas sees cultural modernity as creating a rational world view with autonomous branches of reason dealing with issues of science, morality, and art in terms of truth, normative rightness, and authenticity; that is, there are separate rationality structures – cognitive–instrumental (science), moral–practical (morality), and aesthetic–expressive (art). Modernization leads to the "colonization of the lifeworld" by the one-sided development of cognitive–instrumental rationality. Habermas is generally in favor of the process of cultural modernization. Yet critical theory, he thinks, must redress the balance between the different forms of rationality and increase their communicative content through an extension of democracy. This brings him into critical contact with postmodern theory which, he says, departs from social and cultural modernity. Habermas denies postmodernity as an historical era in which struggle and opposition are eliminated, believing instead that late capitalism, full of contradictions and crisis, can be changed through rational critique and political struggle. For Habermas, postmodern theorists move from one extreme to another when they leap from rejecting absolute knowledge into relativism, whereas for Habermas, the critique of philosophical foundationalism does not mean that no kind of foundation can be provided for normative critique – in conjunction with the empirical social sciences, philosophy can be used to reconstruct normative learning processes. What Habermas calls the "young conservatives" (Foucault, Derrida, and others) attack modernity and rationality only to move into the sphere of the "spontaneous powers of the imagination, self-experience and emotion," juxtaposing to instrumental reason principles accessible only through evocation, like the will to power (Habermas 1983: 14). Postmodern theory Habermas thinks is a wholesale, anti-modern movement which cannot account for the complexity and ambiguity of modernity; science, for example, is the basis for critical consciousness and a universal foundation for law and morality, as well as technical manipulation.

Habermas shows most respect for Foucault. But he finds Foucault undercutting his own positions. Foucault's claims that all truths are illusory and all discourses express power must be the case for his own work too. Foucault's writings are saturated with oppositional values and legitimate the voices of oppressed groups yet claim value neutrality. Habermas says that genealogy cannot account for its own normative foundation, while the counter-discourses it supports must also be effects of power. Furthermore, while Foucault claims to leave behind subject-centered reason in a (structuralist) theory of subjectless power, this does not escape the conceptual constraints of the philosophy of the subject, which indeed the concept of power is borrowed from:

> Genealogy is overtaken by a fate similar to that which Foucault had seen in the human sciences: To the extent that it retreats into the reflectionless objectivity of a non-participatory, ascetic description of kaleidoscopically changing practices of power, genealogical historiography emerges from its cocoon as precisely the *presentistic, relativistic, cryptonormative* illusory science that it does not want to be ... it follows the movement of a radically historicist extinction of the subject and ends up in an unholy subjectivism. (Habermas 1987: 275–6)

Foucault's theory of modern power is "false in its generality" in that it conflates particular disciplinary and panoptic techniques with the whole structure of societal modernization. Finally, in dissolving history into islands of discourse, filling the space of history with absolutely contingent occurrences, Foucault leaves no place for any over-arching meaning. Foucault's theories prohibit the universality and continuity that Habermas finds necessary for grounding social theory and advancing human freedom (Best 1995).

Comparative Essentialisms

Notice, however, that Habermas confronts postmodern theory with his own declarative (if not evocative) essentialist system: there is a universal core of moral intuition, an inherent human interest in emancipation, communication can occur without domination, speech has an implicit telos, any speech act contains universal validity claims, the ideal speech situation can be recovered, and so on. And when we read poststructural social theories in the light of Deleuze's influential recasting of Nietzsche, there too beneath interpretation, difference, and non-totalization, we find essentialism. Poststructuralism is a different form of essentialist structuralism, a system founded on the forces of "desire," mediated by relations of power, and conceptualized in immanent and eventually metaphysical (often vitalist) terms of fields of nondefinable but all-powerful forces. In an early but subtle critique, Peter Dews (1984: 72) finds the philosophy of desire, together with an aestheticization of politics, closely related to "the flowering of self-expression, the exertion of physical and erotic spontaneity against the ascetic routines of the modern working world, which characterized the events of May '68." The complement to a theory of the production of the subject through the containment of libidinal energy is a theory of power, such as that of Foucault. Here, we would add, the driving force behind action is the eruption of desire in an unconscious safe from empirical verification, but discussed in transhistorical terms, as though it might be an "essence" – hence, desiring-production, flows of desire, channels of power, and the whole Nietzschean geography. In the Foucauldian version, desire is linked to power in that desirous individuals interact, as they must, through power relations. On the one side, desire is a power-generating drive involving resistance to the desiring pursuits of others; on the other side, power represses libidinal energy to produce the "civilized subject" – hence, power has its positive and negative aspects. Here, there are important implications for geography – desire as source of local difference. Yet the poststructural reliance on immanent desire/power is metaphysical in that it too attributes essence to an inherent, and universal force which cannot exactly be described (Habermas's "evocation") let alone "proven" and scarcely pointed to, except through self-declaration. Dews (1984: 95) calls this the "inability of Nietzschean naturalism, of a pure theory of forces, to provide a substitute for the normative foundations of political critique." It is therefore convenient that poststructural thought disdains anything like proof even in its simple guise as the ability to demonstrate (point to) the basic empirical components of a theory. This causes poststructural analysis to swing wildly from immanent forces (desire, power) to individualities, singularities, and pure differences, with unconvincing, unexplained "mediations," like strategies (whose strategies?), inexactly placed between. This gets the postmodern end of this set of theories into inordinate difficulties, which it tries to disguise through terminological vagueness and outrageous theoretical excess – there is a brilliant exposé of this in Neil Smith's (1996) "Rethinking Sleep," carried as an editorial by the very journal it so maliciously parodies! Postmodern theory contains brilliant insights, but in the end is not successful as overall philosophy.

Chapter 7

Feminist Theory and the Geography of Gender

This chapter looks at feminist thought in geography in the context of broader political, philosophical, and social-theoretic tendencies. More than other oppositional ideas, feminist theory grew from ideas generated by the political practices of social movements. Feminism is a system of thought radicalized by women's experiences of multiple forms of oppression: these include gender, class, race, and region. Feminist geography too bears the marks of women's exclusion from the upper echelons of the organized discipline and from a research agenda which long ignored their existence. In addition, feminist geography has had a sophisticated radical view since its first appearance in the middle 1970s (see chapter 3). Feminist theory and feminist geography grew together, with geography often being a medium of radicalization in terms of teaching experience and research. The discipline changed rapidly from a position where the very notion of a feminist conception of space would have been impossible to imagine, let alone teach, to one in which feminist theorists could begin to construct such a conception and even make a living teaching the results. Yet a long struggle separates the first inclinations of feminist geography from the mature theories of the 1990s, and opposition has not disappeared. All this, however, presupposes a story of the formation of feminist social movements, the production of feminist social theory, and the steps taken in making a feminist geography. These topics are discussed in turn.

Women's Movements, Feminist Thought

Feminist theory is informed by a history of women's movements, usually divided into first, second, and third waves. Each wave has counter-currents: struggles occur over women's rights and gender, class, and race differences; strategies vary between groups; the tensions are such that it is difficult, if not impossible, to speak of a single women's movement.

First Wave

In the United States, the 1848 Seneca Falls Convention and its Declaration of Rights and Sentiments, modelled after the Declaration of Independence, called for equality in marriage, for women's property rights and the right to earn equal wages, rights to have child custody, to make contracts, testify in court, inherit property, and the right to vote. The Convention organizers, Elizabeth Cady Stanton and Susan B. Anthony, saw achievement of women's political suffrage as the crucial goal. With the vote, women would gain entrance into public life and through it, legal equality, gateway to liberation from social, political and economic oppression. Moreover, suffrage would unite all women, not just the middle class, because the root of oppression was the same: male domination (Balser 1987: 53–5).

The international women's suffrage movement was influenced by the Second Socialist International and the World's Women Christian Temperance Union (WCTU). The British movement in the early twentieth century was a coalition of working-class women (especially from the textile unions) and socialist middle-class suffragists. The movement aimed, in part, at dissolving the distinction between a private woman's sphere and a public, male arena (Nolan and Daley 1994: 17). It used militant tactics, civil disobedience, and mass demonstrations, all met with arrest and forced prison feeding, which "intensified women's militance around the world" (DuBois 1994: 266). Women's movements in Latin America, Asia, and the Middle East developed, after 1920, in connection with larger working-class movements. Strategies differed according to culture and historical moment: Latin American feminists, for example, projected femininity, domesticity, and motherhood into politics. In general, women challenged men's exclusive control of political rights and reaffirmed difference according to women's special, positive abilities and biologically based distinctions (Lavrin 1994: 198–9). Women were faced with a dilemma, whether to join men's organizations, or create their own separate associations. Despite women's persistent (and partly successful) efforts to achieve the vote, in 1940 half the world's people lived still in countries without female franchise (Nolan and Daley 1994: 9). Eventually, the achievement of suffrage in most western countries, an expanding economy, and the appeal of mass consumption demobilized the first wave of feminist movements.

Second Wave

The second wave of feminism began with the radicalization of women during the anti-Vietnam-war and civil rights movements of the 1960s. While women and men participated equally in these political movements, women were often denied leadership positions, and were silenced when they tried to raise issues of women's rights, for example within the activist organization Students for a Democratic Society (SDS). As one SDS organizer said, women "made peanut butter, waited on tables, cleaned up and got laid. That was their role" (Evans 1979: 160). Partly in response, women began organizing consciousness-raising groups which became critical, strategic components of feminist struggles. The notion that "the personal is political" questions oppression in women's lives; it validates personal experience as a basis for collective action; and it allows people to place issues previously considered personal and private into the realm of the political and public (Sarachild 1973: 132). For women who blamed themselves for their situation, it named fundamental causal structures and processes. This was a time of optimism, debate, and the publication of feminism's formative literature. Originally written in 1949, Simone de Beauvoir's *The Second Sex* (1978) had been translated into English in 1953. Betty Friedan's *The Feminine Mystique* (1963) was highly influential in sparking the second wave (Tobias 1997), followed by Shulamith Firestone's *The Dialectic of Sex* (1970), Kate Millett's *Sexual Politics* (1970), and Gayle Rubin's essay "The Traffic in Women: Notes on the Political Economy of Sex" (1975), also influential in the development of feminist consciousness, theory, and strategy. The National Organization of Women (NOW), formed in 1966, connected liberals with socialists. Women of color often joined the Student Non-Violent Coordinating Committee (SNCC), and other similar organizations, working for civil rights before women's rights. Criticisms from women of color, internal divisions, and the entry of women into better positions in the labor force were influential if not in ending, then certainly in diminishing, the second wave of feminism by the 1980s.

Third Wave

A number of factors shaped the development of the third wave, often labelled "postfeminist." Feminism increasingly became an academic critique of knowledge. Women's studies, although not widely institutionalized until the late 1980s, became a critical platform for a more progressive education in colleges and universities. As the New Right feared, the university provided a liberal space for women's movements, but elsewhere a conservative backlash against women and minorities silenced many and enacted new forms of cultural and legal regulation. A number of discourses concerning abortion, welfare, work, crime (especially drug-related), and immigration, coalesced around women's questions.

Contemporary feminist practice, whether in North America, Europe, or the Third World, among academics or activists, now reflects debates begun by women of color and lesbians in the late 1970s. Critical discourses emerged on the politics of location and sexuality. An early statement from the Combahee River Collective (1984) questions the notion of a common women's identity as basis for political strategy. Poets and writers, notably bell hooks and Audre Lorde in the United States, criticized the women's movement for downplaying sexual, racial, and class differences; these authors identify several communities of which they are not wholly a part. Works by Chandra Mohanty (1991a; 1991b) and Adrianne Rich (1986) represent a move from a politics of common identity, for example sisterhood, with its assumptions of similarly structured oppression, to a politics of location, which requires individuals and groups to recognize their own responsibility in a situation. If women are neither victims nor truth tellers, the alternative is a self-conscious struggle to redefine dominant cultural narratives and practices. Lorde, Mohanty, and others call for a dramatic shift in the practice of collective politics.

The United Nations Decade for Women (1975–85) encouraged the growth of feminist groups worldwide (Friedman 1995; Miles 1996). Each world conference has a parallel non-governmental organization (NGO) forum, the site often of fierce debate. In the Mexico and Copenhagen conferences (1975, 1980), a noticeable First World–Third World divide opened around western feminists' inattention to race and imperialism. By the time of the 1985 Nairobi conference, Third World women, a clear majority, were defining the issues. Over the decade of the 1980s, women from the First and Third Worlds developed a basis for solidarity in spite of ideological and cultural differences. The fourth World Conference on Women was held in September 1995 in Beijing. Its Platform for Action concerns the human rights of women – rights to education, food, health, greater political power, and freedom from violence (Bunch, Dutt, and Fried 1995).

Women in the Third World organize around economic, environmental, legal, military, cultural, and physical threats, and resistance to dictatorship, militarism, fundamentalism, economic dependence, and violence against women. Women's movements are not necessarily organized around feminist agendas but promote women's perspectives: examples include the Chipko Movement of the Himalayas, the Green Belt Movement in Kenya, the Self-Employed Women's Association in India, and Mothers of the Disappeared movements in Latin America (Miles 1996: 86). Increasingly, groups posit culturally specific feminisms as a political base. Yet also feminists around the world unite around issues of economic justice, human rights, and degradation of the environment, the idea being unity through diversity.

Feminist studies, particularly those stemming from the second wave of women's movements, take the form mainly of radical political ontologies – that is, attempts to understand life structures in feminist terms, including attempts at posing new questions and adopting transformative political positions; these are matched (sometimes inexactly) by feminist epistemologies – that is, questions about the structures and validation systems of the knowledges employed, these questions being posed for political rather than merely academic or purely intellectual reasons. The chapter moves from feminist theory in its ontological and epistemological guises to feminist geography, its history, arguments, and focal interests.

Political Ontologies–Political Epistemologies

In the view of Alison Jaggar, feminists seek to end women's subordination (humanly imposed restrictions on freedom) using the women's liberation movement as a political instrument. Jaggar, a professor of philosophy at the University of Colorado, outlines four conceptions of women's liberation: liberal, Marxist, radical, and socialist feminisms. We follow her outline here.

Liberal Feminism

This set of positions derives from classical liberal theory. Liberal theory basically states that human beings have intrinsic value as rational agents, with rationality being the mental capacity for moral reasoning and calculation. On the basis of an equal capacity to reason, liberal feminism wishes to apply human rights of dignity, autonomy, and self-fulfillment to women as well as men. Liberal feminism is committed to neopositivist conceptions of objectivity which supposedly eliminate social interests, values, and emotions from consideration; theories produced by the rational, detached observer are universally applicable. Liberal feminists claim no special privilege for women, but only equal rights and opportunities for all. But for Jaggar, liberal feminism's Cartesian assumption that the mind is separable from the body, its particular valuation of reasoning and its abstract individualism present intractable metaphysical and epistemological problems. Therefore, classical Marxism criticizes liberal theory as bourgeois ideology, and instead poses class as key to understanding women's oppression.

Marxist Feminism

Rather than emphasizing universal rationality, Marxist feminism sees humans as a biological species with needs met by praxis (conscious physical labor). Social forms of labor determine the fundamental features of society and its inhabitants, *including* their forms of rationality. Hence, women's nature is formed by the interaction between praxis, biological constitution, and physical and social environments. Understanding women in a specific society basically means examining its social relations of production. Engels (1942) argues that early societies had a sexual division of labor, with men producing means of subsistence and women working in the household. Developments of the forces of production in the male sphere gave men social dominance. Wanting to control the inheritance of wealth, men instituted monogamy as an instrument of the economic dependence and subordination of women. For Engels, women's subordination results from the institution of class society and is maintained because it serves the interests of capital. Jaggar finds problems of biologism, functionalism, and faulty anthropological data in this early approach.

For Marxist feminism, the liberal notion of science as a value-free activity may originally have defined an area of thought free from church and state interference, but since the nineteenth century has served reactionary purposes, obscuring the political assumptions lurking in science (Sohn-Rethel 1975; Rose and Rose 1976). For Marxists, by comparison, there is no outside point allowing a neutral perspective on the world. This does not necessarily make Marxism relativistic: positivist Marxism has a correspondence theory of truth which suggests that objective facts may be found through experimentation; structural Marxism proposes a coherence theory of truth (i.e. truth depends on a theory's comprehensiveness and lack of contradiction); practical or interventionist Marxism says that the ultimate criterion of theoretical adequacy is revolutionary potential; and Lukács's "totalistic Marxism" argues that we should "prefer the standpoint of the class whose interest most closely approximates humanity's – the point of view of the proletariat is epistemologically preferable to that of the bourgeoisie because it is driven to demystify reality and reveal the underlying causes of its own domination" (Jaggar 1983: 362–3; Lukács 1971).

In brief, traditional Marxist feminists want radical women to adopt the standpoint of the working class.

Radical Feminism

Radical feminism generated mainly by the women's liberation movement of the 1960s consists of a *series* of positions united by commitment to eradicating the systematic causes of women's oppression. Explanation initially emphasized the sex-roles played by men and women, the identities assumed by people playing these roles, and the need for androgyny, or the elimination of social and psychological distinctions between genders. In a second line of explanation, the discovery of universal and transhistorical male privilege is interpreted in biologically materialist terms, as with notions of the male as natural predator and the female as natural prey (Brownmiller 1975).

Shulamith Firestone's *The Dialectic of Sex* (1970) adapts Marxism in theorizing procreative reproduction, rather than productive labor, as the moving force of history. In this conception, the biological family is the base of society and economy part of the superstructure. Class struggle occurs between two distinct biological and reproductive classes: women who are weaker due to reproductive physiology; and stronger men with dependent families. The mother–child interdependency shapes the psychology of all females (and infants) in each society while biologically based social institutions reinforce male domination. For Firestone, developments in the forces of reproduction (contraception, test-tube babies) now make it possible to transform the biological basis of women's subordination in the sense that genital sex distinctions would no longer have the same cultural significance. In the place of the biologically based would come consciously designed and chosen social reproductive practices.

Other radical feminist theories link women's special powers to female biology or, in some versions, to relations with nature. Susan Griffen (1980: 226), for example, says that "we are nature," that women have special ways of conceiving the world which emphasize feelings rather than men's reasoning. Closeness to nature becomes the main source of women's strength and power. The human ideal is the woman with empathy, intuition, and protectiveness, an emotional as well as a rational being. However, other radical feminists, particularly those influenced by French structural and poststructural ideas (Christine Delphy, Hélène Cixous, Luce Irigaray), deny naturalistic theories, believing that even human biology is socially constructed (i.e. a process of cultural selection). For Jaggar, too, natural and biological theories confuse historical continuity with causal explanation. Biological constitution, she argues, interacts with social and cultural factors so that the body is an effect as well as a cause of social organization.

Despite internal differences, Jaggar proposes that radical feminism has a consistent epistemology based in a certain view of reality: women know things that men do not know. Radical feminist epistemology explores strategies for furthering this special knowledge: for example, consciousness raising is a collective, dialogic, supportive technique aimed at praxis. This approach has similarities with Marxist analysis. But radical feminism differs in accepting the reliability of human faculties like intuition, and often accepts the spiritual power derived from mystical connections with the universe (Griffen 1980) – an (unreal) anathema to most Marxists. In contrast to patriarchal thought, characterized by hierarchical divisions and distinctions, oppositions and dualisms, radical feminism conceives the world as an organic, dynamic whole, as structures of relations (for example between observer and observed), as a circle, with knowledge moving in upward spirals (Morgan 1977; Daly 1978). In brief, radical feminist knowledge is created directly from the particular experiences of women and is different from that of men.

Socialist Feminism

Socialist feminism is committed to the Marxist notion of the historical and social creation of human nature, a process which includes gender, race, ethnicity, and other distinctions, as well as class. In socialist feminism, causal emphasis is placed on the sexual division of labor, or different types of social praxis, as bases of physical and psychological differences between men and women. Here, the notion of praxis is broadly interpreted: Iris Marion Young (1979), for example, explores under "praxis" socially determined ways men and women experience space, objects, and their own bodies. The central idea, however, is that women are constituted by the social relations they inhabit and the types of labor they perform. Beginning with the Marxian notion of production for the satisfaction of physical needs, socialist feminism argues that needs for bearing and raising children are equally fundamental, as well as needs of sexual satisfaction and emotional nurturing, all of which require (usually female) labor. Gender struggles over reproductive activity are fundamental, yet often ignored by traditional Marxist theory.

Various socialist feminist theories elucidate several implications of this basic position. Nancy Chodorow (1978) argues that the individual's most intense early relationships involve love of the mother, the female reproductive worker. To become masculine, boys must separate themselves via hostility towards their mothers, generating lifelong contempt for women, denying their emotional needs, and creating rigid and punitive superegos. Girls achieve femininity by being like their mothers, retaining their capacity for empathy, and developing superegos open to persuasion and vulnerable to the judgements of others. Boys grow into achievement-oriented men adapted to work outside the home; girls grow into women adapted to emotional work inside or outside the home. Yet, for Jaggar, this is a universalistic, ahistorical theory. Relations between economy, procreation, and male dominance, she argues, are better conceptualized by Ann Ferguson and Nancy Folbre's (1981) "sex-affective production," the historically specific sets of activities which restrict women's options and remuneration. Socialist feminists in general theorize procreative activities and public sphere production as mutually interdependent, neither ultimately determining the other. Public/private distinctions, socialist feminists think, rationalize the exploitation of women. Socialist feminism calls for reproductive democracy, including family and procreative decisions, as well as control over commodity production. Jaggar (1983: 148–63) favors socialist feminism but finds problems in its (Freudian) psychoanalytic theory, its notion of procreation as a form of production, and its conceptualization of production and reproduction.

With affinities to classical Marxism, socialist feminist epistemology asserts that women's position gives a more reliable, less distorted view than the experience and positions of capitalists or working-class men. Women suffer special forms of exploitation and oppression which yield a particular epistemological standpoint; this enables a less biased, more comprehensive, view of reality. Such a women's standpoint, often reflected in naive and unreflective world views, can be enhanced through a collective process of political and scientific struggle. From the point of view of socialist feminism, the scientific revolution of the sixteenth and seventeenth centuries was not only typically bourgeois, but also established masculine conceptualizations as the ideal. Thus, the organic conception of nature as mother, to be respected and cherished, gave way to nature as unruly female, to be tamed, and finally to a passive, inert dead nature, exploitable with impunity (Merchant 1980). Socialist feminists argue also that women's work is different from men's – thus, Dorothy Smith (1974) says that women perform work in the bodily mode, men the abstract, conceptual mode, while Nancy Hartsock (1985) says that women's domestic labor mediates men's contact with natural substances, all these having epistemological consequences. Other socialist feminists argue, from the view of gender theory and object relations, that different processes of separation from the mother in gender-structured societies result in different ways for women and men to understand themselves, their relations to others and to nature. Such preoccupations are reflected in the fundamental categories of western science. Sandra Harding (1982), for example, says that the (positivist) conception of nature as a collection of inert atoms, connected by mechanistic causal relations, and represented by abstract, quantitative mathematical formulae, derives from an unconscious male preoccupation with separation and control (see also Hartsock 1983; Flax 1983). In other words, *feminist standpoint theory* claims that the distinctive social experiences of women are bases for an autonomous epistemology.

For Jaggar (1983: 384), the socialist feminist conception of women's standpoint is a "politically appropriate and theoretically illuminating interpretation of such generally acknowledged conditions [of theoretical adequacy] as impartiality, objectivity, comprehensiveness, verifiability and usefulness." Socialist feminism shows that reconstructing reality requires transformation at a level which masculinist philosophy cannot even begin to comprehend.

Materialism, Feminism, Standpoint Theory

This last set of socialist feminist positions was developed with particular effect by Hartsock's (1985) *Money, Sex and Power*, an important work deriving from Marxism, but also critical of it. Nancy Hartsock, professor of political science at the University of Washington, argues the relation between Marxist theories constructed from the standpoint of workers, and feminist theories built from the position of women. Standpoint theory posits a series of levels of reality, in which the deeper level includes and explains surfaces or appearances. Feminist standpoint theory amplifies the liberatory possibilities embodied in women's experience. The feminist standpoint is related to the proletarian standpoint, but is more thoroughgoing, particularly because women do most of the work involved in reproducing labor power. The male worker's contact with nature outside the factory is mediated by women – hence, the female experience is deeper. That is, women's experience in reproduction represents a unity with nature that goes beyond the proletarian experience of material/metabolic interchange. Motherhood results in the construction of female existence centered in a complex relational nexus and focused on the woman's body. The man's experience is characterized by a duality of concrete versus abstract deriving from the separation between household and public life. Such dualism marks phallocentric social theory, a system of hierarchical dualisms (abstract/concrete, mind/body, culture/nature, ideal/real, stasis/change, etc.) By comparison:

> Women's construction of self in relation to others leads in an opposite direction – towards opposition to dualisms of any sort; valuation of concrete, everyday life; a sense of variety of connectedness and continuities with other persons and with the natural world. If material life structures consciousness, women's relationally defined existence, bodily experience of boundary challenges and activity transforming both physical objects and human beings must be expected to result in a world view to which dichotomies are foreign. (Hartsock 1985: 242)

A feminist standpoint, Hartsock thinks, may be based on the commonalities within women's experiences, but it is not obvious or self-evident – it needs reading out, developing, propagating. Hence, for Hartsock, women's life activity forms the basis of a specifically feminist materialism. Generalizing the human possibilities present in the life activity of women to the whole social system would raise for the first time in history "the possibility of a fully human community, a community structured by a variety of connections rather than separation and opposition" (Hartsock 1985: 247).

The Science Question in Feminism

Questions of feminist epistemology, many outlined for the first time in the late 1970s and early 1980s, became central foci of feminist concern by the mid to late 1980s. In *The Man of Reason*, Genevieve Lloyd (1984) argued that the ideal rationality developed in the seventeenth century by Descartes, Spinoza, and others was characterized by maleness, so that when philosophers speak of human ideals they are talking about ideals of manhood. Sandra Harding (1986), a professor of philosophy at the University of Delaware, argues that feminist criticisms of science move from a reformist to a revolutionary position: from a position merely of improving science, to a position favoring transformation of the foundations of science and the cultures according it value:

> The radical feminist position holds that the epistemologies, metaphysics, ethics, and politics of the dominant forms of science are androcentric and mutually supportive; that despite the deeply ingrained Western cultural belief in science's intrinsic progressiveness, science today serves primarily regressive social tendencies; and that the social structure

of science, many of its applications and technologies, its modes of defining research problems and designing experiments, its ways of constructing and conferring meanings are not only sexist but also racist, classist, and culturally coercive. In their analysis of how gender symbolism, the social division of labor by gender, and the construction of individual gender identity have affected the history and philosophy of science, feminist thinkers have challenged the intellectual and social orders at their very foundation. (Harding 1986: 9)

What are taken to be humanly inclusive concepts, objective methodologies, and transcendental truths bear instead the mark of gender, class, race, and culture. Such feminist criticisms are particularly important, Harding thinks, when applied to the natural sciences. Scientific rationality permeates public and private life and the social use of science is a direct generator of political power. Rational knowledge must be shown to serve the interests of social progress to legitimate scientific/industrial empires: "Neither God nor tradition is privileged with the same credibility as scientific rationality in modern cultures" (Harding 1986: 16). Yet equity studies document massive discrimination against women in science and the ways science is used in the service of sexist and racist social projects. Even the possible existence of any pure science is challenged in terms of the selection and definition of problematics and the design and interpretation of research. Techniques of literary criticism, used to "read science as a text," reveal the hidden social meanings of supposedly value-neutral claims and practices. Finally, feminist epistemologies lay the basis for an alternative understanding of the kind of experience in which to ground the beliefs honored as knowledge. Such feminist critiques of science, Harding says, challenge personal identity to its prerational core.

Yet feminism faces epistemological problems justifying the claims of its own politicized research. Harding outlines the positions and problems of three sets of epistemological attitudes towards science. *Feminist empiricism* argues that stricter adherence to the existing norms of inquiry by women scientists can correct social biases in science. Harding counters this, pointing out that while empiricism holds that scientific method itself is sufficient to account for increases in scientific objectivity, one can argue instead that movements for social liberation (like the bourgeois and proletarian revolutions) are more likely to increase the objectivity of science. And while empiricism insists that its methodological norms apply to the "context of justification" (to the testing of hypotheses and interpretation of evidence), the "context of discovery" (identification and definition of problems) remains a powerful source of social bias. Harding therefore prefers *feminist standpoint theory*, originating in Hegelian and Marxian thought (especially Lukács). As we have seen, this position argues that men's dominating position results in partial, perverse understandings, whereas women's subjugated position gives the potential for more complete understanding. However, this position is unlikely to appeal to those not already convinced, especially natural scientists, while postmodernists are skeptical about the possibility of a *single* feminist standpoint (Flax 1986). Thus, *feminist postmodernism* challenges the universalizing assumptions of the other two positions, emphasizing the fractured identities created by modern life and the multiple nature of theorizing. In response, Harding questions whether feminists should give up trying to provide *one* true feminist story about reality when confronted by powerful alliances between science and sexist, racist social projects. She concludes that feminist epistemological discourses have their own problems and contradictory tendencies, yet feminist criticism has already enhanced the understanding of androcentrism in science, moving "from the Woman Question in science to the more radical Science Question in feminism" (Harding 1986: 29).

Likewise, Evelyn Fox Keller (1990: 42) investigates the "historically pervasive association between masculine and objective," more specifically "between masculine and scientific." The claim used to be openly made, Keller says, that women lack rigor and clarity of mind and therefore can not, should not, be scientists. The women's movement made such assertions at least sound offensive. But Keller finds a continuing belief in science's intrinsic masculinity expressed in language and metaphors – "hard" (masculine) science as opposed to "soft" (feminine) subjective knowledge, the synonymy between feminine and sentimentality, and so on. Clearly, she says, identifying scientific thought with masculinity is deeply embedded in culture. The complement to the scientific mind is said to be nature, viewed ubiquitously as female. The metaphoric marriage between thought and nature, with science as its offspring, sets the scientific project within the patriarchal tradition – hence, the persistent description of the goals of science in terms of "conquering" or "mastering" (feminine) nature. For Keller, it would be naive to suppose that connotations of masculinity and conquest affect only the uses, and not the structure, of science. Science bears the imprint of genderization in all its aspects.

Scientific ideology prescribes a specific relation between knower (mind) and knowable (nature) that leads to knowledge. But, for Keller, characterizing the relation between knower and known in terms of distance and separation, subject and object, denies worldly relations and objectifies nature. The marriage between knower and known is consummated through reason rather than feeling, observation rather than immediate sensory experience, with modes of intercourse defined to ensure emotional and physical inviolability. The scientific mind is set apart from the knowable, masculinity connotes autonomy, separation, distance, and the radical rejection of any commingling of subject and object. In characterizing scientific and objective thought as masculine, the very activity of acquiring knowledge is thereby genderized. The arguments Keller summarizes came to be widely held feminist skepticisms about science by the late 1980s.

For a somewhat contrary feminist epistemological view we turn to the writings of Mary Hawkesworth (1989). Hawkesworth finds it implausible that women, because they are oppressed, or because they are women, know truth better than men. Privileging women's perspective suggests there is a uniform female experience. If standpoint theories reject a uniform experience, they either have to explain why some women see the truth and others do not, or "collapse into trivial and potentially contradictory pluralism that conceives of truth as simply the sum of all women's partial and incompatible views" (Hawkesworth 1989: 546). Instead, Hawkesworth explores the (conventionalist) notion of cognition as a human practice influenced by social processes and theory-laden conventions. "Knowledge, then, is a convention rooted in the practical judgements of a community of fallible inquirers who struggle to resolve theory-dependent problems under specific historical conditions" (Hawkesworth 1989: 549). Rationality and reason, in this view, become multiple and expansive. Yet some things, Hawkesworth finds, can quite definitely be known. Cognition as a human practice is useful to feminism because it avoids the pitfalls of psychological and functionalist arguments by "focusing on the theoretical constitution of the empirical realm" (Hawkesworth 1989: 551). Feminism needs to find modes of analysis appropriate for specific kinds of problems and then to provide detailed analyses of concrete situations.

Under Western Eyes

Yet exactly as these political–ontological and political–epistemological positions were being established, the entire (western) feminist project was subjected to devastating critique from women of color, lesbians, and Third World women. Audre Lorde, a black lesbian scholar, argues that while the oppression of women has no boundaries it is not identical within those boundaries. To imply that all women suffer the same oppression just because they are women loses sight of the varied tools of patriarchy, and ignores how these tools are used by women against each other:

> Racism and homophobia are real conditions of all our lives in this place and this time. I urge each one of us here to reach down into that deep place of knowledge inside herself and touch that terror and loathing of the difference that lives there. See whose face it wears. Then the personal as political can begin to illuminate all our choices. (Lorde 1981a: 101)

For Lorde, differences between women should be seen as a fund of strengths – they are, as she puts it, "polarities between which our creativity can spark like a dialectic" (Lorde 1981a: 99). Without community, she thinks, there is no liberation. But community cannot mean shedding differences, nor the "pathetic pretence" that differences between women do not exist. The failure of academic feminists to recognize difference as strength is a failure to reach beyond the first patriarchal lesson – divide and conquer – which, for Lorde, must be transformed into define and empower.

Lorde's notion of the place of knowledge – that is, differentials in the power to theorize difference – is expressed with particular force by Third World women. Trinh Minh-ha (1989) thinks that difference should not be defined by the dominant sex, but then neither should it be defined by the dominant (western) culture. Under the aegis of "cartographies of struggle" Chandra Mohanty (1991a; 1991b) critically examines works which produce the "Third World woman" as a singular, monolithic subject in a process of "discursive colonization." By this she means the appropriation and codification of scholarship and knowledge by analytical categories which take feminist interests articulated in the west as primary referent. Colonization implies a relation of structural domination involving suppression of the heterogeneity of Third World subjects. Feminist writers:

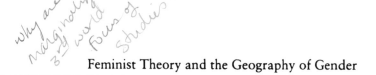

discursively colonize the material and historical heterogeneities of the lives of women in the third world, thereby producing/re-presenting a composite, singular "third world woman" – an image which appears arbitrarily constructed, but nevertheless carries with it the authorizing signature of Western humanist discourse. (Mohanty 1991b: 53)

Much feminist work on women in the Third World, she says, is characterized by assumptions of privilege and ethnocentric universality, and is inadequately self-conscious about the effects of western scholarship. Analyses based on cross-culturally singular, monolithic notions of patriarchy or male dominance lead to a similarly reductive notion of "third world difference," a systematization of the oppression of women that itself exercises oppressive power. In doing this, western feminist discourse employs three analytical principles: notions of gender, sexual difference, or patriarchy are applied universally without being specified in local contexts; uncritical modes of "proof" of universality employ an arithmetic method, adding up fragmented examples to make a supposed universal fact; an homogenous notion of the oppression of women as a group prevails – monolithic images of Third World women ignore the complex relationships between specific historical materialities and general discursive representations. The implication is that the accession to power by women as a group is sufficient to dismantle the existing social system. The colonialist move is that western feminists alone become the true subjects of this counter-history, while Third World women never rise above the debilitating generality of their object status. Mohanty finds disconcerting similarities between such feminist positions and the project of western humanism in general. Humanism involves the recuperation of the "East" and "Woman" as Other in a binary logic where the first term (Identity, Universality, Truth), which is in fact secondary and derivative, is privileged over, and colonizes, a second term (difference, temporality, error), which is in fact primary and originative – that is, only because Woman and East are defined as peripheral or Other can Western Man represent himself as center or Same. "It is not the center that determines the periphery, but the periphery that, in its boundedness, determines the center" (Mohanty 1991b: 73–4). Feminists such as Julia Kristeva (1980) and Hélène Cixous (1981) deconstruct the latent anthropomorphism in western discourse; Mohanty suggests a parallel strategy, a latent ethnocentrism in feminist writing on women in the Third World.

Feminism as Postmodernism

Mohanty's statement made from a position of feminism's Other profoundly disrupted the prevailing mode of discourse which had taken the form of competing political positions within an assumed western and privileged realm. The very notion of a singular progressive women's movement began to be questioned, hesitantly because of the stakes involved, but increasingly and insistently. Also, as the 1980s turned into the 1990s, the full force of the postmodern turn in philosophy and social theory began to affect feminist theory. To put the matter in extreme terms, postmodern feminism finds modern reason to be normalizing, western, masculine prejudice whose "enlightenment" embodies a colonizing scientific rationalism. Postmodern feminists think that western reason makes oppressive, universalizing, and dogmatically assumed truth claims by opposing the masculine knowing subject to a known (often feminized) conquered object. For some postmodern feminists, Enlightenment and feminism are opposed in principle, for others the matter is not that clear-cut. We begin with a series of views which, while critical of certain of its aspects, find compatible or useful arguments and positions in postmodern theory (Fraser and Nicholson, Flax). We then turn to positions more skeptical of postmodernism's potential for feminist understanding and politics (DiStefano, Harding). We conclude the section on feminist social theory with a hybrid position – Haraway's "situated knowledges."

Encountering Postmodernism

For Nancy Fraser, professor of philosophy at Northwestern University, and Linda Nicholson, professor of philosophy at the State University of New York at Albany, there are good reasons for exploring the relations between feminism and postmodernism: both criticize the institution of philosophy and its relation to the larger culture; and both develop paradigms of social criticism not reliant on traditional philosophical underpinnings (Nicholson 1990). Yet the two come from opposite directions: postmodernism emerges from a critique of philosophy and extends to social criticism; feminists develop critical political perspectives from which they draw conclusions about the status of philosophy. The two end up with complementary strengths and weaknesses, each having criticisms of the other: postmodern reflections on feminism uncover its disabling vestiges of essentialism; feminist reflections on postmodernism reveal its androcentrism and political naiveté. An encounter between the two should integrate their respective strengths while eliminating their respective weaknesses: for Fraser and Nicholson, this is the prospect of a postmodern feminism.

Among other things, postmodernists seek conceptions of social criticism which do not rely on traditional philosophical underpinnings. Thinkers like Rorty and Lyotard argue that philosophy is no longer a viable or credible enterprise and can no longer ground politics and social criticism. Rather, with the demise of a modernist founding discourse, postmodern criticism floats free of any universal theoretical ground, becoming pragmatic, ad hoc, contextual, and local. Even so, Fraser and Nicholson argue, philosophy (with all its postmodern changes) still determines the character of social criticism; this has important consequences in terms, for example, of a premature closing of criticism's possibilities. Fraser and Nicholson (1990: 25) are critical too of the (postmodern) philosophy employed in social criticism: thus, Lyotard "throws out the baby of large historical narrative with the bath water of philosophical metanarrative."

What might happen, they ask, if instead of beginning with philosophy, we begin with a social object, like the subordination of women? Many genres rejected by postmodernists, including metanarratives and analyses of macrostructures, would still be needed. Meta- and macro-analyses, they add, can be conceived in nonfoundationalist ways. The practical imperatives of political practice incline feminists towards modes of theorizing which resemble the metanarratives criticized by postmodernists, as with feminist theories claiming to empirically identify causes and features of sexism operating cross-culturally. In Fraser and Nicholson's view, these are "quasi-metanarratives" tacitly presupposing essentialist assumptions about the nature of human beings and the conditions of social life.

Thus, the problem, for Fraser and Nicholson, is to combine poststructural incredulity towards metanarratives with the social-critical power of feminism. This means conceiving a version of criticism that can handle sexism in both its endless variety *and* its monotonous similarity. Towards this end, Fraser and Nicholson argue:

1 Postmodern criticism does not need to abandon large historical narrativist analyses of societal macrostructures.
2 Theory must be explicitly historical, attuned to the cultural specificity of different societies and periods.
3 Even so, postmodern feminist theory should be non-universalistic, so that when its focus is cross-cultural or trans-epochal it would use comparative rather than universal methods, and be attuned to changes and contrasts rather than the production of general laws.
4 Postmodern feminist theory would replace the idea of the subject in history with plural and complexly constructed conceptions of social identity. (Fraser and Nicholson 1990: 34–5)

With notions like these they try to construct a new version of feminism attuned to postmodern philosophy but selective in drawing only certain and modified ideas from it.

Ambivalent Relations

In a wonderfully complex, subtle, and argumentative essay, Jane Flax (1990), professor of political science at Howard University, argues more strongly that feminist theory belongs mainly on the terrain of postmodern philosophy. Flax finds western culture in the midst of a transformation as fundamental as the shift from medieval to modern society. This generates problems that some philosophies confront better than others. For Flax, psychoanalysis, feminist theory, and postmodern philosophy best represent the quandaries of our time. These are partially constituted by Enlightenment beliefs. Yet their insights come also from the breakdown of these beliefs. Each type of theory examines at least one significant facet of the present transitional condition by understanding and (re)constituting the self, gender, knowledge, social relations, and culture without resorting to linear, teleological, hierarchical, holistic, or binary ways of thinking and being. Flax focuses on feminist theory's goals of analyzing gender relations, the situation of women, and male domination; she wants to clear a space in which re-evaluating and altering gender arrangements becomes possible through feminist political action. Flax believes that further developments in feminist theory should draw on wider philosophical contexts, specifically the analysis of social relations and postmodern philosophy.

Considered as a type of postmodern philosophy, feminist theory shares the growing uncertainty about the appropriate grounding and explanatory methods for the interpretation of human experience. Postmodern discourses are deconstructive in that they seek to distance theory from central beliefs about truth, knowledge, power, the self, and language that legitimate contemporary western culture. Flax argues that Enlightenment philosophers (such as Kant) did not see women as capable of attaining freedom from traditional forms of authority through the use of modern methods. In response to their exclusion from the rights of modernity, Flax thinks that women should insist that concepts like the autonomy of reason, objective truth, and beneficial progress through scientific discovery ought to apply to their experiences too. Those who have been excluded might well believe that reason will triumph. And if there is no objective basis for distinguishing true from false belief, power alone will adjudicate competing truth claims. Because of such (pro-modernist) arguments, Flax thinks that feminist theory's relation to the postmodern project of deconstruction must be ambivalent (i.e. there is a need for retaining connections with the modernist humanist project).

Even so, despite the attraction of the (apparently) logical, orderly world of the Enlightenment, Flax (1990: 42) contends that feminist theory belongs more on the terrain of *post*modern philosophy: "Feminist notions of the self, knowledge, and truth are too contradictory to those of the Enlightenment to be contained within its categories. The way(s) to feminist future(s) cannot lie in reviving or appropriating Enlightenment concepts of the person or knowledge." Thus, some feminist theorists have begun to sense that the motto of the Enlightenment, "have courage to use your own reason" (Kant), rests on a gender-rooted sense of self and on self-deception. Some feminists, like other postmodernists, suspect that all transcendental claims reflect and reify the experience of a few persons, mostly white male westerners.

For Flax, no a priori assumption can be made that there will be a single determinant of gender relations in any particular culture. Thus, while Rubin (1975) locates the origin of gender systems in the transformation of biological sex into gender, for Flax, this rests on problematic oppositions like (biological) sexuality versus the social nature of gender. Likewise, socialist feminists locate the fundamental cause of gender arrangements in the organization of production, or the sexual division of labor, but, as Balbus (1982) argues, this rests on Marx's original application of historically specific categories (derived from analyzing a particular form of production) to human life in all historical periods. Socialist feminists, she says, replicate this mistake by accepting the idea that labor is the essence of being human. This distorts many kinds of activity including those traditionally performed by women (pregnancy, childrearing, sexuality). And again, the emphasis placed, this time by French poststructural feminists, on language in the construction of gender relations seems problematical to Flax. For, in this thinking, texts take on a life of their own, or become the world, as with the (Derridian) claim that nothing exists outside the text – so everything becomes a comment on a text, as though the model human activity is literary criticism or writing. Such an approach obscures the projection of its own activity onto the world and denies the existence of the variety of social practices that enter into the construction of language itself; that is, for Flax, ways of life constitute language and texts just as much as language or text constitute ways of life. Lack of attention to concrete social relations (as in Lacan's work) obscures relations of domination. Furthermore, the prescription by French feminists of "writing from the body" seems to Flax incoherent given the still-presumed disjunction between sign/mind/male and body/nature/female – since the body is pre-social and pre-linguistic, Flax (1990: 48) asks, "what could it say?"

Postmodern philosophy suggests that an absolute truth about gender relations would require an outside Archimedean point from which the whole can be seen without distortion, a position which postmodern philosophy questions. Furthermore, the work of Foucault among others should sensitize theorists to the interconnections between knowledge claims (especially absolute or neutral knowledge) and power relations. The search for Archimedes' point may conceal entanglement in an episteme in which truth claims may take only certain forms, an episteme which requires the suppression of discourses threatening the authority of the dominant one – hence, within feminist theory, a search for a defining theme may require the suppression of different voices. Thus, the very search for a root cause of gender relations may, in Flax's view, reflect a mode of thinking grounded in particular forms of gender relations in which domination is present:

> Perhaps reality can have "a" structure only from the falsely universalizing perspective of the dominant group. That is, only to the extent that the person or group can dominate the whole will reality appear to be governed by one set of rules or be constituted by one privileged set of social relations. Criteria of theory construction such as parsimony or simplicity may be attained only by the suppression or denial of the experiences of the other(s). (Flax 1990: 49)

Feminists should suggest that even the praise of the female may be in part motivated by a wish to keep women in a restricted (and restrictive) place. So any feminist standpoint will necessarily be partial. No one can speak for "woman" because no such person exists, except within a specific set of social relations:

> Indeed the notion of a feminist standpoint that is truer than previous (male) ones seems to rest upon many problematic and unexamined assumptions. These include an optimistic belief that people act rationally in their own interests and that reality has a structure that perfect reason (once perfected) can discover. Both of these assumptions in turn depend upon an uncritical appropriation of the Enlightenment ideas discussed earlier. Furthermore, the notion of such a standpoint also assumes that the oppressed are not in fundamental ways damaged by this social experience. On the contrary, this position assumes that the oppressed have a privileged (and not just different) relation and ability to comprehend a reality that is out there waiting for our representation. It also presupposes gendered social relations in which there is a category of beings, who are fundamentally like each other by virtue of their sex – that is, it assumes that women, unlike men, can be free of determination from their own participation in relations of

domination such as those rooted in the social relations of race, class, or homophobia. (Flax 1990: 56)

Flax believes, to the contrary, that there is no force or reality (e.g. history, reason, progress, science, transcendental essence) outside social relations and activity that rescues people from partiality and difference. Feminists belong with those who seek to further decenter the world, although they should reserve the right to be suspicious. Like other forms of postmodernism, feminist theories should encourage tolerance, ambivalence, ambiguity, and multiplicity. Reality would thus appear even more unstable, complex, and disorderly – in this sense Freud (1961) was right when he declared that women are the enemies of civilization.

by whose definition!

Strategic Forms

Such positions, greeting postmodernism with an ambivalent and suspicious "enthusiasm," were countered by feminist social theorists who find potentials in a critique of western humanism (Johnson 1994). Thus, Christine DiStefano (1990) argues that feminism is firmly, if ambivalently, located in the modernist ethos with its insistence on the importance of gender. The feminist case against postmodernism consists of several claims:

> First, that postmodernism expresses the claims and needs of a constituency (white, privileged men of the industrialized West) that has already had an Enlightenment for itself and that is now ready and willing to subject that legacy to critical scrutiny. Secondly, that the objects of postmodernism's various critical and deconstructive efforts have been the creations of a similarly specific and partial constituency (beginning with Socrates, Plato, and Aristotle). Third, that mainstream postmodernist theory (Derrida, Lyotard, Rorty, Foucault) has been remarkably blind and insensitive to questions of gender in its own purportedly politicized rereadings of history, politics, and culture. Finally, that the postmodernist project, if seriously adopted by feminists, would make any semblance of a feminist politics impossible. To the extent that feminist politics is bound up with a specific constituency or subject, namely, women, the postmodernist prohibition against subject-centered inquiry and theory undermines the legitimacy of a broad-based organized movement dedicated to articulating and implementing the goals of such a constituency. (DiStefano 1990: 75–6)

Thus, DiStefano says, postmodernism is as entrenched in the dilemmas of difference as are the modernist and anti-modernist alternatives. In the "post-rationalist" view, the female subject dissolves into a perplexing plurality of differences, none of which can be theoretically or politically privileged over others.

A Principled Ambivalence

Thus, many left feminists urge skepticism about anti-Enlightenment criticisms. Irigaray (1985) asks, is postmodernism the "last ruse" of patriarchy? Hartsock (1987) says that postmodernism appears to side with marginal groups but finds hindrance rather than help – postmodern theories give little guidance at their best, and at worst merely recapitulate the effects of Enlightenment theories. Feminist theorists like Flax and DiStefano are ambivalent about the choice between modernism and postmodernism. However, rather than attempting to resolve this ambivalence (by favoring one side) Sandra Harding (1990: 86) argues that "such an ambivalence should be much more robust and principled" – that is, she argues for a self-conscious and theoretically articulated ambivalence which derives originally from the tensions and contradictions in the worlds inhabited by feminists.

Exploring this principled ambivalence, Harding asks an apparently naive question – in light of the position of Rorty, Lyotard, Foucault, and other critics that epistemology polices our thoughts, why do feminists need epistemology at all? Epistemologies, she says, are justificatory strategies which present themselves as challenging, in the domain of knowledge claims, the conservative notion that "might makes right." In this sense, Harding supports epistemology (in terms of feminist development of theories of knowledge) against the claims of Foucault, Rorty, and others that epistemologies end up rationalizing the legitimacy of the beliefs of the powerful. Also, feminists need a defense against, and an alternative to, the traditional discourses of: objectivism, which argues that scientific claims are value-free and without a point of view; and against interpretationism, which finds feminist and non-feminist interpretations (of why rape occurs for example) equally defensible. "Objectivism and interpretationism do not allow feminists to generate scientific problems, to define what should count as empirical evidence, and to determine what constitutes an adequate explanation or understanding. Woman the knower can find no place in either of these two, intimately linked, mainstream epistemologies" (Harding 1990: 88–9). The development of feminist justification strategies serves also to guide choices in theory, research, and politics.

Who are the women that feminist theory and politics should be accountable to? On the one hand, there is the feminist vision of understanding differences between women as richness and opportunity for cultural enhancement and understanding. On the other hand, differences between women may be due to structures of domination. Theories of knowledge are needed which recognize such differences and enable feminists to counter exploitative relations *between* women, as well as the more usually expressed purpose of guiding understandings which energize the struggle against the subordination of *all* women.

In response to all these needs, Harding says, two main justificatory strategies are developed. First, feminist empiricism argues that sexism and androcentrism in scientific inquiry are consequences of distortions (badly done science) due to social biases, prejudices, superstitions, and ignorance, and can be eliminated by stricter adherence to the existing norms of scientific inquiry. This theory of knowledge satisfies a range of justificatory needs in its emphasis on accumulating empirical support, its apparent conservative position, and its extendibility to other emancipatory movements. Harding argues that there are tendencies towards postmodernism in feminist empiricism: a knower who begins analysis from a particular situation (e.g. that of a woman scientist) cannot be the Enlightenment's transhistorical, unitary individual. In such a case, the feminism of this epistemology undermines its empiricism, moving feminist empiricism, inadvertently, towards postmodernism. Second, feminist standpoint theory takes notions that appear only dimly in feminist empiricism in directions which empiricists would never accept. Feminist standpoint theorists argue that while knowledge is supposed to be grounded in experience, western science originates in a limited and distorted kind of social experience. The activities assigned to women provide the basis of potentially more complete and less distorted knowledge claims than do men's experience. It is exactly the "bifurcated consciousness" of woman alienated from her own experiences through using the dominant (male) conceptual schemes, that generates the greater adequacy of feminist inquiry. Thus, standpoint theory reasserts the possibility of science providing less distorted representations of the world but does not myopically beatify a mythical scientific method. It resolves certain problems more satisfactorily than feminist empiricism, such as the importance of the context of discovery for the eventual picture of science, its undermining of the point-of-viewlessness of objectivism while refusing the relativism of interpretationism, its call for theory to draw on the experiences of working-class women, women of color, lesbians, and its insistence on the importance of political activism to the advance of understanding. Harding argues that standpoint theory more explicitly articulates and radically develops anti-Enlightenment tendencies only implicit in feminist empiricism. Feminist standpoint theorists are opposed to the idea that ahistorical principles of inquiry can ensure more perfect representations of the world while they hold that movements for social liberation advance the growth of knowledge and that changes in social relations tend to produce new ideas. "Movements of social liberation make possible new kinds of activity, and it is on the basis of this activity that new sciences can emerge" (Harding 1990: 98). Furthermore, standpoint epistemologies articulate the suspicion of feminist empiricists that a unitary consciousness is an obstacle to understanding. For such reasons it is possible to see feminist standpoint theory in tension with central Enlightenment assumptions.

Even so, Harding concludes, it is difficult to see how a specifically feminist alternative could completely abandon Enlightenment assumptions while remaining feminist. Feminism stands on Enlightenment ground in its belief that improved theories contribute to social progress. Even feminist postmodernists subscribe to Enlightenment assumptions in that, Harding thinks, "they appear to agree with Enlightenment tendencies that all possible science and epistemology – anything deserving these names – must be containable within modern, androcentric, western, bourgeois forms" (Harding 1990: 99) and their assumption, like the most positivist Enlightenment thinkers, "that if one gives up the goal of telling one true story about reality, one must also give up trying to tell less false stories" (Harding 1990: 100). She thinks that feminist inquiry can aim at producing less partial representations without asserting their absolute, universal or eternal adequacy. Thus, both feminist science thinkers and their feminist postmodern critics "stand with one foot in modernity and the other in the lands beyond" (Harding 1990: 100). At this moment in history, she thinks, feminism needs *both* Enlightenment and postmodern agendas.

Situated Knowledges

Feminist reactions to the postmodern critique of science thus produced a creative series of hybrid epistemologies based on the various ambivalent positions occupied by women in the world. Feminists feel free to take what they wish from a postmodernism which in part corresponded with their own developing perspectives, and to criticize other ideas, even some with which they basically agree. This results of such a "critical ambivalence" are no better exemplified than in Donna Haraway's notion of situated knowledges, a perspective conversant with, even sympathetic to, postmodern arguments which favors still a modified version of objectivity.

For Haraway, professor of the history of consciousness at the University of California, Santa Cruz, feminists may respond flexibly to the modern/postmodern dichotomy on objectivity yet still be trapped between its two poles. Many feminists see all forms of knowledge, including science, to be social constructions, while objectivity is thought of as parable or ideology and a poor guide to how scientific knowledge is actually made – in this view, science is a contestable text and a power field. But Haraway confesses that the further social constructionism goes, especially in its postmodern form, the more nervous she gets. Feminists may begin by showing the radical historical specificity of every layer of the construction of science. But they "end up with a kind of epistemological electro-shock therapy which ... lays us out on the table with self-induced multiple personality disorder" (Haraway 1991: 186). For social constructionism, she says, becomes an excuse for not learning science ("its only another text"). In critical reaction, some feminists hold out for objectivity; but in a different way, as with feminist empiricism. The problem is how to have: radical historical contingency; a postmodern insistence on irreducible difference and radical multiplicity of local knowledges; yet a commitment to faithful accounts of a real world; what Harding (1986) calls the need for a "successor science project"?

Haraway begins to answer by re-placing metaphorical reliance on vision, the sensory system much maligned in feminist discourse. For the most part, the eyes are used by feminists and others to signify a perverse capacity for distancing the knowing subject from the world in the interests of power. Visualization becomes "unregulated gluttony" and the "god-trick of seeing everything from nowhere." But Haraway insists instead on the particularity and embodiment of vision. This allows the construction of a usable doctrine of a feminist objectivity she calls *situated knowledges*. In this, objectivity is concerned with particular and specific embodiment, and not the false vision of transcendence. For "only partial perspectives promise objective vision" (Haraway 1991: 190). There is no unmediated photographic process of vision in such scientific accounts, but only highly specific visual possibilities, each with a detailed, active, partial way of organizing the world. "Feminist objectivity is about limited location and situated knowledge, not about transcendence and splitting of subject and object. In this way, we might become answerable for what we learn how to see" (Haraway 1991: 190).

For Haraway, feminism attempts to theorize the grounds for trusting the vantage points of the subjugated (seeing from the peripheries and the depths). The positionings of the subjugated are not exempt from critique, but are preferred because they are least likely to deny the critical, interpretative core of knowledge (in this we see the remnants of a feminist standpoint). The question is *how* to see from below. Such a preferred positioning is as hostile to relativism as it is to totalization and single vision. The alternative is partial, locatable, critical knowledges sustaining webs of connection in politics and conversations in epistemology, whereas relativism is being nowhere yet claiming to be everywhere (it too is a "god-trick"). With other feminists, Haraway argues for a practice of objectivity that privileges contestation, deconstruction, construction, webbed connections, transformation, mobile positioning, and "passionate detachment." Innocence is impossible in the kind of affinity politics she favors – that is, seeing from the standpoints of the subjugated in order to see well. Identity or "being" is always problematic and contingent, vision and position are questions of power, people are not immediately present to themselves, and self-identity is a bad visual system. The "boys in the human sciences" call this doubt concerning self-presence, that single point of will and consciousness, "the death of the subject," but this judgement seems bizarre to Haraway – she prefers to call generative doubt "the opening of non-isomorphic subjects, agents, and territories of stories unimaginable from the vantage point of the cyclopean, self-satiated eye of the master subject" (Haraway 1991: 192). The split, contradictory self is able to join with another to see together without the self claiming to be the other: in this, objectivity is partial connection, critical positioning. The positions of the dominators, by comparison, are self-identical, disembodied, transcendent, and born again. Positioning is therefore the key practice grounding knowledge arranged around the imagery of vision:

> I am arguing for politics and epistemologies of location, positioning, and situating, where partiality and not universality is the condition of being heard to make rational knowledge claims. These are claims on people's lives; the view from a body, always a complex, contradictory, structuring and structured body, versus the view from above, from nowhere, from simplicity. Only the god-trick is forbidden. (Haraway 1991: 195)

So the only way to find larger vision is to be somewhere in particular. The feminist science question revolves around objectivity as positioned rationality. Its images are made from joining partial views and halting voices into a collective subject position, a series of views from somewhere.

Haraway finally attempts to resolve the ambiguity about the related questions of the status of objects of knowledge and the faithfulness of accounts, no matter how mediated, to a real world. Feminists and others shy away from scientific objectivity in part because the object of knowledge is presented as a passive, inert thing – that is, the object of knowledge is only matter for the seminal power of the knower. The status of agency is denied the object. This is called by Sofoulis (1988) "resourcing," the homogenizing of the world's body into resources for man's perverse projects. Haraway is nervous about feminism's resourcing sex for re-presentation as gender which "we" can control. It seems impossible to escape an appropriationist logic of domination built into nature/culture binarism. But, she says, situated knowledges require that objects of knowledge be pictured as actors and agents, not screens, grounds, or resources. Accounts of the "real world" therefore do not depend on a logic of discovery, but a social relation of conversation: the world neither speaks itself nor disappears in favor of a master coder. This is not a version of realism, which Haraway finds to be a poor way of engaging with the world's active agency. Instead, she sides with ecofeminists in the view that the world is an active subject. This acknowledging of the agency of the world includes a sense of its independent sense of humor, the world as witty agent; not primal mother, but coyote or trickster, so that we keep searching for fidelity in knowledge, knowing all the while we are hoodwinked. Thus, feminist objectivity makes room for surprises, ironies at the heart of knowledge production. "I like to see feminist theory as a reinvented coyote discourse obligated to its enabling sources in many kinds of heterogeneous accounts of the world" (Haraway 1991: 199). In a similar feminist practice, the body, object of biological discourse, becomes an engaging being, agent not resource. This means reworking the relations between sex and gender, with the boundary between animal and human at stake (as well as that between machine and organism). In her "Cyborg Manifesto" for late twentieth-century feminism, Haraway (1991: 149–81) restates many of these ideas, saying:

> By the late twentieth century, our time, a mythic time, we are all chimeras, theorized and fabricated hybrids of machine and organism; in short we are cyborgs. The cyborg is our ontology; it gives us our politics. The cyborg is a condensed image of both imagination and material reality, the two joined centers structuring any possibility of historical transformation. (Haraway 1991: 150)

She thinks that this cyborg imagery helps express two crucial arguments: that the production of universal, totalizing theory is a major mistake, missing most of reality; and that taking responsibility for the social relations of science and technology means refusing an anti-science metaphysics, a demonology of technology. Haraway would rather be a cyborg than a goddess.

Where then does this leave feminist theory? As we have seen, there is no such thing as a singular ontology, nor a given epistemology, nor even a feminist politics shared in all essential aspects by a coherent movement. Yet especially in the works of Hartsock, Harding, and Haraway we find a radical position discussed and differed on, yet proposed at least as project, which derives from the socialist end of the feminist spectrum, propagates a feminist standpoint, listens to criticisms from women who differ, learns from postmodernism without being convinced, and insists still, with Haraway, on the possibility of objective but situated knowledges. This complex, hybrid series of positions was widely adopted by left-feminists in the early 1990s. It produced the semblance of a new left consensus, including the adherence of many feminist geographers.

Feminist Geography

Feminist geography was initially closely associated with radical geography and went through similar phases of development. Arguments made by the two movements were similar, indeed often made by the same people, simultaneously radical and feminist. Early radical geography called for topical change in geographical focus towards urgent social issues, feminists for a geography of women. Both went through humanistic and Marxist phases in the 1970s – Alison Hayford, a prominent feminist geographer (see chapter 3), was influential in promoting Marxist ideas in radical geography, although as Mackenzie (1989a: 115) says, many feminists were skeptical about Althusserian structuralism, which seemed to be as "depopulated and abstract as gravity models and nearly as inhospitable to feminist questions." And just as social problems were thrust on radical geographers by the press of capitalist contradictions, so in looking beneath spatial problems, feminist geographers discovered the "divided city." Suzanne Mackenzie (1989a), a professor of geography at Carleton University in Ottawa, Canada, argues that women's daily activities, carried out in opposition to the current urban form, and women's political actions in calling for day care, new designs for neighborhoods, and better transit systems were instrumental in getting academics to notice that space was divided into men's public and productive spheres and women's private and reproductive spheres; from Marxist theory came the further realization that the public–private dichotomy was fundamental to capitalist society as differentiated sites of production and reproduction (Lloyd 1975; Saegart 1981; Werkele 1981; Werkele, Peterson, and Morley 1980). In terms of academic geography, an analytical focus on the intersection of production and reproduction spaces allowed geographers to incorporate gender as a fundamental parameter in environmental processes (Mackenzie and Rose 1983; Rose 1984).

In 1984, a cooperative of feminist scholars–practitioners in the Women and Geography Study Group of the Institute of British Geographers published *Geography and Gender* (Women and Geography Study Group 1984). This followed earlier theoretical articles on women (Hayford 1974), empirical studies of women and space (Tivers 1978), and surveys of research on women in geography (Monk and Hanson 1982; Zelinsky, Monk, and Hanson 1982). But the cooperative study was the first sustained effort at outlining a critique of human geography and an alternative feminist approach. For the Women and Geography Study Group, geographical works portray humanity so much in terms of *man* and his environment that women's existence is denied. The group advocated change not simply by adding women to geography, but by developing "an entirely different approach to geography as a whole" (Women and Geography Study Group 1984: 21). Feminist geography, they say, looks at how socially created gender structures form and transform space in a project dedicated to ending gender inequalities through social change. The cooperative chose four topics as examples of feminist approaches to mainstream geography. *Feminist urban geography* is interested in conventionally neglected aspects of land use, especially the effects of a separation of the public sphere of waged work from the private sphere of family and home; attacking this separation, and creating a new form of built environment, they think, should be a feminist priority.

Women's increased participation in the public sphere is studied in terms of the composition of the workforce, patterns of women's employment, regional inequalities, topics which they find best examined by attending to women's everyday lives. Studies of the effects of the *separation between home and waged work* on women's access to facilities and public services should emphasize gender-based inequalities. Feminist geography needs to reconsider women's activity in changing the *developing world.* Basically, the cooperative argued that feminist geography must concern itself with changing gender relations, within and outside the discipline, by doing research not on people, but with them: "feminism challenges us to examine our personal, political and academic lives" (Women and Geography Study Group 1984: 146). With this, feminist geography entered as a fully theorized, socially engaged dimension of a changing discipline.

However, there remained a strong sentiment among some feminist geographers that despite such attempts at considering the social relations of gender within human geography, gender (along with race) was still relegated to a position of epiphenomenon in urban and economic geography, and that feminists were consequently left out of defining "the project" of reconstituting geography. Susan Christopherson (1989), a professor of planning at Cornell University, thought that a feminist perspective on theory and method would transform human geography in a number of ways: the selection of problems deemed significant for inquiry, as with women's poverty and "family values"; the content of theoretical concepts in terms of the metaphors and definitions of a wider range of human experiences; and the question of scale which changes when the usual spatial hierarchies are questioned. Christopherson found the discipline changing in terms of greater diversity of people "allowed into the discipline," working-class people, women, a few minorities, people who bring different experiences and want to do research that is self-empowering rather than self-denigrating. She found the new geographers alienated from positivist and Marxist research agendas, and called for a transformed geography to express "faith in the legitimacy of subjectivity, and thus provide a basis for resistance to authority, including our own" (Christopherson 1989: 87). Yet she did not expect this to happen, for the development of powerful abstract theories is intensely social and elitist, requiring resources, knowing who to cite and who is (quickly) out of fashion, involving fear of being left out, or being labelled, or not dealing with the "in" subject. So, for Christopherson, there was a theoretical crisis in geography rooted in alienation from the abstract post-positivist discourses vying for dominance, and rooted in a growing political consciousness emerging from experiences of gender, race, and class. Christopherson called for multiplication of theoretical perspectives through dialogue, mutual learning, and respect.

The period of the middle to late 1980s saw two kinds of divide opening in feminist-radical geography: between feminist and masculinist radical geography; between perspectives within feminist geography, especially as poststructural and postmodern theory entered the discussion. A number of competing perspectives emerged within feminist geography which can be categorized like the earlier distinctions of schools of feminist social thought. These are outlined by McDowell.

Feminist Approaches

In a series of articles, Linda McDowell (1993a; 1993b), a professor of geography at Cambridge University, provides an intellectual history of feminist geography and its links with feminist social theory. Feminist approaches within geography, McDowell says, address three central concerns: space, place, and nature. The geography of gender involves spatial variations in gender relations, the social construction of gender identities in particular milieux, the ways nature is related to gendered distinctions, and similar issues. McDowell interprets these different emphases in terms of Harding's (1986) distinction between feminist empiricism, feminist standpoint theory, and postmodern feminism, a trinity she finds similar to DiStefano's (1990) rationalist, anti-rationalist, and post-rationalist feminisms, these being similar again to the positions outlined earlier by Jaggar (1983).

Feminist empiricist geography shares the rational, humanist ideals of the Enlightenment but objects to the exclusion of women from respect as human beings; hence, "difference" must be repudiated so that women may assume their rightful place in society (DiStefano 1990: 67). The initial purpose of feminist geography, therefore, was to illustrate the unfairness of the exclusion of women from the discipline and, more generally, from the "public realm," hence, a politics emphasizing equal (women's) rights. Feminist empiricist geography maps women's subordination and documents variations in status (Seager and Olson 1986), studies the geography of women's rights (Holcomb, Kodras, and Brunn 1990), and looks at differences in poverty rates among black female-headed households (Holcomb and Jones 1990), to give but a few examples. Thus, feminist empiricism objects to women's exclusion from the public arena justified by "natural" association with the home, childbirth, and unpaid reproductive labor. Feminist urban geographers see human geography's exclusive concern with public activities taking the Enlightenment distinction between public and private for granted. Human geography, they find, excludes pressing questions such as daily life, household and domestic activities. Descriptive feminist studies document that women lead more spatially restricted lives than men. These studies show that the contemporary city embodies conventional gender divisions (Harman 1983) literally because the environment is "man-made" in terms of architecture and planning (Hayden 1983). Most of this work assumes that the agency of a rational state will ameliorate women's subordinate position once this is adequately demonstrated. Likewise with work that documents problems faced by women in urban areas, the housing problems of single women for instance, or women's fear in cities, or the effects of urban design and layout on women (McDowell 1983). While such studies point up differences in living standards between men and women, in McDowell's view they tend to be descriptive and reliant on male (and western) statistical indicators. Much of the early feminist research emphasizes the gendered structure of urbanization and the spatial division of waged and domestic work (Mackenzie and Rose 1983), although studies of gender inequalities focus increasingly on the interdependence of waged work and reproductive labor (Hanson and Pratt 1988; 1995). For McDowell, many of these latter feminists find common interest either with the structural Marxist school of geographical thought, even though it marginalized gender issues, or (in the middle 1980s) emphasize a middle way centered on human agency.

Feminist standpoint theory, anti-rationalism, or radical feminism rejects the rationalist vision of equality and valorizes instead female difference and female knowledge. While few geographers are self-consciously standpoint theorists, many rely on gender as their central analytical category, and are involved in rediscovering women's experiences and particular relationships with landscape and place. Thus, Mackenzie (1989a; 1989b) investigates women making their own geographies, Janice Monk and Vera Norwood (1987) look at women's responses in literature and art to the landscapes of the North American Southwest, and Liz Bondi (1992) addresses the gender symbolism of the urban environment, again to mention just a few examples. Critics of feminist standpoint argue that it has an essentialist notion of identity as a universalized (female) other, but McDowell points out that geography investigates variations between places, so feminist geography cannot avoid stressing differences among women (Katz and Monk 1993). Although it does not embrace a postmodern deconstruction of the category "woman," McDowell refers to this work as "context specific," focused on women, but recognizing differences especially in terms of place-based constitution.

Postmodern or post-rational feminism finds the very notion of gender implicated in a disastrous, oppressive fiction of "woman" which rides roughshod over differences between and within women – that is, gender ignores other subjugated arenas of difference (DiStefano 1990: 65). From this view, both the rationalist and anti-rationalist feminist paradigms should be rejected and the subject "woman" replaced by decentered, partial, and fractured identities. The first reaction by feminist geographers to this bombshell was suspicion (of postmodernism) and reluctance to abandon the notion that gender matters (Christopherson 1989; Bondi and Domosh 1992; McDowell 1992; Massey 1994). For McDowell, this does not signify a "retreat to modernist notions of truth," but stimulates debate on the salience of place in the construction of multiple female identities. Overall, she finds feminist geography moving towards Harding and Haraway's partial or situated knowledges. Haraway argues the need for a geometry of differences which breaks out of binaries, dialectics, and nature/culture models, wants maps of tensions and resonances and concepts of embodiment as a node in a set of fields, ideas McDowell finds similar to the work of Massey (1994). Mohanty's notion of community as contested cartographies and imagined communities poses new questions for feminist geographers. Similarly, the notion of contradictory, multiple subjects and the role of location in this positioning is similar to Peter Jackson's (1991) argument for the construction of historically and geographically specific forms of masculinity (and femininity). For McDowell, feminist geography contains a hybrid set of positions with intercutting perspectives. Her own position favors the contradictory version of feminist objectivity proposed by Harding and Haraway in a feminism that insists that some differences are more important than others.

Gender and Space

Feminist social theory has long shown considerable interest in the relations between gender and space. In Daphne Spain's (1992: 3) terms, spatial arrangements reinforce status differences between women and men – gendered spaces reduce women's access to knowledge and are used by men to reproduce power. Some feminists argue that women attempt to take up as little space as possible in the public sphere by positioning their bodies in unobtrusive ways. Thus, in "Throwing Like a Girl," Iris Marion Young (1989) argues that women learn to situate themselves in space in more removed ways than men. Yet universal views of the relations between women as a whole and space in general can be criticized in that different groups of women have different relations to space – hence, Henrietta Moore (1986) examines socially constructed differences in women's and men's access to private and public spheres, while Sara Mills (1996) proposes that colonial space might be gendered in specific and complex ways. This kind of work carried out in feminist social science in general intersected with the development within geography of a feminist school of thought specifically conceptualizing space, place, and environment. In the early period of feminist–geographic research and writing, in the late 1970s and early 1980s, feminist positions were modified either from political philosophies such as Marxism, established traditions of geographic thought such as urban geography, or combinations of the two. During the 1980s theoretical debates began to outline other feminist–geographic positions, drawing more freely from the broader reach of feminist social theories. This set off a series of debates on feminism, patriarchy, and geography. Perhaps the main debate of the 1980s concerned the concept of patriarchy.

The Patriarchy Debate

This debate was initiated by Jo Foord and Nicky Gregson (1986), both at the Centre for Urban and Regional Development Studies at the University of Newcastle, England. Feminist geographers, Foord and Gregson argue, did important early work on *gender roles* and spatial patterns, the goal being to understand forms of women's subordination. Nevertheless, this work produced only a partial understanding of women's position which, for Foord and Gregson, limited the development of a workable theoretical framework. Realizing limitations in gender-role theory, feminist geographers introduced the further notion of *gender relations* – the idea that roles and inequalities derive from power relations between men and women. Yet Foord and Gregson still find gender relations misplaced in theoretical analysis, while patriarchy is marginalized, particularly by socialist feminists. Based on realist methods of abstract analysis, they argue that "patriarchy can be conceptualised as a particular form of the general category gender relations" and that this helps in finding "the basic characteristics of patriarchy" (Foord and Gregson 1986: 187).

The initial impetus for work in feminist geography came from the political demands of the women's movement – putting women first, making women visible, changing the content and direction of research (Tivers 1978). But feminist geographers were also influenced by socialist feminism and Marxist geography (Bowlby, Foord, and Mackenzie 1980) – hence, an emphasis on production and reproduction, and related social and spatial divisions. Much of the empirical work on making women visible adopted Anne Oakley's (1972) concept of gender roles, the idea that people conform to socially proscribed roles, activities, forms of behavior, and even female and male characteristics, such as passivity or aggressiveness; in geography, gender-role theory is used in explaining the effects of women's roles as mothers and housewives on their paid employment (Tivers 1985), or women's assumed dexterity or ability to do routine work, or women's suitability for certain occupations (the nimble fingers syndrome). Research influenced by socialist feminism analyses these roles in relation to historically and spatially specific modes of production and class differences, the social and spatial separation of production from reproduction, home from work, domestic from waged labor, women's from men's lives, and so on. But, for Foord and Gregson, feminist geography sees the emphasis on women's inequality (in terms, for example, of limited access to the public sphere) pre-empting analysis of common practices, processes, and structures producing women's subordination as a whole, and therefore not being particularly useful, while gender-role theory is likewise a static social theory with a restricted understanding of people's active participation in creating social structures.

Some exploratory conceptualizations see gender relations, specified in terms of the formation of *gender identities* (femininity, masculinity), as particular expressions of patriarchy. But this is an undertheorized area in feminist geography. Socialist feminists, Foord and Gregson think, have difficulties with this concept. Patriarchy was originally used as a universal term for male dominance thought of as an autonomous and superior structure. Socialist feminists reconceptualized the term as the symbolic power of fathers (Mitchell 1975), or the material and ideological control of women's sexuality and labor (Barrett 1980) in "sex/gender systems" (Cockburn 1983), as part of a project to unify Marxism and feminism, capitalism and patriarchy. Yet fifteen years of socialist feminist work, they say, has not been able to produce this theoretical synthesis. Hence, Foord and Gregson suggest that patriarchy be theorized as an object of analysis related solely to gender relations.

For the meticulous conceptualization of patriarchy they suggest realist methods of analysis isolating the basic characteristics and necessary relations of patriarchy from its contingencies (see chapter 3). Foord and Gregson argue that patriarchy, defined as men's domination of women, is a particular form of a more general object, gender relations. These relations are transhistorical and transspatial in nature, because people are always gendered, and are embedded in all forms of social relations (part of the complex production, reproduction, social relations, which makes up human existence). Yet, for Foord and Gregson, the elements of this complex are not necessarily related one to another in a realist sense. Hence, capitalism and patriarchy are contingently related structures which interlock in the specificity of particular places and times, and gender relations are critical to capitalism only at the level of empirical analysis. Hence, attempts by socialist feminists to combine capitalism and patriarchy as a single object of analysis must prove unsatisfactory. For Foord and Gregson, gender relations are an object of analysis in their own right. The basic characteristics are the two genders. Initially it might seem that the internal (necessary) gender relations are: biological reproduction and heterosexuality (both transhistorical relations); and marriage and the nuclear family (both historically and spatially specific). But Foord and Gregson argue that marriage and nuclear families are contingent to gender relations as an object of analysis. Patriarchy necessarily involves heterosexuality and biological reproduction, in which men dominate the process of species reproduction, specifically women's fertility. In patriarchal heterosexuality, female sexuality is defined, constructed, and understood in male terms. Patriarchal gender relations are reproduced through discourse and power. Foord and Gregson think that this clarifies the chaotic conception of patriarchy. Empirical work in feminist geography can provide case studies of how the causal properties of patriarchal gender relations work out in particular places, for example in a locality framework, or how specific contingencies, such as urban structures, reproduce patriarchal gender relations, this kind of study employing intensive qualitative methods (as with ethnomethodology).

This Foord–Gregson position on patriarchy was subject to considerable discussion. Linda McDowell (1986) fundamentally disagrees with the realist notion of patriarchy as a separate structure, arguing instead that women's oppression in capitalist societies should be explained through class analysis at both the theoretical and empirical levels. She agrees that gender relations are founded on biological differences but differs when Foord and Gregson move from the general nature of relations to the particular form of women's oppression under patriarchy. Here, there is little indication of why oppressive relations develop and are maintained. McDowell argues that this requires a simultaneous understanding of class relations between exploiter and exploited, relations which are central to the analysis of patriarchy rather than being contingent – women's oppression has a material basis. McDowell finds the oppression of women in the exploited class to have a different origin than in the capitalist class; indeed, she agrees with Angela Carter (1979: 12) that the notion of a universal female experience is "a clever confidence trick." Following Quick (1977) and Vogel (1983), McDowell outlines an approach unifying Marxist and feminist analyses of production and reproduction as a basis for geographical analyses of the empirical variety of women's experiences.

The basic site of women's oppression is the social reproduction of labor power, particularly women's ability to bear children. Rather than this being a biologically determinist position, McDowell sees reproduction relations as social constructs in Foucault's (1979b) sense of the construction of categories, definitions, and institutions. Marx argues that the working day must include necessary labor reproducing labor power. Vogel adds that socially necessary labor has several components, including domestic labor which enables necessities to be consumed in appropriate forms, providing means of subsistence for dependants, and ensuring generational replacement. The generational replacement process depends on a gender division of labor (i.e. the conception, carrying, and delivery of children) and threatens the immediate appropriation of surplus labor. For McDowell (following Vogel 1983), the potential contradiction for the capitalist class between an immediate need for appropriating surplus labor and long-term requirements for reproducing a class to perform this surplus labor is the key issue behind various strategies of male supremacy within the exploited class, the main focus being the provision by men of means of subsistence to women during childbearing (i.e. material dependence). Social constructions of male sexuality and the dominance of family forms are historical resolutions of this contradiction (between surplus and reproduction) rather than necessary elements of gender relations. Women participate also in surplus production directly, but in ways dependent on their responsibilities in necessary reproductive labor, the emphasis on one or the other changing with historical circumstances – the reduction of domestic labor is a contested area and divisions occur within families. Hence, the working-class family household is "an historically evolving form where capitalist social reproduction is undertaken primarily by women" (McDowell 1986: 319) with a key, but contradictory, role in capitalist accumulation. The oppression of working-class women comes from the way they undertake domestic labor necessary for capitalist reproduction. While all women share common experiences of subordination in capitalist societies, and there is a degree of real solidarity across class lines, the class position of women is theoretically distinct – Jacqueline Kennedy Onassis was not a sister. While McDowell shares much of Foord and Gregson's research agenda, she thinks that a class analysis of women's subordination in the context of the overall reproduction of capitalist societies leads to a more complete understanding than the theoretical separation of the exploitative institutions of patriarchy and capitalism.

Lawrence Knopp and Mickey Lauria (1987) find two analytical errors in Foord and Gregson's reconceptualization of patriarchy. The first is the notion that capitalism and patriarchy are conceptually independent objects of analysis, the argument being that an understanding of gender relations is not necessary for understanding capitalism. Knopp and Lauria argue conversely that gender relations, and their specific forms such as patriarchy, cannot be understood without the more general category of social relations (modes of production). For them, the social organization of gender into relations of power is part of the particular form of a mode of production, and gender relations are not an object of analysis in their own right. The second error, for Knopp and Lauria, is the characterization of necessary gender relations in terms of biological reproduction and heterosexuality. Foord and Gregson's justification for the latter view is especially weak. Sexuality is theorized as biologically or psychologically fixed rather than a contingent form of gender relations. In general, for Knopp and Lauria (1987: 51–2), "gender relations constitute a subset of the broader category 'social relations' and . . . biological reproduction is a subset of the more general category 'production,'" hence, patriarchy "must be theorized conjointly with social relations in the capitalist mode of production."

Jaclyn Gier and John Walton (1987) find the application of realist epistemology to feminist theory, which reduces gender relations to matters of necessary and contingent relations, does not help an understanding of patriarchy. For Gier and Walton (1987: 57), gender is not transhistorical but is culture-bound and historically specific: "the term 'gender' is more appropriately used to translate the phenomena of human sex difference into the epiphenomena of meanings which are produced by human thought, language, and society." Only the necessity of sexual difference in biological reproduction is transhistorical. Any conceptualization of patriarchy which does not focus on cultural and historical specificity promotes crude biological determinism. For Gier and Walton (1987: 58), this comes down to differences over philosophical approach – they find Foord and Gregson selecting an epistemology "off the peg" and imposing it on feminism without realizing the problems with realism (see also the discussion in chapter 5).

Louise Johnson criticizes Foord and Gregson's objective of formulating a single theory of women's oppression. For Johnson (1987: 212), such a project is tied to a patriarchal conception of all-embracing theory: "Their objective to create an overarching theory to explain *all* women's oppression using criteria and a concept somehow detached from history and social context puts their discussion *into* the realm of patriarchal knowledge, not in opposition to it." This causes Foord and Gregson to read the history of feminist ideas on patriarchy as indecisive, lacking clarity and coherence, as a prelude to reconceptualization. Johnson finds the possibility of abstraction deciding between necessary and contingent relations open to serious doubt. Hence, there are problems with the singular objective, their characterization of the patriarchy debate, and their reconceptualization. For Johnson, the priority is challenging the discipline, creating an oppositional discourse rather than working within the confines of what remains patriarchal geography.

In reply, Foord and Gregson find many of these criticisms misunderstanding their realist methodology. In realism, they say, what matters is the "conjunction of basic characteristics with complex historical contingencies" and not questions of the origins of women's oppression (Gregson and Foord 1987: 372). The realist method suggests three interrelated levels of analysis, general, particular, and individual, and they move from the most abstract (gender relations) to particular forms (patriarchal gender relations) in an analytical process necessary for making sense of the individual instances which make up research agendas. Many of the criticisms apply to the second level of analysis, specifically the idea of a separation between capitalism and patriarchy. For Foord and Gregson, this framework allows the flexibility of seeing mode of production and gender relations as distinct objects of analysis which interlock as particular social forms but not as conceptual categories. Further, they find this not to be a universal theory for it emphasizes historical specificity and contingency. They resist the notion of an exclusively feminine way of thinking and want feminism to engage in wider analytical and political debates (as with realism, locality, etc.), especially in geography where feminism only begins to challenge what has gone before.

The patriarchy debate established some of the basic positions in feminist geography, clearly drawing on the more general feminist literature: Foord and Gregson restate ideas from radical feminism; McDowell, Knopp, and Lauria criticize and restate from positions of (Marxist) socialist feminism; Johnson relies on poststructural philosophies. Yet there remains in this debate a stronger sense of feminist project than in the humanistic–Marxist controversy a few years earlier. In other words, there is, in feminist geography, a sense of collaboration in the construction of a range of positions united by a common purpose, the ending of the oppressions of women, which survives even sharp disagreements. The same can be said of a second major debate conducted in the middle 1990s on feminist research methodologies.

Feminist Research Methods

Paralleling this move to more complex ontological and epistemological positioning, there was an increased interest in research methods, appropriate research problems, and other methodological issues, the idea being to differentiate a feminist geography with a distinct methodology. Again, the best initial survey comes from McDowell (1992). Women were excluded from geographical research, McDowell argues, in part because of methodological factors, like the unavailability of data on women's waged work, let alone unpaid (household) labor. Studies either focus on men to the exclusion of women or drop women when problems of analysis become methodologically intractable. Male researchers privilege men as respondents without considering the systematic biases this introduces into analysis. Hence, the question becomes should there be a distinct feminist research methodology? Inside and outside geography there is general agreement on feminists searching for methods "consonant with their values and aims as feminists, and appropriate to feminist topics" (McDowell 1992: 405), but less agreement on what these methods might be. However, there is a general feminist insistence on collaborative methods in which the typically unequal power relations between researcher and informant are broken down. "As women interviewing women, commonalities of experience should be recognized and become part of a mutual exchange of views" (McDowell 1992: 405). For, as Grosz (1986: 199) says, the notion of the researcher as disembodied, rational, sexually indifferent subject, a mind unlocated in space, time, or relationships, attributes a status normally reserved for angels rather than the mere academic. Feminists often adopt a strategy for collaborative relationships with participants in their/our research employing qualitative methodologies of some kind: in-depth interviews, participant observation, ethnographic research, often in small-scale and case study work which validates personal experience. Intersubjectivity rather than objectivity is the ideal.

Field-Work in Feminist Geography

However, methods like participant observation and ethnographic research are not immune from power differentials. In a "Symposium on Feminist Participatory Research" (Farrow, Moss, and Shaw 1995), a group of geographers contemplate their experiences with feminist *participatory research*. These methods demonstrate solidarity with oppressed people through research and want to radically change social reality with, rather than for, disempowered people (Maguire 1987). Incorporating critical theory into methodology, feminists search for emancipatory, action-oriented research which merges scholarship with political action (Mies 1982, 1983; Reinharz 1992). Thus, Heather Farrow (1995) wants the research question and the research work to be conducted by the researched people and the researcher, recognizing the power differences between them; from research practice in Namibia she finds limits to what outsiders can research. Pamela Moss (1995a) argues that feminists must deal with differences in the ways power is constituted in research and in the conditions forming researcher and researched. Barbara Shaw (1995) finds the situation further complicated when Northern research workers, funded with money and time, study the lives of people in the South; she thinks that her position as Other could not effectively be overcome during participatory research in Goa (India). These feminists conclude that participatory research is complicated and restrictive, involving reflexivity as part of the research process, and that processes of marginalization are embedded in the academy.

Similar conclusions are reached during a discussion on *field-work* in feminist geography. Heidi Nast (1994) finds feminist discussions of the relations between researcher and researched especially pertinent to field-oriented research, with its periodic, short, and intense relationships. In feminist theory, field research involves political commitment, with techniques engendering critical, reflexive forms of engagement designed to include those typically excluded from study. Indeed, Cindi Katz (1994) finds the borders between research and politics, and between "in the field" and "not in the field," artificial yet pragmatically necessary. Research involving conversations with "natives" necessarily involves marking off a physical space to define a site of inquiry in which the researcher is displaced so as to discern things difficult to see at home. Katz wants a method of displacement that avoids treating places as vessels for holding cultural attributes, as museums or mausoleums. Defining "the field" in a situation where the fieldworker is imposed on the time–space of others brings the academic field of power into play. The social actor/scholar is interpolated in the research project and these figure in her development. Katz (1994: 72) says of herself: "I am always, everywhere, in 'the field'" and "my subject position is constituted in spaces of betweenness," neither inside nor outside; from such a standpoint she thinks it may be possible to frame questions of theoretical interest as well as practical significance to those with whom the work is concerned.

Audrey Kobayashi (1994) sees feminists of color challenging the authority of white middle-class women to speak for those on the margin so that they (white women) withdraw completely from research in territories which they cannot claim. This changes the way field-work is done by challenging the myth of neutral detachment and encouraging respect for communities. The issue of white women's domination can be resolved at one level, Kobayashi says, by linking professional research with a commitment to political change, at another by using research methods that (ideally) involve mutual concern and trust: "Feminist methods that stress mutual respect and involvement, shared responsibility, valuing difference, and non-hierarchical ways of achieving ends are not simple or shallow gestures of accommodation, nor are they just an alternative methodology. Such methods define an approach to political change" (Kobayashi 1994: 76). These political ends are achieved only when the previously disempowered are given voice. The question of "Who speaks for whom?" can be answered only on the basis of a history of involvement and an understanding of the construction of difference.

Kim England (1994) problematizes field-work (where the research worker directly confronts those researched) at a time when objectivity is being questioned by the postmodern turn in the social sciences. Traditional neopositivism provides epistemological security from which to venture into research. Detachment, distance, and impartiality reduce the personal to the status of nuisance factor. Following Stanley and Wise (1993), England says that the notion of an open and culturally constructed social world, in which the "field" is constantly changing, should be embraced rather than dismissed. Hence, the only inevitability in research is unreliability and unpredictability; this means less rigid conceptualizations of the appropriate method, with flexibility and the openness of the researcher to the challenges of field-work:

> For me, part of the feminist project has been to dismantle the smokescreen surrounding the canons of neopositivist research – impartiality and objectivist neutrality – which supposedly prevent the researcher from contaminating the data ... As well as being our object of inquiry, the world is an intersubjective creation and, as such, we cannot put our commonsense knowledge of social structures to one side. (England 1994: 81)

Indeed, she finds treating people like objects to be morally unjustifiable. Those researched should be treated like people, not mines of information to be exploited by collectors of "facts." Of several relationships with the researched, feminists usually prefer the role of supplicant seeking reciprocal relations based in empathy with people having greater knowledge of the immediate question; feminists also prefer using dialogical methods. That is, England (1994: 82) wants a geography in which "intersubjectivity and reflexivity play a central role." While she finds appropriation (if "only" textual in nature) an inevitable consequence, the lives and loves of the researched being grist for the ethnographic mill, she is not convinced by the viability of some popular solutions like sharing the prepublication text with the researched, or writing multivocal texts, for the text is finally the responsibility of the researcher. For England, the unequal power relations in research have to be approached by exposing the partiality of the researcher's perspective. Field-work is conducted in the world between researcher and researched, a world already interpreted by people living in it: research is an account of the betweenness of the world of researcher and researched.

For Melissa Gilbert (1994), critiques of universality and the objectivity of feminist research, together with its emancipatory purpose, occur in the areas of epistemology and methodology rather than in research methods. During research on working-class women in Worcester, Massachusetts, Gilbert found these aspects of feminist research highly problematical. One problem is the category "woman" in the claim that women researchers have an insider's view, or in the confirmation of a unified subjectivity of shared consciousness through gender. Gilbert's research leads her to agree with Daphne Patai (1991: 144) that the purported solidarity of female identity is a fraud with good intentions, indeed, she extends this by questioning the possibility of a feminist research methodology: there is a need to theorize different women's experiences in the ways feminists challenge the world. Her experience also makes her ambivalent about the feminist notion of a supportive, trusting relationship between researcher and researched – for example, what are the power dynamics when the interviewer encounters racism among women being interviewed? Also, when analyzing data and writing up research she finds the proposed methods of overcoming power inequalities, such as presenting conclusions to the researched, to be limited in applicability and relinquishing of obligation to interpret. Such methodologies, she concludes with Patai (1991: 149), do not challenge the inequalities on which the research process rests.

Should Women Count?

In a similar manner, quantitative methods (or "counting") came under feminist critical scrutiny. As Doreen Mattingly and Karen Falconer-Al-Hindi (1995) say, feminist challenges to the epistemology of academic research mean rethinking methodological practices such as quantification. Quantitative research is criticized for its tendency to derive universal causality from inferential statistics and for the static nature of the categories it employs (Hartsock 1985). Sharing the critique of conventional objectivity with humanistic approaches, feminists find with Haraway (1991) that being objective means making one's position known, and limiting one's conclusions, rather than making grand claims. A combination of quantitative and qualitative techniques might be most valuable for such feminist research. Sarah McLafferty (1995) agrees that feminist critiques center on the myth of objectivity, the view that quantitative techniques are neutral and impartial. In geography, many quantitative researchers now accept that subjectivity is present in all research. But quantitative techniques hide their subjectivity and thus carry more weight as the language of (formal) science than qualitative techniques. Quantitative techniques were developed in the physical sciences for the study of interchangeable objects; these techniques are then transferred to social scientific analyses of diverse groups of people – for example, grouping women without recognizing the complex divisions among them. But, for McLafferty, this does not necessarily mean that quantitative techniques cannot incorporate diversity. She also believes studying broad divisions like gender to be important: "Denying this would seem to me to deny the very basis of feminist geography and feminism itself" (McLafferty 1995: 437). Important aspects of women's lives can be measured and comparisons with men provide a potent summary of gender inequalities. Counting can be used to reveal the broad contours of difference. She has no easy response to the criticism that quantitative techniques break the living connections between researcher and researched, but finds that these techniques can identify places and people for in-depth qualitative study and place results in broader context. Quantitative and qualitative techniques can thus enrich each other.

Pamela Moss (1995a; 1995b) is unsatisfied with feminist empiricist, standpoint theoretical, and postmodern accounts of objectivity and counting. With Hawkesworth (1990) she suggests a feminist epistemology that "explicitly locates objectivity where human cognition is acknowledged within people's multiple power positionings in society ... and where counting is a tool, not to strengthen a claim or privilege a position, but rather to contextualize and ascertain structural relations of everyday life" (Moss 1995b: 445). This objectivity is located in "betweenness," the fact that feminist researchers can never not work with others separate and different from themselves (Nast 1994: 57). Accepting this means, for Moss (1995b: 445), that "an agenda for research in feminist geography would be to sort through our positionings and those of 'others' ... to build narratives inclusive of 'others.'" She finds the positionings within betweenness multifaceted and embedded in the texture of everyday life, a texture comprising multiple mediations of "facts," "truths," and "power." The question for Moss is not whether women should count, but how to do so, and how to counter the claim that quantification has a monopoly on truth. Numbers give context to representations, preventing the individualization of experiences. She wants a feminist epistemology that locates a mediated objectivity that everyone has a part in constructing; this mediation takes place in betweenness at various scales; and is embedded in ways of knowing.

Victoria Lawson (1995) argues that quantitative techniques are extensively used by feminist empiricist approaches but are resisted by standpoint and poststructural feminists. Yet she finds provocative the ideas expressed by Sprague and Zimmerman (1993: 266) that social change requires evidence, and that to empower themselves women need access to quantified information. She therefore argues that some quantitative techniques are compatible even with poststructural feminist research goals. Even so, she adopts a critical attitude towards quantitative methods as presently constituted. The focus on qualitative techniques tends to reinforce an existing quantitative/qualitative dualism between objective and rigorous (superior) and subjective and opinionated (inferior) which obscures overlaps in the actual operations using both kinds of approach. She finds the link between quantitative methods and masculinist science insufficiently interrogated – for Lawson, this coupling is historically produced and not inevitable. In quantitative geography, techniques for gathering information are conflated with theories of what can be known. Yet techniques are not synonymous with philosophical positions (Bennett 1985). Also, following Haraway's (1991) notion of knowledge as a view always from somewhere, she argues that feminists can *count* from somewhere too. Objects take on meaning relationally along multiple axes (Staeheli and Lawson 1994) and quantitative techniques can answer particular types of questions within these relational ontologies. Quantitative techniques powerfully demonstrate processes of oppression – for example:

> Women comprise 50% of the world's population, do two-thirds of the world's work hours, receive 10% of the world's income and own less than 1% of world property, according to the International Labour Organization. (Bronstein 1982: 11)

Yet this kind of analysis is criticized by standpoint and poststructural feminists because in using an unproblematized concept of gender it masks as much as it exposes – for example, disaggregated by race, class, or region these data would reveal even more intense inequalities. Hence, the call by McDowell (1992) among others for theorizing significant differences. Lawson (1995: 453) supports this call by arguing that "counting has the potential to provoke questions about significant differences" and that quantitative analysis "poses questions about *differences* between gendered subjects rather than about the *similarities* that conventionally form the basis for categorizing and counting." In geography, quantification is used to stabilize categories that fix complex social processes. For Lawson, descriptive uses of counting can reveal key relationships identified theoretically by poststructural approaches. But conflating descriptive counting with statistical inference is problematic, for inferential statistics assume normalcy, representativeness, generalization, replicability, all parts of an atomistic, closed world view. Hence, counting can only be descriptive of carefully contextualized relations when researchers employ relational ontologies. Quantitative techniques are valuable for certain kinds of research questions, substantive issues of material experiences for instance, but not for questions concerned with subjectivity and identity where the focus of research is "uncountable" and discursive methods and in-depth interviews are called for. Schooled in quantification, Lawson finds it difficult even after a decade of struggle to read the objectification that results in a different way. However, she advocates interweaving several methods, including counting, as part of a process of separating techniques from ontological positions.

The notion of combinations of quantitative and qualitative methods, raised by several writers, is taken up by Diane Rocheleau (1995) in the context of political ecology, an area where researchers often work at the boundary between positivist and critical paradigms. For Rocheleau, feminist research has moved from taking the identity of women as a group for granted to working on affinities, coalitions, and the notion that scientists can construct shared bodies of knowledge derived from distinct experiences (Haraway 1991). This, however, raises questions about the boundaries of the groups when affinities change over time and context – questions of who counts, who is counted, in what context? Also, the notion of partial objectivities challenges scientists to stretch and combine the subjective into something that can be verified through a variety of methods including quantitative techniques. Poststructural thought, emphasizing visual imagery and stories as sources of insight into the separate realities of diverse groups, opens new epistemological space for combining methods, such as combining resource mapping from remotely sensed data with personal life histories and participatory mapping methods. Rocheleau finds these combinations allowing freedom of inquiry and leading to practical interactions between numbers, pictures, maps, and stories. Drawing on her research experience with a social forestry project in the Dominican Republic, she advocates using "counter-maps" drawn from the bottom up to "represent a variety of gendered and otherwise differentiated perspectives on land, resources, and the possible futures of people and the ecosystems that they both create and inhabit" (Rocheleau 1995: 464). As opposed to "maps-as-usual" drawn by government agencies, these images place rural people at the center to depict the gendered sharing embodied in individual and community practices. Once made visible, these can be named, categorized, and mapped as a fact, ideal, or norm, as a point of departure for changes in land use, property regimes, and livelihoods. Rocheleau wants to combine quantitative, qualitative, and visual research methods into new composite tools in a feminist poststructural perspective that serves the interests of rural women and men.

Feminism and Geography

Such theoretical and methodological work conducted under the aegis of feminist geography shows an area of the discipline undergoing rapid development by (mainly) women geographers united by a common sense of project, yet differing in political–ontological and epistemological perspective. However, this picture of a feminist geography triumphant is only part of the story. Feminist geography has differentiated itself from masculinist geography through fierce, profound critique. From the early 1990s on, the position of feminist geography was consolidated by a major critique of masculinist geography and the beginnings of an alternative feminist vision of space provided by Gillian Rose, a professor of geography at Edinburgh University. Feminist geographers, Rose (1993) says, argue that domination of the discipline of geography by men has serious consequences for its production of acceptable knowledge. For Rose, thinking within the existing parameters of the discipline means occupying a "masculine subject position." While claiming to cover everything, the actually existing masculinist geography erases women's existence. Under the premise that identity is relational rather than inherent, Rose argues that masculinity both depends on femininity and is evaluated higher than the feminine in the constellations of ideas and associated practices called "scientific discourses." Central to her argument is Haraway's (1991: 183–201) notion of the "master subject" – the subject constituted as white, bourgeois, heterosexual, and masculine – who sees different others only in relation to his own powerful self, as his "Other." Feminists argue that this structure of (masculine) Same and (feminine) Other is embedded in the western production of knowledge, in the scientific revolution, Enlightenment, and subsequent thought (Keller 1985; Le Doeuff 1987). Reason is not gender-neutral. Rather, masculine rationality assumes the knower can separate himself from his body, emotions, and values so that his thoughts are objective. The assumption that thought is untainted by social position allows a claim for universality and exhaustiveness. For Rose, geographers share this view in their role as "detached explorers" producing transcendent visions of neutral truths about the entire world. The power of the master subject appears also in an unobtrusive prose style which, by deflecting attention from its author, invests writing with the authority of rational man, as the objective expression of reason. But just as Same requires an Other, male rationality requires a female irrationality, the notion of women ruled by the passion of their bodies, incapable of producing legitimate knowledge. The white bourgeois heterosexual masculinities attracted to geography imagine their feminine Other to be all they deny in themselves, the bodily, emotional, passive, natural, and irrational, or what de Lauretis (1987) calls "Woman" the imagined fantasy figure.

How, Rose asks, do women resist the (partly internalized) subject position of Woman? Feminism's engagement with hegemonic discoursers of gender creates two basic strategies of feminist critique (Snitow 1990): building the identity "woman" and giving it political meaning – but this can end up reinstating the patriarchal idea of "Woman," and tearing down the category "woman" – but then what unites women as feminists? As it is practically impossible to choose one strategy over the other, Rose advocates strategic mobility and diversity as feminism's greatest strengths – hence, Rose adopts different critical strategies for different geographies.

Rose finds two kinds of masculinity dominating geography, distinguished by their relation to a feminine Other. "Social scientific masculinity" asserts its authority by claiming access to a transparently real geographical world and represses reference to its Other while claiming total knowledge. Rose uses *time-geography* as illustration: for example, its "oddly minimalist account of the body," its reduction of human agency to *paths in space*: "Time-geography embodies an agency ... [that] inhabits a masculine (no)body" (Rose 1993: 34). With some accounts (Gould 1981), she finds space articulated as infinite, unbounded, transparent in the sense of the spatial freedom of men. Hence, in time-geography human agency and the space it moves in are masculine, constructed in the image of the master subject. For all its claims to universality and objectivity, time-geography unproblematically assumes a highly specific theorization of society and space – what she terms "masculinism's false exhaustiveness of the Same" (Rose 1993: 38). Erasure of specificity allows the master subject to assume he can see and know everything. Such "heroism" not only depends on masculinity but constitutes it in denying other possibilities.

"Aesthetic masculinity" establishes power by claiming heightened sensibility to human experience and admits the existence of its Other to achieve unique profundity. Rose uses *humanistic geography's* conception of place as a location full of memory, experience, and significance as case study. For Rose, humanists show a general concern for the submission of ordinary people to authority rather than analyzing specific power relations. Further, humanistic geography claims access to the essence of place in an authoritarian manner she finds to be masculinist because essence is theorized in terms of an implicit masculine norm. Rather than repressing its female Other, as with time-geography, it engenders its Other through masculine notions of woman. Place is the feminized Other, idealized as Woman, and discussed as lost mother – place is mysterious, unknowable, feminine. Hence, the paradox of humanistic geography – "it seeks exhaustive knowledge of something that it argues is unknowable" (Rose 1993: 60). This produces an "aesthetic masculinity" claiming to know through sensitivity to an obscure yet profound human experience.

Thus, for Rose, both the opaque knowability of place, and the transparent knowability of space, are masculine understandings which depend, in different ways, on a feminized Other. Rose herself relies on Keller's (1985) argument that the search for knowledge is shaped by ideologies, especially of gender, resting on emotional substructures. Keller finds that the masculine subject's identification of himself as center against all non-masculine Others emerges as a distinction between subject and object and in thinking through binary, hierarchized oppositions (the masculine term favored over the feminine). For Rose, one such dualism, between nature and culture, a central metanarrative of western thought, is crucial to the discipline of geography, culture being thought of as masculine, nature as feminine. Hence, Margaret Fitzsimmons (1989) finds human geography implicitly structured around this binary distinction: culture, city, and space (masculine) are opposed to nature, countryside, and primitive (feminine). Likewise, Andrew Sayer (1991a) finds theory, generality, and abstraction opposed to empirics, specificity, and the concrete, terms Rose finds engendered through the nature/culture distinction, theory being masculine, specifics feminine. For Rose, time-geography and humanistic geography likewise are two parts of a binary structured field of knowledge, the social scientific masculinity of time-geography (A) limits the arena of humanistic geography (not-A), each requiring the other to make sense, for example space and place needing each other. Keller's account of science suggests that one side (masculine) of an oppositional structure is always valued over the other (feminine). But Rose critically analyses the geographic tradition of "field-work" to find this dualism unstable in the discipline and geographical discourse more mobile; geographers, she says, are fascinated by, as well as hostile to, the (natural, feminine) Other. For Rose, the question then becomes strategy. While some radical feminists (as with gyn-ecology) invert the power relation by valorizing the feminine, natural side (Griffen 1980), Rose criticizes this as accepting the patriarchal conflation of women and nature. Rose prefers challenging and displacing the nature–culture dualism by oscillating between different forms of resistance, exploring beyond A and not-A by drawing on different experiences to produce different kinds of knowledge.

This leads Rose to consider the possibility of a space which does not replicate the masculinist exclusions of Same and Other. She concentrates on the spatial imagination of the "subject of feminism" (de Lauretis 1987) – that is, a particular sense of identity which, in avoiding the exclusions of the master subject, imagines spaces not structured by masculinist claims to exhaustiveness. The construction of the subject of feminism is a political project, including a practice and a way of knowing, which tries to displace the patriarchal dualism of Man and Woman by asserting the importance of other axes of identity (class, race) in a desire to find something else. The construction of woman has frequently been referred to in terms of a politics of location and images of multidimensional, shifting, contingent, and paradoxical spaces, and radically heterogeneous geometries. Such paradoxical spaces are lived, experienced, and felt; articulate arguments about power and identity; and can challenge the exclusions of masculinist geography.

In more detail – while spatial images proliferate in social understanding, in part through the globalization of life, Rose thinks that feminists' use of such imagery has a trajectory of its own, related more to the geography of everyday life. Also, feminists talking about space evoke a sense of difficulty, a desire for absence, an image of confinement. Women are expected to look right for the panoptical male connoisseur residing even in their own consciousness. The threat of constant evaluation encourages women to see themselves as bodies placed with other objects in a space experienced as alien, a hazardous arena far from the transparent space conceptualized by masculinist geography. Yet the sense of space that results can also dissolve divisions between mind and body, metaphorical and real, in a feminist space resonating with both emotion and analysis. The masculine claim to know, experienced as violent claims to space, invokes suffering and resistance from women. Masculinism claims universal spatial conquest, yet there is an Other space, part of the territory of the same, but perceived as outside. Feminists also imagine somewhere beyond this territorial logic. Understanding the subject of feminism as a site of such differences – what Haraway (1991: 170) calls "geometries of difference and contradiction" – enriches the feminist spatial imaginary and ruptures the geography of the master subject. The resulting "*paradoxical space*" has simultaneous insideness and outsideness, is center and margin at once, and enables an "outsider within" stance which can critique the authority of masculinism. Separatism is advocated, despite controversy, as breathing space or as space of interrelation and means of thinking about coalition and resistance. These tentative ideas are illustrated by readings of bell hooks (1990) on growing up on the margins of a Southern US town and M. B. Pratt (1984) on the experiences of a white Christian lesbian. These, for Rose, are paradoxical geographies and political projects which challenge the transparent geography of hegemonic subjectivity to create not so much a space of resistance as an entirely different geometry:

> This space is paradoxical because . . . it must imagine the position of being both prisoner and exile, both within and without. It must locate a place which is both crucial to, yet also denied by, the Same; and it must locate a place both defined by that Same and dreaming of something quite beyond its reach. Paradoxical space, then, is a space imagined in order to articulate a troubled relation to the hegemonic discourses of masculinism. (Rose 1993: 159)

Rose refuses to demand that geographers acknowledge paradoxical space as emancipatory, for it is merely one strategy currently adopted by a critically mobile feminism which may not always be emancipating. She asks instead for a geography that acknowledges the grounds of its knowledge to be unstable, shifting, uncertain, and contested. Space as a disciplinary concept is precarious and fluctuating, destabilized by internal contradictions of the geographical desire to know, and by resistance from marginalized victims of that desire. Her conclusion is that there are many geographies with different compulsions, desires, and effects, complementing and contesting one another.

Space, Place, and Gender

In the end, a feminist geography has to produce conceptions of space and nature that are its own, that derive from women's experiences, the insights of feminist theories, and other similar committed sources. There are signs that this view begins to emerge in Rose's work. At several points in her numerous essays Doreen Massey also returns to the theme which forms the title of her *Space, Place and Gender* (1994). Reflecting its origins in Marxism, Massey's work puts the case for a particular way of thinking about space and place in terms of social relations, originally class relations, but increasingly emphasizing gender. Geography matters, she says, in terms of the construction of gender, while variations in gender relations are significant elements in the production of imaginative geographies and uneven development. Here, the idea is that space must be conceptualized integrally with time, in terms of space–time. This is an extension of the notion that space is constructed out of social relations which are inherently dynamic (space as "dynamic simultaneity"). It is also a view which implies that the lived world is a "simultaneous multiplicity of spaces: cross-cutting, intersecting, aligning with one another, or existing in relations of paradox or antagonism" (Massey 1994: 3). Most evidently this is because the social relations of space are experienced differently, variously interpreted by people holding positions in it, including the observer (the person choosing the frame of reference about space). This argument, for Massey, means that space is not simply opposed to time as absence or lack; it "releases the spatial from the realm of the dead" (Massey 1994: 4); it relates spatiality to the social and to power; it makes spatial organization integral to the production of the social. Moreover, thinking about space in this way challenges influential conceptualizations of places as bounded sites of authenticity, singular, fixed, and unproblematic in their identities – for Massey, this rests on the view of space as stasis. When space is thought of in terms of social interrelations at all scales, place emerges as a particular articulation, or moment of interrelations, which are not confined to the local, but stretch beyond to the global. This challenges views of places as timeless identities. Place identities are always unfixed, contested, and multiple, the product of specificities of mixes of links and connections, place as open and porous. Instituting horizons, establishing boundaries, and securing the identities of places are attempts to stabilize the meaning of particular envelopes of space–time or come to grips with the "unutterable mobility and contingency" of space–time.

Massey interprets this politically as social contestation over the power to label space–time. She thinks that the unity of space and place must be rethought in different terms, as group or national identity, but also as gender. In the latter sense, she finds the western dichotomy between masculine and feminine informing the division between time and space, so that time is coded masculine (history, progress, civilization, politics, transcendence) and space feminine (stasis, passivity, depoliticization). She wants to challenge all such violent dichotomies. Similarly with place, the construction of the specific means through interrelations rather than imposing boundaries means that localities can be present in one another; the need for counter-positioned identities is culturally masculine, defensive, designed for domination, and should be abandoned. Just as personal identities are thought to be multiple, shifting, unbounded, so are the identities of places – indeed, the two are related in a double articulation. Massey finds notions of the local having malleable meanings but with a real consistency of gender association: because, it is said, women lead more local lives than men. Thus, feminism is often said derogatively to be a local struggle compared with the universalism of class struggle, and place is interpreted as important in the search for identity in times of time–space compression. For Massey, the conceptualization of place as haven away from globalization, as a site of indulgence in nostalgia, derives from an association between Woman and Nature, or a nonexistent lost authenticity which lends itself to reactionary politics. She contests this view of place – it does not encapsulate the lives of real women, for the home may be as much a place of conflict as repose, and many women have to leave home and community to forge their own identities. For Massey, one gender-disturbing message in terms of identity and place is "keep moving!"

Conclusion

Women's movements struggle for equality, rights, and opportunity in the liberal sphere, for justice, power, and emancipation in the radical sphere, and for difference, voice, and identity in the postmodern sphere. It is an expression of academic conceit that this chapter moves quickly from the real struggles of women in everyday life to their representations in theory and abstract politics. So the chapter catalogues the intellectual development of a series of movements but particularly of ideas. In this way, it joins that (masculine) strategy of abstracting ideas from their contexts and subjecting the reader to heavy doses of concentrated text, with little relief from descriptive passages, no doubt as a power play. Yet this is a power strategy itself in context, in this case the existing intellectual power structure of an already established discipline which, as Christopherson (1989) revealingly points out, pays attention to the heavy, the dense, and the abstract. Thus, a first step in constructing a feminist alternative might involve doing the same only better! A second strategy is doing it differently as well. A third is criticism continually. Feminist thought has proven open to self-criticism at a level no other form of political thinking dares. Through self-criticism, feminist thought has changed directions several times, from the universality of woman to the differences between women, from women close to nature to femininity as a social construction, from modern to postmodern, structural to poststructural. Yet there remains a strong sense not of a singular project, but linked projects – feminist geography retains in many ways a commitment to radical humanism (Johnson 1994).

Feminist geography emerged as a disciplinary descendant of the women's movement and as part of radical geography. With feminist thought in general, the concern of feminist geographers moves from the establishment of ontological positions to discussions of epistemology and method, and to the differentiation of specific visions of the nature of space, place, and environment. Drawing on the epistemological contributions of feminist theory, feminist geography has added empirical evidence, theories of space and place, and an especially useful contribution in the area of methodology. Feminist geographers began by pointing out the summary exclusion of women from the discipline's theoretical constructs and empirical work. Eventually, they argued the context-specific and place-based constitution of gender and moved on to deconstruct the category "woman." In this, we begin to see the possibility of distinctive feminist positions on space based on different experiences, space as material yet representational, space as differentiated rather than homogenous, space as dynamic rather than static, space as the opposite of the positive conception.

Yet feminist geography remains at an early stage in the development of an autonomous theoretical content. By this is meant a system of statements, backed by epistemological justifications, ontological delimitations, and especially empirical exemplifications, establishing a definite range of positions, that express something approaching a consistent set of viewpoints. In the disciplinary context ("disciplinary" in both senses of the term), this must provide a particular perspective on geographic themes of nature and space – basically, feminist geography must develop a gendered theory of environmental space. There are abundant signs (in the work of McDowell, Rose, Massey, etc.) that such a theory is under development and that different conceptions of space – "paradoxical space" for example – will be involved. But the paradoxical problem with paradoxes lies in the tendency for involution to turn into convolution with nothing much emerging beyond vague indications of what might be implied, and this has to be the case for feminist conceptions of space. Feminist notions of space, place, and environment cannot emerge solely from critiques of masculinist geography. Nor can feminist theory be spatialized just by reading the personal accounts of marginalized (or privileged) women – the literature is too thin on the ground, and literary means are only one source of information. Instead, feminist geographic theory stands in almost desperate need of empirical work employing exactly the range of research methods so abundantly discussed to further the development of a body of linked concepts which express a coherent range of positions (for examples see Hanson and Pratt 1995; McDowell and Court 1993; 1994). Feminist geography needs to develop alternate theories of space, place, and environment which speak to the experiences of doubly and triply oppressed peoples, *despite* the problems of speaking for others. For the first generation of scholars to emerge from oppressed groups bear a special responsibility. During a brief moment, they have enormous power to change things in liberal, academic, guilty circles. As this chapter records, the recent history of feminist thought and feminist geography is one of rapidly growing sophistication and enhanced political awareness, yet one of potentials only partly realized.

Chapter 8

Conclusion

Geography entered modern knowledge as a science of the classification of worldly facts. It has retained its list-like character in the popular imagination and for part of its teaching practice. But the academic geography enamoured of by intellectuals has long transcended this classificatory activity. Behind every fact lies a causal structure waiting to be interpreted. Behind spatial variations in the characteristics of nature and humanity lie arrangements of factors whose geography makes a difference. In the early modern geographical imagination, haunted still by ghosts, goblins, and gods, geographical facts were the signifying presence of an eventually spiritual intent. The landscape was read as pattern which revealed the systematic will of the world spirit. Even scientists like Darwin still believed in an original god-cause, a metaphysics of divine presence beyond the physics of real processes. As the nineteenth century "progressed," to use the optimistic language of the time, positivism discarded god from the list of usual suspects in the direct causes of the event. Positivism resembles its religious predecessor in that it surveys the surface of events for causal factors; it differs in finding causes (except the original) to be real, material, and definitely knowable, rather than spiritual, immaterial, and "knowable" in the end only through faith. Thus, positivism begins a process of disenchantment which takes philosophy from divination to groundlessness, from looking for meaning to denying that life has significance, that there is anything beneath the surface, that it is possible to find truth (figure 1.1). Positivism differs from religion too in the ruling interests it serves, economic rather than ecclesiastical, progressive rather than conservative, the bourgeoisie rather than the nobility. In this sense of serving powerful interests, geography entered modern knowledge as prejudiced "scientific" understanding. Mere classification became obsolete in a move to directly functional ideology – environmental determinism legitimated as natural the progressive European conquest of the world's lands and peoples. Yet this could be explained scientifically by a discipline which told the truth in the language of facts. Strange "facts" were these – geographies of human energy, scientific surveys of intelligence – but they sufficed to cement geography's place in the modern curriculum.

Knowledge is organized into disciplines by the diversity of the requisites of power.

Disciplines so formed must also respond to changes in power systems if they are to retain efficacy. Geography will always carry the mark of environmental determinism on its forehead. Yet geographical thought has also an autonomy of purpose and method, and a fluidity of emphasis and concern, which allow a partial escape from the dictates of power systems but only at the cost of a diminution of fame. Thus, as the requisites of power shifted in emphasis from colonial control over the external arena of global space to the colonization of internal consciousness, geography lost its way, lost direct functionality, meandered through a vaguely neo-Kantian revival of its classificatory past in descriptive regional geography obviously, but in human geography and the cultural geography of landscapes less obviously. Geography as the areal differentiation of the earth's surface into unique regions, weakly "analyzed" using a thinly disguised environmentalism, drifted through the interwar period, lacking immediate functionality, except perhaps in societies with local planning traditions (Britain), too esoteric and far too amorphous to regain power in other societies suddenly in need of regional planning (the United States). A discipline in drift is a discipline ripe for the taking or for dismemberment. So with the return of soldiers from the war, or from government agencies organizing the war effort, came too a new urgency, resolutely modern, powerfully positivist, scientifically optimistic, functionally engaged with power, a new geography concerned not with regional description but with spatial analysis. This different geographical imagination was greatly influenced by views from outside the discipline, from the resurrection of classical landscape rationalism, from sociology, social physics, economics and regional science. For the rational modernist imbued with scientific method, space was experienced not as collections of unique things, but as homogenous expanse stretching into the remote reaches of a conquered globe. This quantitative, spatial geography dealt in generalities and similarities rather than unique instances, in location theory rather than regional description, and used mathematical and statistical methods rather than poetic description or muddy-booted, mind-sodden field-work. Yet one wonders whether the search for generality missed, and still misses, something that these quaint areal differentiators were trying to discover. The notion of generality captures sameness but ignores, even hides, difference. And difference originates new things, even as recombinations of the old. The trouble was that the quantitative positivist methods of the new geography proved too cumbersome as theoretical devices for integrating studies of the unique into analyses of generality. Areal differentiation also had no way of integrating its unique descriptions into general theory. Both were deficient, unsatisfying, ready again to be transcended.

Geography as Social Theory

Regional geography can be read as a version of Kantian idealism; quantitative geography appeals to logical positivism for perspective and method; but only recently have the connections between geography and philosophy been more tightly drawn through the medium of social theory. The savaging of areal differentiation by the quantifiers returned with a vengeance when they too, the quantifiers, came under critical attack from humanists and radicals simultaneously if not always in synchrony. "With a vengeance" because both turned the heavy guns of philosophy onto what turned out to be only precariously established "scientific" positions. "With a vengeance" because positivism provided geography with a functional base, a position of usefulness to power which, along with the practice of physical geography by dedicated, usually conventional, "hard scientists," gives the philosophical avant-garde of human geography the freedom to spend their intellectual energies in Bataillian delights of criticism and free speculation. This kind of utilitarian underwriting of the discipline continues to the present with geographic information systems, which prove to be highly functional and well rewarded. We might remember too that legion of part-timers, graduate students, temporary appointments, and junior faculty who labor still in "World Regional Geography" courses, under the watchful eyes of departmental dictators, producing old-fashioned academic value (fact memorization) from which the intellectual elite draw surplus measured in terms of salary, freedom, and disciplinary status. "With a hidden vengeance" therefore against that which originates and sustains the critic (always the most ferocious form of vengeance!). And yet exactly because the new critical geography interacts with formal knowledge in philosophical and social-theoretic terms, it too contributes to the legitimacy of geography, makes geography intellectually respectable not only on campus, but with governments filled with university graduates and even corporations tinged by humanist rationalism. A discipline can support only a few true radicals; the rest have functional utility, oblique though this often may seem. "With a cunning vengeance" then because the critic is safely ensconced (with tenure) in an institution resting compatibly within the relations of a power system – power takes its revenge on the safely vengeful critic.

What came to be known as humanistic geography derived much of its considerable critical power from existentialism and phenomenology. Both had long histories of criticism; both were reconstructive in the philosophical and social theoretical senses. The existential phenomenological critique rejects the Cartesian dualism between mind and body underlying Enlightenment rationality and its most famous offspring, positivist science. For existential phenomenologists, Cartesian dualism misinterprets the subject by emphasizing rational consciousness at the expense of emotional subjectivity and bodily presence, reduces objects to the measurable qualities of things, and mischaracterizes subject–object relations by careless removal from everyday experience into a never-never-land of abstract observation. Existential phenomenology wants to return people, including scientists, to the study of the lifeworld, the historical field of lived experience, in a cathartic spasm of rebirth and renewal – in two senses: as a kind of democratization of the objects and processes of study, and in the sense of lifeworld as primary constituent of thought world. Here, "scientific method" becomes hermeneutics, a science of interpretation, source of understanding rather than abstract knowledge, a science of possibilities at its best. Humanistic geography interprets lifeworld (too readily) as the contextualization of experience in place, with place conceptualized not as point in space, nor even landscape, but as community, field of care, center of significance, all linked formatively and reflexively to human identity. Such a reconceptualization transforms space into a mosaic of places, an entirely different surface than the abstract space of positivist geography – indeed, nowhere can we see more clearly the effects of beginning from a different philosophical viewpoint than in the differences between existential place and positivistic space. Yet also there are problems with a humanistic geography of places, problems which have their origins exactly in existential phenomenology. For the human relation to place is phrased far too frequently in the ghostly terms of "deep spiritual and psychological attachment," while the literature resounds with a lexicon of experience, meaning, intention, and sense, all terms easier to use than to say what they mean (except that they sound nice). Particularly difficult is the notion of an inherent intentionality, not as struggle to survive, nor even as vitalist dynamic essence, but as a spiritual urge to bestow meaning – here, medieval mysticism survives in the modern theory of the subject. Again, for all its talk of intersubjectivity and community, humanistic geography has little conception of social relations (hence, the "intentional" individual) and therefore little idea of spatial relations (hence, its emphasis on isolated places rather than landscapes). If landscape is a mosaic of places, what organizes the mosaic, what ties places together? Such questions lead to a basic issue, which remains even after sophisticated internal and external critique: existential phenomenology rests on a nostalgic assumption of original, untainted, prescientific understanding based on a pure (precapitalist) experience primordially of place. When and where this happened is conveniently left unexamined. For is it not exactly the problem that human beings have always misunderstood themselves, their social relations, and their relations with nature? And therefore there never was a time when crystal-clear understanding emerged in perfectly pure places?

With historical materialist human geography, the social production of existence extends to its meaning – that is, meaning is found, or rather constructed, under conditions not of one's choosing. Meaning emerges under conditions of domination, of which Marxism emphasizes natural compulsion and class control of the material production of existence. Marxism's project is to understand relations of domination in order to change them, exactly so that a liberated humanity can find meaning in life. In Marxism, "the production of existence" is initially taken literally to mean the material transformation of nature by the labor process – that is, the exertion of social forces organized through the fundamental relations between people in the active creation of life. This entails a basic assumption of essential position: some social practices and relations are fundamental in the sense that they allow existence to take place and change. These are the basic activities of social reproduction, especially, in classical Marxism, practices which enable the material production of life, those physically producing bodies, necessary objects, places to live. Yet this statement of position does not "reduce" life to its direct production; it is merely a starting point from which analysis proceeds. During material activity, within the confrontations and contradictions of the making of social life, meanings emerge and ideologies are constructed, all under conditions of domination: hence, consciousness comes to express domination in multiple, ideological ways. Thus are societies interpreted through the lens of social reproduction.

As this materialist understanding seeped into geography during a long period of re-education and politicization, the relations in which the discipline specialized – relations with nature, social and economic relations across space, relations to places and within landscapes – were integrated into the total system of relations which constitute human existence. Thus, nature is seen again as origin and source of the production of existence, space is the medium in which reproductive relations occur, life elements and practices happen in places bound together through social relations. In this way, geography was integrated into critical social theory – indeed, placed at the heart of a materialist understanding of the world and its peoples; with this too, geography matured as a discipline. In Sartre's existential Marxism, and with Lefebvre, reproduction is understood as praxis. This is perhaps best exemplified as "project" in Sartre's terms, or as a real yet also imagined process with Lefebvre, "imagined" in the sense of represented. While Marxism brings to geography the notion of the production of space, even the "production" of nature at its (excessive) extreme, these latter theorists give production that aspect of creative agency which prevents geographic analysis from dwelling on anonymous forces and peopleless relations. The structuralist project should be reread from this position. It stresses the synchronic system of relations, linguistically mediated, in which humans are immersed – indeed which gives them a subject position to occupy – that is, places them in a system and even calls them into action (with the understanding that a call may not be answered). In social semiotics, space is the medium marked by *signifying* material practices which, again, stresses the representational aspect of human practice. Even Althusserian Marxism (totalities as structures in dominance) de-emphasizes economy as the immediately determining moment and re-places emphasis on the state, ideology, and culture as active constituents in reproduction. In this, space and environment are theorized as being marked by systems of practices, political, cultural, representational, organized only in the last instance by the economic. The notion of overdetermination, borrowed from Freud (via Lacan) and rethought in dialectical terms, offers the possibility of theorizing changing complexes of such active forces organized under multiple conditions of power and domination. By extension, this methodology conceptualizes the social reproductive forces as embedded in the space and nature they transform. Or, rather than *acting* on a separate natural environment, or a space differentiated from practice, forces *are* spatial in organization, have materialities which *are* environmental. With this, the notion of a space different and separate from social forces becomes impossible; the separation of a spatial domain is mere temporary analytical device. Structuralism attempts also to retain the idea of causality in systems characterized by mutual constitutivity. Nevertheless, Marxism, especially in its structural guise, was misunderstood profoundly, particularly by geographers. Either this mis-understanding was deliberate, or perhaps careless, or these aspects of signification, overdetermination, and mutual constitutivity, cannot have been fully explained at the time when structuralism was a main focus of interest.

Thus, instead of developing structuralist ideas within the corpus of geography, leftist critical thought diverted into structuration theory and realism, the main (but not sole) practical disciplinary product being locality studies. Structuration theory attempts, only partly successfully, yet at great length, to fill the gap which yawns between social structure and human agency. Here, the most interesting part of structuration theory from a geographical point of view is the use of place, or locale, as resource setting, socialized system of meaning, and network of power relations in which human action continually remakes social structures. Yet exactly the geographic aspect, the production of global structures through localized practices, proves most difficult to theorize, let alone exemplify, even by geographers committed to local, empirical research. Space as medium and outcome of social practice turns out to be excruciatingly difficult to understand. Likewise in realism, the division between abstract and concrete research runs into particular difficulties exactly when space is considered – realist analysis moves mechanically from the recognition that "space as such" is a contentless abstraction (so why even consider it?), to the notion that spatial relations cannot be theorized in general (which does not necessarily follow), to the idea that concrete spatial effects can be known only through empirical research (which makes abstract geographical theory impossible). Ten years of debate and empirical enquiry stretching through the 1980s failed to challenge these assumptions. We conclude that structuration and realism were interesting experiments, which leave useful ideas in their wake, but in the end were inconclusive even in coming close to "proving" their main claims. This is perhaps the reason why the discussion of localities in geography terminated suddenly around 1990, why structuration and even realism are scarcely mentioned during the new round of controversy, centered on postmodernism and feminism, which emerged in the 1990s.

Indeed, the notion of agency, especially in the form of the conscious subject, is anathema to poststructuralism – structuration theory's "agency" is incompatible with poststructuralism. Hence, the theory of the individual in poststructural thought is structuralist, in the linguistic sense of the creation of the person by the symbolic order (language, discourse) and Nietzschean, in the sense of its emphasis not on consciousness, but body, desire, and power – no wonder "identity" proves easier to mention in the title of books and articles than to find adequately theorized or fully exemplified in their contents! No wonder too that society, even in the preferred poststructural sense of symbolic order, is nevertheless conceptualized as a "dispersed regularity." In this, dispersed system origins are non-originary, presences countered by absences, meanings always deferred in the endless play of signifiers. These positions emerge from a view postmodern in its incredulity towards metanarratives of any kind, but especially those central beliefs of critical modernism – universal truth, justice, rationality, liberation, causality, and even coherence. Instead, postmodernism looks to the margins, to forgotten or subjugated narratives, to difference rather than similarity – thus, in the extreme, to the schizo-subject living in a schizo-revolutionary realm of flows, intensities, and becomings. Yet even this proposes still the possibility of a creative, if schizophrenic, critical response to the modern world. With other theorists, postmodernity is a universe of nihilism, where meaning of any kind has long since disappeared, and people float in a void of prescribed sign-pleasures and dominating sign-objects. The reaction of Anglo-American intellectuals to this wild beast of a postmodern philosophy is to tame it by rephrasing the postmodern as an historical period, cultural logic, or condition of late capitalism, and therefore part of a sequence explainable in economic terms. Likewise, postmodernism in geography consists almost entirely of a series of partial encounters during which fragments of postmodernism are attached to thought structures derived from Marxism – postmodern culture with post-Fordism for instance. Yet postmodernism has a heightened concern with the dimension of space, paralleling its conceptualization of the symbolic order, which offers more than fragments better synthesized elsewhere. This is not an orderly, essentialized space organized by rational practice and centralized power, but a space of dispersion, a fragmented space of otherness and difference, a space in which nothing is universal but everything is local and specific. Likewise, the position of space in theory is transformed from mirror of sociality to playground of difference. Such a space is analogous to a text which escapes author-ity; such a space is an erotic landscape of desire. In such a space, difference is a dynamic, productive moment, not something left over. In the extreme, geography becomes entirely deconstructive in that writing difference is impossible – although it must occasionally risk making sense to make space for an Other conveniently yet to come. In less extreme versions, space is the soil in which difference can flourish. In all cases, space is rethought from plane of similarity to profusion of possibilities.

If geography is about difference in contexts of similarity then it has much to learn from feminist thought. For the notion of difference is debated fiercely by feminists, originally in terms of differences with men, increasingly in terms of differences within the different. And if contemporary human geography is involved in a search for different epistemologies, then again it has much to learn, for the critique of conventional science – this time as masculinity scarcely disguised, or as false universality – again has a long, contentious history in feminist thought. The two variants of difference, conceptually, methodologically, come together in the notion of situated knowledges – claiming objectivity because of immersion in particular circumstances. Feminist geography, itself immersed in feminist theory, moves from spatial differences between women and men in general to the construction of gender identities in particular spaces. Opposed to masculinist conceptions of space inherent in the received wisdom it receives, feminist geography begins to construct an alternative paradoxical space, which it proposes researching using new, critical methods. In this developing feminist conception, place identities are unfixed, contested, multiple and places open and porous, far different from the places of humanism, the space of positivism, or Marxism's economic landscapes. Yet such notions (contested, multiple, etc.) are yet to be specified, ideas whose evolution is often retarded by too stifling a political correctness.

Thus, geography exits modern knowledge in a form which resembles its entry, interest in difference if not in differentiation, but with thinking at a level which demonstrates the influence of a succession of philosophies, at a level which shows its entry into modern, and now postmodern, social theory.

Geography as Spatial Theory

In the introduction, we argued that geography is the study of relations between society and nature, space being the surface expanse of natural environment worked up by social forces into humanized landscapes. As the book developed, it soon became apparent that this relation is part of a broader and even more fundamental relation between mind and matter, or culture and nature, and that issues of some significance, like the natural or spiritual origins of consciousness, and the character of representations of people and earth, are involved in geographical understanding. In this increasingly broad discussion, the question has continually recurred: how to conceptualize space and nature? Two main philosophical approaches were explored: idealism and realism/materialism. In idealism, the knower imposes order on the world, one fundamental dimension of this order being space. In Kantian transcendental idealism, the self imposes a prior structure on sense impressions, including those of space and time, while space reflects the nature of the knowing subject rather than the object coming to be known. Thus, Kant finds space to be an abstract frame of reference which can .be examined independently of matter. This Kantian philosophy of space, space as the container projected by the mind as an organizing framework for objects and events, is the source of much of the early philosophy of regional geography: thus, the Hettner–Hartshorne notion of regionalism and uniqueness. This is an *idealist–absolute* conception of space in that the origins of mind (consciousness) are metaphysically "explained" while the space discovered by that mind is empty and infinite.

In scientific realism, by contrast, space is a substantial extension existing independently of, yet prior to, the mind which indeed becomes knowledgeable by encountering objects in space. In this way, real space structures the contents of the mind, creates its inner space, and is the source of human conceptions of space. But here, two conceptual problems occur which trace through modern geography as central quandaries of our discipline. In the first, the tendency is for philosophical thought to abstract space from matter – thus, in Newton's conception, absolute space exists separately from matter, constituting a universal receptacle in which objects are located – space as a frame of reference or coordinate system (Smith 1984: 67–8). While this absolute space is said to be a thing in itself existing independently of matter, it is abstracted from matter, and not projected by a prior mind, hence, it amounts to a *realist–absolute* conception of space. Relative space, by contrast, consists of relations between pieces of matter, relations between objects which have material substance: this is a *realist–relative* conception of space. For Harvey (1973: 13), space can be regarded as absolute, a thing in itself, existing independently of matter; as relative, a relationship which exists only because objects exist and relate with each other; or "relational space" can, in the fashion of Leibnitz, be regarded as contained in objects (i.e. objects contain their relationships with other objects); space is not absolute, relative, or relational in and of itself, but can be one, or all, depending on circumstances.

Some of the difficulties in conceptualizing the relation between absolute and relative real space surface in *realist philosophy*. For Harre, science consists of knowledge of the existence of the constitutions and natures of real things. Space is the totality of places where things can exist at a given time. This totality can be considered as a system of relations – for example, things related by "betweenness." But also, places can be considered in abstraction from the particular things occupying them. For Sayer (1985: 52), following Harre, while space is constituted by objects it is not reducible to them and is independent of the types of object present – this is a realist notion of absolute space. Yet given that "space as such" is a contentless abstraction, for Sayer there can be no "science of space," as in the positivist geographic tradition of absolute space. Thus, abstract social theory, in the transcendental realist tradition, considers space only as far as the necessary spatial properties of objects (extent, form, etc.) are involved. Such properties are relatively insignificant and abstract claims for the influence of absolute (real) space are indifferent. This changes with concrete research on relative (real) space, for the causal powers possessed by objects are activated (or not) depending on the contingent relations between them. In criticism, we argued that earth space is never, in reality, mere in-betweenness, but is always stretches of (socially altered) natural environment. Things cannot be separated from the relations which form them. Thus, space consists of objects in their relations across environment and not the alienated relations alone. From this restated realist view there can be an abstract science of absolute real space, one of relative real space, and, in the tradition of Ollman's internal relations, a relational theory of real space.

Moving to a second group of related problems, these concern how space is remade by human action, how it is represented in mind, discourse and culture, and how representations relate to human actions in space. Much of this book involves the various aspects of this set of "problems." Let us deal initially with the making of space. In *existential phenomenology*, Heidegger finds inadequate the western philosophy of space as container; a more adequate view is "spatiality," practical involvement generating a fundamental sense of space. Thus, the primary sense of space is not abstract and geometric but embodied – there is a fundamental spatiality embedded in existence. The hermeneutic of space searches for an ontological, existential understanding of the universal structural characteristics of human spatiality as the precondition for understanding more exact places and spaces. In this argument, the absolute space of Galileo, Descartes, and Newton, characterized as homogenous expanse, equivalent in all directions, and not perceptible to the senses, is not the genuine, objective space: instead, space is the geographic form of places created by practical concerns. Space encountered in practical ways (through work, dwelling, etc.) then becomes a theme for science through formalization: abstract spaces of various kinds and degrees of generality can be projected by mental abstraction; ultimately, the possibility exists for a purely mathematical space. However, the notion of "concern" in existential phenomenology can be questioned as a descendant of Husserl's (a priori) intentionality, itself a residue of Kantian transcendental idealism.

In *historical materialism*, conceptions of space are produced by different types of human activities: there is a history of theories of space forming part of the history of human experiences. The development of second out of first nature, with advance of the forces of production, is the material basis of a theoretical differentiation between absolute, natural, physical space and relative, social space. But Smith's (1984) account is critical of the dualism of space and society implicit in this view; instead he sees the Marxist tradition dialectically intertwining space and society. Thus, Smith substitutes the "production of space" as means of demonstrating that practice and space are integrated at the level of the concept of space. Our criticism is that "production" is too strong a term, especially when space is considered to be stretches of nature – the "social construction of nature" is surely an arrogant, even dangerous, exaggeration, and terms like the physical transformation or social conception of space/nature are preferable. In any case, space is *transformed* by social forces acting under the influence of social relations, so that socialized space is a class phenomenon in Marxism, a gendered phenomenon in socialist feminism. Structuralist theories, such as that of the early Castells, specify the component parts of the production of space using the organizing concept of mode of production: hence, there are economic, political, and ideological spaces articulated differentially. Spatial dialectics theorizes the dynamics of developments in spatial components, both instances and regions, while social semiotics examines space-making as a signifying process. Here, the tendency is towards an increased emphasis on ideas, ideologies, discourses, and concepts as forces in the transformation of natural expanse into social space. At this point, another related aspect of the "problem" of space occurs, in that the ideas guiding the social construction of space have autonomy from material practice – the discussion threads back again towards transcendental idealism! Here, we might recall Lefebvre's discussion.

Lefebvre distinguishes fields of space: physical (nature), mental (abstraction), and social (everyday life) united into a single theory by the social production of social space. The triad of spatial concepts employed in analyzing space consists of: spatial practices; representations of space; and representational space lived through images and symbols. Lefebvre also proposes a movement from "absolute space," original natural space, to "abstract space," abstract labor under capitalism produces an abstract space of things/signs and their merely formal, quantitative relations, which erase (absolute) distinctions derived from nature and body. Homogenization in abstract space is opposed by differential space, as distinctions (uneven development) are also generated by contradictory space-transforming processes. The main innovation here is the inclusion of representations in the social transformation of absolute into social space, and the subsequent emphasis on representational space, space as lived not only materially but also through representations – this shows the influence of semiotics in social theory and geography. Yet there remains a question of the relation between materiality and representationality even in this complex formulation. The ghost of Kant haunts the geographical imagination as a specter rising from the intellectual graveyard. As a careful review of the "social construction of nature" by Judith Gerber (1997: 3) concludes, overcoming the original Cartesian dualism between nature and society entails not only changes in language and categories but requires investigation of the "complex processes at work when the physical, the mental and the social interact."

So let us turn to recent proposals. A "trialectic" disciple of Lebebvre, Soja (1996) argues that mainstream geography has a dual mode of thinking: Firstspace, fixed on the concrete materiality of spatial forms; and Secondspace, conceived in ideas about space (cognitive representations). Soja finds another form of spatial awareness emerging, a thirding of the spatial imagination simultaneously real, imagined, and more ("real-and-imagined"): hence, the notion of Thirdspace. Examples might include Foucault's spaces of dispersion (Philo 1992), Rose's (1993) paradoxical spaces which dissolve divisions between mind and body, metaphorical and real, and Massey's (1994) space as "dynamic simultaneity," the lived world as simultaneous multiplicity of intersecting spaces held precariously together by relations of paradox or antagonism. Yet it is easier to "dissolve" the dreaded binary, real and imaginary, by melding them into one term (real-and-imagined) than it is to synthesize what remain as somewhat distinct spheres of existence, the hopelessly mental and the all too mortal. Thus, we seem to be left with two current positions: a poststructural *discursive idealist* conception of space, in which imaginaries structure multiple spaces; and a radical humanist *discursive materialist* view, in which imaginaries arise from prior real spaces to help structure the practices currently altering contemporary spaces. While both schools have conceptions of absolute, relative, and relational spaces, the tendency is for absolute space to recede from the geographical memory, and relative and relational spaces (represented, representational, and materially altered) to fascinate this area of social thought. Geography is changed almost beyond recognition in style and sophistication, yet it is dominated still by ancient themes. Is this an eternal return of almost-the-same?

Bibliography

Ackerman, E. A. 1945. Geographic training, wartime research, and immediate professional objectives. *Annals of the Association of American Geographers* 35: 121–43.

Ackerman, E. A. 1958. Geography as a fundamental research discipline. Department of Geography, University of Chicago, Research Paper 53.

Ackerman, E. A. 1963. Where is a research frontier? *Annals of the Association of American Geographers* 53: 429–40.

Aglietta, M. 1979. *A Theory of Capitalist Regulation: The US Experience*, trans. D. Fernbach. London: New Left Books.

Agnew, J. and J. Duncan (eds) 1989. *The Power of Place: Bringing Together Geographical and Sociological Imaginations*. Boston: Unwin Hyman.

Agnew, J., D. N. Livingstone, and A. Rogers (eds) 1996. *Human Geography: An Essential Anthology*. Oxford: Blackwell.

Albaum, M. 1973. *Geography and Contemporary Issues*. New York: John Wiley.

Alonso, W. 1964. *Location and Land Use: Toward a General Theory of Land Rent*. Cambridge: Harvard University Press.

Althusser, L. 1965. *Lire le Capital*. Paris: F. Maspero.

Althusser, L. 1969. *For Marx*, trans. B. Brewster. Harmondsworth: Penguin.

Althusser, L. 1971. *Lenin and Philosophy and Other Essays*. London: Verso.

Althusser, L. 1976. *Essays on Ideology*. London: New Left Books.

Althusser, L. and E. Balibar, 1968. *Reading Capital*. London: New Left Books.

Anderson, B. 1983. *Imagined Communities*. London: Verso.

Anderson, P. 1980. *Arguments Within English Marxism*. London: Verso.

Anderson, P. 1983. *In the Tracks of Historical Materialism*. Chicago: University of Chicago Press.

Antipode 1978–9. *Anarchism and Environment*: double issue, 10(3) and 11(1).

Anzaldua, G. 1987. *Borderlands? La Frontera*. San Francisco: Spinsters/Aunt Lute Press.

Anzaldua, G. and C. Moraga (eds) 1981. *Making Face/Making Soul*. San Francisco: Spinsters/Aunt Lute Press.

Archer, K. 1987. Mythology and the problem of reading in urban and regional research. *Society and Space* 5: 384–93.

Ashcroft B., G. Griffiths, and H. Tiffin 1989. *The Empire Writes Back: Theory and Practice in Post-Colonial Literatures*. London: Routledge.

Ayer, A. J. 1952. *Language, Truth and Logic*. New York: Dover.

Ayer, A. J. (ed.) 1959. *Logical Positivism*. New York: Free Press.

Bachelard, G. 1938. *La Formation de espirit scientifique*. Paris: J. Urin.

Bachelard, G. 1951. *L'Activité rationaliste de la physique contemporaire*. Paris: Presses Universitaires de France.

Bachelard, G. 1958. *The Poetics of Space*. Boston: Beacon Press.

Bachelard, G. 1971. *Epistemologie*. Paris: Presses Universitaires de France.

Baffoun, A. 1985. Future of feminism in Africa. *ECHOE, AAWORD Newsletter* 2/3: 4–6.

Balbus, I. D. 1982. *Marxism and Domination*. Princeton: Princeton University Press.

Balser, D. 1987. *Sisterhood and Solidarity: Feminism and Labor in Modern Times*. Boston: South End Press.

Baran, P. 1957. *The Politics of Economic Growth*. New York: Monthly Review Press.

Barnes, B. 1977. *Interests and the Growth of Knowledge*. Andover: Routledge and Kegan Paul.

Barnes, T. 1992. Reading the texts of theoretical economic geography: the role of physical and biological metaphors. In Barnes, T. and J. Duncan (eds) 1992. *Writing Worlds: Discourse, Text and Metaphor in the Representation of Landscape*. London: Routledge, 118–35.

Barnes, T. and J. Duncan (eds) 1992. *Writing Worlds: Discourse, Text and Metaphor in the Representation of Landscape*. London: Routledge.

Barrett, M. 1980. *Women's Oppression Today: Problems in Marxist Feminist Analysis*. London: New Left Books.

Bartels, D. 1973. Between theory and metatheory. In R. J. Chorley (ed.), *Directions in Geography*. London: Methuen.

Barthes, R. 1967. *Writing Degree Zero*. London: Jonathan Cape.

Barthes, R. 1972. *Mythologies*. London: Jonathan Cape.

Bassin, M. 1987. Imperialism and the nation state in Friedrich Ratzel's political geography. *Progress in Human Geography* 11: 473–95.

Bataille, G. 1985. *Visions of Excess: Selected Writings, 1927–1939*, ed. A. Staekl. Minneapolis: University of Minnesota Press.

Baudrillard, J. 1968. *Le Système des objects*. Paris: Denoel-Gouthier. Trans. 1996 by J. Benedict as *The System of Objects*. London: Verso.

Baudrillard, J. 1972. *Pour une critique de l'economie politique du signe*. Paris: Gallimard.

Baudrillard, J. 1975. *The Mirror of Production*, trans. M. Poster. St Louis: Telos Press.

Baudrillard, J. 1979. *De la seduction*. Paris: Gonthier.

Baudrillard, J. 1981. *For a Critique of the Political Economy of the Sign*. St Louis: Telos Press.

Baudrillard, J. 1983. *Simulations*. New York: Semiotexte.

Baudrillard, J. 1984. Interview: games with vestiges. *On the Beach* 5: 19–25.

Baudrillard, J. 1986. *America*. London: Verso.

Baudrillard, J. 1987. *Forget Foucault*. New York: Semiotexte.

Baudrillard, J. 1988. *Jean Baudrillard: Selected Writings*, ed. M. Poster. Stanford: Stanford University Press.

Baudrillard, J. 1996. *The System of Objects*, trans. J. Benedict. London: Verso.

Bauman, Z. 1978. *Hermeneutics and Social Science*. New York: Columbia University Press.

Bell, D. 1973. *The Coming of Post-Industrial Society*. New York: Basic Books.

Bell, D. and G. Valentine 1995. *Mapping Desire*. London: Routledge.

Bennett, R. J. 1985. Quantification and relevance. In R. J. Johnston (ed.), *The Future of Geography*. London: Methuen, 211–24.

Bennington, G. and J. Derrida 1993. *Jacques Derrida*. Chicago: University of Chicago Press.

Benton, T. 1984. *The Rise and Fall of Structural Marxism: Althusser and His Influence*. New York: St Martin's Press.

Benton, T. 1989. Marxism and natural limits: an ecological critique and reconstruction. *New Left Review* 178: 51–81.

Berger, D. C. and T. Luckmann 1966. *The Social Construction of Reality: A Treatise in the Sociology of Knowledge*. Harmondsworth: Penguin.

Berger, J. 1972. *Ways of Seeing*. Harmondsworth: Penguin.

Berman, M. 1983. *All That Is Solid Melts Into Air: The Experience of Modernity*. London: Verso.

Bernal, J. D. 1971. *Science in History*. Cambridge: MIT Press.

Bernstein, R. 1992. *The New Constellation: The Ethical–Political Horizons of Modernity/Postmodernity*. Cambridge: MIT Press.

Berry, B. J. L. 1964. Approaches to regional analysis: a synthesis. *Annals of the Association of American Geographers* 54: 2–11.

Berry, B. and W. Garrison, 1958. Alternate explanations of urban rank–size relationships. *Annals of the Association of American Geographers* 48: 83–91.

Berry, B. and F. Horton 1970. *Geographical Perspectives on Urban Systems*. Englewood Cliffs, NJ: Prentice-Hall.

Berry, B. and A. Pred 1961. *Central Place Studies: A Bibliography of Theory and Applications*. Philadelphia: Regional Science Institute.

Best, S. 1995. *The Politics of Historical Vision: Marx, Foucault, Habermas*. New York: Guilford.

Best, S. and D. Kellner 1991. *Postmodern Theory: Critical Interrogations*. New York: Guilford.

Bhaba, H. 1990. The third space. In J. Rutherford (ed.), *Identity, Community, Culture, Difference*. London: Lawrence and Wishart, 207–21.

Bhaba, H. 1994. *The Location of Culture*. London: Routledge.

Bhaskar, R. 1978. *A Realist Theory of Science*. Hassocks, Sussex: Harvester.

Bhaskar, R. 1979. *The Possibility of Naturalism*. Hassocks, Sussex: Harvester.

Bhaskar, R. 1986. *Scientific Realism and Human Emancipation*. London: Verso.

Bhaskar, R. 1989. *Reclaiming Reality: A Critical Introduction to Contemporary Philosophy*. London: Verso.

Bhaskar, R. 1993. *Dialectic: The Pulse of Freedom*. London: Verso.

Billinge, M., D. Gregory, and R. Martin (eds) 1983. *Recollections of a Revolution: Geography as Spatial Science*. New York: St Martin's Press.

Binnie, J. 1997. Coming out in geography: towards a queer epistemology? *Society and Space* 15: 223–7.

Blaikie, P. 1985. *The Political Economy of Soil Erosion in Developing Countries*. New York: Longman.

Blaikie, P. and H. Brookfield 1987. *Land Degradation and Society*. London: Methuen.

Blaut, J. 1961. Space and process. *Professional Geographer* 13(4): 1–7.

Blaut, J. 1962. Object and relationship. *Professional Geographer* 14(6): 1–7.

Blaut, J. 1970. Geographic models of imperialism. *Antipode* 2: 65–85.

Blaut, J. 1976. Where was capitalism born? *Antipode* 8: 1–11.

Blaut, J. 1994. *The Colonizer's Model of the World*. London: Guilford.

Bloor, D. 1976. *Knowledge and Social Imagery*. Andover: Routledge and Kegan Paul.

Blum, V. and H. Nast 1996. Where's the difference? The heterosexualization of alterity in Henri Lefebvre and Jacques Lacan. *Society and Space* 14: 559–80.

Blunt, A. and G. Rose (eds) 1994. *Writing Women and Space: Colonial and Postcolonial Geographies*. New York: Guilford.

Boggs, C. 1976. *Gramsci's Marxism*. London: Pluto.

Bogue, R. 1989. *Deleuze and Guattari*. London: Routledge.

Bondi, L. 1990. Progress in geography and gender: feminism and difference. *Progress in Human Geography* 14: 438–46.

Bondi, L. 1991. Gender divisions and gentrification: a critique. *Transactions of the Institute of British Geographers* 16: 190–8.

Bondi, L. 1992. Gender and dichotomy. *Progress in Human Geography* 16: 98–104.

Bondi, L. and M. Domosh 1992. Other figures in other places: on feminism, postmodernism and geography. *Society and Space* 10: 199–213.

Botting, P. 1973. *Humboldt and the Cosmos*. London: Sphere.

Bourdieu, P. 1977. *Outline for a Theory of Practice*. Cambridge: Cambridge University Press.

Bourdieu, P. 1991. *The Political Ontology of Martin Heidegger*. Stanford: Stanford University Press.

Bowen, M. 1981. *Empiricism and Geographical Thought: From Francis Bacon to Alexander von Humboldt*. Cambridge: Cambridge University Press.

Bowie, M. 1979. Jacques Lacan. In J. Sturrock (ed.), *Structuralism and Since*. Oxford: Oxford University Press, 116–53.

Bowie, M. 1991. *Lacan*. Cambridge: Harvard University Press.

Bowlby, S., J. Foord, and S. Mackenzie 1980. Feminism and geography. *Area* 14: 19–25.

Bowlby, S., J. Lewis, L. McDowell, and J. Foord 1989. The geography of gender. In R. Peet and N. Thrift (eds), *New Models in Geography*. London: Unwin Hyman, vol. 2, 157–75.

Boyer, R. 1986. *La Theorie de la regulation: une analyse critique*. Paris: La Decouverte.

Braithwaite, R. B. 1953. *Scientific Explanation*. New York: Harper.

Breitbart, M. 1975. Impressions of an anarchist landscape. *Antipode* 7: 44–9.

Breitbart, M. 1978. The theory and practice of anarchist decentralism in Spain, 1936–1939: the integration of community and environment. PhD Dissertation, Clark University.

Brewer, A. 1984. *A Guide to Marx's Capital*. Cambridge: Cambridge University Press.

Bronstein, A. 1982. *The Triple Struggle*. Boston: South End Press.

Brownill, S. and S. Halford 1990. Understanding women's involvement in local politics: how useful is a formal/informal dichotomy? *Political Geography Quarterly* 9: 396–414.

Brownmiller, S. 1975. *Against Our Will: Men, Women and Rape*. New York: Simon and Schuster.

Bruhnes, J. 1952. *Human Geography*. London: Harrap.

Buch-Hanson, M. and B. Nielson 1977. Marxist geography and the concept of territorial structure. *Antipode* 9: 1–12.

Bunch, C., M. Dutt, and S. Fried 1995. *Beijing 1995: A Global Referendum on the Human Rights of Women*. Rutgers, NJ: Center for Women's Global Leadership.

Bunge, W. 1966. *Theoretical Geography*, 2nd edn. Lund Studies in Geography Series C, no. 1. Lund: C. W. K. Gleerlup.

Bunge, W. 1969. The first years of the Detroit Geographical Expedition: a personal report. *Field Notes* Discussion Paper 1.

Burger, P. 1984. *Theories of the Avant-Garde*. Manchester: University of Manchester Press.

Burnett, P. 1973. Social change, the status of women and models of city form and development. *Antipode* 5: 57–62.

Burton, I. 1963. The quantitative revolution and theoretical geography. *Canadian Geographer* 7: 151–62.

Butler, J. 1990. *Gender Trouble: Feminism and the Subversion of Identity*. New York: Routledge.

Butler, J. 1993. *Bodies that Matter: On the Discursive Limits of Sex*. New York: Routledge.

Buttimer, A. 1971 *Society and Milieu in the French Geographic Tradition*. Chicago: Rand McNally.

Buttimer, A. 1974. Values in geography. Washington: Association of American Geographers Commission on College Geography, Resource Paper 24.

Buttimer, A. 1976. Grasping the dynamism of lifeworld. *Annals of the Association of American Geographers* 66: 277–92.

Buttimer, A. 1980a. Home, reach and the sense of place. In A. Buttimer and D. Seamon (eds), *The Human Experience of Space and Place*. London: Croom Helm, 166–87.

Buttimer, A. 1980b. Social space and the planning of residential areas. In A. Buttimer and D. Seamon (eds), *The Human Experience of Space and Place*. London: Croom Helm, 21–54.

Buttimer, A. 1980c. Introduction. In In A. Buttimer and D. Seamon (eds), *The Human Experience of Space and Place*. London: Croom Helm, 13–18.

Buttimer, A. and D. Seamon (eds) 1980. *The Human Experience of Space and Place*. London: Croom Helm.

Callari, A., S. Cullenberg, and C. Biewener (eds) 1995. *Marxism in the Postmodern Age*. New York: Guilford.

Callinicos, A. 1976. *Althusser's Marxism*. London: Pluto.

Callinicos, A. 1985. *Marxism and Philosophy*. Oxford: Oxford University Press.

Callinicos, A. 1990. *Against Postmodernism: A Marxist Critique*. London: St Martin's Press.

Cangelheim, G. 1943. *La Normal et la pathologique*. Paris: Presses Universitaires de France.

Cangelheim, G. 1988. *Ideology and Rationality in the History of the Life Sciences*. Cambridge: MIT Press.

Cannon, S. F. 1978. *Science in Culture: The Early Victorian Period*. New York: Dawson and Science History Publications.

Caputo, J. D. 1978. *The Mystical Element in Heidegger's Thought*. Athens, Ohio: Ohio University Press.

Caputo, J. D. 1987. *Radical Hermeneutics*. Bloomington: Indiana University Press.

Carnap, R. 1935. *Philosophy and Logical Syntax*. London: K. Paul, Trench, Trubner.

Carnap, R. 1958. *Meaning and Necessity: A Study in Semantics and Model Logic*. Chicago: University of Chicago Press.

Carney, J., R. Hudson, and J. Lewis (eds) 1980. *Regions in Crisis*. London: Croom Helm.

Carter, A. 1979. *The Sadeian Woman*. London: Virago.

Carter, E., J. Donald, and J. Squires 1993. *Space and Place: Theories of Identity and Location*. London: Lawrence and Wishart.

Cassirer, E. 1951. *The Philosophy of the Enlightenment*. Princeton: Princeton University Press.

Castells, M. 1977. *The Urban Question: A Marxist Approach*, trans. A. Sheridan. Cambridge, Mass.: MIT Press.

Castells, M. 1978. *City, Class and Power*, trans. E. Lebas. New York: St Martin's Press.

Castoriadis, C. 1991. The social historical: mode of being, problems of knowledge. In C. Castoriadis, *Philosophy, Politics, Autonomy*. New York: Oxford University Press, 33–46.

Castree, N. 1995. The nature of produced nature: materiality and knowledge construction in Marxism. *Antipode* 27: 12–48.

Castree, N. 1996. Birds, mice and geography: Marxism and dialectics. *Transactions of the Institute of British Geographers* 21: 342–62.

Chapman, J. D. 1966. The status of geography. *Canadian Geographer* 10: 133–44.

Chodorow, N. 1978. *The Reproduction of Mothering: Psychoanalysis and the Sociology of Gender*. Berkeley: University of California Press.

Chouinard, V. and R. Fincher 1983. A critique of "Structural Marxism and Human Geography". *Annals of the Association of American Geographers* 73: 137–46.

Christaller, W. 1933. *Die Zentralen Orte in Suddeutschland*. Jena: Gustav Fischer Verlag. Trans. in C. W. Baskin 1957. A critique and translation of W. Christaller's *Die Zentralen Orte in Suddeutschland*. PhD dissertation, University of Virginia.

Christopherson, S. 1989. On being outside "the project." *Antipode* 21: 83–9.

Cixous, H. 1981. The laugh of the Medusa. In S. E. Mark and I. de Courtivron (eds), *New French Feminisms*. New York: Schocken.

Clark, M. 1990. *Nietzsche on Truth and Philosophy*. Cambridge: Cambridge University Press.

Clifford, J. and G. E. Marcus (eds) 1986. *Writing Culture: The Poetics and Politics of Ethnography*. Berkeley: University of California Press.

Cloke, P., C. Philo, and D. Sadler 1991. *Approaching Human Geography: An Introduction to Contemporary Theoretical Debates*. New York: Guilford.

Cockburn, C. 1983. *Brothers: Male Dominance and Technical Change*. London: Pluto.

Cohen, G. A. 1978. *Karl Marx's Theory of History: A Defence*. Princeton: Princeton University Press.

Cohen, I. J. 1989. *Structuration Theory: Anthony Giddens and the Constitution of Social Life*. New York: St Martin's Press.

Colletti, L. 1972. *From Rousseau to Lenin*. London: New Left Books.

Colletti, L. 1973. *Marxism and Hegel*. London: New Left Books.

Combahee River Collective 1984. A black feminist statement. In A. M. Jaggar and P. S. Rothenberg (eds), *Feminist Frameworks*. New York: McGraw Hill, 202–9.

Comte, A. 1988. *Introduction to Positive Philosophy*. Indianapolis: Hackett.

Connolly, J. M. and T. Keutner (eds) 1988a. *Hermeneutics Versus Science? Three German Views*. Notre Dame: University of Notre Dame Press.

Connolly, J. M. and T. Keutner 1988b. Introduction: interpretation, decidability, and meaning. In J. M. Connolly and T. Keutner (eds), *Hermeneutics Versus Science? Three German Views*. Notre Dame: University of Notre Dame Press, 1–67.

Cooke, P. 1986. The changing urban and regional system in the United Kingdom. *Regional Studies* 20: 243–51.

Cooke, P. 1987. Clinical inference and geographic theory. *Antipode* 19: 407–16.

Cooke, P. 1989a. *Localities: The Changing Face of Urban Britain*. London: Unwin Hyman.

Cooke, P. 1989b. Locality-theory and the poverty of "spatial variation". *Antipode* 21: 261–73.

Cooke, P. 1990. *Back to the Future*. London: Unwin Hyman.

Corey, K. 1972. Advocacy in planning: a reflective analysis. *Antipode* 4: 42–63.

Cornu, A. 1957. *The Origins of Marxian Thought*. Springfield, Ill.: C. C. Thomas.

Corragio, J. L. 1977. Social forms of space organization and their trends in Latin America. *Antipode* 9: 14–28.

Cosgrove, D. 1984. *Social Formation and Symbolic Landscape*. London: Croom Helm.

Cosgrove, D. 1989. Geography is everywhere: culture and symbolism in human landscapes. In D. Gregory and R. Walford (eds), *Horizons in Human Geography*. Totowa: Barnes and Noble, 118–35.

Cosgrove, D. and S. Daniels (eds) 1987. *The Iconography of Landscape*. Cambridge: Cambridge University Press.

Cox, K. and R. Golledge 1969. *Behavioural Problems in Geography: A Symposium*. Evanston: Northwestern University Press.

Cox, K. and A. Mair 1989. Levels of abstraction in locality studies. *Antipode* 21: 121–32.

Cox, K. and A. Mair 1991. From localised social structures to localities as agents. *Environment and Planning A* 23: 197–213.

Crook, S. 1991. *Modernist Radicalism and its Aftermath*. London: Routledge.

Crush, J. 1995. *Power of Development*. London: Routledge.

Culler, J. 1973. The linguistic basis of structuralism. In D. Robey (ed.), *Structuralism: An Introduction*. Oxford: Clarendon Press, 20–36.

Culler, J. 1982. *On Deconstruction: Theory and Criticism after Structuralism*. Ithaca: Cornell University Press.

Cutler, A., B. Hindess, P. Hirst, and A. Hussain 1977. *Marx's Capital and Capitalism Today*, 2 vols. London: Routledge and Kegan Paul.

Dallmayr, F. 1993. *The Other Heidegger*. Ithaca: Cornell University Press.

Daly, M. 1978. *Gyn/Ecology: The Metaethics of Radical Feminism*. London: The Women's Press.

Daniels, S. 1989. Marxism, culture and the duplicity of landscape. In R. Peet and N. Thrift (eds), *New Models in Geography*. London: Unwin Hyman, vol. 2, 196–220.

Dardel, E. 1952. *L'Homme et la terre: nature de realité geographique*. Paris: Presses Universitaires de France.

Darwin, C. 1964. *The Origin of Species*. Cambridge: Harvard University Press.

Davis, A. 1982. *Women, Race and Class*. London: The Women's Press.

Davis, W. M. 1900. Physical geography in the high school. *School Review* 8: 388–404.

Davis, W. M. 1909. *Geographical Essays*. Boston: Ginn.

Dear, M. 1986. Postmodernism and planning. *Society and Space* 4: 367–84.

Dear, M. 1988. The postmodern challenge: reconstructing human geography. *Transactions of the Association of American Geographers* 13: 262–74.

Dear, M. 1994. Postmodern human geography: a preliminary assessment. *Erdkunde* 48: 2–13.

de Beauvoir, S. 1978. *The Second Sex*, trans. H. M. Parshley. New York: Knopf.

Debord, G. 1983. *Society of the Spectacle*. Detroit: Black and Red.

de Certeau, M. 1984. *The Practice of Everyday Life*. Berkeley: University of California Press.

de Certeau, M. 1986. *Heterologies: Discourse on the Other*. Manchester: Manchester University Press.

de Lauretis, T. 1987. *Technologies of Gender*. Bloomington: Indiana University Press.

Deleuze, G. 1983. *Nietzsche and Philosophy*. New York: Columbia University Press.

Deleuze, G. 1984. *Kant's Critical Philosophy: The Doctrine of the Faculties*. Minneapolis: University of Minnesota Press.

Deleuze, G. 1988. *Foucault*. Minneapolis: University of Minnesota Press.

Deleuze, G. and F. Guattari 1983. *Anti-Oedipus: Capitalism and Schizophrenia*. Minneapolis: University of Minnesota Press.

Deleuze, G. and F. Guattari 1987. *A Thousand Plateaus*. Minneapolis: University of Minnesota Press.

Deleuze, G. and F. Guattari 1994. *What Is Philosophy?* New York: Columbia University Press.

Demeritt, D. 1996. Social theory and the reconstruction of science and geography. *Transactions of the Institute of British Geographers* 21: 484–503.

Derrida, J. 1974. *Of Grammatology*, trans. G. Spivak. Baltimore: Johns Hopkins University Press.

Derrida, J. 1978. *Writing and Difference*, trans. A. Bass. Chicago: University of Chicago Press.

Derrida, J. 1981. *Margins of Philosophy*. Chicago: University of Chicago Press.

Derrida, J. 1994. *Specters of Marx*. New York: Routledge.

Descartes, R. 1956. *Discourse on Method*. New York: Liberal Arts Press.

Descartes, R. 1968. *The Philosophical Works of Descartes*, trans. E. Haldane and G. R. T. Ross. Cambridge: Cambridge University Press.

Descombes, V. 1980. *Modern French Philosophy*. Cambridge: Cambridge University Press.

Detroit Geographical Expedition 1972. The Trumbull community. *Field Notes* Discussion Paper 4.

Deutsche, R. 1991. Boys town. *Society and Space* 9: 5–30.

Dewey, J. 1958. *Experience and Nature*. New York: Dover.

Dewey, J. 1979. *The Quest for Certainty*. New York: Paragon.

Dews, P. 1984. Power and subjectivity in Foucault. *New Left Review* 144: 72–95.

DiStefano, C. 1990. Dilemmas of difference: feminism, modernity and postmodernism. In L. Nicholson (ed.), *Feminism/Postmodernism*. New York: Routledge.

Doel, M. 1993. Proverbs for paranoids: writing geography on hollowed ground. *Transactions of the Institute of British Geographers* 18: 377–94.

Doel, M. 1994. Deconstruction on the move: from libidinal economy to liminal materialism. *Environment and Planning A* 26: 1041–59.

Doel, M. 1996. A hundred thousand lines of flight: a machinic introduction to the nomad thought and scrumpled geography of Gilles Deleuze and Felix Guattari. *Society and Space* 14: 421–39.

Dreyfus, H. L. and P. Rabinow 1983. *Michel Foucault: Beyond Structuralism and Hermeneutics*. Chicago: University of Chicago Press.

Driver, F. 1985. Power, space, and the body: a critical assessment of Foucault's *Discipline and Punish*. *Society and Space* 3: 425–46.

Driver, F. 1992. Geography's empire: histories of geographical knowledge. *Society and Space* 10: 23–40.

DuBois, E. C. 1994. Woman suffrage around the world: three phases of suffragist internationalism. In C. Daley and M. Nolan (eds), *Suffrage and Beyond: International Feminist Perspectives*. New York: New York University Press, 252–76.

DuBois, M. 1991. The governance of the third world: a Foucauldian perspective on power relations in development. *Alternatives* 16: 1–30.

Duncan, J. 1990. *The City as Text: The Politics of Landscape Interpretation in the Kandyan Kingdom*. Cambridge: Cambridge University Press.

Duncan, J. and N. Duncan 1988. (Re)reading the landscape. *Society and Space* 6: 117–26.

Duncan, J. and D. Ley 1982. Structural Marxism and human geography: a critical assessment. *Annals of the Association of American Geographers* 72: 30–59.

Duncan, S. 1989. What is a locality? In R. Peet and N. Thrift (eds), *New Models in Geography*. London: Unwin Hyman, vol. 2, 221–52.

Duncan, S. 1994. Theorising differences in patriarchy. *Environment and Planning A* 26: 1177–94.

Duncan, S. and M. Savage 1989. Space, scale and locality. *Antipode* 21: 179–206.

Duncan, S. and M. Savage 1991. Commentary. *Environment and Planning A* 23: 155–64.

Dunford, M. 1990 Theories of regulation. *Society and Space* 8: 297–321.

Dunford, M. and D. Perrons 1983. *The Arena of Capital*. New York: St Martin's Press.

Dunn, E. S. 1954. *The Location of Agricultural Production*. Gainesville: University of Florida Press.

Dunn, J., J. O. Urmson, and A. J. Ayer 1992. *The British Empiricists*. Oxford: Oxford University Press.

Dupre, L. 1966. *The Philosophical Foundations of Marxism*. New York: Harcourt, Brace and World.

Eagleton, T. 1983. *Literary Theory: An Introduction*. Minneapolis: University of Minnesota Press.

Eagleton, T. 1987. Awakening from modernity. *Times Literary Supplement*, 20 February.

Eagleton, T. 1991. *Ideology: A Critical Reader*. London: Verso.

Eco, U. 1973. Social life as a sign system. In D. Robey (ed.), *Structuralism: An Introduction*. Oxford: Clarendon Press, 57–72.

Edie, J. M. 1962. Introduction. In P. Thevanaz, *What Is Phenomenology?* Chicago: Quadrangle, 13–36.

Edwards, M. 1989. The irrelevance of development studies. *Third World Quarterly* 11: 116–35.

Elgie, R. 1970. Rural inmigration, urban ghettoization and their consequences. *Antipode* 2: 35–54.

Elkins, T. H. 1989. Hettner and regional geography in the German-speaking lands in the first forty years of the twentieth century. In N. Entrikin and S. Brunn (eds), *Reflections on Richard Hartshorne's The Nature of Geography*. Washington: Association of American Geographers, 17–34.

Elliot, G. 1986. The Odyssey of Paul Hirst. *New Left Review* 159: 81–105.

Elliot, G. (ed.) 1994. *Althusser: A Critical Reader*. Oxford: Blackwell.

Engels, F. 1940. *Dialectics of Nature*. New York: International Publishers.

Engels, F. 1942. *The Origin of the Family, Private Property and the State*. New York: International Publishers.

Engels, F. 1976. *Anti-Duhrung*. New York: International Publishers.

England, K. 1994. Getting personal: reflexivity, positionality and feminist research. *Professional Geographer* 46: 80–9.

Entrikin, J. N. 1976. Contemporary humanism in geography. *Annals of the Association of American Geographers* 66: 615–32.

Entrikin, J. N. 1985. Humanism, naturalism and geographic thought. *Geographical Analysis* 17: 243–7.

Entrikin, J. N. 1989. Introduction: *The Nature of Geography* in perspective. In N. Entrikin and S. Brunn (eds), *Reflections on Richard Hartshorne's "The Nature of Geography"*. Washington: Association of American Geographers, 1–15.

Entrikin, J. N. 1991. *The Betweenness of Place: Towards a Geography of Modernity*. Baltimore: Johns Hopkins University Press.

Epstein, S. 1987. Gay politics, ethnic identity: the limits of social constructionism. *Socialist Review* 17: 9–54.

Ernst, R., L. Hugg, R. Crooker, and R. Ayotte 1974. Competition and conflict over land use change in the inner city. *Antipode* 6: 70–97.

Escobar, A. 1984–5. Discourse and power in development: Michel Foucault and the relevance of his work to the third world. *Alternatives* 10: 377–400.

Escobar, A. 1988. Power and visibility: development and the invention and management of the third world. *Cultural Anthropology* 3: 428–43.

Escobar, A. 1992. Imagining a post-development era? Critical thought, development and social movements. *Social Text* 31/32: 20–56.

Escobar, A. 1995. *Encountering Development: The Making and Unmaking of the Third World*. Princeton: Princeton University Press.

Evans, S. 1979. *Personal Politics: The Roots of Women's Liberation in the Civil Rights Movement and the New Left*. New York: Vintage.

Eyles, J. and D. Smith (eds) 1988. *Qualitative Methods in Human Geography*. Cambridge: Polity.

Farias, V. 1989. *Heidegger and Nazism*. Philadelphia: Temple University Press.

Farrow, H. 1995. Researching popular theater in Southern Africa: comments on a methodological implementation. *Antipode* 27: 75–81.

Farrow, H., P. Moss, and B. Shaw. 1995. Symposium on feminist participatory research. *Antipode* 27: 71–4.

Febvre, L. 1925. *A Geographical Introduction to History*. London: Kegan, Paul.

Ferguson, A. and N. Folbre 1981. The unhappy marriage of patriarchy and capitalism. In L. Sargent (ed.), *Women and Revolution*. Boston: South End Press.

Ferguson, K. 1993. *The Man Question: Visions of Subjectivity in Feminist Theory*. Berkeley: University of California Press.

Feyerabend, P. 1978. *Against Method*. London: Verso.

Finch, H. L. 1995. *Wittgenstein*. Rochport, Mass.: Element.

Firestone, S. 1970. *The Dialectic of Sex*. New York: Quill.

Fisher, E. and L. Gray MacKay 1996. *Gender Justice: Women's Rights Are Human Rights*. Cambridge: Unitarian Universalist Service Committee.

Fitzsimmons, M. 1989. The matter of nature. *Antipode* 21: 106–20.

Flad, H. 1972. The urban American Indians of Syracuse, New York: human exploration of urban space. *Antipode* 4: 46–63.

Flax, J. 1983. Political philosophy and patriarchal unconscious. In S. Harding and M. B. Hintikka (eds), *Discovering Reality*. Boston: D. Reidel, 245–81.

Flax, J. 1986. Gender as a social problem: in and for feminist theory. *American Studies* 31: 193–213.

Flax, J. 1990. Postmodernism and gender relations in feminist theory. In L. J. Nicholson (ed.), *Feminism/Postmodernism*. New York: Routledge, 39–62.

Foord, J. and N. Gregson 1986. Patriarchy: towards a reconceptualization. *Antipode* 18: 186–211.

Foord, S. 1991. Landscape revisited: a feminist reappraisal. In C. Philo (ed.), *New Words, New Worlds: Reconceptualising Social and Cultural Geography*. Aberystwyth: Cambrian Printers, 151–5.

Forster, E. 1989. How are transcendental arguments possible? In E. Schaper and W. Vossenkuhl (eds), *Reading Kant: New Perspectives on Transcendental Arguments and Critical Philosophy*. Oxford: Basil Blackwell, 3–20.

Foucault, M. 1967. *Madness and Civilization*. New York: Vintage.

Foucault, M. 1972. *The Archaeology of Knowledge and the Discourse on Language*. New York: Pantheon.

Foucault, M. 1973. *The Order of Things*. New York: Vintage.

Foucault, M. 1977. Nietzsche, genealogy, history. In *Michel Foucault: Language, Counter-Memory, Practice*, ed. D. F. Bouchard. New York: Cornell University Press.

Foucault, M. 1978. *The Birth of the Clinic: An Archaeology of Medical Perception*. London: Tavistock.

Foucault, M. 1979a. *Discipline and Punish*. New York: Vintage.

Foucault, M. 1979b. *The History of Sexuality*, vol. 1: *An Introduction*. London: Allen Lane.

Foucault, M. 1980. *Power/Knowledge: Selected Interviews and Other Writings, 1972–1977*, ed. C. Gordon. New York: Pantheon.

Foucault, M. 1983. On the genealogy of ethics: an overview of work in progress. In H. L. Dreyfus and P. Rabinow, *Michel Foucault: Beyond Structuralism and Hermeneutics*. Chicago: University of Chicago Press, 229–52.

Foucault, M. 1986a. *Death and the Labyrinth: The World of Raymond Roussel*. London: Athlone.

Foucault, M. 1986b. Of other spaces. *Diacritics* 16: 22–7.

Foucault, M. 1986c. *The History of Sexuality*, vol. 2: *The Use of Pleasure*. New York: Vintage.

Foucault, M. 1988. *The History of Sexuality*, vol. 3: *The Care of the Self*. New York: Vintage.

Frank, A. G. 1969. *Capitalism and Underdevelopment in Latin America*. New York: Monthly Review Press.

Fraser, N. and L. Nicholson 1990. Social criticism without philosophy: an encounter between feminism and postmodernism. In L. Nicholson (ed.), *Feminism/Postmodernism*. New York: Routledge, 19–38.

Freud, S. 1961. *Civilization and Its Discontents*. London: Hogarth.

Friedan, B. 1963. *The Feminine Mystique*. New York: W. W. Norton.

Friedman, E. 1995. Women's human rights: the emergence of a movement. In J. Peters and A. Wolper (eds), *Women's Rights Human Rights: International Feminist Perspectives*. New York: Routledge, 18–35.

Friedman, S. 1995. Beyond white and other: relationality and narratives of race in feminist discourse. *Signs* 21: 1–49.

Frodeman, R. 1992. Being and space: a re-reading of existential spatiality in *Being and Time*. *Journal of the British Society for Phenomenology* 23: 33–41.

Fukuyama, F. 1989. The end of history? *The National Interest* 16: 3–18.

Gadamer, H-G. 1975. *Truth and Method*. New York: Continuum.

Gadamer, H-G. 1977. *Philosophical Hermeneutics*. Berkeley: University of California Press.

Galois, B. 1976. Ideology and the idea of nature: the case of Peter Kropotkin. *Antipode* 8: 1–16.

Garrison, W. 1959a. Spatial structure of the economy: I. *Annals of the Association of American Geographers* 49: 232–9.

Garrison, W. 1959b. Spatial structure of the economy: II. *Annals of the Association of American Geographers* 49: 471–82.

Garrison, W. 1960. Spatial structure of the economy: III. *Annals of the Association of American Geographers* 50: 357–73.

Garrison, W. and D. Marble 1957. The spatial structure of agricultural activities. *Annals of the Association of American Geographers* 47: 137–44.

Geertz, C. 1973. *The Interpretation of Cultures*. New York: Basic Books.

Geertz, C. 1983. *Local Knowledge*. New York: Basic Books.

Gerber, J. 1997. Beyond dualism – the social construction of nature and the natural *and* social construction of human beings. *Progress in Human Geography* 21: 1–17.

Gibson, K. and R. Horvath 1984. Abstraction in Marx's method. *Antipode* 16: 12–24.

Gibson-Graham, J. K. 1994. "Stuffed if I know!": reflections on post-modern feminist social research. *Gender, Place and Culture* 1: 205–25.

Giddens, A. 1978. Positivism and its critics. In T. Bottimore and R. Nisbet (eds), *A History of Sociological Analysis*. New York: Basic Books, 237–86.

Giddens, A. 1979a. Structuralism and the theory of the subject. In A. Giddens, *Central Problems in Social Theory*. Berkeley: University of California Press, 9–48.

Giddens, A. 1979b. *Central Problems in Social Theory*. Berkeley: University of California Press.

Giddens, A. 1981. *A Contemporary Critique of Historical Materialism*. Berkeley: University of California Press.

Giddens, A. 1984. *The Constitution of Society: Outline of a Theory of Structuration*. Berkeley: University of California Press.

Giddens, A. 1985. Time, space and regionalisation. In D. Gregory and J. Urry (eds), *Social Relations and Spatial Structures*. New York: St Martin's Press, 265–95.

Giddens, A. 1987. *The Nation State and Violence*. Berkeley: University of California Press.

Giddens, A. 1989. A reply to my critics. In D. Held and J. Thompson (eds), *Social Theory of Modern Societies: Anthony Giddens and His Critics*. Cambridge: Cambridge University Press, 249–301.

Giddings, P. 1984. *When and Where I Enter: The Impact of Black Women on Race and Sex in America*. New York: Bantam.

Gier, J. and J. Walton 1987. Some problems with reconceptualising patriarchy. *Antipode* 19: 54–8.

Gilbert, M. 1994. The politics of location: doing feminist research at home. *Professional Geographer* 46: 90–5.

Glacken, C. 1963. *Traces on the Rhodean Shore*. Berkeley: University of California Press.

Godelier, M. 1978. Infrastructures, societies and history. *New Left Review* 112: 84–96.

Goffman, E. 1963. *Behaviour in Public Places*. New York: Free Press.

Goffman, E. 1972. *Interaction Ritual*. London: Allen Lane.

Goffman, E. 1974. *Frame Analysis*. New York: Harper.

Golledge, R. and H. Timmermans 1990. Applications of behavioural research in spatial problems: 1 Cognition. *Progress in Human Geography* 14: 57–99.

Gottdiener, M. 1985. *The Social Production of Urban Space*. Austin: University of Texas Press.

Gottdiener, M. 1987. Space as a force of production: contribution to the debate on realism, capitalism and space. *International Journal of Urban and Regional Research* 11: 405–16.

Gottdiener, M. 1995. *Postmodern Semiotics*. Oxford: Blackwell.

Gottdiener, M. and A. Lagopoulos 1986. *The City and the Sign: An Introduction*. New York: Columbia University Press.

Gould, P. 1963. Man against his environment: a game theoretic framework. *Annals of the Association of American Geographers* 53: 290–7.

Gould, P. 1979. Geography 1957–1977: the Augean period. *Annals of the Association of American Geographers* 69: 139–51.

Gould, P. 1981. Space and rum: an English note on espacien and rumian meaning. *Geografisker Annaler* 63B: 1–3.

Grace, H. 1991. Business, pleasure, narrative: the folktale of our times. In R. Diprose and R. Farrell (eds), *Cartographies: Poststructuralism and the Mapping of Bodies and Spaces*. Sydney: Allen and Unwin, 113–25.

Graham J. 1990. Theory and essentialism in Marxist geography. *Antipode* 22: 53–66.

Graham, J. 1992. Anti-essentialism and overdetermination: a response to Dick Peet. *Antipode* 24: 141–56.

Gramsci, A. 1971. *Selections from the Prison Notebooks*. New York: International Publishers.

Greenhut, M. L. 1956. *Plant Location in Theory and Practice: The Economics of Space*. Chapel Hill: University of North Carolina Press.

Gregory, D. 1978. *Ideology, Science and Human Geography*. New York: St Martin's Press.

Gregory, D. 1981. Human agency and human geography. *Transactions of the Institute of British Geographers* NS 6:1–18.

Gregory, D. 1982. *Regional Transformation and Industrial Revolution: A Geography of the Yorkshire Woolen Industry*. Minneapolis: University of Minnesota Press.

Gregory, D. 1989. Presences and absences: time–space relations and structuration theory. In D. Held and J. Thompson (eds), *Social Theory of Modern Societies: Anthony Giddens and His Critics*. Cambridge: Cambridge University Press, 185–214.

Gregory, D. 1994. *Geographical Imaginations*. Oxford: Blackwell.

Gregory, D. 1995. Lefebvre, Lacan and the production of space. In G. Benko and U. Strohmayer (eds), *Geography, History and Social Sciences*. Dordrecht: Kluwer, 15–44.

Gregory, D. and J. Urry (eds) 1985. *Social Relations and Spatial Structures*. New York: St Martin's Press.

Gregson, N. 1989. On the irrelevance of structuration theory. In D. Held and J. Thompson (eds), *Social Theory of Modern Societies: Anthony Giddens and His Critics*. Cambridge: Cambridge University Press, 235–48.

Gregson, N. and J. Foord 1987. Patriarchy: comments on critics. *Antipode* 19: 371–5.

Greimas, A. J. 1966. *Semantique Structurale*. Paris: Larousse.

Griffen, S. 1980. *Women and Nature: The Roaring Inside Her*. New York: Harper Colophon.

Grossman, L. 1984. *Peasants, Subsistence Ecology and Development in the Highlands of Papua New Guinea*. Princeton: Princeton University Press.

Grosz, E. 1986. *Futurefall: Excursions into Post-Modernity*. Sydney: Power Institute of Fine Arts.

Guelke, L. 1971. Problems of scientific explanation in geography. *Canadian Geographer* 15: 38–53.

Guyer, P. 1989. The rehabilitation of transcendental idealism. In E. Schaper and W. Vossenkuhl (eds), *Reading Kant: New Perspectives on Transcendental Arguments and Critical Philosophy*. Oxford: Basil Blackwell, 140–67.

Habermas, J. 1971. *Knowledge and Human Interests*, trans. J. Shapiro. Boston: Beacon.

Habermas, J. 1975. *Legitimation Crisis*. Boston: Beacon.

Habermas, J. 1983. Modernity: an incomplete project. In H. Foster (ed.), *The Anti-Aesthetic*. Port Townsend: Bay Press.

Habermas, J. 1984–7. *The Theory of Communicative Action*, 2 vols, trans. T. McCarthy. London: Heinemann.

Habermas, J. 1987. *The Philosophical Discourse of Modernity*, trans. F. G. Lawrence. Cambridge: MIT Press.

Habermas, J. 1992. *Postmetaphysical Thinking*. Cambridge: MIT Press.

Hagerstrand, T. 1952. The propagation of innovation waves. Lund Studies in Geography, Series B, Human Geography 4. Lund: Gleelup.

Hagerstrand, T. 1970. What about people in regional science? *Papers of the Regional Science Association* 24: 7–21.

Hagerstrand, T. 1975. Space, time and human conditions. In A. Karlquist (ed.), *Dynamic Allocation of Urban Space*. Farnborough: Saxon House.

Hagerstrand, T. 1982. Diorama, path and project. *Tidscrift voor Economische en Sociale Geografie* 73: 323–39.

Hammond, M., J. Howarth, and R. Keat 1991. *Understanding Phenomenology*. Oxford: Basil Blackwell.

Hannah, M. 1993. Foucault on theorizing specificity. *Society and Space* 11: 349–63.

Hannah, M. and U. Strohmayer 1992. Postmodernism (s)trained. *Annals of the Association of American Geographers* 82: 308–10.

Hanson, S. and G. Pratt 1988. Reconceptualizing the links between home and work in urban geography. *Economic Geography* 64: 299–321.

Hanson, S. and G. Pratt. 1995. *Gender, Work and Space*. New York: Routledge.

Haraway, D. 1989. *Primate Visions: Gender, Race and Nature in the World of Modern Science*. London: Verso.

Haraway, D. 1991. *Simians, Cyborgs and Women: The Reinvention of Nature*. New York: Routledge.

Harding, S. 1982. Is gender a variable in conceptions of rationality? *Dialectica* 36: 2–3.

Harding, S. 1986. *The Science Question in Feminism*. Ithaca: Cornell University Press.

Harding, S. 1990. Feminism, science, and the anti-Enlightenment critiques. In L. Nicholson (ed.), *Feminism/Postmodernism*. New York: Routledge, 83–106.

Harman, E. 1983. Capitalism, patriarchy and the city. In C. Baldock and B. Cass (eds), *Women, Social Welfare and the State in Australia*. Sydney: Allen and Unwin, 53–70.

Harre, R. 1970. *The Principles of Scientific Thinking*. Chicago: University of Chicago Press.

Harre, R. 1972. *The Philosophies of Science: An Introductory Survey*. London: Oxford University Press.

Harre, R. and E. H. Madden 1975. *Causal Powers: A Theory of Natural Necessity*. Totowa, NJ: Rowman and Littlefield.

Harre, R. and P. F. Secord 1972. *The Explanation of Social Behavior*. Totowa, NJ: Rowman and Littlefield.

Harris, R. 1986 Translator's introduction to *Course in General Linguistics* by F. de Saussure. La Salle, Ill.: Open Court, ix–xvi.

Harrison, M. and H. Cummings 1972. The American Indian: the poverty of assimilation. *Antipode* 4: 77–87.

Hartshorne, R. 1939. *The Nature of Geography: A Critical Survey of Current Thought in the Light of the Past*. Lancaster, Penn.: Association of American Geographers.

Hartshorne, R. 1959. *Perspective on the Nature of Geography*. Chicago: Rand McNally.

Hartsock, N. 1983. The feminist standpoint: developing the ground for a specifically feminist historical materialism. In M. Hintikka and S. Harding (eds), *Discovering Reality*. Dordrecht: Reidel.

Hartsock, N. 1985. *Money, Sex and Power*. Boston: Northeastern University Press.

Hartsock, N. 1987. Rethinking modernism: minority vs majority theories. *Cultural Critique* 7: 187–206.

Hartsock, N. 1990. Foucault on power: a theory for women? In L. Nicholson (ed.), *Feminism/Postmodernism*. New York: Routledge, 157–75.

Harvey, D. 1969. *Explanation in Geography*. London: Arnold.

Harvey, D. 1973. *Social Justice and the City*. Baltimore: Johns Hopkins University Press.

Harvey, D. 1974. Population, resources and the ideology of science. *Economic Geography* 50: 256–77.

Harvey, D. 1975 The geography of capitalist accumulation: a reconstruction of the Marxian theory. *Antipode* 7: 9–21.

Harvey, D. 1982. *The Limits to Capital*. Chicago: University of Chicago Press.

Harvey, D. 1985a. *The Urbanization of Capital*. Oxford: Basil Blackwell.

Harvey, D. 1985b. *Consciousness and the Urban Experience*. Oxford: Basil Blackwell.

Harvey, D. 1987. Three myths in search of a reality in urban studies. *Society and Space* 5: 367–76.

Harvey, D. 1989. *The Condition of Postmodernity: An Enquiry into the Origins of Cultural Change*. Oxford: Basil Blackwell.

Harvey, D. 1992. Postmodern morality plays. *Antipode* 24: 300–26.

Harvey, D. 1996. *Justice, Nature and the Geography of Difference*. Oxford: Blackwell.

Harvey, D. and L. Chatterjee 1974. Absolute rent and the structuring of space by governmental and financial institutions. *Antipode* 6: 22–36.

Harvey, D. and A. Scott 1987. The practice of human geography: theory and empirical specificity in the transition from Fordism to flexible accumulation. In B. Macmillan (ed.), *Remodelling Geography*. Oxford: Basil Blackwell, 217–29.

Hawkes, T. 1977. *Structuralism and Semiotics*. Berkeley: University of California Press.

Hawkesworth, M. E. 1989. Knowers, knowing, known: feminist theory and claims of truth. *Signs: Journal of Women in Culture and Society* 14: 533–57.

Hawkesworth, M. E. 1990. *Beyond Oppressions*. New York: Continuum.

Hay, A. M. 1979. Positivism in human geography: response to critics. In R. J. Johnston and D. T. Herbert (eds), *Geography and the Urban Environment*, vol. 2. New York: Wiley, 1–26.

Hayden, D. 1983. *Redesigning the American Dream*. New York: W. W. Norton.

Hayford, A. 1974. The geography of women: an historical introduction. *Antipode* 6: 1–19.

Hegel, G. W. F. (ed.) 1967. *The Phenomenology of Mind*. New York: Harper.

Heidegger, M. 1958. An ontological consideration of place. In *The Question of Being*. New York: Twayne.

Heidegger, M. 1959. *An Introduction to Metaphysics*, trans. R. Manheim. New Haven: Yale University Press.

Heidegger, M. 1962. *Being and Time*, trans. J. Macquarrie and E. Robinson. New York: Harper and Row.

Heidegger, M. 1963. *Kant and the Problem of Metaphysics*, trans. J. S. Churchill. Bloomington: Indiana University Press.

Heidegger, M. 1969a. *The Essence of Reason*, trans. T. Malick. Evanston: Northwestern University Press.

Heidegger, M. 1969b. Art and space. *Man and World* 6: 3–8.

Heidegger, M. 1971. *Poetry, Language, Thought*. New York: Harper and Row.

Heidegger, M. 1977. Letter on humanism. In D. F. Krell (ed.), *Martin Heidegger: Basic Writings*. London: Routledge and Kegan Paul, 197–242.

Heidegger, M. 1990. The self assertion of the German university. In G. Neske and E. Kettering (eds), *Martin Heidegger and National Socialism*. New York: Paragon House, 5–13.

Held, D. and J. Thompson (eds) 1989. *Social Theory of Modern Societies: Anthony Giddens and His Critics*. Cambridge: Cambridge University Press.

Heller, A. and F. Feher 1991. *The Grandeur and the Twilight of Radical Universalism*. New Brunswick, NJ: Transaction Publishers.

Hempel, C. G. 1952. *Fundamentals of Concept Formation in Empirical Science*. Chicago: University of Chicago Press.

Hempel, C. G. 1965. *Aspects of Scientific Explanation*. New York: Free Press.

Hempel, C. G. and P. Oppenheim 1948. Studies in the logic of explanation. *Philosophy of Science* 15: 135–75.

Hesse, M. 1974. *The Structure of Scientific Inference*. Berkeley: University of California Press.

Hettner, A. 1927. *Die Geographie: Ihre Geschichte, Ihre Wesen und Ihr Methoden*. Breslau: Hirt.

Hindess, B. and P. Hirst 1975. *Pre-Capitalist Modes of Production*. London: Routledge and Kegan Paul.

Hirsch, J. 1978. The state apparatus and social reproduction: elements of a theory of the bourgeois state. In J. Holloway and S. Picciotto (eds), *State and Capital*. London: Edward Arnold, 57–107.

Hirsch, J. 1984. Notes towards a reformulation of state theory. In S. Haenninen and L. Daldan (eds), *Rethinking Marx*. Berlin: Argument Verlag, 155–60.

Hirst, P. and Zeitlin, I. M. 1991. Flexible specialization versus post Fordism: theory, evidence and policy implications. *Economy and Society* 20: 1–56.

Hobsbawm, E. 1994. The structure of capital. In G. Elliot (ed.), *Althusser: A Critical Reader*. Oxford: Blackwell, 1–9.

Hofstadter, R. 1955. *Social Darwinism in American Thought*. Boston: Beacon.

Holcomb, B. and J-P. Jones 1990. Work, welfare and poverty among black female-headed families. In J. Kodras and J-P Jones (eds), *Geographic Dimensions of US Social Policy*. London: Edward Arnold, 200–17.

Holcomb, B., J. Kodras, and S. Brunn 1990. Women's issues and state legislation: fragmentation and inconsistency. In J. Kodras and J-P Jones (eds), *Geographic Dimensions of US Social Policy*. London: Edward Arnold, 178–99.

Holt-Jensen, A. 1988. *Geography: History and Concepts*. Totowa, NJ: Barnes and Noble.

Hook, S. 1962. *From Hegel to Marx: Studies in the Intellectual Development of Karl Marx*. Ann Arbor: University of Michigan Press.

hooks, b. 1984. *Feminist Theory: From Margin to Center*. Boston: South End Press.

hooks, b. 1990. *Yearning: Race, Gender and Cultural Politics*. Boston: South End Press.

hooks, b. 1991. *Breaking Bread: Insurgent Black Intellectual Life*. Toronto: Between the Lines.

hooks, b. 1994. *Outlaw Culture*. New York: Routledge.

Horkheimer, M. and T. Adorno 1991. *Dialectic of Enlightenment*. New York: Continuum.

Horvath, R. 1971. The "Detroit Geographical Expedition" experience. *Antipode* 3: 73–85.

Howard, D. 1977. *The Marxian Legacy*. New York: Urizen.

Hoy, D. C. 1985. Jacques Derrida. In Q. Skinner (ed.), *The Return of Grand Theory in the Human Sciences*. Cambridge: Cambridge University Press, 41–64.

Hudson, B. 1977. The new geography and the new imperialism 1870–1918. *Antipode* 9: 12–19.

Hulme, P. 1988. *Colonial Encounters*. London: Methuen.

Huntington, E. 1915. *Civilization and Climate*. New Haven: Yale University Press.

Hurst, M. E. E. 1973. Establishment geography: or how to be irrelevant in three easy lessons. *Antipode* 5: 40–59.

Husserl, E. 1970. *The Crisis of European Sciences and Transcendental Phenomenology: An Introduction to Phenomenological Philosophy*, trans. with an introduction by D. Carr. Evanston: Northwestern University Press.

Husserl, E. 1977. *Cartesian Meditations*, trans. D. Cairns. The Hague: Martinus Nijhoff.

Hyland, G. 1970. Social interaction and urban opportunity: the Appalachian in-migrant in the Cincinnati Central City. *Antipode* 2: 68–83.

Irigaray, L. 1985. *This Sex Which Is Not One*. Ithaca: Cornell University Press.

Isard, W. 1956. *Location and Space-Economy*. New York: Wiley.

Isard, W. and J. Cumberland 1950. New England as a possible location for an integrated iron and steel works. *Economic Geography* 26: 245–59.

Jackson, P. 1989. *Maps of Meaning*. London: Unwin Hyman.

Jackson, P. 1991. The cultural politics of masculinity: towards a social geography. *Transactions of the Institute of British Geographers* 16: 199–213.

Jackson, P. and J. Penrose 1993. *Constructions of Race, Place and Nation*. London: UCL Press.

Jaggar, A. 1983. *Feminist Politics and Human Nature*. Totowa, NJ: Rowman and Littlefield.

Jakobson, R. 1962. *Selected Writings*. New York: Holt, Rinehart and Winston.

James, P. E. 1952. Toward a further understanding of the regional concept. *Annals of the Association of American Geographers* 42: 195–222.

Jameson, F. 1984. Postmodernism, or the cultural logic of late capitalism. *New Left Review* 146: 53–92.

Jameson, F. 1991. *Postmodernism, or, the Cultural Logic of Late Capitalism*. Durham: Duke University Press.

Jaspers, K. 1967. *Philosophical Faith and Revelation*, trans. E. B. Ashton. New York: Harper and Row.

Jay, M. 1973. *The Dialectical Imagination: A History of the Frankfurt School and the Institute of Social Research 1923–1950*. Boston: Little, Brown.

Jay, N. 1981. Gender and dichotomy. *Feminist Studies* 7: 38–56.

Jessop, B. 1989. Capitalism, nation-states and surveillance. In D. Held and J. Thompson (eds), *Social Theory of Modern Societies: Anthony Giddens and His Critics*. Cambridge: Cambridge University Press, 103–28.

Jessop, B. 1990. Regulation theories in retrospect and prospect. *Economy and Society* 19: 153–216.

Johnson, H. G. 1971. The Keynesian revolution and monetarist counterrevolution. *American Economic Review* 16: 1–14.

Johnson, L. 1987. (Un)realist perspectives: patriarchy and feminist challenges in geography. *Antipode* 19: 210–15.

Johnson, P. 1994. *Feminism as Radical Humanism*. Boulder: Westview.

Johnston, R. J. 1980. *Geography and Geographers: Anglo-American Human Geography since 1945*. New York: Wiley.

Johnston, R. J. 1983. *Philosophy and Human Geography*. London: Edward Arnold.

Johnston, R. J., D. Gregory, and D. M. Smith (eds) 1994. *The Dictionary of Human Geography*, 3rd edn. Oxford: Blackwell.

Joynt, C. B. and N. Reschler 1961. The problem of uniqueness in history. *History and Theory* 1: 150–62.

Kant, I. 1965. *Critique of Pure Reason*. New York: St Martin's Press.

Kaplan, G. 1992. *Contemporary Western European Feminism*. New York: New York University Press.

Kasbarian, J. A. 1996. Mapping Said: geography, identity, and the politics of location. *Society and Space* 14: 529–57.

Katz, C. 1994. Playing the field: questions of fieldwork in geography. *Professional Geographer* 46: 67–72.

Katz, C. and J. Monk (eds) 1993. *Full Circles: Geographies of Women Over the Life Course*. New York: Routledge.

Kaufmann, W. 1974. *Nietzsche: Philosopher, Psychologist, AntiChrist*. Princeton: Princeton University Press.

Kay, J. 1991. Landscapes of women and men: rethinking the regional historical geography of the US and Canada. *Journal of Historical Geography* 17: 435–52.

Keat, R. and J. Urry 1975. *Social Theory as Science*. London: Routledge and Kegan Paul.

Keith, M. and S. Pile (eds) 1993. *Place and the Politics of Identity*. London: Routledge.

Keller, E. F. 1990. *Conflicts in Feminism*. New York: Routledge.

Keller, E. F. 1985. *Reflections on Gender and Science*. New Haven: Yale University Press.

Kellner, D. 1989. *Jean Baudrillard: From Marxism to Postmodernism and Beyond*. Stanford: Stanford University Press.

Kierkegaard, S. 1936. *Philosophical Fragments*. Princeton: Princeton University Press.

Kierkegaard, S. 1941. *Concluding Unscientific Postscript*, trans. D. F. Swenson. Princeton: Princeton University Press.

Knopp, L. 1992. Sexuality and the spatial dynamics of capitalism. *Society and Space* 10: 651–69.

Knopp, L. and M. Lauria 1987. Gender relations as a particular form of social relations. *Antipode* 19: 48–53.

Kobayashi, A. 1994. Coloring the field: gender, "race" and the politics of fieldwork. *Professional Geographer* 46: 73–9.

Kockelmans, J. 1965. *Martin Heidegger: A First Introduction to His Philosophy*. Pittsburgh: Duquesne University Press.

Kockelmans, J. 1984. *On the Truth of Being: Reflections on Heidegger's Later Philosophy*. Bloomington: Indiana University Press.

Kohnke, K. C. 1991. *The Rise of Neo-Kantianism: German Academic Philosophy Between Idealism and Positivism*, trans. R. J. Hollingdale. Cambridge: Cambridge University Press.

Kojeve, A. 1969. *Introduction to the Reading of Hegel. Lectures on the Phenomenology of Spirit*, assembled by Raymond Queneau, ed. A. Bloom, trans. J. H. Nichols Jr. New York: Basic Books.

Koloday, A. 1984. *The Land Before Her: Fantasy and Experience of the American Frontiers, 1630–1860*. Chapel Hill: University of North Carolina Press.

Kristeva, J. 1980. *Desire in Language: A Semiotic Approach to Literature and Art*. Oxford: Basil Blackwell.

Kristeva, J. 1986. *About Chinese Women*. New York: M. Boyars.

Kropotkin, P. 1898. *Fields, Factories and Workshops*. London: T. Nelson.

Kropotkin, P. 1902. *Mutual Aid: A Factor of Evolution*. London: Heinemann.

Kropotkin, P. 1924. *Ethics: Origin and Development*. New York: Tudor Publishing.

Kropotkin, P. 1978. *Selected Writings on Anarchism and Revolution*. Cambridge: MIT Press.

Kropotkin, P. 1991–5. *Collected Works*, 11 vols. Montreal: Black Rose.

Kuhn, T. S. 1962. *The Structure of Scientific Revolutions*. Chicago: University of Chicago Press.

Kuhn, T. S. 1970. Reflections on my critics. In I. Lakatos and A. Musgrove (eds), *Criticism and the Growth of Knowledge*. Cambridge: Cambridge University Press.

Lacan, J. 1968. *The Language of the Self*. Baltimore: Johns Hopkins University Press.

Lacan, J. 1977. *Ecrits: A Selection*. Paris: Editions du Seuil.

Lacan, J. 1981. *The Four Fundamental Concepts of Psycho-Analysis*. New York: Norton.

Laclau, E. 1990. *New Reflections on the Revolution of Our Time*. London: Verso.

Laclau, E. and C. Mouffe 1985. *Hegemony and Socialist Strategy: Towards a Radical Democratic Politics*. London: Verso.

Lacoste, Y. 1973. An illustration of geographical warfare: bombing of the dykes on the Red River, North Vietnam. *Antipode* 5: 1–13.

Lagopoulos, A. and K. Boklund-Lagopoulou 1992. *Meaning and Geography*. Berlin: Mouton de Gruyter.

Lakatos, I. (ed.) 1968. *The Problem of Inductive Knowledge*. Amsterdam: North Holland.

Lamarck, J. B. 1914. *Zoological Philosophy*, trans. H. Elliot. London: Macmillan.

Lapple, D. and P. van Hoogerstraten 1980. Remarks on the spatial structure of capitalist development: the case of the Netherlands. In J. Carney, R. Hudson, and J. Lewis (eds), *Regions in Crisis*. London: Croom Helm, 117–66.

Lavrin, A. 1994. Suffrage in South America. In M. Nolan and C. Daley (eds), *Suffrage and Beyond: International Feminist Perspectives*. New York: New York University Press.

Lawson, H. 1985. *Reflexivity: The Post-Modern Predicament*. LaSalle, Ill.: Open Court.

Lawson, V. 1995. The politics of difference: examining the quantitative/qualititative dualism in post-structuralist feminist research. *Professional Geographer* 47: 449–57.

Leacock, E. and R. Lee 1982. *Politics and History in Band Societies*. Cambridge: Cambridge University Press.

Leborgne, D. and A. Lipietz 1988. New technologies, new modes of regulation: some spatial implications. *Society and Space* 6: 263–80.

Lecourt, D. 1975. *Marxism and Epistemology: Bachelard, Canguilheim and Foucault*, trans. B. Brewster. London: New Left Books.

Le Doeuff, M. 1987. Women in philosophy. In T. Moi (ed.), *French Feminist Thought*. Oxford: Blackwell, 181–209.

Lefebvre, H. 1968. *Dialectical Materialism*. London: Jonathan Cape.

Lefebvre, H. 1969. *The Sociology of Marx*. New York: Random House.

Lefebvre, H. 1970. *La Revolution urbaine*. Paris: Gallimard.

Lefebvre, H. 1971. *Everyday Life in the Modern World*, trans. S. Rabinovitch. New York: Harper.

Lefebvre, H. 1972. *La Pensée Marxiste et la ville*. Paris: Casterman.

Lefebvre, H. 1976. Reflections on the politics of space, trans. M. Enders. *Antipode* 8: 30–7.

Lefebvre, H. 1991. *The Production of Space*, trans. D. Nicholson-Smith. Oxford: Basil Blackwell.

Lefort, C. 1978. Marx: from one vision of history to another. *Social Research* 45: 615–66.

Leibniz, G. W. F. 1949. *New Essays Concerning Human Understanding*. LaSalle, Ill.: Open Court.

Leibniz, G. W. F. 1953. *Discourse on Metaphysics*. Manchester: Manchester University Press.

Lemart, C. and G. Gillan 1982. *Michel Foucault: Social Theory and Transgression*. New York: Columbia University Press.

Lenin, V. I. 1972a. Conspectus of Hegel's book *The Science of Logic*. In V. I. Lenin, *Collected Works* 38: 85–238.

Lenin, V. I. 1972b. From materialism and empirico criticism: critical comments on a reactionary philosophy. In K. Marx, F. Engels, and V. Lenin, *On Historical Materialism*. New York: International Publishers, 431–46.

Lenin, V. I. 1975. *Imperialism: The Highest Stage of Capitalism*. Peking: Foreign Languages Press.

Lévi-Strauss, C. 1966. *The Savage Mind*. Chicago: University of Chicago Press.

Lévi-Strauss, C. 1973. *Tristes tropiques*, trans. J. and D. Weightman. London: Cape.

Lévi-Strauss, C. 1977. *Structural Anthropology*. Harmondsworth: Penguin.

Ley, D. 1974. The city and good and evil: reflections on Christian and Marxist interpretations. *Antipode* 6: 66–74.

Ley, D. 1977. Social geography and the taken-for-granted world. *Transactions of the Institute of British Geographers* NS 2: 498–512.

Ley, D. 1978. Social geography and social action. In D. Ley and M. Samuels (eds), *Humanistic Geography: Prospects and Problems*. Chicago: Maaroufa Press, 41–57.

Ley, D. 1980. Geography without man: a humanistic critique University of Oxford, School of Geography, Research Paper 24.

Ley, D. 1981. Behavioral geography and the philosophies of meaning. In K. Cox and R. Golledge (eds), *Behavioral Problems in Geography: A Symposium Northwestern University Studies in Geography* 17. Evanston, Ill., 209–30.

Ley, D. and M. Samuels (eds) 1978a. *Humanistic Geography: Prospects and Problems*. Chicago: Maaroufa Press.

Ley, D. and M. Samuels 1978b. Introduction: contexts of modern humanism. In D. Ley and M. Samuels (eds), *Humanistic Geography: Prospects and Problems*. Chicago: Maaroufa Press.

Lilla, M. 1993. *G. B. Vico: The Making of an Anti-Modern*. Cambridge: Harvard University Press.

Lipietz, A. 1980. The structuration of space, the problem of land, and spatial policy. In J. Carney, R. Hudson, and J. Lewis (eds), *Regions in Crisis: New Perspectives in European Regional Theory*. New York: St Martin's Press, 60–75.

Lipietz, A. 1986. New tendencies in the international division of labor: regimes of accumulation and modes of regulation. In A. J. Scott and M. Storper (eds), *Production, Work, Territory*. Winchester, Mass.: Allen and Unwin, 16–40.

Lipietz, A. 1992a. *Towards a New Economic Order: Post Fordism, Ecology and Democracy*. New York: Oxford University Press.

Lipietz, A. 1992b. A regulationist approach to the future of urban ecology. *Capitalism, Nature, Socialism* 3: 101–10.

Lipietz, A. 1993. From Althusserianism to "regulation theory." In E. A. Kaplan and M. Sprinker (eds), *The Althusserian Legacy*. London: Verso, 99–138.

Livingstone, D. 1984. Natural theology and neo-Lamarckism: the changing context of nineteenth-century geography in the United States and Great Britain. *Annals of the Association of American Geographers* 74: 9–28.

Livingstone, D. 1992. *The Geographical Tradition*. Oxford: Blackwell.

Livingstone, D. 1995. The space of knowledge: contributions towards a historical geography of science. *Society and Space* 13: 5–34.

Lloyd, B. 1975. Women's place, man's place. *Landscape* 20: 10–13.

Lloyd, G. 1979. The man of reason. *Metaphilosophy* 10: 18–37.

Lloyd, G. 1984. *The Man of Reason: "Male" and "Female" in Western Philosophy*. London: Methuen.

Lojkine, J. 1976. Contributions to a Marxist theory of capitalist urban systems. In C. Pickvance (ed.), *Urban Sociology: Critical Essays*. London: Tavistock, 99–146.

Lorde, A. 1981a. The master's tools will never dismantle the master's house. In C. Morroga and G. Anzaldua (eds), *The Bridge Called Me Back: Writings by Radical Women of Color*. Watertown, Mass.: Persephone Press, 98–101.

Lorde, A. 1981b. An open letter to Mary Daly. In C. Morroga and G. Anzaldua (eds), *The Bridge Called Me Back: Writings by Radical Women of Color*. Watertown, Mass.: Persephone Press, 94–7.

Lorde, A. 1984. *Sister Outside*. Trumansberg, NY: Crossing Press.

Losch, A. 1954. *The Economics of Location*. New Haven: Yale University Press.

Lovejoy, A. O. 1964. *The Great Chain of Being*. Cambridge: Harvard University Press.

Lovering, J. 1987. Militarism, capitalism and the nation state: towards a realist synthesis. *Society and Space* 5: 283–302.

Lovering, J. 1989. Postmodernism, Marxism, and locality research: the contribution of critical realism to the debate. *Antipode* 21: 1–12.

Lowenthal, D. 1961. Geography, experience and imagination: towards a geographical epistemology. *Annals of the Association of American Geographers* 51: 241–60.

Lugones, M. 1994. Purity, impurity, and separation. *Signs* 19: 458–79.

Lukács, G. 1971. *History and Class Consciousness*. Cambridge, Mass.: MIT Press.

Lukerman, F. 1964. Geography as a formal intellectual discipline and the way in which it contributes to human knowledge. *Canadian Geographer* 8: 167–72.

Luxembourg, R. 1951. *The Accumulation of Capital*. London: Routledge and Kegan Paul.

Lynch, K. 1968. *The Image of the City*. Cambridge: MIT Press.

Lyons, J. 1973. Structuralism and linguistics. In D. Robey (ed.), *Structuralism: An Introduction*. Oxford: Clarendon Press, 5–19.

Lyotard, J-F. 1971. *Discours, figure*. Paris: Klinksieck.

Lyotard, J-F. 1974. *Economie libidinal*. Paris: Minuit.

Lyotard, J-F. 1984. *The Postmodern Condition*. Minneapolis: University of Minnesota Press.

Lyotard, J-F. 1988. *The Differend*. Minneapolis: University of Minnesota Press.

Lyotard, J-F. 1989. *The Lyotard Reader*, ed. A. Benjamin. Oxford: Blackwell.

Lyotard, J-F. and J-L. Thebaud 1985. *Just Gaming*. Minneapolis: University of Minnesota Press.

MacDonnell, D. 1986. *Theories of Discourse: An Introduction*. Oxford: Basil Blackwell.

Mach, E. 1959. *The Analysis of Sensations and the Relation of the Physical to the Psychical*. New York: Dover.

Machado, R. 1992. Archaeology and epistemology. In *Michel Foucault Philosopher*, trans. T. Armstrong. London: Routledge, 3–18.

Mackenzie, S. 1984. Editorial introduction. *Antipode* 16: 3–10.

Mackenzie, S. 1989a. Women in the city. In R. Peet and N. Thrift (eds), *New Models in Geography*. London: Unwin Hyman, vol. 2: 109–26.

Mackenzie, S. 1989b. Restructuring the relations of work and life: women as environmental actors, feminism as geographical analysis. In A. Kobayashi and S. Mackenzie (eds), *Remaking Human Geography*. London: Unwin Hyman, 40–61.

Mackenzie, S. and D. Rose 1983. Industrial change, the domestic economy and home life. In J. Anderson, S. Duncan, and R. Hudson (eds), *Redundant Spaces: Industrial Decline in Cities and Regions*. London: Academic Press, 155–99.

Mackinder, H. 1907. *Britain and the British Seas*. Oxford: Clarendon Press.

Mackinder, H. 1911. The teaching of geography from an imperial point of view. *Geographical Teacher* 6: 79–86.

Mackinder, H. 1931. The human habitat. *Scottish Geographical Magazine* 47: 321–35.

MacKinnon, C. 1982. Feminism, Marxism, method and the state: an agenda. *Signs* 7: 515–44.

Macquarrie, J. 1972. *Existentialism*. Harmondsworth: Penguin.

Maguire, P. 1987. *Doing Participatory Research: A Feminist Approach*. Amherst, Mass.: Center for International Education, University of Massachusetts.

Maier, A. 1986. Thomas Kuhn and understanding geography. *Progress in Human Geography* 10: 345–69.

Mandel, E. 1976. *Late Capitalism*. London: New Left Books.

Mandel, E. 1978. *The Second Slump*. London: New Left Books.

Mandel, E. 1980. *Long Waves in Capitalist Development*. Cambridge: Cambridge University Press.

Marcel, G. 1949. *Being and Having*. New York: Harper Brothers.

Marcus, G. E. 1986. Contemporary problems of ethnography in the modern world system. In J. Clifford and G. F. Marcus (eds), *Writing Culture: The Poetics and Politics of Ethnography*. Berkeley: University of California Press, 165–93.

Marx, K. 1963. *The Poverty of Philosophy*. New York: International Publishers.

Marx, K. 1964a. Critique of Hegel's philosophy of right. In *Early Writings*, trans. T. Bottomore. New York: McGraw–Hill.

Marx, K. 1964b. *The Economic and Philosophic Manuscripts of 1844*. New York: International Publishers.

Marx, K. 1969. Theses on Feuerbach in *Karl Marx and Frederick Engels: Selected Works*. Moscow: Progress Publishers, vol. 1, 13–15.

Marx, K. 1970. *A Contribution to the Critique of Political Economy*. Moscow: Progress Publishers.

Marx, K. 1973. *Grundrisse: Foundations of the Critique of Political Economy*, trans. M. Nicolaus. Harmondsworth: Penguin.

Marx, K. 1976. *Capital: A Critique of Political Economy*, vol. l, trans. B. Fowkes. Harmondsworth: Penguin.

Marx, K. 1981. *Capital: A Critique of Political; Economy*, vol. 3, trans. D. Fernbach. Harmondsworth: Penguin.

Marx, K. and F. Engels 1970. *The German Ideology*. New York: International Publishers.

Massami, B. 1992. *A User's Guide to Capitalism and Schizophrenia: Deviations from Deleuze and Guattari*. Cambridge: MIT Press.

Massami, B. 1996. Becoming Deleuzian. *Society and Space* 14: 395–406

Massey, D. 1973. Towards a critique of industrial location theory. *Antipode* 5: 33–39.

Massey, D. 1974. *Social Justice and the City*: a review. *Environment and Planning A* 6: 229–35.

Massey, D. 1978. Regionalism: some current issues. *Capital and Class* 6: 106–25.

Massey, D. 1984. *Spatial Divisions of Labor: Social Structures and the Geography of Production*. New York: Methuen.

Massey, D. 1991. Flexible sexism. *Society and Space* 9: 31–57.

Massey, D. 1993. Power geometry and a progressive sense of place. In J. Bird, B. Curtis,

T. Putnam, G. Robertson, and L. Tickner (eds), *Mapping the Futures*. London: Routledge, 59–69.

Massey, D. 1994. *Space, Place and Gender*. Minneapolis: University of Minnesota Press.

Massey, D. and J. Allen (eds) 1984. *Geography Matters! A Reader*. Cambridge: Cambridge University Press.

Massey, D. and R. Meegan 1982. *The Anatomy of Job Loss*. London: Methuen.

Mattingly, D. and K. Falconer-Al-Hindi 1995. Should women count? A context for the debate. *Professional Geographer* 47: 427–35.

Mauss, A. 1967. *The Gift*. New York: Norton.

May, J. A. 1970. *Kant's Concept of Geography and Its Relation to Recent Geographical Thought*. Toronto: University of Toronto Press.

McCarthy, T. 1978. *The Critical Theory of Jürgen Habermas*. Cambridge: Polity.

McCarthy, T. 1985. Reflections on rationalization in the *Theory of Communicative Action*. In R. Bernsten (ed.), *Habermas and Modernity*. Cambridge: MIT Press, 176–91.

McDowell, L. 1983. Towards an understanding of the gender division of urban space. *Society and Space* 1: 59–72.

McDowell, L. 1986. Beyond patriarchy: a class-based explanation of women's subordination. *Antipode* 18: 311–21.

McDowell, L. 1989. Women, gender and the organisation of space. In D. Gregory and R. Walford (eds), *Horizons in Human Geography*. Totowa, NJ: Barnes and Noble, 136–51.

McDowell, L. 1991. Life without father and Ford: the new gender order of post-Fordism. *Transactions of the Institute of British Geographers* 16: 400–19.

McDowell, L. 1992. Doing gender: feminism, feminists and research methods in human geography. *Transactions of the Institute of British Geographers* NS 17: 399–416.

McDowell, L. 1993a. Space, place and gender relations: Part I. Feminist empiricism and the geography of social relations. *Progress in Human Geography* 17: 157–79.

McDowell, L. 1993b. Space, place and gender relations: Part II. Identity, difference, feminist geometries and geographies. *Progress in Human Geography* 17: 305–18.

McDowell, L. and G. Court 1993. Missing subjects: gender power and sexuality in merchant banking. *Economic Geography* 70: 229–51.

McDowell, L. and G. Court 1994. Performing work: bodily representations in merchant banks. *Society and Space* 12: 727–50.

McDowell, L. and D. Massey 1984. A woman's place in geography matters. In J. Allen and D. Massey (eds), *Geography Matters*. Cambridge: Cambridge University Press.

McGrane, B. 1989. *Beyond Anthropology: Society and the Other*. New York: Columbia University Press.

McLafferty, S. 1995. Counting for women. *Professional Geographer* 47: 436–42.

McPherson, C. B. 1973. *Democratic Theory: Essays in Retrieval*. Oxford: Oxford University Press.

Megill, A. 1985. *Prophets of Extremity: Nietzsche, Heidegger, Foucault, Derrida*. Berkeley: University of California Press.

Melnick, A. 1989. *Space, Time, and Thought in Kant*. Dordrecht: Kluwer.

Mercer, D. and J. Powell 1972. Phenomenology and related non-positivistic viewpoints in the social sciences. Monash Publications in Geography, Victoria, Australia.

Merchant, C. 1980. *The Death of Nature: Women, Ecology and the Scientific Revolution*. New York: Harper and Row.

Merleau-Ponty, M. 1962. *Phenomenology of Perception*, trans. C. Smith. London: Routledge and Kegan Paul. Reprinted 1981.

Merrifield, A. 1995. Lefebvre, Anti-Logos and Nietzsche: an alternative reading of *The Production of Space*. *Antipode* 27: 294–303.

Merton, R. K. 1968. *Social Theory and Social Structure*. New York: Free Press.

Mies, M. 1982. *The Lace Makers of Narsapur*. London: Zed Press.

Mies, M. 1983. Towards a methodology for feminist research. In G. Bowles and R. D. Klein (eds), *Theories of Women's Studies*. London: Routledge and Kegan Paul, 117–39.

Mies, M. 1986. *Patriarchy and Accumulation on a World Scale*. London: Zed Books.

Miles, A. 1996. *Integrative Feminisms: Building Global Visions 1960s–1990s*. New York: Routledge.

Millett, K. 1970. *Sexual Politics*. London: Virago.

Miller, B. 1992. Collective action and rational choice: place, community and the limits to individual self-interest. *Economic Geography* 68: 22–42.

Mills, S. 1996. Gender and colonial space. *Gender, Place and Culture* 3: 125–47.

Minh-ha, T. T. 1989. *Woman, Native, Other: Writing Postcoloniality and Feminism*. Bloomington: Indiana University Press.

Mitchell, J. 1966. Women, the longest revolution. *New Left Review* 40: 11–37.

Mitchell, J. 1975. *Psychoanalysis and Feminism*. Harmondsworth: Penguin.

Mohanty, C. 1991a. Cartographies of struggle: third world women and the politics of feminism. In C. T. Mohanty, A. Russo, and L. Torres (eds), *Third World Women and the Politics of Feminism*. Bloomington: Indiana University Press, 1–51.

Mohanty, C. 1991b. Under western eyes: feminist scholarship and colonial discourses. In C. T. Mohanty, A. Russo, and L. Torres (eds), *Third World Women and the Politics of Feminism*. Bloomington: Indiana University Press, 51–81.

Monk, J. and S. Hanson. 1982. On not excluding half of the human in human geography. *Professional Geographer* 34: 11–23.

Monk, J. and V. Norwood (eds) 1987. *The Desert Is No Lady: Southwestern Landscapes in Women's Writing and Art*. New Haven: Yale University Press.

Moore, H. 1986. *Space, Text and Gender*. Cambridge: Cambridge University Press.

Morgan, R. 1977. *Going Too Far: The Personal Chronicle of a Feminist*. New York: Random House.

Morrill, R. 1969–70. Geography and the transformation of society. *Antipode* 1: 6–9 and 2: 4–10.

Moss, P. 1995a. Reflections on the "gap" as part of the politics of research design. *Antipode* 27: 82–90.

Moss, P. 1995b. Embeddedness in practice, numbers in context: the politics of knowing and doing. *Professional Geographer* 47: 442–9.

Mouffe, C. 1995. Post-Marxism: democracy and identity. *Society and Space* 13: 259–65.

Murgatroyd, L. 1989. Only half the story: some blinkering effects of "malestream" sociology. In D. Held and J. Thompson (eds), *Social Theory of Modern Societies: Anthony Giddens and His Critics*. Cambridge: Cambridge University Press, 147–61.

Murray, D. 1988. *Marx's Theory of Scientific Knowledge*. Atlantic Highlands: Humanities Press.

Murray, M. (ed.) 1978. *Heidegger and Modern Philosophy: Critical Essays*. New Haven: Yale University Press.

Muth, R. 1969. *Cities and Housing*. Chicago: University of Chicago Press.

Nagel, E. 1962. *The Structure of Science*. New York: Harcourt, Brace and World.

Nash, C. 1986. Reclaiming vision: looking at landscape and the body. *Gender, Place and Culture* 3: 149–69.

Nast, H. 1994. Opening remarks on "women in the field." *Professional Geographer* 46: 54–66.

Nicholson, L. (ed.). 1990. *Feminism/Postmodernism*. New York: Routledge.

Nietzsche, F. 1967. *On the Genealogy of Morals*, trans. W. Kaufmann and R. J. Hollingdale. New York: Vintage.

Nietzsche, F. 1968. *The Will to Power*, trans. W. Kaufmann and R. J. Hollingdale. New York: Random House.

Nietzsche, F. 1979. *Truth and Philosophy: Selections from Nietzsche's Notebooks of the 1870s*. Atlantic Highlands: Humanities Press.

Nolan, M. and C. Daley 1994. International feminist perspectives on suffrage: an introduction. In M. Nolan and C. Daley (eds), *Suffrage and Beyond: International Feminist Perspectives*. New York: New York University Press, 1–22.

Norberg-Schulz, C. 1969. Meaning in architecture. In C. Jencks (ed.), *Meaning in Architecture*. New York: G. Brazilier.

O'Keefe, P., K. Westgate, and B. Wisner 1976. Taking the naturalness out of natural disasters. *Nature* 260: 566–7.

O'Tuathail, G. 1996. *Critical Geopolitics*. Minneapolis: University of Minnesota Press.

Oakley, A. 1972. *Sex, Gender and Society*. London: Temple Smith.

Ollman, B. 1976. *Alienation: Marx's Conception of Man in Capitalist Society*. Cambridge: Cambridge University Press.

Olsson, G. 1980. *Birds in Egg: Eggs in Bird*. London: Pion.

Olsson, G. 1983a. Pretexts, texts and contexts. Paper given at the Institute of British Geographers Meeting, Edinburgh, 6 January.

Olsson, G. 1983b. Toward a sermon of modernity. In M. Billinge and D. Gregory (eds), *Recollections of a Revolution: Geography as Spatial Science*. New York: St Martin's Press, 73–85.

Olsson, G. 1991. *Lines of Power/Limits of Language*. Minneapolis: University of Minnesota Press.

Outhwaite, W. 1994. *Habermas: A Critical Introduction*. Cambridge: Polity.

Palmer, B. D. 1990. *Descent into Discourse: The Reification of Language and the Writing of Social History*. Philadelphia: Temple University Press.

Palmer, R. E. 1969. *Hermeneutics: Interpretation Theory in Schleirmachr, Dilthey, Heidegger, and Gadamer*. Evanston: Northwestern University Press.

Parekh, B. 1982. *Marx's Theory of Ideology*. Baltimore: Johns Hopkins University Press.

Pareto, V. 1965. *Les Systems socialistes* Geneva: Droz.

Parsons, T. 1949. *The Structure of Social Action*. Glencoe: Free Press.

Parsons, T. 1951. *The Social System*. Glencoe: Free Press.

Parsons, T. and E. Shils 1964. *Toward a General Theory of Action*. New York: Harper and Row.

Patai, D. 1991. US academics and third world women: is ethical research possible? In S. B. Gluck and D. Patai (eds), *Women's Words: The Feminist Practice of Oral History*. New York: Routledge.

Paterson, J. L. 1984. *David Harvey's Geography*. London: Croom Helm.

Peet, R. 1972. Editorial policy. *Antipode* 4: iv.

Peet, R. 1972. *Geographical Perspectives on American Poverty*. Worcester: Antipode Monographs in Social Geography.

Peet, R. 1977a. *Radical Geography*. Chicago: Maaroufa Press.

Peet, R. 1977b. The development of radical geography in the United States. *Progress in Human Geography* 1: 64–87.

Peet, R. 1978. Materialism, social formation, and socio-spatial relations: an essay in Marxist geography. *Cahiers de Geographie du Quebec* 22: 147–57.

Peet, R. 1981. Spatial dialectics and Marxist geography. *Progress in Human Geography* 5: 105–10.

Peet, R. 1985. The social origins of environmental determinism. *Annals of the Association of American Geographers* 75: 309–33.

Peet, R. 1989a. World capitalism and the destruction of regional cultures. In R. J. Johnston and P. J. Taylor (eds), *A World in Crisis? Geographical Perspectives*, 2nd edn. Oxford: Basil Blackwell, 175–99.

Peet, R. 1989b. Conceptual problems in neo Marxist industrial geography. *Antipode* 21: 35–50.

Peet, R. 1991. *Global Capitalism: Theories of Societal Development*. London: Routledge.

Peet, R. 1992. Some critical questions for anti-essentialism. *Antipode* 24: 113–30.

Peet, R. 1993. Review of J. Duncan, *The City as Text. Annals of the Association of American Geographers*, 83: 184–7.

Peet, R. 1996. A sign taken for history: Daniel Shays' memorial in Petersham, Massachusetts. *Annals of the Association of American Geographers* 86: 21–43.

Peet, R. and N. Thrift (eds) 1989. *New Models in Geography*, 2 vols. London: Unwin Hyman.

Peet, R. and M. Watts (eds) 1996. *Liberation Ecologies: Nature, Development and Social Movements*. London: Routledge.

Philo, C. 1984. Reflections on Gunnar Olsson's contribution to the discourse of contemporary human geography. *Society and Space* 2: 217–40.

Philo, C. (ed.) 1991a. *New Words, New Worlds: Reconceptualising Social and Cultural Geography*. Aberystwyth: Cambrian Printers.

Philo, C. 1991b. Introduction. acknowledgements and brief thoughts on older words and older worlds. In C. Philo (ed.), *New Words, New Worlds: Reconceptualising Social and Cultural Geography*. Aberystwyth: Cambrian Printers, 1–13.

Philo, C. 1992. Foucault's geography. *Society and Space* 10: 137–61.

Philo, C. 1994. Escaping flatland: a book review essay inspired by Gunnar Olsson's *Lines of Power/Limits of Language. Society and Space* 12: 229–52.

Piaget, J. 1970. *Structuralism*. London: Routledge and Kegan Paul.

Piaget, J. 1972a. *Genetic Epistemology*. New York: Columbia University Press.

Piaget, J. 1972b. *Insights and Illusions of Philosophy*. New York: New American Library.

Pickles, J. 1985. *Phenomenology, Science and Geography: Spatiality and the Human Sciences*. Cambridge: Cambridge University Press.

Pickvance, C. 1976. Housing, reproduction of capital and reproduction of labour power: some recent French work. *Antipode* 8: 58–68.

Pile, S. 1993. Human agency and human geography revisited: a critique of "new models" of the self. *Transactions of the Institute of British Geographers* 18: 122–39.

Pile, S. 1996. *The Body and the City: Psychoanalysis, Space and Subjectivity*. London: Routledge.

Pile, S. and N. Thrift 1995. *Mapping the Subject: Geographies of Cultural Transformation*. London: Routledge.

Piore, M. J. and C. F. Sable 1984. *The Second Industrial Divide: Possibilities for Prosperity*. New York: Basic Books.

Pollock, G. 1988. *Vision and Difference: Femininity, Feminism and Histories of Art*. London: Routledge.

Popper, K. 1965. *The Logic of Scientific Discovery*. New York: Harper.

Popper, K. 1972. *The Open Society and Its Enemies*. Princeton: Princeton University Press.

Popper, K. and J. C. Eccles 1977. *The Self and Its Brain: An Argument for Interactionism*. Berlin: Springer-Verlag.

Poster, M. 1975. *Existential Marxism in Post-War France: From Sartre to Althusser*. Princeton: Princeton University Press.

Poulantzas, N. 1978. *State, Power, Socialism*. London: Verso.

Pratt, G. 1993. Reflections on poststructuralism and feminist empirics, theory and practice. *Antipode* 24: 51–63.

Pratt G. and S. Hanson 1988. Gender, class and space. *Society and Space* 6: 15–35.

Pratt, M. B. 1984. Identity: skin blood heart. In E. Bulkin, M. B. Pratt and B. Smith (eds), *Yours in Struggle*. Brooklyn: Long Haul Press, 9–63.

Pred, A. 1981a. Social reproduction and the time geography of everyday life. *Geografiska Annaler* 63B: 5–22.

Pred, A. 1981b. Of paths and projects: individual behavior and its societal context. In R. Golledge and K. Cox (eds), *Behavioral Geography Revisited*. London: Methuen, 231–55.

Pred, A. 1983. Structuration and place: on the becoming of sense of place and structure of feeling. *Journal for the Theory of Social Behavior* 13: 157–86.

Pred, A. 1986. *Place, Practice and Structure: Social and Spatial Transformation in Southern Sweden, 1750–1850*. Totowa, NJ: Barnes and Noble.

Preteceille, E. 1976. Urban planning: the contradiction of capitalist urbanization. *Antipode* 8: 69–76.

Pudup, M. B. 1988. Arguments within regional geography. *Progress in Human Geography* 12: 369–90.

Quick, P. 1977. The class nature of women's oppression. *Review of Radical Political Economics* 9: 42–53.

Quine, W. V. O. 1953. *From a Logical Point of View*. Cambridge: Cambridge University Press.

Raban, J. 1974. *Soft City*. New York: E. P. Dutton.

Rabinow, P. (ed.) 1984. *The Foucault Reader*. New York: Pantheon.

Rapp, R. and E. Ross. 1986. The 1920s: Feminism, consumerism and political backlash in the US. In J. Friedlander (ed.), *Women in Culture and Politics: A Century of Change*. Bloomington: Indiana University Press, 52–61.

Ratzel, F. 1896. *History of Mankind*, trans. A. J. Butler. London: Macmillan.

Reinharz, S. 1992. *Feminist Methods in Social Research*. New York: Oxford University Press.

Relph, E. 1970. An inquiry into the relations between phenomenology and geography. *Canadian Geographer* 14: 193–201.

Relph, E. 1976. *Place and Placelessness*. London: Pion.

Relph, E. 1981. *Rational Landscapes and Humanistic Geography*. Beckenham: Croom Helm.

Relph, E. 1986. Violent and non-violent geographies. In L. Guelke (ed.), *Geography and Humanistic Knowledge*. University of Waterloo, Department of Geography Publication Series 25, 69–85.

Resnick, S. and R. Wolff 1987. *Knowledge and Class: A Marxian Critique of Political Economy*. Chicago: University of Chicago Press.

Resnick, S. and R. Wolff 1992. Reply to Richard Peet. *Antipode* 24: 131–40.

Rich, A. 1986. *Blood, Bread and Poetry: Selected Prose 1979–1985*. New York: Norton.

Ricoeur, P. 1965. *De l'Interpretation*. Paris: Editions du Seuil.

Ricoeur, P. 1971. The model of the text: meaningful action considered as text. *Social Research* 38: 529–62.

Ricoeur, P. 1973. The hermeneutical function of distanciation. *Philosophy Today* 17: 129–41.

Ritter, C. 1874. *Comparative Geography*. Philadelphia: J. B. Lippincott.

Robbins, D. 1991. *The Work of Pierre Bourdieu*. Boulder: Westview.

Rocheleau, D. 1995. Maps, numbers, text and context: mixing methods in feminist political ecology. *Professional Geographer* 47: 458–66.

Rockmore, T. 1995. *Heidegger and French Philosophy*. London: Routledge.

Rorty, R. 1979. *Philosophy and the Mirror of Nature*. Princeton: Princeton University Press.

Rorty, R. 1991. *Objectivity, Relativism, and Truth*. Cambridge: Cambridge University Press.

Rose, D. 1984. Rethinking gentrification: beyond the uneven development of Marxian urban theory. *Society and Space* 2: 47–74.

Rose, G. 1989. Locality studies and waged labour: an historical critique. *Transactions of the Institute of British Geographers* 14: 317–28.

Rose, G. 1993. *Feminism and Geography: The Limits of Geographical Knowledge*. Minneapolis: University of Minnesota Press.

Rose, G. 1995. Tradition and paternity: same difference? *Transactions of the Institute of British Geographers* 20: 414–16.

Rose, H. and S. Rose 1976. *Ideology Of/In the Natural Sciences*. Boston: G. K. Hall.

Rossi, I. 1974. Intellectual antecedents of Lévi-Strauss' notion of unconscious. In I. Rossi (ed.), *The Unconscious in Culture: The Structuralism of Claude Lévi-Strauss*. New York: E. P. Dutton, 7–30.

Rubin, G. 1975. The traffic in women: notes on the political economy of sex. In R. Reiter (ed.), *Toward an Anthropology of Women*. New York: Monthly Review Press, 157–210.

Rupp, L. J. 1985. The women's community in the National Woman's Party, 1945 to the 1960s. *Signs* 10: 715–40.

Sachs, W. (ed.) 1992. *The Development Dictionary: A Guide to Knowledge as Power*. London: Zed Books.

Sack, R. 1997 *Homo Geographicus: A Framework for Action, Awareness and Moral Concern*. Baltimore: Johns Hopkins University Press.

Sack, R. 1980 *Conceptions of Space in Social Thought: A Geographic Perspective*. Minneapolis: University of Minnesota Press.

Said, E. 1979. *Orientalism*. New York: Vintage.

Said, E. W. 1993. *Culture and Imperialism*. New York: Knopf.

Santos, M. 1977. Society and space: social formation as theory and method. *Antipode* 9: 3–13.

Sarachild, K. 1973. Consciousness raising: a radical weapon in red stockings: feminist revolution. Pamphlet.

Sarap, M. 1988. *An Introductory Guide to Post-Structuralism and Postmodernism*. New York: Harvester Wheatsheaf.

Sartre, J-P. 1957. *The Transcendence of the Ego*, trans. F. Williams and R. Kirkpatrick. New York: Noonday Press.

Sartre, J-P. 1958. *Being and Nothingness: An Essay on Phenomenological Ontology*, trans. H. E. Barnes. New York: Philosophical Library.

Sartre, J-P. 1966. *Being and Nothingness: A Phenomenological Essay on Ontology*. New York: Washington Square Press.

Sartre, J-P. 1968. *Search for a Method*, trans. H. E. Barnes. New York: Vintage.

Sartre, J-P. 1976. *Critique of Dialectical Reason*. Atlantic Highlands, NJ: Humanities Press.

Sauer, C. 1941 Foreword to historical geography. *Annals of the Association of American Geographers* 31: 11–24.

Sauer, C. 1952. *Agricultural Origins and Dispersals*. New York: American Geographical Society.

Sauer, C. 1956. The agency of man on earth. In W. Thomas (ed.), *Man's Role in Changing the Face of the Earth*. Chicago: University of Chicago Press, 49–69.

Sauer, C. 1963. *Land and Life*, ed. J. Leighly. University of California Press.

Saunders, P. 1985. Space, the city and urban sociology. In D. Gregory and J. Urry (eds), *Social Relations and Spatial Structures*. New York: St Martin's Press.

Saunders, P. 1989. Space, urbanism and the created environment. In D. Held and J. Thompson (eds), *Social Theory of Modern Societies: Anthony Giddens and His Critics*. Cambridge: Cambridge University Press, 215–34.

Saunders, P. and P. Williams 1986. The new conservatism: some thoughts on recent and future developments in urban studies. *Society and Space* 4: 393–9.

Saussure, F. de 1986. *Course in General Linguistics*, trans. R. Harris. LaSalle: Open Court.

Savage, M., J. Barlow, S. Duncan, and P. Saunders 1987. "Locality research": the Sussex programme on economic restructuring, social change and the locality. *Quarterly Journal of Social Affairs* 3: 27–51.

Sayer, A. 1979. Theory and empirical research in urban and regional political economy. University of Sussex Urban and Regional Studies, Working Paper 14.

Sayer, A. 1984. *Method in Social Science: A Realist Approach*. London: Hutchinson.

Sayer, A. 1985. The difference that space makes. In D. Gregory and J. Urry (eds), *Social Relations and Spatial Structures*. New York: St Martin's Press, 49–66.

Sayer, A. 1987. Hard work and its alternatives. *Society and Space* 5: 395–9.

Sayer, A. 1991a. Behind the locality debate. *Environment and Planning A* 23: 283–308.

Sayer, A. 1991b. *Radical Geography and the Crisis Of Marxist Political Economy*. Sussex: Centre for Urban and Regional Research.

Sayer, A. 1995. *Radical Political Economy: A Critique*. Oxford: Blackwell.

Schaeffer, F. K. 1953. Exceptionalism in geography: a methodological examination. *Annals of the Association of American Geographers* 43: 226–49.

Schatzki, T. D. 1993. Theory at bay: Foucault, Lyotard, and Politics of the local. In J. P. Jones, W. Natter and T. R. Schatzki (eds), *Postmodern Contentions: Epochs, Politics, Space*. New York: Guilford, 39–64.

Schleiermacher, F. 1977. *Hermeneutics: The Handwritten Manuscripts*, trans. J. Duke and J. Forstman. Atlanta, GA: Scholars Press.

Schmidt, A. 1971. *The Concept of Nature in Marx*. London: New Left Books.

Schmidt-Renner, G. 1966. *Elementare Theorie de Okonomischen Geographie*. Gotha.

Schrift, A. D. 1995. *Nietzsche's French Legacy: A Genealogy of Poststructuralism*. New York: Routledge.

Schutz, A. 1967. *The Phenomenology of the Social World*. Evanston: Northwestern University Press.

Schutz, A. 1970. *On Phenomenology and Social Relations: Selected Writings*, ed. Helmut R. Wagner. Chicago: University of Chicago Press.

Schuurman, F. J. (ed.) 1992. *Beyond the Impasse; New Directions in Development Theory*. London: Zed Press.

Scott, A. J. 1988. Flexible production systems and regional development: the rise of new industrial spaces in North America and Western Europe. *International Journal of Urban and Regional Research* 12: 171–86.

Scott, A. J. and M. Storper 1986a. Industrial change and territorial organization: a summing up. In A. Scott and M. Storper (eds) 1986b. *Production, Work, Territory: The Geographical Anatomy of Industrial Capitalism*. London: Allen and Unwin, 301–11.

Scott, A. and M. Storper (eds) 1986b. *Production, Work, Territory: The Geographical Anatomy of Industrial Capitalism*. London: Allen and Unwin.

Scott, J. 1976. *The Moral Economy of the Peasant*. New Haven, Conn.: Yale University Press.

Saegart, S. 1981. Masculine cities and feminine suburbs: polarized ideas, contradictory realities. In C. Stimpson, E. Dixler, M. Nelson, and K. Yatrakis (eds), *Women and the American City*. Chicago: University of Chicago Press.

Seager, J. and A. Olson 1986. *Women in the World: An International Atlas*. London: Pluto.

Seamon, D. 1979. *A Geography of the Lifeworld*. New York: St Martin's Press.

Searle, J. D. 1969. *Speech Acts*. London: Cambridge University Press.

Semple, E. C. 1903. *American History and Its Geographic Conditions*. Boston: Houghton Mifflin.

Semple, E. C. 1911. *Influences of Geographic Environment on the Basis of Ratzel's System of Anthropo-geography*. New York: Henry Holt.

Sennett, R. 1970. *The Uses of Disorder: Personal Identity and City Life*. New York: Knopf.

Shaw, B. 1995. Contradictions between action and theory: feminist participatory research in Goa, India. *Antipode* 27: 91–9.

Sheehan, H. 1985. *Marxism and the Philosophy of Science: A Critical History*. New Jersey: Humanities Press.

Shils, E. and T. Parsons 1961. *Towards a General Theory of Action*. Cambridge: Harvard University Press.

Shurmer-Smith, P. and K. Hannam 1994. *Worlds of Desire, Realms of Power: A Cultural Geography*. London: Edward Arnold.

Slater, D. 1975. The poverty of geographical inquiry. *Pacific Viewpoint* 16: 159–76.

Slater, D. 1992. Theories of development and politics of the post-modern – exploring a border zone. *Development and Change* 3: 283–319.

Slater, D. 1997. Spatialities of power and postmodern ethics – rethinking geopolitical encounters. *Society and Space* 15: 55–72.

Smelser, N. 1963. *The Sociology of Economic Life*. Englewood Cliffs, NJ: Prentice-Hall.

Smith, D. 1974. Women's perspective as a radical critique of sociology. *Sociological Inquiry* 44: 7–13.

Smith, D. M. 1997. Back to the good life: towards an enlarged conception of social justice. *Society and Space* 15: 19–35.

Smith, N. 1979. Geography, science and post-positivist modes of explanation. *Progress in Human Geography* 3: 356–83.

Smith, N. 1981. Degeneracy in theory and practice: spatial interactionism and radical eclecticism. *Progress in Human Geography* 5: 111–18.

Smith, N. 1984. *Uneven Development: Nature, Capital and the Production of Space*. Oxford: Basil Blackwell.

Smith, N. 1987a. Dangers of the empirical turn: some comments on the CURS initiative. *Antipode* 19: 59–68.

Smith, N. 1987b. Rascal concepts, minimalizing discourse, and the politics of geography. *Society and Space* 5: 377–83.

Smith, N. 1989. Geography as museum: private history and conservative idealism in *The Nature of Geography*. In N. Entrikin and S. Brunn (eds), *Reflections on Richard Hartshorne's The Nature of Geography*. Washington: Association of American Geographers, 89–120.

Smith, N. 1996. Rethinking sleep. *Society and Space* 14: 505–6.

Smith, N. K. 1933. *Immanuel Kant's Critique of Pure Reason*. London: Macmillan.

Smith, R. G. 1997. The end of geography and radical politics in Baudrillard's philosophy. *Society and Space* 15: 305–20.

Snitow, A. 1990. A gender diary. In M. Hirsch and E. Fox Keller (eds), *Conflicts in Feminism*. New York: Routledge, 9–43.

Sofoulis, Z. 1988. *Through the Lumen: Frankenstein and the Optics of Re-origination*. University of California at Santa Cruz, PhD thesis.

Sohn-Rethel, A. 1975. Science as alienated consciousness. *Radical Science Journal* 2/3: 65–101.

Soja, E. 1980. The socio-spatial dialectic. *Annals of the Association of American Geographers* 70: 207–25.

Soja, E. 1986. Taking Los Angeles apart: some fragments of a critical human geography. *Society and Space* 4: 255–72.

Soja, E. 1989. *Postmodern Geographies: The Reassertion of Space in Social Theory*. London: Verso.

Soja, E. 1996. *Thirdspace: Journeys to Los Angeles and Other Real-and-Imagined Places*. Cambridge: Blackwell.

Soja, E. and Hadjimichalis, C. 1979. Between geographical materialism and spatial fetishism: some observations on the development of Marxist spatial analysis. *Antipode* 11: 3–11.

Solomon, R. C. 1972. *From Rationalism to Existentialism: The Existentialists and their Nineteenth Century Backgrounds*. New York: Harper and Row.

Spain, D. 1992. *Gendered Spaces*. Chapel Hill, NC: University of North Carolina Press.

Spencer, H. 1864. *First Principles*. New York: D. Appleton.

Spencer, H. 1882. *The Principles of Sociology*. New York: D. Appleton.

Spiegelberg, H. 1978. *The Phenomenological Movement: A Historical Introduction*. The Hague: Martinus Nijhoff.

Spinoza, B. de 1959. *Ethica*. London: Dent.

Spivak, G. 1988. *In Other Worlds*. New York: Routledge.

Spivak, G. 1990. *The Post-Colonial Critic*, ed. S. Harasym. New York: Routledge.

Sprague, J. and M. Zimmerman 1993. Overcoming dualisms: a feminist agenda for sociological methodology. In P. England (ed.), *Theory on Gender/Feminism in Theory*. New York: Aldine de Gruyter, 255–80.

Staeheli, L. A. and V. Lawson 1994. A discussion of "women in the field": the politics of feminist field work. *Professional Geographer* 46: 96–102.

Stanley, L. and S. Wise. 1993. *Breaking Out Again: Feminist Ontology and Epistemology*. London: Routledge.

Stedman Jones, G. 1978. The Marxism of the early Lukács. In *Western Marxism: A Critical Reader*, ed. New Left Review. London: Verso, 11–60.

Stephenson, D. 1974. The Toronto Geographical Expedition. *Antipode* 6: 98–101.

Stewart, J. Q. 1947a. Empirical mathematical rules concerning the distribution and equilibrium of population. *Geographical Review* 37: 461–85.

Stewart, J. Q. 1947b. Suggested principles of "social physics." *Science* 106: 179–80.

Stewart, L. 1995. Bodies, visions and spatial politics: a review essay. *Society and Space* 13: 609–18.

Stock, B. 1986. Texts, readers and narratives. *Visible Language* 20: 89–95.

Stock, B. 1990. *Listening for the Text: On the Uses of the Past*. Baltimore: Johns Hopkins University Press.

Stoddart, D. 1966. Darwin's impact on geography. *Annals of the Association of American Geographers* 56: 683–98.

Stoddart, D. (ed.) 1981. *Geography, Ideology and Social Concern*. Oxford: Basil Blackwell.

Stone, M. 1975. The housing crisis, mortgage lending and class struggle. *Antipode* 7: 22–37.

Storper, M. 1987 The post-Enlightenment challenge to Marxist urban studies. *Society and Space* 5: 418–26.

Storper, M. and A. J. Scott 1986. Overview: production, work, territory. In A. Scott and M. Storper (eds), *Production, Work, Territory: The Geographical Anatomy of Industrial Capitalism*. Boston: Allen and Unwin, 1–15.

Storper, M. and A. Scott 1989. The geographical foundations and social regulation of flexible production complexes. In J. Wolch and M. Dear (eds), *The Power of Geography: How Territory Shapes Social Life*. Boston: Unwin Hyman, 21–40.

Strohmayer, U. and M. Hannah 1992. Domesticating postmodernism. *Antipode* 24: 29–35.

Strong, T. B. 1988 *Friedrich Nietzsche and the Politics of Transfiguration*. Berkeley: University of California Press.

Sturrock, J. 1979a. *Structuralism and Since: From Lévi-Strauss to Derrida*. Oxford: Oxford University Press.

Sturrock, J. 1979b. Roland Barthes. In J. Sturrock, *Structuralism and Since: From Lévi-Strauss to Derrida*. Oxford: Oxford University Press, 52–80.

Susman, P., P. O'Keefe, and B. Wisner 1983. Global disasters, a radical interpretation. In K. Hewitt (ed.), *Interpretations of Calamity*. Boston: Allen and Unwin, 263–83.

Therborn, G. 1978. The Frankfurt school. In *Western Marxism: A Critical Reader*, ed. New Left Review. London: Verso, 83–139.

Thevanaz, P. 1962. *What Is Phenomenology?* Chicago: Quadrangle.

Thomas, W. (ed.) 1956. *Man's Role in Changing the Face of the Earth*. Chicago: University of Chicago Press.

Thomas, W. 1959. Introductory [to "Man, time and space in Southern California"]. *Annals of the Association of American Geographers* 49: 4–7.

Thompson, E. P. 1966. *The Making of the English Working Class*. New York: Vintage.

Thompson, E. P. 1978. *The Poverty of Theory*. New York: Monthly Review Press.

Thrift, N. 1983. On the determination of social action in space and time. *Society and Space* 1: 23–57.

Thrift, N. 1985. Bear and mouse or bear and tree? Anthony Giddens's reconstruction of social theory. *Sociology* 19: 00–00.

Thrift, N. 1987. No perfect symmetry. *Society and Space* 400–7.

Thrift, N. and D. Parkes 1980. *Times, Spaces, and Places*. Chichester: John Wiley.

Tickell, A. and J. Peck 1992. Accumulation, regulation and the geographies of post-Fordism: missing links in regulationist research. *Progress in Human Geography* 16: 190–218.

Tickell, A. and J. Peck 1995. Social regulation after Fordism: regulation theory, neo-liberalism and the global–local nexus. *Economy and Society* 24: 357–86.

Timpanero, S. 1975. *On Materialism*. London: New Left Books.

Tivers, J. 1977. Constraints on urban activity patterns: women with young children. Department of Geography, King's College, University of London, Occasional Paper 6.

Tivers, J. 1978. How the other half lives; the geographical study of women. *Area* 10: 302–6.

Tivers, J. 1985. *Women Attached*. London: Croom Helm.

Tivers, J. 1988. Women with young children: constraints on activities in the urban environment. In J. Little, L. Peake, and P. Richardson (eds), *Women in Cities: Gender and the Urban Environment*. New York: New York University Press, 84–97.

Tobias, S. 1997. *Faces of Feminism: An Activist's Reflections on the Women's Movement*. Boulder: Westview Press.

Todorov, T. 1984. *The Conquest of America: The Question of the Other*. New York: Harper and Row.

Toffler, A. 1970. *Future Shock*. New York: Bantam Books.

Touraine, A. 1971. *Post-Industrial Society*, trans. L. Mayhew. New York: Random House.

Touraine, A. 1985. An introduction to the study of social movements. *Social Research* 52: 749–87.

Touraine, A. 1988. *Return of the Actor: Social Theory in Post Industrial Society*. Minneapolis: University of Minnesota Press.

Tuan, Y-F. 1971. *Man and Nature*. Washington: Association of American Geographers.

Tuan, Y-F. 1974. *Topophilia: A Study of Environmental Perception, Attitudes and Values.* Englewood Cliffs, NJ: Prentice-Hall.

Tuan, Y-F. 1976. Humanistic geography. *Annals of the Association of American Geographers* 66: 266–76.

Tuan, Y-F. 1977. *Space and Place: The Perspective of Experience.* Minneapolis: University of Minnesota Press.

Turner, B. S. 1994. *Orientalism, Postmodernism and Globalism.* London: Routledge.

Turner, J. C., M. A. Hogg, P. V. Oakes, S. D. Ruches, and M. S. Wethrell 1987. *Rediscovering the Social Group.* Oxford: Blackwell.

Ullman, E. 1953. Human geography and area research. *Annals of the Association of American Geographers* 43: 54–66.

Ullman, E. 1957. *American Commodity Flows.* Washington: University of Washington Press.

Ullman, E. 1980. *Geography as Spatial Interaction,* ed. R. Boyce. Seattle: University of Washington Press.

Unwin, T. 1992. *The Place of Geography.* Harlow: Longman.

Urry, J. 1981. Localities, regions and social class. *International Journal of Urban and Regional Research* 5: 455–74.

Urry, J. 1985. Social relations, space and time. In D. Gregory and J. Urry (eds) *Social Relations and Spatial Structures.* New York: St Martin's Press, 20–48.

Urry, J. 1986. Locality research: the case of Lancaster. *Regional Studies* 20: 233–42.

Urry, J. 1987. Society, space and locality. *Society and Space* 6: 435–44.

Venturi, R. 1972. *Learning from Las Vegas.* Cambridge: MIT Press.

Vico, G. B. 1984. *The New Science of Giambattista Vico,* trans. T. G. Bergin and M. H. Fisch. Ithaca: Cornell University Press.

Vidal de la Blache, P. 1926. *Principles of Human Geography,* trans. M. Bingham. London: Constable.

Vogel, L. 1983. *Marxism and the Oppression of Women.* London: Pluto.

von Bertalanffy, L. 1951. General systems theory: a new approach to unity of science. *Human Biology* 23: 303–61.

von Humboldt, A. 1847. *Cosmos: Sketch of a Physical Description of the Universe.* London: Longman, Brown, Green and Longmans.

von Thunen, J. H. 1966. *Von Thunen's Isolated State.* Oxford: Oxford University Press.

Wagner, H. R. (ed.) 1970. *Alfred Schutz: On Phenomenology and Social Relations.* Chicago: University of Chicago Press.

Waterhouse, R. 1981. *A Heidegger Critique.* Sussex: Harvester.

Watson, S. and K. Gibson (eds) 1995. *Postmodern Cities and Spaces.* Oxford: Blackwell.

Watson, T. W. 1955. Geography: a discipline in distance. *Scottish Geographical Magazine* 71: 1–13.

Watts, M. 1983a. On the poverty of theory: natural hazards research in context. In K. Hewitt (ed.), *Interpretations of Calamity.* Boston: Allen and Unwin, 23–62.

Watts, M. 1983b. *Silent Violence: Food, Famine and Peasantry in Northern Nigeria.* Berkeley: University of California Press.

Watts, M. 1993. Development I: Power, knowledge, discursive practice. *Progress in Human Geography* 17: 257–72.

Weber, A. 1929. *Alfred Weber's Theory of the Location of Industries,* trans. C. J. Friedrich. Chicago: University of Chicago Press.

Weber, M. 1978. *Economy and Society: An Outline of Interpretive Sociology.* Berkeley: University of California Press.

Werkele, G. 1981. Women in the urban environment. In C. Stimpson, E. Dixler, M. Nelson, and K. Yatrakis (eds), *Women and the American City*. Chicago: University of Chicago Press.

Werkele, G., R. Peterson, and D. Morley 1980. Introduction. In G. Werkele, R. Peterson, and D. Morley (eds), *New Space for Women*. Boulder, Colorado: Westview Press.

Werlen, B. 1993. *Society, Action and Space: An Alternative Human Geography*. London: Routledge.

Westkott, M. 1990. Feminist criticism of the social sciences. In J. M. Nielsen (ed.), *Feminist Research Methods*. Boulder: Westview Press, 58–68.

Whatmore, S. 1997. Dissecting the autonomous self: hybrid categories for a relational ethics. *Society and Space* 15: 37–53.

White, H. 1987. *The Content of the Form*. Baltimore: Johns Hopkins University Press.

White, H. 1993. Review of *The Production of Space* by Henri Lefebvre. *Design Book Review* 29/30: 90–3.

White, S. 1988. *The Recent Work of Jürgen Habermas: Reason, Justice and Modernity*. Cambridge: Cambridge University Press.

Wild, J. 1962. Preface. In P. Thevanaz, *What Is Phenomenology?* Chicago: Quadrangle, 7–9.

Willey, T. E. 1978. *Back to Kant: The Revival of Kantianism in German Social and Historical Thought 1860–1914*. Detroit: Wayne State University.

Williams, R. 1973. *The Countryside and the City*. New York: Oxford University Press.

Williams, R. 1977. *Marxism and Literature*. Oxford: Oxford University Press.

Williams, R. 1979. *Politics and Letters*. London: New Left Books.

Williams, R. 1981. *Culture*. London: Fontana.

Williams, S. W. 1981. Realism, Marxism and human geography. *Antipode* 13: 31–8.

Wisner, B., K. Westgate, and P. O'Keefe 1976. Poverty and disaster. *New Society* 9: 546–8.

Wittfogel, K. 1929. Geopolitik, geographischer materialismus. *Unter den Banner des Marxismus* 3: l, 4, 5. Trans. by G. L. Ulmen (1985) as Geopolitics, geographical materialism and Marxism. *Antipode* 71: 21–72.

Wittgenstein, L. 1922. *Tractatus Logico-Philosophicus*. London: Kegan Paul.

Wittgenstein, L. 1968. *Philosophical Investigations*. London: Macmillan.

Wolpert, J. 1964. The decision process in a spatial context. *Annals of the Association of American Geographers* 54: 537–58.

Women and Geography Study Group of the Institute of British Geographers 1984. *Geography and Gender: An Introduction to Feminist Geography*. London: Hutchinson.

Wood, E. 1986. *The Retreat from Class: A New "True" Socialism*. London: Verso.

Wright, E. O. 1978. *Class, Crisis, State*. London: New Left Books.

Wright, E. O. 1989. Models of historical trajectory: an assessment of Giddens's critique of Marxism. In D. Held and J. Thompson (eds), *Social Theory of Modern Societies: Anthony Giddens and His Critics*. Cambridge: Cambridge University Press, 77–102.

Wright, J. K. 1966. *Human Nature in Geography*. Cambridge: Harvard University Press.

Wright, J. K. 1965. *The Geographical Lore of the Times of the Crusades: A Study in the History of Medieval Science and Tradition in Western Europe*. New York: Dover.

Yapa, L. 1996. What causes poverty? A postmodern view. *Annals of the Association of American Geographers* 86: 707–28.

Yeung, H. W. 1997. Critical realism and realist research in human geography: a method or a philosophy in search of a method? *Progress in Human Geography* 21: 51–74.

Young, I. M. 1979. Self determination as a principle of justice. *Philosophical Forum* 11: 172–82.

Young, I. M. 1989. Throwing like a girl: a phenomenology of feminine bodily comportment, morality and spatiality. In J. Allen and I. M. Young (eds), *The Thinking Muse: Feminism and Modern French Philosophy*. Bloomington: Indiana University Press, 51–70.

Young, I. M. 1990. *Justice and the Politics of Difference*. Princeton: Princeton University Press.

Zeitlin, I. M. 1967. *Marxism: A Re-Examination*. New York: D. Van Nostrand.

Zelinsky, W., J. Monk and S. Hanson. 1982. Women and geography: a review and prospectus. *Progress in Human Society* 6: 317–66.

Zimmerman, E. 1933. *World Resources and Industries*. New York: Harper and Row.

Zipf, G. K. 1949. *Human Behavior and the Principle of Least Effort*. Cambridge: Addison-Wesley.

Index

Lightning Source UK Ltd.
Milton Keynes UK
25 August 2009